SHOUT TO THE TOP

SHOUT TO THE TOP

the jam AND PAUL WELLER

AN INSIDE STORY BY DENNIS MUNDAY

OMNIBUS PRESS
LONDON / NEW YORK / PARIS / SYDNEY / COPENHAGEN / BERLIN / MADRID / TOKYO

Jacket designed by Josh Labouve
Picture research by Sarah Bacon, with thanks to Simon Kelly.

ISBN13: 978.1.84609.401.9
ISBN: 1.84609.401.1
Order No: OP51436

Exclusive Distributors
Music Sales Limited,
14/15 Berners Street;
London, W1T 3LJ.

Music Sales Corporation,
257 Park Avenue South,
New York, NY 10010, USA.

Macmillan Distribution Services,
53 Park West Drive,
Derrimut, Vic 3030,
Australia.

To the Music Trade only:
Music Sales Limited,
8/9 Frith Street,
London W1D 3JB, UK.

Typeset by Phoenix Photosetting, Chatham, Kent
Printed by MPG Books, Bodmin, Cornwall

A catalogue record for this book is available from the British Library.
Visit Omnibus Press on the web at www.omnibuspress.com

Contents

Introduction

When I entered the record biz, I always dreamt of working with a famous band, but I never really expected it to become a reality, and even now, I expect to wake up and find that it's all been a dream. When I joined Polydor, I had no idea where it would lead and when I was promoted to become their jazz A&R manager, it was a dream come true, as jazz music as always been my first love. For the next four years, I worked with some truly stellar artists, like Ella Fitzgerald, Oscar Peterson, Count Basie, and Dizzy Gillespie. I also worked with the legendary jazz producer Norman Granz who taught me about dealing with artists and producing records. If my career in the music business had ended there, I would have been quite happy, as I had a ball. Following this I was promoted to look after Polydor's American acts, which were really no hopers, as the label was struggling to make an impact in America, and I can't say I enjoyed this period one bit.

In 1977, Chris Parry signed The Jam to Polydor although I never realised at the time how much this would change my life. The following year I had a large slice of luck when The Jam's Product Manager, Tim Chacksfield, left Polydor and I inherited his roster. The next few years were among the most exciting times of my life, and although The Jam came to a premature but necessary end, Paul Weller launched The Style Council, and I have many warm memories of working with this band. Both The Jam and the Council meant a lot to me personally, and for different reasons. As far as The Jam goes, I have a foot in both the camps, and it is shame that there is such a gulf between Rick and Bruce, and Paul and John Weller, particularly as The Jam and Paul Weller are now icons of British music. At the time, and after the split, it was difficult working with the four of them, as I always had more than one master – don't forget Polydor paid my wages.

The Council were never going to have the same impact as The Jam, Paul made sure of this, but it was a very important stepping-stone to his successful solo career, and he exorcised many demons during this period. Working with both bands, I became friends with Paul, Bruce, Rick, and John, as well as Mick Talbot and Steve White, and was part of their inner sanctum. This caused me no end of personal problems with Polydor, and had an adverse affect on my career, but I have no regrets.

Since the early nineties, I've been responsible for the most of their back catalogue releases, the high points being the two box sets. I've also followed Paul's solo career and watched him become an icon of the British music industry, with the ultimate accolade, a Brit in 2006 for his outstanding achievements to British Music. Although I played no part in his solo career, I have written a few chapters about this period, as it has intertwined with my life. In fact, hardly a day goes past when someone isn't e-mailing me, or talking to me about the man and the two great bands he fronted.

When I first met John and Paul I was quick to notice the similarity between my working class background, and theirs, as well as the many teenage fans that followed The Jam and later the Council. I grew up on a notorious council estate in South-East London, and in many ways their lifestyle mirrored my own youth. Like most switched on kids, I listened to the new wave of *Britpop*, which snowballed rapidly, and sounded the death knoll for the artists from the fifties. The music of the sixties influenced a new generation, and like a turbo charged Dyson cleaner, out went rock'n'roll, box jackets, motorcycles, and greasy haircuts. In came a New Model Army, the Mods, with their smart, short haircuts, dressed in sharp Ivy League Mohair suits, with a dash of European flair, loafers, and scooters. We were a new generation, with a new attitude, and the first teenagers to do their own thing. Like the Jam and Council fans, my generation was football mad, my team was West Ham, and I was an Iron, through and through. In 1966, when Bobby Moore lifted the Jules Rimet trophy, it was a victory for the Hammers as well as England. It was a heady time to be a teenager, not only had we won the World Cup, British music dominated the airwaves.

In reminiscing about the sixties, it's fashionable to talk about what a great time it was to be a teenager, but it wasn't quite as swinging as it's often made out to be. Oh yeah, if you had money, it swung like a bitch in heat, but for Joe Normal you worked Monday to Friday and looked forward to having it large at the weekend. My brother Robert and I were confirmed Mods, and followed the dress code. No self-respecting Mod would be seen out in anything less than a tailor-made Mohair suit, and if you could afford it, you went to your local Jewish tailor and got him to knock you up one in tonic. Bruv' and I didn't earn that sort of dough, and had to make do with a

Mohair and wool mixture that was less expensive, and had our suits made at one of the many chains of clothes shops that were about in the sixties. It wasn't cheap being a dedicated follower of fashion, but as far as I am concerned, it's the most stylish look of the last 50 years. The sportswear fad and baggy jeans, which is so predominant these days, pales into comparison, and as for style, it has as much class as a box of Brillo pads. Even when we went for a Sunday lunchtime pint, we would exchange our Levis and Fred Perry for a suit and a freshly pressed button down shirt and tie. You wouldn't be seen dead in a tracksuit, or an off the peg suit, not even an Armani. A lot of credit has to be given to the Labour Government who relaxed the rules on hire purchase (credit) and allowed my generation to dress in style, and pay for it on a monthly basis. When I left school I earned £6.50p a week, and the only way I could afford to look good was to pay for it over the next two years.

At the weekends, the West End of London was the place to head for and the in-crowd made a beeline for Soho, and the great club scene that existed there. It was where it was at, and there were many venues to visit. In Wardour Street alone there was the [old] Marquee, The Whisky-A-Go-Go [in the eighties renamed as the {trendy} WAG club], and in the basement, The Flamingo. After an evening's entertainment at the Whisky we would disappear downstairs, pilled up for an all nighter. There was the 100 Club in Oxford Street where you could see the best in jazz and blues, as well as the latest R&B bands. In the mid-seventies, it would rejuvenate its image by having the cream of punk and new wave performing nightly. The funny thing is, Bossa Nova, a jazz trend in the early sixties translates as new wave – some difference though. I betcha' they didn't gob at Astrud Gilberto when she sang 'The Girl From Ipanema'!

The local scene in your hood was almost as good, and you could see live bands in just about every other pub and it was possible to see big groups, even in a small 'niche' club. Georgie Fame, The Spencer Davis Group, The Animals, Jimi Hendrix, John Mayall, Cream and Derek & The Dominoes were some of the 'names' I was lucky to see, and it didn't cost an arm and leg either. Several times, I visited the Ram-Jam club in Brixton, which later re-branded itself as the Fridge. There weren't many white faces present, but I don't recall any racist abuse, and everybody mixed freely. However, there was always an undercurrent of racism, which viciously surfaced during the seventies and eighties, and has never really gone away. Most of the venues were 'flea pits', but had character, and most weekends would be packed to the rafters with fans, baying [like dogs] at their favourite bands. Inside it was like a Turkish bath, and no matter how hot it got, you never loosened your tie, you kept your jacket buttoned up, sweating your bollocks off, trying to look cool. Would I remove my jacket, no way, after all, looking good was the answer. At the time, thinking it was hip, I refused tickets to see The Beatles play the Odeon at Lewisham, preferring to go and see the guv'nor, Georgie Fame, across the road. This was probably the right choice, as the girls' screaming drowned out The Beatles singing, but at least I heard Georgie.

As well as the vibrant club and pub scene, there were the summer festivals to look forward to, including the Richmond Jazz & Blues festival, which was the forerunner of the Reading Festival where The Jam played. There was also a great English soul scene, with many bands' records going on to become favourites with the Northern Soul crowd. I recall artists like, A Band Of Angels, Jimmy James, Sandra Barry, Timebox, Riot Squad, Alan Bown Set, The Mike Cotton Sound, Keith Powell, and Billie Davis who at the time recorded a stunning version of 'Angel Of The Morning'.

At the age of 15, a mate introduced me too modern jazz. He was more hip than the rest of us, the Fonz of our gang: good lookin', pulls all the girls, every posse has a geezer like this. I used to go round his house in the evenings and we would disappear into his bedroom where the walls and ceiling were painted black, and he would play me records from his jazz collection. Another friend, who was a blues freak, introduced me to this brand of music, and my Bruv' was mad on Blue-Beat and Ska. He had a stack of 45s, which he would blast out of our Dansette record player. My generation had an eclectic taste, and our influences came from a broad spectrum of music and listened to Soul, Ska, R&B, the blues, as well as bands like the Stones, The Small Faces, The Kinks, The Action, and The Who.

As far as pop music goes Georgie Fame is my biggest influence. His affect on me was enormous, enough for me to go out and buy a Hammond organ. I spent two years learning to play, read, and write music, desperately trying to emulate him, and the likes of Jimmy Smith. I realised after 18 months of hard graft this was never going to happen, and I gave up and sold the organ. Many of my musician friends told me I had given up too quickly and I should carry on. For me, my playing was monkey see, monkey do, and I didn't have the natural talent required to become a good musician. At one time, it bothered me greatly that I didn't persevere, but having achieved all that I have during my career, has more than made up for this early disappointment.

It was great being a teenager in the sixties but I am certain that every generation enjoys their youth, whatever decade it is. In my case working with The Jam and the Council gave me a second youth. Anyway, who wants to grow up? I'm nearly 60, but going on 17 and I don't intend to change!

It wasn't The Jam, The Sex Pistols or The Clash that turned me on to new wave, it was The Damned's debut single, 'New Rose', and I vividly recall the moment I heard this song. It was a Saturday morning, I was in my kitchen listening to the Kid Jensen show on Radio 1, and he announced he was going to play their new single. It took me by surprise, up to that moment punk records were played only in the evenings. No one had dared to give this music an airing during the day; after all, it might be contagious. From the opening intro, paying homage to the old sixties record, *'Leader Of The Pack' by* the Shangri La's, I was hooked, and listening to this song was a real bristle brush experience. I loved Brian James wonderful slashing guitar riffs, the throbbing drums, Dave Vanian's strident vocals, and thought, 'What the fuck is this'! First thing Monday morning I stopped at HMV to acquire the single before going to the office, and for rest of the day, instead of hearing the dulcet tones of Ella Fitzgerald wafting out of my office, all you heard was 'New Rose'. Whatever music I'm into, I have to play it loud, and when I liked a tune, I'd blast it out it all day.

Among the cognoscenti The Jam are considered one of the most influential and important bands of their generation. There's no doubt that The Sex Pistols blasted down the doors of mediocrity when they released their debut album *Never Mind The Bollocks*. However, the two milestone recordings of that decade proved to be The Clash's first album, and The Jam's *In The City*. Proof of this was the release of The Jam box set in 1997, some twenty years after they signed to Polydor. It went on to be one of the best selling box sets in the UK, and a top ten record, outselling much bigger artists and bands. The Council are now looked at in a better light, and were a ray of sunshine, amongst the synthesised pop music in the eighties.

This book is an insider's view of working with Paul and both these great bands, and what it was like working for Polydor. Regardless of what people might say, I have never been a yes man, I have always spoken my mind, and I've tried to tell my story like it was. I have been frank with my opinions and comments, and whilst some people might not agree with them, they are mine, and they are honest. Working with Paul, The Jam and the Council had a huge affect on my career and my life, as I know it did on the fans of both bands, but I was luckier as I got to work close up with both bands.

Dennis Munday
Vermegliano
Ronchi Dei Legionari
Italia

March 2006

PART 1

THE JAM

CHAPTER 1

Shaken, And Stirred In My Loafers

When I began working with The Jam, I knew very little about their career prior to their signing with Polydor. I knew they came from Woking and they lived on a council estate and all went to a secondary modern school that turned out to be called Sheerwater. I'd visited Woking but recalled very little about the town, other than that they had a reasonable amateur football team. The Stranglers, Rick Parfitt of Status Quo, and The Vapors, who Bruce and John co-managed, were all local lads. Woking's other claim to fame was the film of H.G Well's novel, *The War Of The Worlds*, was filmed on Horsell Common. Nearby Guildford was more up-market and middle-class, with its own university, and had produced the likes of Eric Clapton – from nearby Ripley – and Peter Gabriel who, like the rest of Genesis, went to Charterhouse public school in Godalming. Sham 69, one of The Jam's rivals, lived down the road, and put the town of Hersham on the map, though its doubtful the residents were entirely delighted by this.

There was nothing out of the ordinary about The Jam's early career. It was pretty much what all bands go through, though most of them split up when college or serious employment beckons. In 1972, Paul befriended Steve Brookes at school, and they got together, practiced their guitars, and took their first steps at song writing, with The Beatles heavily influencing their early efforts. In 1973, they recruited Dave Waller on guitar and Neil 'Bomber' Harris on drums. Dave was a budding poet and a big influence on Paul, but he was also a troubled lad, unable to handle the small town mentality of Woking. Overindulgence in booze and hard drugs tragically cost him his life in August 1982.

During the summer of 1973, Paul 'Rick' Buckler replaced Harris on drums, and Paul's dad, John Weller, began managing the band. John was raised the hard way, in the building trade, and if you couldn't duck and dive with the best in this game you wouldn't survive. John served in the British army, seeing active service in Korea, and was a keen amateur boxer as a teenager, becoming good enough to box for England and an ABA featherweight champion. To my surprise, he grew up in Lewisham and south east London, where I grew up. John met and married Ann Craddock, and settled in Walton Road in Woking. Shortly after Paul was born on May 25, 1958, they moved to Stanley Road, a street now synonymous with the name Paul Weller.

John and Anne made serious sacrifices for Paul and, unlike most parents, encouraged his musical ambitions instead of forcing him to accept a regular job. There's no doubt that John and Anne have always spoiled 'Soldier', as they often refer to Paul, something rotten, and he could do no wrong in their eyes. As a manager John knew nothing about the music business, and was very naïve, but he was a good hustler and single-minded in his dedication to his talented son and The Jam. He had total and unshakeable faith in Paul's abilities as a songwriter and would be by his side throughout his career. Unlike Paul, Bruce and Rick were doing the nine to five, mixing The Jam with their day jobs until things started rolling for them all.

There's no doubt that John Weller has played a pivotal role in The Jam and Paul's career, but if his son had been a songwriter of the *vin ordinaire*, it's unlikely that he would have made it in the record business, and more than likely spent the rest of life laying bricks. In the early days it was said that having John as their manger was a weakness, although history would prove this wrong. John's biggest ambition was to see The Jam play the famous Madison Square Garden arena in New York, something that was never realised.

In the autumn of 1973, they made their first recordings, 'Blueberry Rock' and 'Takin' My Love'. Shortly after this, frustrated with his inability to master the guitar, Dave Waller left the band and the trio went into a studio in North London for their second demo sessions. A surviving photo of the band at this time is a cracker; their uniform of flared trousers, kipper ties and shoulder length hair is as far removed as you could get from their later razor-sharp Mod image. It was around this time that they christened themselves The Jam, and I recall being told that it was Paul's younger sister Nicky who came up with the name one morning while the Weller family was having breakfast.

In 1974 they auditioned for a second guitarist, and Bruce Foxton joined the band, which now takes on a more familiar look. At the time, Paul was playing bass, and would later switch instruments with Bruce. Paul also discovered The Who, and after hearing their 1965 single 'My Generation' became interested in the Mod youth cult of the sixties, buying his first scooter, a Lambretta GP 150. They started to augment their live act with covers from the Motown, Stax, and the Atlantic labels, and Paul purchased his first Rickenbacker, a guitar favoured by The Who's Pete Townshend, and the American band, The Byrds.

The Jam auditioned for EMI music publishing during early 1975, but nothing came of it and they continued playing the pub and club circuit. Paul had seen Doctor Feelgood and began to model his guitar playing on the jerky rhythm and lead technique of Wilko Johnson, a style that would soon become a trademark sound of The Jam. That summer, Paul heard The Who's *My Generation* album, on which the trailblazing Shepherds Bush quartet pioneered what they termed 'Maximum R&B', a hybrid of soul and rock pumped up with frenzied guitar chords and frantic drums. The early Who had a huge effect on Paul and influenced not only The Jam's music but also the way they dressed. Paul adopted the sharp sixties Mod look and pop-art imagery with an almost religious zeal, though later on he would chastise his fans for their lack of individualism, for mimicking the fashion that he and The Jam adopted. Another sixties group, The Small Faces, inspired Paul even more and during The Jam's career he practically cloned himself on their singer Steve Marriot, copying not only his fashion sense, but his haircut too. To this day, he still is a huge fan, collecting any recordings and memorabilia he can find, and he has recorded many of their songs.

After a gig at the Fulham Greyhound, Steve Brookes parted company with the band, citing musical differences as the reason. This is record biz speak for the benefit of the press but generally translates as ego problems. Although they advertised for a replacement, they were unable to find a suitable candidate and remained a three piece for the rest of their career. Fortuitously, they also failed an audition for the TV talent show *Opportunity Knocks*.

During 1974 and 1975, The Jam played over a hundred and fifty live gigs, mostly in the Woking area. Many bands which break big have a club that was special to them during their formative years; for The Beatles it was the

Cavern and for the Jam it was Michael's in Woking, where they had a residency. They recorded numerous demo sessions, laying down both original material and cover versions. I have heard quite a few of these early recordings, and they reflect where the band and Paul's song writing talents were at the time.*

1976 was a decisive year for Paul and The Jam. A new generation of teenagers was emerging who were uninterested in most of the pop and rock music beloved of previous generations. Records by The Sex Pistols, The Clash and The Damned signalled the arrival of punk which would go on to make a dramatic mark socially as well as musically, and Paul Weller took note. Faced with the confrontational style of the Pistols and The Clash, he abruptly changed his attitude towards music and the importance of lyrics.

Still a small town band, there was a need to expose The Jam to a wider audience and they took the unusual step of performing a short live set in a Soho street market. This did the trick and *Melody Maker* gave them a review, as did the influential punk fanzine, *Sniffin' Glue*. On October 21 they supported The Sex Pistols at Dunstable's Queensway Hall, performing for the last time as a quartet with Bob Gray on piano. In a *Melody Maker* review of the gig, Caroline Coon tagged them as being revivalists, which would stalk the band and Paul throughout their careers. As they played more gigs in London their following started to grow and soon people were queuing up to see them. Given the impact punk was having on the record business, it was only a matter of time before a record company snapped them up.

At the time all this was happening, I was Polydor's jazz A&R manager, and spent most of my time listening to jazz, but I still kept a weather eye out on what was happening in other music scenes. I have to be truthful, and admit I wasn't sure about the punks. Yes, the Pistols, and The Clash were great, on the cutting edge of a new generation's music, but these two were lone diamonds scattered among the glass. It had nothing to do with my age at the time (29), or that the music was for a new generation of teenagers. I was uncertain about the quality, and there were too many fringe bands aping the fashion, playing the same venues and just jumping on the bandwagon.

The Jam and their music wasn't exactly punk, but they aligned themselves with the movement and hung on to its shirttails for all their worth.

* For a more in-depth account of The Jam's career, I recommend Steve Brooke's autobiography, *Keeping The Flame*, which is the best account of this period.

Fortunately for them punk transmuted into new wave – a sort of slightly more sophisticated version, as personified by the likes of Elvis Costello and Ian Dury. Prior to their signing with Stiff, just about every record company had turned down Costello while Dury had failed to make any commercial headway with Kilburn & The High Roads, though music critics were certainly on their side. The record business at this time was too set in its ways, complacently believing that the rock music it had sold for the last ten years would keep selling forever; it was conservative, unprepared and indifferent to any new brand of rock.

In contrast to what the record companies believed, there was a new generation of fans who wanted a change and wanted it badly. Many of my colleagues at Polydor were negative, and adopted a superior attitude to punk and new wave, making smug comments like, "It won't last five minutes", or "They won't be around for long". They couldn't, or perhaps simply didn't want to come to terms with any new trend in music, and felt threatened by the anarchy that accompanied it. As punk's popularity snowballed, the record companies had no choice, and every label went out looking for a punk band to sign, though to most the music and attitude were completely alien. It wasn't just the way they dressed, it was the 'couldn't give a fuck attitude'. Whereas in the past bands looking for a record deal had been deferential towards A&R men, these punks were just as likely to spit in their faces and pour a pint of beer over their heads. Here was a new youth culture who wanted music that didn't sound like anything that had gone before, and to dress in *their* fashions, walk *their* walk, and talk *their* talk.

It isn't difficult to understand punk's appeal. Unlike the sixties, it wasn't much fun being a teenager in the mid-seventies when jobs weren't as freely available as they once were. Teenagers became part of a 'lost generation', and I was genuinely troubled by the plight of many fans I came across. When I insisted they had a future, I recall one Jam fan asking me: "What fucking future Den, the dole queue?" Here was a generation abandoned, adrift in a sea of confusion and futility. This was their Modern World, an era when some arsehole Tory politician would tell you to, "Get on your bike and move away", all because you couldn't find employment in your own town; never mind about your family and friends, or your community.

By the time punk arrived in the mid-seventies, Polydor's best selling artists were Slade, The Bee Gees, Focus, Eric Clapton, The New Seekers and the two German stalwarts of MOR music, James Last and Bert Kaempfert. In 1976, however, a likable New Zealander called Chris Parry was hired as an A&R manager, and he would change not only the face of Polydor but my life as well. At the time, he was the only A&R man at Polydor who saw punk's potential, and thus formed part of its vanguard. Chris was desperate to sign The Sex Pistols but Malcolm McClaren chose EMI, phoning Polydor from their offices to let them know they weren't going to get the band. Chris demoed The Clash, and we got close to signing them but they decided to go with CBS.

On Shane McGowan's recommendation, Chris went to see The Jam at the Marquee and was so impressed he decided to offer them a deal. Having missed out on the Pistols and The Clash, it was third time lucky, and for the princely sum of £6,000, Chris signed The Jam. Working class to the core it turned out that John Weller, didn't have a bank account, and dealt only in cash so Chris had to cash the advance cheque and hand over the readies. At the time there was no doubt that the Pistols and The Clash were making the waves and The Jam some way behind.

Both the Pistols and the Clash had signed contracts to record at least one album, but The Jam was signed to a singles deal only with an option to pick up their first album if the label so desired. It would appear that Polydor were hedging their bets on the band and wanted a get out of jail card should the first couple of singles fail to make any impact on the charts. Although The Jam didn't get anywhere near as big an advance as the Pistols (£40, 000), or the Clash (£100,000), John Weller made the shrewdest move of his career by signing them to Polydor. He recognised that at the beginning of their career, it was more important to get on the first rung of the ladder than to argue over how much money was paid up front. Once in the frame, The Jam's progress would depend purely on the band and Paul's developing talent as a song writer. If and when they took off, John knew that the record company would be happy to renegotiate their contract, and the cash would start flowing in. Their first demo session was scheduled for January 1977, but was cancelled due to an IRA bomb scare. On February 9, 1977, Chris took them into Anemone studios and recorded four 8-track demos, including the debut single 'In The City', plus 'Time For Truth', 'Sounds From The Street' and 'I've Changed My Address'.

In the mid-seventies, Polydor was a hive of activity and among the many artists they signed was the likable eccentric John Otway whose first two singles were produced by Pete Townshend. Interest from a bankable superstar always upped the ante and Polydor gave John a golden handcuff deal for three straight albums, at the extraordinary price of £70,000 an album. I recall the execs flapping around like demented seals at feeding time, extolling the virtues of his prodigious (sic) talent, and telling anyone who was daft enough to listen as he was going to be Polydor's next big star.

Instead of bringing in a name producer, Chris Parry decided to produce the band himself and brought in Vic Smith as co-producer. Vic had been a house engineer for Decca at their legendary studios in Hampstead, working alongside many top producers and I recalled seeing his name credited on several John Mayall albums that I'd bought in the sixties. Although from my generation, I found him a strange cove, with a penchant for safari suits. Although I worked with him for several years, I never really got to know him.

Chris had a hidden motive for bringing in Vic. At the time Polydor wouldn't give their A&R managers points on the groups they signed or produced. All you received at the end of the month was your salary cheque, regardless of whether a record you'd originated sold ten copies or a million. To get round this, A&R men did the odd 'dodgy' deal to make a few quid for their endeavours. Chris knew if a band broke into the big time he would be earning peanuts while the artist and record company would be cleaning up. A&R men were well paid, but the knowledge that he was lining Polydor's pockets must have frustrated Chris, and there's no doubt in my mind this attitude prompted him to eventually set up his own label.

In March 1977, Chris, Vic and the band went into Polydor's studios, and recorded their first single, 'In The City' b/w 'Takin' My Love'. The company's studio wasn't exactly state of the art, and was used mostly by in-house bands recording their demos, although the likes of Hendrix, The Bee Gees and Rory Gallagher had all previously worked in this tiny studio. I suspect the reason for doing this was to save money. Even though the cost would come out of The Jam's future earnings, it would save Polydor having to stump up the cash for an outside studio.

There were four great debut singles from this new wave of music: The Damned's 'New Rose', the Pistols, 'Anarchy In The UK', The Clash's 'White Riot' and The Jam's 'In The City'. Polydor released The Jam's debut single on April 29, 1977, and as far as debut singles go, they couldn't want for more. The lyrics were an accurate reflection of the time, and of the fans who were fast following the band. More than 25 years later, I still get excited when I hear this song, even though it was written for another generation. At the age of 17, The Who's 'My Generation' succinctly summed up the period I was living through, and for me 'In The City' encapsulates what was happening in 1977. Co-incidentally, both songs contain lines that date the song from their conception. In 'My Generation', Daltrey sings, 'I hope I die before I get old', whilst eleven years later Weller belts out, 'In the city there's a thousand faces all shining bright/and those golden faces are under twenty-five'. With its pumping bass the B-side 'Takin' My Love' is a nod towards Paul's R&B roots and the Feelgoods.

Although the record sold well and went to number 40 in the singles chart, it didn't set the world alight. Nevertheless, Polydor's ageing limbs were stirring and this modest success kick-started the company insofar as they went on to sign two other punk acts, Sham 69 and Siouxsie & The Banshees. Slowly Polydor was taking on the look of a contemporary record company as opposed to a home for aging rock bands and geriatric German dance bandleaders.

The Jam made their debut on *Top Of The Pops* and recorded their first John Peel session. On Radio 1, Peely was in the forefront of punk, and a big supporter of The Jam, playing an important part in launching their career. For the first two years he was always given the first copy of their promo singles as apart from Mike Reed, and Janice Long, no Radio 1 DJs played this kind of music, daytime radio totally ignoring new wave.

It was around this time that I first clapped eyes on the boys, an encounter I recall vividly. I was attending a meeting in the press office to discuss one of my jazz artists, and Paul, Bruce and Rick were in doing interviews. They were reading music papers and chatting up the girls when I caught sight of them, and it shook me to the core. In their black mohair suits, they looked the very image of me when I was a Mod in the sixties. I was both shaken *and* stirred, unlike James Bond's famous Martinis.

Following the success of the single Polydor went ahead and picked up their option for an album, which was recorded in 11 days and released on May 20, and also titled *In The City*, it reached number 20 in the charts. Debut albums are often the easiest for a band to record as most of the songs are taken from their live act, built up over a long period. Prior to signing to Polydor they'd played endless one nighters, honing their talents on the pub and workingmen's club circuit, where they were able to try out their own material, as well as blasting out their favourite covers. When I first heard the album, I was surprised just how far away from The Clash, The Damned and the Pistols The Jam were, and I can understand why Polydor may have been a little reticent in offering an album deal as they were definitely out of step with their contemporaries. However, by the time Polydor released this album, The Jam had built up a solid following, and it incorporated enough Weller originals for them to be positive about their future.

The tracks that appealed to me were the title track, 'I Got By In Time', with its Motown influences and I really liked 'Sounds From The Street', even though it was a bit rock'n'roll, a touch of California meets Surrey.

What hit me about 'Slow Down' was their banzai approach to this great Larry Williams song. I first heard this played in the sixties, when I was the same age as the Jam's fans, and this song was staple fare for the many R&B and blues bands playing pubs and clubs up and down the motorways. 'Time For Truth' saw Paul dipping his feet into political water, and although the sentiments were naïve, it was an early signpost to his future.

The one tune that stood out for me was 'Away From The Numbers'. I was genuinely amazed that a teenager was capable of writing such an accomplished tune. The structure of the song is far superior to the rest, with lyrics that belie Paul's relative lack of maturity. It's like he went to Horsell Common and borrowed H. G. Well's time machine and beamed himself forward to his *All Mod Cons* period and returned with this tune. The album overall does sound like a debut album, but 'Numbers' doesn't belong on anyone's debut record; it hasn't dated and sounds as good now as it did then. While the rest of the tracks are solid rather than exceptional, exactly the kind of songs you find on debut albums of a young band.

In The City differs from debut albums by The Jam's contemporaries in ways beyond its R&B and soul influence. While Paul's rhythm and lead guitar style announces a guitarist of unusual merit, many of the tracks feature Paul and Bruce singing in tandem, making the songs more tuneful with less of the gung-ho chanting that dominates their rival's anthem-like songs. If you listen closely, you can hear the beginning of what turned out to be The Jam sound, with all three members making a telling contribution.

Bill Smith was an in-house designer at Polydor who as well as designing the singles bags, did a wonderful job for The Jam's debut album sleeve. The stark image with The Jam logo spray-painted on pristine white tiles with a moody photo of the boys completed the package. The inner bag contained the lyrics, something that all bands ought to do, well, the ones who write decent songs should, and throughout his career, all of Paul's albums would feature his lyrics. The first single and album sleeves set the tone for Jam packaging, which rarely went below excellent.

On July 8, following up the success of the album they released a new single, 'All Around The World' b/w 'Carnaby Street', which reached number 13 in the charts. It was customary for record companies to take a second single from an album to boost its sales, but this practice was not adhered to with The Jam. They always insisted on releasing a new single after every album and to their credit followed this custom for the remainder of their career. It probably pissed off certain folk at Polydor, as it went against all the accepted marketing rules – but at the same time it promoted The Jam as a band with integrity, who weren't about to rip off their fans.

Although the second single went 23 places higher than 'In The City' it's clearly not as good, either musically or lyrically, but what is unusual about this song is the call-and-response vocals interplayed by Paul and Bruce. Most bands at the time had a lead vocalist with the rest of the band bawling out the chorus with football terrace frenzy. I don't like the affected cockney 'Oi' that kicks the song off, and the lyrics show Paul trying to put a distance between The Jam and the punk movement in general. I was never sure why he took this attitude as if punk hadn't come along when it did, it's quite possible that jam would be remembered only for spreading on bread with butter.

The high chart position was an indication that their fan base was increasing, and a summer release would have helped. Most bands are reluctant to release records at this time of the year, knowing their fans are basking on the beach on the Costa Del Plenty. The B-side was Bruce's first chance at writing a song and given that I was walking down Carnaby Street in the sixties, I agree with his cynicism. If anything, it's worse than ever now. Bruce was never able to write with either the subtlety or the metre that Paul could summon up but 'Carnaby Street' isn't a bad song, and Bruce gets his message across.

It was around this time that Paul met and fell for Gill Price, whom I recall was a big Buzzcock's fan. In the beginning, Paul, Bruce and Rick would have spent most of their time in each other's company, playing together, pulling birds or getting pissed. After falling for Gill things changed, and when they eventually moved to London there became two circles, and Paul started to move away from Bruce and Rick.

Coming from Woking, a suburban town in the stockbroker belt of Surrey, Paul was still naïve and his parameters of life narrow. Gill came from Bromley, which is just outside of London, and she was worldlier, and more knowledgeable about literature, and art. She opened his eyes, broadened his horizons and through her inspiration he started to write love songs, a theme that would continue throughout his song-writing career. It must have been a wonderful experience for both of them as they were young, and head over heels in love with each other. There is no doubt Paul received support from John, Bruce and Rick, but creative people need someone close who is not in competition, and is sensitive to their fluctuating, artistic temperament. Gill turned out to be a very important figure in his life, but it was perhaps a tad early in both their lives to settle down, and he couldn't have been easiest bloke to live with.

Although their love affair lasted until the early eighties, it was a tempestuous romance, right up to the end.

Their third single, released on October 21, 1977 was the abrasive, 'The Modern World' b/w 'Sweet Soul Music', 'Back In My Arms Again' and 'Bricks And Mortar'. The three extra tracks, all live, were recorded at their London gig at the 100 club on September 11. The lyrics are an early indication that Paul wasn't going to take crap from authority figures, and show how driven he was to do everything his way, regardless of the consequences. Although a better song than their second single, 'Modern World', reached only number 36 in the charts, which disappointed Paul. The live B-side is the band dipping their bread into Stax and Motown's gravy and is a snapshot of their early live act.

Timing is critical for the release of a single, and coming out eight weeks before Christmas would have affected the chart position of 'Modern World'. Most big acts release their singles to hit the Christmas market and the competition in the charts is fierce. Even with the success The Jam was enjoying, they weren't getting their singles aired on daytime radio, and the establishment was still anti-punk. It was necessary to censor the lyrics of this single for radio purposes and the word 'fuck' replaced. If this change hadn't taken place, no radio station would have played the uncensored version and it would have struggled to make the top 50. Even now, more than 25 years after it came out, radio stations haven't changed, and while I agree with Paul's sentiments about this kind of censorship, it was a necessary change. It wouldn't be the last time that Polydor would censor a Jam single. If this chart position affected Paul's confidence, it shouldn't have, as it's one of his best early efforts.

The acid test for all bands comes with their second album, without a doubt the most crucial stage of their career. Most bands release one album a year, and record companies tend to give new bands the much-needed time to write their second album, so I was never quite sure why it was necessary to rush out The Jam's second album so quickly. Following the success of *In The City* and their singles, not to mention their increasing profile in the music press, it might have been better for them to carry on touring for the remainder of 1977, consolidating their position by building up their fan base rather than going straight back into the studios to record.

John Weller was new to the game of managing a band and when Polydor offered him £20,000 for the second album, he bit their hand off – right up to the shoulder! A more experienced manger would have given it more thought, as it would put immense pressure on Paul as a songwriter. The band's finances would have been a worry to John, as at best they were only breaking even. Twenty grand at this time must have looked like a million dollars.

Between mid-August and September, they quickly recorded the album for release on November 18. Considering the pressure on this teenage band, *This Is The Modern World* ain't half as bad as it was made out to be, with even Paul in a recent interview stating that half of it was rubbish. Not so – given the age Paul and the band were at and the pressure they were under they did well to come up with an album of this calibre. It went to 22 in the charts and I'll bet the sales weren't far off their debut album.

Although the second album was rushed, it showed that Paul and the band had taken a step forward, albeit a small one. The literature and poetry that they were reading was beginning to influence the songs and Paul's writing skills were slowly maturing. Bruce contributes two songs, 'London Traffic' and 'Don't Tell Them You're Sane'. The first is a prescient warning about London's traffic problems written more than twenty years before Ken Livingstone had the bottle to do something about the volume of cars that pollute the city centre. Bruce's second track deals with a young lad unfairly institutionalised in a mental asylum and was inspired by Ken Kesey's great book, *One Flew Over The Cuckoo's Nest,* as was Paul's song, 'The Combine'. Neither of Bruce's efforts is as lyrically strong as Paul's contributions, but this isn't surprising considering how quickly he was thrown into the spotlight, with Polydor's insistence on releasing a second album so soon after the first.

Because the album was rushed, many of the songs have an unfinished feel about them and perhaps needed more work. 'Life From A Window', 'In The Street Today', and 'Tonight At Noon' all suffer from not being played enough live and being recorded too early in their evolution. Paul borrowed the subject matter of 'Tonight At Noon' from two poems by Adrian Henri, the well-known Liverpool Beat poet. Dave Waller, who co-wrote 'In The Street', his last contribution to the Jam songbook, introduced Paul to him.

The Orwell influenced 'Standards', with its 'Can't Explain' intro is one of the better tracks, and brings to mind one of many quirks between The Jam and myself that went beyond the sixties music we had in common. Coming from Plumstead I was more than a little unworldly and after leaving school I read extensively, with Orwell among my favourite authors. By my early twenties, I'd read everything he'd written and considered him to be the one Britain's finest writers.

Finally, 'I Need You' is a really good tune, and whenever I hear any version of 'In The Midnight Hour', it takes me back to 1965, I'm down The

Black Cat club in Woolwich, in my green mohair, and I heard Wilson Pickett's classic for the first time. This track was included on the album as they were stuck for original material. It wouldn't be the last time that this would occur.

This Is The Modern World wasn't well received by the music press or at Polydor, which was no fault of the band. It was recorded in a hurry and rushed out far too quickly, leaving the group insufficient time to do justice to the songs. Polydor's handling of the situation doesn't do them any favours, as they were an experienced major label, and knew the score. Although there was talk of wanting the record in time for the Christmas market, this was a red herring, as outside ofThe Jam's following, I doubt that many Christmas stockings would have had this album stuffed in it. There was also talk of a live album, which would have been a big mistake as the band didn't have the repertoire, and as exciting as they were on stage, they were not mature enough as musicians to warrant a live album so early on in their career.

All this points to a company wanting to make a fast buck, probably because those in control though that punk, and by extension The Jam, was going to burn out quickly, and the best policy was to take advantage of their financial situation and John's naivety. It would have made no difference to Polydor when the second album came out and it doesn't take a great deal of hindsight to realise that the band would have been better served if it was released later. The company could still have advanced the money to help John out, and released a new single, postponing the album until mid-1978. This would have given Paul the time to write more songs, and the band to play them in before recording a second album. As it was, the problems caused by rushing out *This Is The Modern World* would have a knock-on effect when it came to the third album, which would eventually give me serious problems, and drive a wedge between The Jam and Polydor.

Whatever is said about the album, it does stand the test of time, and many bands over the last four decades have had problems with their second albums. *With The Beatles,* The Beatles second LP, wasn't that much different from their debut as at this point in their career they were still on a learning curve. The Rolling Stones were struggling too, composing only three original songs for their second album, for which they mostly had to loot the tombs of Memphis and Chicago, and down the line U2 seem to have had a problem coming up with material of a high standard for *October*.

When The Beatles released their first two albums, everyone raved about them, but nobody at the time had any inkling that for the next 40 years every band would be measured by their benchmark. They were the new breed, and along with the likes of the Stones, Kinks and Who were laying down the foundations for the next four generations of rock bands. The sixties groups were lucky as there was nothing much from the past with which to draw a comparison, unlike The Jam and their contemporaries. For everyone, the giant steps came later.

Nevertheless, it still puzzles me as to why it was necessary to rush The Jam's second album out and not wait six months for the band to come up with new material. It was common practice by record companies to release an album every year, giving artists plenty of time to write and prepare material for the 'difficult' second album. The Jam went from obscurity to the charts rapidly, and although they didn't crash into the top ten, there was enough success for the company to think positively. Given the limited time, Paul had to write the songs, and the band to record it, *This Is The Modern World* was a success. I don't think any band of that era, or any other, given the same time frame, could have done better with their second album and it could have been a lot worse.

Following the release of *This Is The Modern World*, Paul went through an artistic crisis, and was unable to come up with any new songs for a fourth single, which put Bruce firmly in the spotlight. Of the three tracks featured, he wrote two, including the A-side. Given that he was still a novice songwriter, this was an enormous responsibility to shoulder and it can't have been easy. The Jam's first three singles and both their albums had been successful and they were now a name band. Anything that smelled of failure would be closely scrutinised.

On February 24, 1978, Polydor released, 'News Of The World' b/w 'Aunties And Uncles' and 'Innocent Man'. A tirade against tabloid newspapers, it wasn't a bad effort and went to number 27 in the charts, 9 places higher than 'The Modern World', and 13 places higher than their debut single. Since 'In The City' their fan club had increased, and the band by now had moved on from the pubs and clubs to playing larger venues, like The Friars at Aylesbury, the Odeon at Canterbury, The Apollo in Glasgow, and the Hammersmith Odeon. There is no doubt that this higher chart position was down to the band's much increased following. The Jam's momentum was moving forward at the right pace.

Over the years, Bruce's song writing abilities have come under scrutiny. I don't think for one minute, he ever tried or even thought he could emulate Paul in this department. He just wanted to write a good song for The Jam, and receive recognition for his own contribution to their songbook. 'News Of The World', might not be up to the standard of 'In The City' or 'The

Modern World', but it certainly holds its head high amid The Jam's early repertoire.

If Paul was going through a crisis when it came to the fourth single, Chris Parry, as an experienced A&R man, should have been able to deal with this, and help him through a lean time. At one point, Chris was offered a lucrative contract to come in with John and help manage The Jam, but I suspect he found John hard work as his knowledge of the business was minimal. Chris saw The Jam one way, while John and the band had different opposing views. Some of this difference of opinion centred on America.

There were certainly problems with the US market and the band did themselves no favours by displaying an overt anti-American attitude on their first tour of the USA, in October 1977. They appeared at CBGBs in New York, Rat's Kellar in Boston and the Whisky-A-Go-Go in Los Angeles, but it wasn't an enjoyable tour – Chris Parry described it as a 'nightmare' – with the boys taking an instant dislike to the US, a view that affected the band's career right up to the end. In adopting this stance, they sacrificed American sales. Chris Parry knew that to be truly successful you had to achieve success in America as that's where the big bucks are, but this kind of success would elude not only The Jam, but also The Style Council and Paul as a solo artist. I never quite understood their, and particularly Paul's, stance on the USA, given his musical influences.

There is no doubt the States wasn't ready for English punk, they were used to music that came from the ocean or the wide open spaces as opposed to city streets. However, there is no question in my mind The Jam's attitude alienated them from this massive market, and this would have given Chris second thoughts about becoming involved in their management. By the beginning of 1978, Chris was making plans and thinking of his own future, one that didn't necessarily include The Jam or Polydor.

The Sex Pistols blazed the trail for punk when they released their first single 'Anarchy In The UK', in 1976 and although well publicised, it reached no higher than number 38 in the charts. 'God Save The Queen' and 'Pretty Vacant' came out in 1977 and both singles stormed the charts reaching numbers two and six respectively. Their 1977 debut album, *Never Mind The Bollocks*, caused a public furore, with EMI refusing to press it, but this didn't stop it making the number one slot, and staying in the charts for more than year.

Meanwhile, The Clash released two singles in 1977, 'White Riot' and 'Complete Control', but neither made much impact on the singles chart, going to 38 and 28 respectively. However, their debut album went to number 12, eight place higher than *In The City*. Looking back, it's hard to believe that The Damned's great single 'New Rose' never made the charts at all, but their debut album, *Damned Damned Damned* went to 36. Elvis Costello faired better as his single, 'Watching The Detectives' went to 15, and his debut album, *My Aim Is True* went to 14. Another of The Jam's rivals were Generation X, fronted by the peroxide Billy Idol, whose first single, 'Your Generation' went to 36 in the charts.

At the time, The Stranglers were the most successful 'punk' band after the Pistols, though they were a good deal older than the rest of the pack, a fact they preferred to keep to themselves. In 1977, they released four singles, which all charted. '(Get A) Grip (On Yourself)' went to 44, 'Peaches' went to eight, 'Something Better Change' went to nine, and 'No More Heroes' also went to eight. Like The Jam, they released two albums that year, with their debut album *Stranglers IV: Rattus Norvegicus* going to number four, while their follow up album, *No More Heroes* hit the number two spot.

While the new wave had announced its arrival in a rash of newspaper headlines and was adopted by the fiercely partisan music press, the number one records of the year told another story. It was the same old faces: David Soul, Abba, Kenny Rogers, John Travolta & Olivia Neutron-Bomb, Julie Covington and The Brotherhood Of Man, and Paul McCartney had the Christmas number one with 'Mull Of Kintyre'. Punk had won a battle, but winning the war against mediocrity was going to be an uphill climb.

1977 was a good year for The Jam. Along with Costello, the Pistols, Stranglers and Clash, they'd made headway. They were about to enter my life in a big way but I had no inkling of the storm gathering around them.

CHAPTER 2

Look Out – Here Comes Jim Cook's Spy

To be successful in the record business, it's not enough to be talented, you need to be lucky and in the right place at the right time. Had Chris Parry signed either the Pistols or The Clash, its unlikely Polydor would have gone for The Jam, and it's anyone's guess where they would have ended up. Their early repertoire of Martha & The Vandellas, Wilson Pickett, The Who and Dr Feelgood wasn't synonymous with punk generally and Polydor only signed them because all the other labels were signing up bands with short spiky hair and an angry attitude, and even then, it was a suck it and see singles deal.

My own career in the record business was kick-started by a chance meeting when I was eighteen and between jobs, and I decided to go up to the West End to visit a few record shops. I regularly visited Rymington Van Wyk's in Leicester Square, and became friendly with the guys working there and casually mentioned that I was at a loose end, and looking for work. One suggested I apply for a job at the main HMV store, at 363, Oxford Street, and after passing the interview went on to work there for four years. Later, I was extremely fortunate to be offered a job with Polydor, for had I decided to go down the pub that day, I am not sure where I would have ended up. My first year was spent as the gofer for the tape marketing manager, before becoming Polydor jazz A&R man, a job that I enjoyed immensely as I was left alone and had a free hand. By 1977, the position became obsolete and I was promoted to looking after Polydor's American roster. During this period, I worked with rock bands, but it wasn't an enjoyable experience. On a trip to America to see Ritchie Blackmore's Rainbow, I got into a serious ruck with Ritchie, which nearly ended up with me chinning him. He was a thoroughly unpleasant bloke, and after this incident, I was fired from working on Rainbow.

At the back end of 1976, I'd written and recorded a punk single, 'I'm A Punk Star' b/w 'Me Brain Done Hurt', with some of my mates at Polydor. It was a hoot, but my song writing was more Abbott & Costello than Weller and Strummer – trust me, I'm an A&R man, I know these things! Because of the fuss that EMI made over the Pistols debut album, Polydor refused to press 500 promo records, which disappointed the band, as it meant our names were never going to be enshrined on vinyl. Tim Chacksfield sang backing vocals and was the Jam's product manager, and in 1978, he quit Polydor for a better position with another record company, his departure left a vacancy, and I saw my chance to move on.

At a meeting with my boss George McManus, I suggested the company move me sideways to Tim's position and promote my mate John Perou to take over my slot. The management agreed and I was more than happy, as by now I'd had enough of rock music. Allied to this, Polydor's American arm was worse than useless, forever struggling to get bands into the charts. The promotion coincided with the release of The Jam's fifth single and they were demoing songs for their third album, although at the time I had no idea what was going down.

I moved up the ladder with an air of expectancy, only to be brought down to earth rapidly, as unbeknown to me war had been declared between The Jam and Polydor. I'd heard the rumblings of discontent about the second album, and they'd delivered a number of tracks, mostly written by Bruce, which the company dismissed out of hand as not being good enough. Chris Parry subtly told Bruce to give up trying to write songs and get back to his day job, playing the bass, which went down like a lead balloon. This failed session led to journalists and fans believing there was a lost third Jam album, which has never existed, but the myth persists to this day. Even Paul mentioned it in an interview with *Uncut* magazine in March 2006.

Paul was going through a dry patch, which had more to do with the band having to record their second album so quickly after their first than being able to deliver the goods. The company was asking too much, expecting a young band and songwriter to come up with three albums in nineteen months, particularly as the third was going to be make or break for them. With all the attention that was now being paid to Paul, and the need to re-awaken his song writing, he moved out of the London flat he shared with Gill and returned home to his parent's house in Woking to write the songs for The Jam's next album.

The next few months were a real baptism of fire, with the band and John Weller at odds with the company. The shit was about to hit the fan and for a while it turned out to be a real nightmare. My promotion was far from a dream move.

John called for a meeting to discuss the fifth single and The Jam's third album, but I wasn't looking forward to attending. I could imagine the mood the boys would be in, and when I entered the studio, the atmosphere was decidedly unfriendly. Paul was very sullen, with an inner hostility about him. Unlike most other teenagers, he was almost always reticent, moody, and serious. Bruce was always immaculately dressed, and the only time I saw a hair out of place on his head was after the heavy drinking sessions that took place on tour. He could be moody bugger too and prone to fits of artistic temperament. Several times, I witnessed him lobbing teddy out of the pram. But at other times, he could be a warm and friendly bloke, and he always wore The Jam on his sleeve. Rick was the most laid back of the three, and wasn't so prone to outbursts of temperament. One thing I can say with absolute honesty about John, Paul, Bruce, and Rick, was that they were deadly serious about The Jam. They knew where they were going and what they wanted.

During the meeting, everyone had a pop at me, telling me that Polydor had gone over the top and letting me know exactly what they thought about the company. During these early days, my relationship with them was particularly difficult, and for quite a while, I was known as 'Jim Cook's spy', (Jim being my boss at Polydor), a sobriquet that wasn't quite true. It's fair to say that I was a company man, but my first loyalty was to the artists and bands I worked with. You have to gain their trust, let them know you are on their side, and you will support them through the hard times, not just when the hits are flowing. I left the meeting subdued, and returned to the office, not certain as to what would happen next.

There was considerable debate about whether to release their cover of Ray Davies's 'David Watts' or Paul's song 'Billy Hunt' as the A-side. Originally, 'Billy Hunt' had been picked with 'English Rose' & 'The Night' as the B-side, and as acetates of the B-sides exist, it must have been on the cards to release these tracks at one time. John and Chris had a chat with

Mickie Most, although I am not sure why they sought his opinion, and decided the single would be a double A-side, with 'David Watts' as the lead track. This kind of move is common practice when you are stuck for an original A-side. You record a classic cover to fill the gap, and crossover the single into the mainstream market and daytime airplay. Polydor was looking for a short cut, and this was a tried and tested method of obtaining chart success.

Most had a middling career as a singer in the early sixties in the style of Marty Wilde and Billy Fury – hence, his surname – and had a small hit with 'Mr Porter' in 1963. By the late seventies, he was a big name in the business, and had a good track record producing pop records. He appeared on a TV talent show, making acidic criticisms about the artists that appeared, who were easy targets for his snide comments. I have no idea whether he liked or was interested in punk music, although it's fair to say that any record exec would have automatically gone for 'David Watts' as it was written by one of the finest British songwriters of the sixties, a known song and, frankly, bloody obvious. After the likes of Mud and Suzie Quatro, it would be interesting to know what Most really thought about 'Billy Hunt'!

'David Watts' b/w 'A Bomb In Wardour Street' came out on August 11, 1978, and in the end reached only 25 in the charts, just two places higher than 'News Of The World'. Paul swaps lead vocals with Bruce and while the single is ok, it lacks the bite that their early singles had. I always preferred the song when they played it live, where it had an edge to it. The apocalyptic 'A Bomb' would be Paul's last punk type song and he would shun new wave, even though it brought his talents and The Jam to the notice of Polydor. Personally, I would have preferred to go with 'Billy Hunt', and although I never thought for one minute that it would have fared any better in the charts, it was a song The Jam's fans could directly identify with. The failure of such a tried and tested method of obtaining (false) success and the perceived failure of *This Is The Modern World* may have sewn seeds of doubt about the band's long-term future. Some thought, if they can't do it with a known song, could they do it with a Weller original? This single was talked up as being a turning point in the Jam's career, something I don't agree with, at least not as far as Polydor were concerned. No matter what the music press wrote, it was the chart position that mattered and a top thirty single made no real impression on the company.

The friction between Chris Parry and the band came to head with their third album. It wasn't just his blatant criticism of Bruce's song writing abilities, he was often absent when they were recording, which led to him being dropped as The Jam's co-producer. Chris's reasons for not being around at the time were, "I was heavily involved in the administrative side of the business at Polydor," which is not strictly true. Whilst The Jam were recording tracks for the third album, Chris spent the time working on his own future, and The Jam and Polydor were the last things on his mind. Having said that, I must pay him his dues and it's my opinion that he was one of the top A&R men of his generation, having signed The Jam and The Cure in 1978. Chris then left Polydor to set up Fiction and achieved considerable success worldwide with Robert Smith and The Cure.

During this period, I had to attend many meetings with my bosses, who were worried about the direction The Jam were taking. At one, it was suggested that now Chris was out of the picture Vic Smith should be given the heave-ho. After his success with The Stranglers, Martin Rushent's name came up as a replacement, and although he was one of the great producers of this era, as far as I was concerned he wasn't the man for job. This wasn't the moment for another change, it was a critical time in their career, and they were in the studios recording their new album. Bringing in a new face at this time would have made it even harder to get a result. Not only that, Vic had established a good relationship with the band, and after all the shit that had gone down, getting rid of him would have caused even more friction. Vic wasn't popular with Polydor, but alongside Chris, he'd done an effective and successful job.

At another meeting, the management hinted to me that The Jam needed a more professional manager, and it would be in my interest to help bring this about. I pointed out that they were talking about Paul's father and at the time, the band trusted John, and Paul, Bruce, and Rick had total confidence in him. This was one move too far, there were enough problems for me to cope with, never mind trying to persuade Paul to fire his old man. As far as Polydor were concerned, The Jam was a problem band, they couldn't be manipulated, they wouldn't change producers, or sack their manager, and the company didn't like having its authority challenged.

The Jam's next single, 'Down In The Tube Station At Midnight' b/w 'So Sad About Us' came out on October 6, 1978, and it turned out to be a classic 'Jam' song, charting at 15, two places lower than 'All Around the World'. When I first heard the tune, I knew it was a good 'un, but must admit to having reservations. No matter how much I liked it, it wasn't 'commercial' enough to give Polydor what it wanted – a top 10 hit. The complicated, wordy, and kaleidoscopic violent storyline was too heavy for daytime radio, and although a top twenty single the company wrote the song off as just another Jam single. The lyrics were about a late night mugging on a tube station and took an anti-violent stance, but outside of the band and their fans, most misconstrued the message, with Radio 1's old crooner, Tony Blackburn making scathing remarks on air about the music and lyrics of a new generation's music. Throughout The Jam and the Council's careers, Paul's messages were often misunderstood or lost, and there would come a time when even his loyal fans were unable to follow his line. The B-side was a cover version of a Who classic recorded as a tribute to drummer Keith Moon, who had died the previous month of an accidental overdose of a drug prescribed to combat alcoholism. Moonie's picture adorned the back of the picture bag. With this hit record, the mood of the company was less hostile, but the problems were still bubbling under the surface.

Both the band and Paul were very English, as exemplified in the storyline of 'Tube Station', and this aspect of their image was reflected in the criticism they received, both good and bad, throughout their career. It certainly held them back from breaking into the lucrative US market, but to achieve this they would have had to compromise everything they stood for. In the sixties, the new wave of Brit Pop that swamped the states encompassed both the Beatles and Herman's Hermits. It was simply pop music, uncommitted, and very few artists or bands made any kind of statement.

By the mid-seventies, there was musical chasm between the States and Britain. Punk was disturbing the cosy slumbers of AOR rock and the dreadful progressive music scene, and was about to alter the face of English music. Despite the valiant attempts of Iggy Pop and the New York bands like The Ramones that emerged from the CBGBs scene, nothing much would change in America until grunge came along in the nineties, led by Kurt Cobain and Nirvana. During the seventies and eighties, there was little chance of any band making it on the western side of the Atlantic playing The Jam's kind of music.

Before recording *All Mod Cons*, Paul's song writing reflected both his tender age, and the music that inspired and influenced him to form a band and write songs. There was an inkling of his talent with 'Away From The Numbers', the first indication that Paul had depth and wasn't going to be just an ordinary songwriter. 'Tube Station' cemented this; it may not have raced up the charts, but it showed how far he had developed from 'In The City'. The first two years of any songwriter's career is the most difficult, no matter who you are. At this point, you rely heavily on borrowing from your influences, and establishing your own style. It was also suggested at the time that Paul and The Jam were coming back with this single, although I am not sure from where, as every single and album had charted, and the band was highly thought of outside of Polydor's boardroom. Typically, people were looking at the glass and seeing it as being half-empty; instead they should have seen it as half-full.

Although the band was still suspicious of me, I would often pop into RAK and Eden studios to see them while they were recording. There was nothing underhanded about this, in the past I always enjoyed a 'friendly' relationship with the artists I'd worked with and wanted the same rapport with Paul, Bruce, and Rick. I really liked being in studios when artists are making their records, it was the most enjoyable part of the job, and it got me out of the office, and away from the politics and the ever ringing telephones.

One Saturday night while the band were recording *All Mod Cons* at RAK in St John's Wood I received a phone call at home, complaining about the boys. I was told they'd wrecked the studio, and asked to come and sort them out. I found this complaint a bit odd, as by now I knew them well enough that they weren't the type to cause malicious damage. When I arrived, I found the four of them legged up but in good spirits. They'd been up the local pub, had a few beers, and returned to the studio, stopping at a local chippy for a late night snack. I surveyed the studio for damage, and all I saw was a sprinkling of chips and sheets of newspaper scattered around the floor. There was no sign of the carnage I was expecting. Being a little pissed off at being dragged out on a Saturday night I had a word with the receptionist, pointing out that the boys were just having a little harmless fun, what's the problem? "It's not the kind of thing that we want at RAK studios," she said. "Mickie doesn't like it, so tell them to cut it out." I'm not sure whether I had a word or not, they were just lads, having a laugh and a few beers. At the time, I recall Led Zeppelin had damaged ABBA's studio with the costs running into thousands. I resolved to leave the phone off the hook at weekends in future.

Polydor released *All Mod Cons* two days before bonfire night on November 3 and the album set off its own firework display. So far, The Jam hadn't managed a top ten single, but the lack of single success, didn't stop it reaching number six in the charts. The album highlighted just what a talented tunesmith Paul had become, and the songs that most impressed me were, 'It's Too Bad', 'To Be Someone', 'Mr Clean', 'English Rose,' and 'In The Crowd'. The first two highlight what a great three-minute pop songwriter Paul was, and while both songs are commercial; this takes nothing away from the superb lyrics of both tunes.

Whenever I am asked what my favourite Jam song is, I reply, 'It's Too Bad'. No matter how many times I hear this, I never get bored, and often play it over and over again. It's a nod to The Who's 'So Sad About Us' and

The Beatles, with its 'yeah yeah' guitar riff. The storyline is of lost love, but whether the lyrics are about his own personal situation, given that he moved back with his parents, is open to question. Lost love has been a popular theme that songwriters throughout the last six decades have written about and all great tunesmiths seem able to conjure up lyrics of this ilk. Having this kind of talent is the difference between writing a sickly, or ordinary (lost) love song and being able to write a memorable tune, and 'It's Too Bad' is one of The Jam's finest.

When writing songs Paul often wrote from the outside looking in, and I recall one Jam fan accurately stating in a music magazine: 'The problem with Weller is, he is always sitting on the fence, and on the outside looking in'. Paul always had a tendency to view the world like this, which is easier than being on the inside looking out. 'To Be Someone' is about a pop star that had it all, and ends up back in the crowd with the rest of us. I have always found Paul's lyrics and The Jam's music absorbing and even though I have listened to this tune hundreds of times, I failed to notice Bruce's opening bass line, which later appeared in 'Start!'. Since starting in the business, I've lost count of how many stars ended up out on their arses with the rest of the crowd, it's a fickle industry to say the least.

Coming from a working class background, his distaste for the class system came through with the stinging 'Mr Clean', a theme that was constant throughout The Jam's career and one that Paul carried on with The Style Council. Inspired by the writing of Ray Davies of The Kinks, the lyrics are a warning that Paul has sussed out the establishment's Mr Clean and he'd better watch out. Given the problems that The Jam had with Polydor, I've often wondered whether the lyrics were aimed at Polydor's senior management, and Paul was having a dig at them.

'In The Crowd', with its references to Wall's ice cream and baked beans on toast, and its clumsy psychedelic ending, is another enduring Weller song. Listening to the lilting introduction, you could be lured into thinking it was going to be another pop song. It was anything but, and the opening gives way to an understated but nevertheless powerful backing track. Part of Paul's song writing talent was to be able to portray strong images and this tune shows how far this had developed in such a short time after the R&B-influenced debut album.

Among the power chords, there was 'English Rose', a song written during the ill-fated tour of America where they supported Blue Oyster Cult, which was a revealing portrait of a young Paul Weller. It wasn't the first ballad that he wrote for The Jam, as he'd written a few Beatle influenced ballads, which were demoed during the band's early days. There is a self-conscious feel to his vocals, the lyrics are very personal with a naïve charm about them, and you can hear just how lonely he was when he wrote it. Not many bands of this era featured acoustic numbers, and it was a brave move on his and The Jam's part to include this on the album.

The remainder of the album featured the three A-sides from their two previous singles and the title track 'All Mod Cons', which may have been another dig at Polydor. 'Fly', with its mixture of acoustic and electric guitars was never played live. 'The Place I Love' is more typical, with an urgent backing track and lyrics that contrast the violence of 'A Bomb'. All three tracks are excellent, but not quite as outstanding as the other tracks on this album.

The album was well received by the music press who showered the band and Paul with richly deserved compliments. I've never placed much faith in what is written in the music papers as I have seen ordinary albums receive five-star reviews, while stunning albums can receive a panning. However, with *All Mod Cons* they got it about right.

Unlike their second album, the band had demoed many of the songs prior to going into Eden and RAK studios in July and August to record the album masters. 'Tonight At Noon', 'David Watts', 'It's Too Bad', 'To Be Someone', 'Mr. Clean', and 'Fly' were all demoed on June 29 in Polydor's studio, and all the arrangements are close to the final recordings. When the band began the real recordings, they had played in many of the songs – and had they been given the same amount of time to prepare their second album, there's no doubt in my mind that it would have turned out differently. *This Is The Modern World* was written and recorded with too much haste, and many of the songs suffered as a result, the band having been unfairly pressurised into following up their debut album too quickly. This was a mistake and Polydor should have known this was risky. They knew Paul, as a songwriter, and the band were immature and just commencing their recording career. Had the third album been released under similar circumstances, it could have met the same fate.

A third album is not usually as difficult a hurdle to overcome as a second, but it's still crucial in any career. The first couple of albums tell you where a band is coming from, while the third defines where they are going. One could almost look on *All Mod Cons* as really The Jam's second album, given that *This Is The Modern World* was released on the back of *In The City* and showed just how far the group had progressed. On this level, *'All Mod Cons'* was an emphatic success: more accomplished in every way, and a giant leap forward from their early recordings. They'd learned how to pace a tune, that it was unnecessary to play everything at 100 mph to get your songs across.

Paul had refined his lead guitar/rhythm guitar technique and his vocals had really come on and so had Bruce and Rick, which gave the band a new, and more dynamic (Jam) sound. Paul's song writing had transcended his teenage period, and there was a more mature feel to what he had to say. Whatever music was influencing Paul, be it The Beatles, The Kinks or The Who or the poetry or the books he was reading, the change was immense, and extremely successful, boding well for The Jam's future.

Being the front man and (main) songwriter, Paul was always seen as the focal point of The Jam. If you're in the rhythm section, or the second guitarist, no matter how good a musician you are, you will always take second place to the man chewing the mike. But in a three-piece group, there is nowhere to run and hide, and the 'engine room' needs to be strong, or the whole group falls apart. Many have tended to underestimate Bruce and Rick's contribution, but it was as paramount as Paul's to the growth of the *band* at this time. They were never just his backing band, and it wasn't just Paul who came of age with this album, so did Rick and Bruce. When he moved in with Gill, he may have moved away from the band in one respect, but as far as *All Mod Cons* goes, The Jam was still a three piece. In addition, Vic's contribution to the album is understated, and I'm as guilty of this, as anyone. It was his deft touches which gave the album the polish that the early Jam singles and albums lacked. At the time, The Jam was still a fledgling band finding their feet, and after the second album it could have gone either way – not that I believed this. It couldn't have been easy for Vic, as the band was battling with Polydor, and I speak as someone who was in the middle of this war. Paul, Bruce, and Rick along with Vic, recorded what turned out to be *the* classic Jam album, and the beginning of a golden era of Jam singles and albums.

The packaging on The Jam's previous singles and albums sleeves had always contained sharp images and great photos, but with this album Bill Smith and the band surpassed all their previous releases. Bill did a fantastic job on *All Mod Cons,* which combined The Jam's very strong Mod image and exploited the imagery of prime influences, The Who. A strange thing happened as I was checking the artwork; I received a call to report to Polydor's MD, AJ Morris, who looked more like a public school headmaster than the MD of record company. I was a little puzzled as to what the meeting could be about, the album was being released on the back of a reasonably successful single, and there was a good buzz about it and I thought what the fuck could be the problem now. I entered his office and noticed he was closely scrutinizing the sleeve and inner bag. Now, the old man wasn't the creative type, administration was his game and I always made it a practice to keep him away from all things artistic. Stupidly I asked: "What's the problem." He replied: "I've been reading the lyrics [I groaned inwardly] and I'm not happy about them." I replied quickly: "Paul is a prolific songwriter, and one of the best of his generation." He retorted: "All well and good Dennis, but can't you get him to cut out the swearing, his songs would be better for it."

I was lost for words, something that doesn't often happen and mumbled something like: "If you censor his lyrics, they lose their impact, after all his songs are about his generation and the swearing is not included just for effect." He wasn't impressed, and asked me to inform Paul to tone it down. I left his office wondering if this chat had really taken place and thinking where the fuck was his head. Then again, he was a big fan of James Last and Andrew Lloyd Webber – 'nuff said.

To make my life even more interesting, in 1978 Polydor signed Siouxsie & The Banshees and Sham 69. Although rivals, they both had their own very different following and initially fared better in the single charts than The Jam, though in the long term neither were able to consolidate their early success and go on to become a major act. Sham 69's light burned brightly but fizzled out spectacularly when Jimmy Pursey and punk imploded.

Jimmy was the Max Bygraves of his generation, and sang street anthems for Sham's fan club to sing along with. Maybe someday a *Sing-a-long-a-Sham* CD will be released. I was never happy attending Sham 69 gigs, always arriving early as the shows turned violent, with sporadic fights breaking out. I would park my company car near the venue for a quick getaway and watch their show from the back of the auditorium, making sure I wasn't more than a couple yards from an exit. When trouble inevitably kicked off, I would make my escape. Indeed, I can't recall watching a Sham gig all the way through. The violence was brutal at times, and more often than not, the claret would be flowing. I still recall a gig at The Roxy, where the fighting was so appalling I left before they completed the third number. There's no doubt, there was also violent undercurrents at Jam concerts, but it was nothing like attending a Sham gig.

1978 was Sham 69's best year as far as the charts went, with their debut single 'Angels With Dirty Faces' reaching 19, whilst their follow up, 'If The Kids Are United' went to number nine. Tony Blair, the Prime Minister of the UK, used this ditty as the background music at the 2005 New Tory party conference, but whoever chose this song obviously had no idea what Sham were like, and I can't think of a better reason for him to step down from the leadership of the country. Their third single, the very mockney

'Hurry Up Harry', a song about going down the pub, went to number 10. Strangely enough, this song was chosen for England's 2006 World Cup song and aptly re-titled 'Hurry Up England'. However, Sham were unable to match this single success with their debut album *Tell Us The Truth*, which only went to 25 in the charts. Like The Jam, they released their second album *That's Life*, far too quickly, just nine months after their debut, and it staggered to 27.

Siouxsie & The Banshees were among the last name punk bands to be picked up, and I remember the day they came into Polydor to sign the contract. As soon as they had put pen to paper, we retired to Polydor's unofficial office, the public bar of The Lamb & Flag in James Street, to celebrate. I expected the band to be overjoyed at getting a deal, but as we drank to their success, it was an anti-climax and their mood sombre and quiet. In fact, they were down right miserable gits. I must admit to having a little crush on Siouxsie, as she was a very attractive girl, more often than not dressed in a mini skirt, stilettos, fishnets, and looking the business. However, it doesn't pay to get involved with the female artists you're working with.

Siouxsie & The Banshees were much wiser than The Jam or Sham 69 and released only one single and album during their first year. Their brilliant debut single 'Hong Kong Garden' raced to number seven and sold in excess of 250,000 copies, earning them a silver disc. Their debut album, *The Scream,* which in my opinion wasn't that far behind The Jam and The Clash's debut albums, went to number 12. Unfortunately, the career of the Banshees virtually stood still from this moment, with the exception of The Beatles' cover 'Dear Prudence', which went to number three some five years after their debut single. In 1980 and 1981, the albums *Kaleidoscope* and *Ju-Ju* went to five and seven respectively and although Siouxsie's career spanned more than ten years, they somehow failed to live up to the expectation that their debut single and album promised.

During the year The Jam's other rivals were either consolidating their positions or on the way out. The rapidly imploding Sex Pistol's solitary contribution to 1978 was their single 'No One Is Innocent', which featured the very guilty great train robber Ronnie Biggs on (uncredited) vocals and went to number seven. This record is best remembered for its B-side, which featured Sid Vicious' truly dreadful version of Frank Sinatra's 'My Way'. By this time, John Lydon had decided to jump ship to form Public Image. Jimmy Pursey was talked of as a replacement, but nothing came of it. The Stranglers released three singles but couldn't match their previous year's success, and The Clash also released three, 'Clash City Rockers', '(White Man) In Hammersmith Palais' and 'Tommy Gun', but none of these made any real impact on the singles charts. However, their second album, *Give 'em Enough Rope* stole The Jam's thunder when it went to number two in the album charts. Elvis Costello also released three singles, '(I Don't Wanna Go to) Chelsea', 'Pump It Up' and 'Radio Radio', which all reached the top thirty while his second album, *This Year's Model*, went to number four, two places higher than *All Mod Cons*. The Damned went off the radar screen, and Generation X just made the top fifty with their single, 'Ready Steady Go', while their debut album crept into the top thirty.

Another rival to The Jam was The Police, whom The Jam once supported and were also a trio. They made their first appearance in the charts this year with the single 'Can't Stand Losing You', which went to number two. I knew their guitarist Andy Summers from my Mod days in the sixties, when he played with Zoot Money's Big Roll Band and vividly recall a gig of theirs where they supported the Spencer Davis Group at The Shakespeare pub in Woolwich. Following this Zoot disbanded his big band and along with Andy formed the short-lived psychedelic band Dantalions Chariot, who played the Seventh National Jazz & Blues Festival in 1967 at the Royal Windsor Racecourse. I never thought of The Police as being the genuine article as far as punk went. Although they dressed the part, they were a pop band whose lyrics bore no resemblance to what most punk bands were singing about. Frontman Gordon Sumner, who went under the sobriquet of Sting, came to the attention of the public via a starring role in the film version of The Who's *Quadrophenia*, an everyday story of Mod life in the sixties, which was released two months prior to their first single.

Whilst The Jam was moving away from punk, new wave music had firmly established itself and had penetrated the singles chart. At the top, it made little difference as the number one records were by Abba, 10cc, John Travolta & Olivia Newton-John, Brian & Michael, The Bee Gees, Boney M, and Brotherhood of Man. The only vaguely punk band of 1978 to see the top slot was The Boomtown Rats, fronted by Bob Geldof, with 'Rat Trap'.

All Mod Cons was a pivotal album of that decade and cemented The Jam's future, and confirmed that they had a long career ahead of them. I was now more accepted, and the troubles with Polydor were swept under the carpet for the time being. I was ecstatic and really looking forward to 1979, hoping, perhaps naively, this undiluted success would have a positive affect on their relationship with Polydor. How wrong could I be? The following year would turn out to be one of the hardest periods of my career, and for a considerable time, I was isolated and fighting a rearguard action.

CHAPTER 3

Polydor Go Off The Boil

In December 1978, *All Mod Cons* won the prestigious *NME* album of the year award and The Jam came second in the Group Poll. For the first time Paul's writing abilities received recognition, when the poll made him the number two songwriter. This acknowledgment was the genuine article, for no matter what the record business think, the fans know what they want and they know a great band when they hear one. The respect paid to Paul, Bruce and Rick was an accurate reflection, of just how popular The Jam had become.

The next phase of their career was crucial, and The Jam needed to consolidate the success of their third album and plan things carefully, as their record deal called for them to deliver three singles and an album every year. As far as singles went, the band and Paul had problems coming up with a song that equalled the (chart) success of 'All Mod Cons'. At the time, Polydor saw this as weakness, failing to realise that The Jam were developing into an album band that made singles. In the singles charts they were up against the likes of The Bee Gees, who were cleaning up after *Saturday Night Fever*, and there was a huge disco boom at the time, and let's not forget, Abba, who by 1978, had racked up seven number one singles.

Prior to 1979, even The Clash was struggling in the singles chart. Their highest chart position was with 'Tommy Gun', which just sneaked into the top twenty. Their debut single, 'White Riot', only reached number 38, but it's unlikely the execs at CBS were having a downer at The Clash's lack of singles success. They knew their (early) singles were unlikely to get serious airplay on Radio 1, and concentrated instead on their albums, using singles simply as a marketing tool. Led Zeppelin never (officially) released a UK single during their career, but Atlantic Records didn't give them a hard time once they started to shift albums. Record companies make far more money from selling albums than singles whose sales by this time had more than halved since the heady days of the sixties.

Polydor was never happy at The Jam's insistence on not taking a single off an album after release, to try to further the sales of the album. They'd built up a large loyal following, and didn't want to rip off their fans. This guaranteed The Jam's longevity, and a fan base that would stick with them throughout their career. Looking back in hindsight, even if we had taken a single off, it wouldn't have made much difference to the overall sales of their albums. Although The Jam crossed over, they never quite managed to release an album, or a single that sold a half million copies plus.

In 1979, punk crossed over into the mainstream market, with The Jam, Ian Dury, Elvis Costello, and Sham 69, all enjoying top ten hit records, with The Clash's 'London Calling', just behind at 11. Punk would eventually implode, and by 1980, the bands on the periphery had fallen by the wayside with only a few going on to have long careers. Given the anarchy that surrounded the music, this was no surprise and had been predicted by the record business from day one. The major labels just couldn't deal with the music or the personalities that punk threw up. It was much easier for them to deal with groups like The Eagles, or dreadful American AOR bands like Boston and Kansas, or even the remains of the English pub rock scene, which actually wasn't much better.

No matter how successful an artist is, a major record company can make or break them, and quite easily fuck up their career. If they go off the boil, or the company decide they are a spent force and have had their moment, they will align themselves with what's coming next and move on quickly. This applied to The Jam; they were still the young pretenders to the throne and needed to consolidate on the success of their third album as early as possible in 1979.

As far as The Jam's seventh single, 'Strange Town', went, it was a bit of a mix and match affair, like two songs welded together which to some extent it was. The bridge was poached from 'Worlds Apart'; a song demoed a year earlier in February 1978, with Paul borrowing the vocal part from the

Buzzcock's 'What Do I Get'. On January 6, they recorded a version of this song, along with 'Simon', another Weller original, which never went beyond the demo phase. There is no doubt that after the blinding success of *All Mod Cons*, the band was under pressure to deliver, and perhaps this weighed heavily on them, particularly Paul. Even the production values of this single are down on the third album, and I'm not suggesting that Vic did a bad job. When you compare 'Strange Town' to what went before, and what followed, it's clear that whilst it's a good song, it wasn't one of their best. Lyrically, it's not as strong and they had two stabs at recording the song, which indicated to me that there were problems from the start. There's hardly any space in the song, and it has a claustrophobic feel, although live, once the song was played in, it came across more directly than the studio version. It was released on March 9 and like 'Tube Station' went to number 15 in the charts

The B-side, 'The Butterfly Collector', is a guv'nor track and without a doubt, a Jam classic, and a song that wouldn't have been out of place on their third album. Influenced by The Kinks 'Shangri La', it is a riveting piece of music, with lyrics exaggerating the lifestyle of Soo Catwoman, a girl who hung out with all the punk bands. I eventually met up with her when she was a member of The Invaders, a band signed to Polydor, and she was the main squeeze of their leader, Sid Sidelnyk, whose brother Steve played percussion with The Style Council and now drums for Madonna. In every respect, it is a better song than the A-side, both lyrically and musically, but there was never a chance of it coming out as a single. The content was too explicit, and after the problems with 'Tube Station', there is no way Radio 1 would have given it airtime. Had it been the A-side, it would have struggled in the charts.

The picture bag for this single has a blurred image of a man standing at a crossroads, which just happened to be Bill Smith, who designed the sleeve.

Although The Jam enjoyed success in the album charts, their singles never sold beyond their hard-core fan base, and if they were going to cross over into the mainstream, they needed to improve the chart performance of their singles. Polydor was certainly looking for an improvement in this area, and when this single only went to 15, and after the heady success of their third album, they falsely saw this low chart position as a failure. Many believed, *All Mod Cons* was their apex and there was a possibility that the band – like the punk movement – was about to implode.

If life wasn't hard enough, Sham 69, and Siouxsie & The Banshees decided to release singles during the same month as The Jam. Sham's fourth single, 'Questions And Answers', only got to number 18 and Siouxsie didn't fair any better. They followed up their top ten record 'Hong Kong Garden' with 'The Staircase (Mystery)', which only reached 24.

Shortly after the release of the three singles, Sham's manager Tony Gordon turned up in my office, shouting and accusing me of favouring The Jam and The Banshees. He immediately went into one, and said I wasn't putting enough effort into Jimmy and Sham 69. A little later Siouxsie's manger Nils Stevenson came in accusing me of favouring The Jam and Sham 69, and apart from fancying Siouxsie [true], I wasn't working hard enough on the Banshees. I felt a little beleaguered and couldn't believe what happened next. Within a few minutes of Nil's departing, John Weller came in. There was no "hello Den," he was straight to the point. "I am pissed off with you; you're not giving The Jam the same fucking attention that you give those other wankers, Sham 69 and the fucking Banshees." John always had a nice turn of phrase and with that stormed out of the office. This left me slightly bewildered, as I (honestly) tried not to favour any of the bands, and did my best for all three. John's tirade did it, and I thought fuck the lot of them, and went home for an early bath.

You couldn't hope to meet different managers than these three. Tony Gordon was very middle-class, well spoken and dressed like a Lincoln Inn's lawyer, and he went on to manage Boy George and The Cult. How he got on with Sham and The Angelic Upstarts, whom he also managed, was beyond me. Nils Stevenson was a waif-like character with hedgehog haircut and his background beggars' belief. His old man was Lord Chief Justice Melford Stevenson (Lord of the Rolls), and I cannot imagine what his father made of his occupation. John was working class through and through. He had a gruff manner about him, and (like Paul) wasn't afraid to throw in the occasional fuck when talking to the directors of the company. He certainly brightened up many of the meetings that I attended.

As 'Strange Town' wasn't a top ten record, the company was disappointed and behind my back someone decided it was the time to chance another tried and tested industry ploy to obtain chart success, specifically to bring in a heavyweight (famous) producer. Evidently, they hadn't learnt anything from the 'David Watts' and the infamous third album period. At the time, the producers making a name for themselves were Steve Lilywhite (Siouxsie), Martin Rushent (Stranglers), and Chris Thomas and Bill Price (Sex Pistols). I knew Martin and Steve personally, and though they were great producers, I never felt they had the right personality to work with The Jam, and particularly Paul. As for Chris Thomas and Bill Price, the fact that they had worked with the Pistols would have put the band off and it's highly unlikely they would have bought into the idea of working with either of them.

If I thought Vic wasn't good enough, I would have said something when Chris Parry got the sack. *All Mod Cons* proved he was the man for the job, but the company didn't see it this way and were still unhappy with him producing the band. The producer they came up with was the legendary Sir George Martin of Beatles fame, whom they saw as the man to smooth out the Jam's sound and make them more acceptable for the American market. Sir George is a legend in the business, one of the all time great producers, but in my opinion, he was the wrong man for The Jam, and I am not writing this comment in hindsight. Had the company asked what I thought of this move, I would certainly have baulked at the idea.

Sir George was from my father's generation and served in the Second World War with the British Fleet Air Arm as a ranking officer. At the time, The Jam went into the studios to record *Setting Sons* he was 53, and had no affinity and very little time for punk music. This is understandable, as during his early career, he produced the likes of Stan Getz and Judy Garland, and comedy records by Peter Cook & Dudley Moore, Peter Ustinov, Bernard Cribbins, and most famously, The Goons. Amongst others, he also produced hits for The Temperance Seven and Sir Cliff Richard.

I have often wondered what would have happened to Sir George and the Beatles if a label other than Parlophone had signed the fab four. It was the right time and the right place for both parties, with Martin becoming an integral part of their music. Nevertheless, he was still the wrong man for The Jam, and I suspect he would have found the lyrical content of many of Paul's songs difficult to deal with. My generation were running the industry and they were having a hard enough time coming to terms with punk, and I can't imagine what my father's generation thought about Mohican haircuts and bondage trousers. I recall my old man giving me a hard time when I came home in a maroon Mohair, telling me to take it back to the tailors. My comments about Sir George might sound sacrilegious, but I have lost count of how many bands he produced who were talked up as 'the next Beatles', before disappearing into obscurity. During his illustrious career, Sir George also produced Jeff Beck, America, Elton John, Jose Carreras, Celine Dion, Little River Band, Cheap Trick, Ultravox, and it's difficult to see where The Jam fit in amongst these very mainstream artists.

I could have understood if Polydor had gone for a more contemporary producer, but by going for Sir George, they were just looking for a short cut to success. The company knew The Beatles were an influence on Paul, and perhaps thought this would sway him. They thought – wrongly – that by dangling him under the boy's noses, it would help remove Vic; however, the band and Paul were having none this and quite rightly stuck by him.

George's services were much in demand, his diary must have been full, and I wonder whether he would have had the time to fit The Jam into his busy schedule. I have a sneaking suspicion that the company made only a cursory approach, exploited the idea as a ruse to off load Vic, whose nose was already out of joint. This move didn't help matters, and for the rest of the time Vic worked with The Jam, he was ambivalent towards Polydor. All Polydor needed to do, was listen to *All Mod Cons*, and 'The Butterfly Collector'. While Vic's talents may not have been up to those of the fifth Beatle, he did a terrific job. With 'Strange Town', it wasn't the production values that were the problem – even Mr Sheen would have problems putting a gloss on this track.

As we approached their eighth single, both sides were dug in, and there was no chance of a ceasefire in hostilities. I was hopeful that the next single, 'When You're Young' would change this, and give everybody what they wanted. When I heard the track, as far I was concerned, it was going to be the single that would crack the charts wide open. For a reason that I'm now not sure of, I wrongly compared it to The Who's classic teen anthem, 'My Generation', although the story line was more pessimistic and bleak. There was no doubt in my mind that in every aspect the song was an improvement on 'Strange Town', and a precursor to the way Paul, Bruce and Rick were developing and an indication of the direction of their next album. Lyrically, it is stronger and not as muddled, with a much more direct storyline, summing up the feelings of the teenage generation at the time. There was even a hint of reggae in the break, perhaps an indication that Paul's lug 'oles were tuning into something different.

The B-side, 'Smithers-Jones', is Bruce's finest contribution to the Jam songbook. The storyline follows a man who after years of committing himself to his employers is unexpectedly sacked, leaving him with an uncertain future. The sentiments are as prevalent now as when the song was written in 1979, with principles and loyalty counting for nowt. I recall one of Paul's so-called yes men telling me the tag Paul wrote for the song made the tune, which is unjust. Yes, Paul's lyrics round off the song nicely, giving it a more solid ending, but this doesn't alter the fact that the song is good enough in its own right, and always went down well with the fans.

The single was released on August 17, but only reached 17 in the charts, and like 'Strange Town', sold around 150,000 copies. I was disappointed with this showing and considered the company culpable, for as far as I was concerned the record and the band were good enough, but Polydor wasn't. To say I was unhappy is an understatement; I was running around the corridors of Polydor like a bear with a sore head, and looking for a scapegoat to blame for the singular lack of chart success. At the same time, Sham 69 had a massive hit record with 'Hersham Boys', which sold in excess of 250,000, and reached number six in the charts. Even though they were one of my bands, it didn't help my mood, which turned blacker by the day.

Paul, too, must have noted the huge success of his rival's single, but I'm not sure whether it really gave him that much grief; he knew he was a more talented songwriter than Jimmy Pursey and 'Hersham Boys' owed a lot to Jimmy Edwards who co-wrote the song. Many of his contemporaries were having bigger hits, but very few were writing lyrics in the same vein as Paul. Blondie's 'Heart of Glass' and 'Sunday Girl', The Police's 'Message In A Bottle' and 'Walking on The Moon' and Gary Numan's 'Are Friends Electric' and 'Cars' were pure pop records. I've always believed that Paul could have written songs of this ilk throughout his career, but chose not too. He wanted The Jam to mean something, and for him to be known as a quality songwriter.

I wrongly blamed our promotion department for the lack of success of 'When You're Young'. Their job is not easy, but it's nowhere near as difficult as an A&R man's job: if the bands you sign don't make it, you're out on your arse. When a promo man fails to get your records played on the radio, they come back with a plethora of excuses: the hook wasn't good enough; or the lyrics were too hard or they're not playing this kind of single at the moment; and your band's wearing the wrong kind of underpants. During the many years I worked in the music business, I heard just about every excuse as to why Radio 1 didn't play my records.

Tony Bramwell was assigned promotional duties for The Jam, and he was a legend in the business. Tony grew up in Liverpool and was childhood friends with The Beatles, going on to work with them throughout their illustrious career. There was no doubting his credentials, he knew everyone who was anyone in the music business, and if he chose too could open doors at Radio 1, *Top Of The Pops* and just about every other radio and TV station in the country. Once, at a singles meeting, he phoned a Radio 1 DJ while he was on air, and asked him to play a Polydor single – and a little later, the single was played. The Jam, however, were not impressed, and unhappy about the way he worked their singles. Tony's rapport with the band wasn't great; as far as they were concerned, it was fuck his track record, he's wasn't doing it for The Jam.

Still steaming about 'When You're Young', I wrote to my bosses with regard to Tony's and the company's attitude towards The Jam. It was several pages long and bluntly pointed out that unlike the other bands on Polydor,

The Jam had a long-term future. I suggested comparisons with artists from the past four decades, listing the two or three that went on to have careers that lasted 30 years. I put the bulk of the blame on the promotion department, and their lack of enthusiasm, for the failure of the single. As far as I was concerned, they were tossers, posers, living off their past reputations. In hindsight, I was well out of order, but I could see the company losing The Jam as interest in the band had begun to wane. Maybe a little bit of paranoia was creeping in, but I was desperate for The Jam to have a successful single, if only to get Polydor off my back.

The memo had no affect on my boss, Jim Cook, the man responsible for signing Sham 69. He came into my office and threw the memo on to my desk proclaiming, "When the ship sinks [punk] it will go down with all hands [bands], nobody will survive." His comments pissed me off. I pointed out how in the past many artists transcended the trend they were a part of initially. As well as The Jam, Elvis Costello and The Clash looked to be to be able to transcend new wave and have prolonged careers. Alas, my comments had no affect. I was getting more frustrated, I knew whatever happened next, there had to be a change.

'The Eton Rifles', a song that Paul had demoed at Polydor's studios earlier, was chosen as the next single. It was the first time he'd written a complete song, without the aid of Bruce and Rick, and the arrangement was presented to them as a fait accompli. Even without the blistering backing track, and in the simplest form on the demo, you can hear what a great song this is.

The song was recorded at the Townhouse Studios in Shepherds Bush and after listening back to the finished track, everyone thought it had a real chance. From the opening power chords, the pace is breathtakingly sustained until the very end. It was one of the most direct singles The Jam had recorded to date. When I first heard it, the prominent Hammond organ solo surprised me as I didn't expect the band to feature this instrument on a single. It was also noticeable how much more muscular and confident Paul's voice is on this track, compared to some of his previous recordings. He was stepping up a gear; in the past, he sometimes sounded tentative, and not completely happy with some of his lyrics or his own performances.

These lyrics were anti-establishment, and anti-middle class, and were supposed to be humorous, but many fans missed the humour. I have never been one to over-intellectualise about music and lyrics, they are as personal to the listener, as they are to the writer, but many times the listener's view is out of synch with what the writer is trying to get across, and mixing humour with a political slant is difficult at the best of times. Throughout his career, Paul's humour has been misconstrued, and as close as I worked with The Jam, the Council and Paul, some of his humour went above my head, and was only apparent when he pointed it out or if I read about it in later interviews. Many great artists over the last five decades have suffered similarly. It's not that fans are obtuse or stupid; their heads are not always where the writers are, and they re-interpret the song to fit their own personal view. Credit also must be given to Vic, whose production on this single is spot on.

The B-side was 'See-Saw', which was covered by the Scottish band The Jolt, also on Polydor, but like other bands who covered Paul's songs, they couldn't quite do it justice. Certainly, during The Jam's days, Paul wrote songs for *The Jam,* making it almost impossible for other artists to cover them. At the time, many fans were confused about this track, as it wasn't in keeping with what The Jam were trying to achieve. I suspect it became the B-side because there weren't enough tunes recorded for the next album, and taking an existing track would have denuded the album and given the band even more problems, and they were getting nearer its release date.

'Eton Rifles' was The Jam's most commercial single to date and provided it got airplay on Radio 1, it looked to be the record to set the charts alight. Unexpectedly, I got a call from John to attend a meeting to discuss the new single. I wasn't looking forward to this one bit, and turned up in full riot gear, expecting it to kick off. To my surprise, the boys and John were very quiet, and there was no histrionics. Paul was his usual moody self, and I fully expected Bruce to blow up, but he didn't. Rick was quiet, and they made it clear how they felt. John categorically stated: "Den, something's got to be done about Tony." He went on to explain that the boys still weren't happy with him, and perhaps it was time for a change. All three made the point that they didn't care about his past success; he wasn't doing the biz for The Jam. Holding my breath, I told them: "Ok I'll have to line someone else up first, and then have a word with AJ [the MD] and see what I can do." Now I knew this wasn't going to be easy, Tony Bramwell was one of the old man's favourites, almost treating him like son, and I had to tread carefully, after all Polydor paid my mortgage. I considered several pluggers for the gig, and in the end plumped for Clive Banks who I'd worked with when he managed a band called The Dodgers. He had a solid reputation, was rated as one of the best promo men in the business, and had done a good job on The Boomtown Rats and The Pretenders.

When I first approached Clive, no one in the company had heard the single, I wanted to keep my powder dry, and I planned to keep it that way. Armed with an acetate of the finished song I went to see him at his office.

Given the problems that Polydor's promo department had in the past, I was a little worried about the lyrics, which alluded to politicians' covert sexual proclivities. I asked Clive whether they were going to be problem with the eggheads at Radio 1. He wasn't worried and was very positive about the single, going on to explain how he was going to work the record. At the end of the meeting, I told him: "As long as I can get this past the MD you've got the job." There was no doubt in my mind, he was the man, and I knew working with The Jam would enhance his own credibility and reputation. I wasn't looking forward to the next step, and I organised a meeting with the MD, Tony Bramwell, and John Weller to discuss the promotion of 'Eton Rifles'.

By the time this meeting took place, I'd played the record to the company, but hadn't mentioned my clandestine meeting with Clive. John opened up the discussion, growling: "The boys are not happy with the way they are being promoted, we're not getting the airplay that the other wankers are." I have to give Tony his due as he promptly admitted that his relationship with The Jam was a problem, and we continued discussing the matter, without coming to any conclusions. John piped up: "Something's gotta be done, what do you think Den?" I glanced at AJ, expecting him to step in, but he had inexplicably gone into silent mode, and it was left to me make a decision. I reluctantly said: "There has to be a change. The Jam's next single is important – we need to bring in someone else." I then mentioned I'd spoken to Clive Banks, and providing everyone was ok about him, he was up for it. I didn't mention the fact that I had played him the single first, as I knew this would have made me as popular as a rattlesnake in a lucky dip.

As far as John and AJ go, I was more than a little pissed off with them. They both had the clout, but not the bottle, to come out and ask Tony to stand aside, and left me to shovel the shit. Once this got around the promotion department, I knew there would be reprisals. A couple of days later, I received a visit from Joey Reddington, an oppo of Tony, who during his career had worked for Paul McCartney and he vented his spleen. Blaming me for Tony's sacking, he called me every name under the sun and his parting remark was a dire threat: "Don't expect us to work on any of *your* bands in the future." They were true to their word, and for sometime after, I know they didn't put the effort into the other [unknown] bands I was working on. One time on entering the promo office, I noticed one of my bands promo singles were stuffed in a rubbish bin.

I've always been worse than useless at office politics, and I may have been wrong to go behind the company's back and maybe given Tony a second chance. But I have no remorse then or now about bringing Banks in as it was the right call. 'Eton Rifles' was a crucial moment in The Jam's career, the company were having serious doubts, and a big hit was essential to remedy this. The single was released on October 26 and Clive delivered the airplay to give The Jam their first top five single, reaching number three. It took them into the big time, and proved to be the springboard for greater things to come. They increased their fan base to a level that would see them regularly sell in excess of a quarter of a million singles, and 'Eton Rifles' was their first single to receive a silver disc. Even though I was still getting grief from our promo lads, I was ecstatic, and looking forward to their fourth album, which they were also recording at The Townhouse.

Much has been written about Polydor exerting pressure on The Jam to complete their fourth album, which isn't quite true, or at least that's not how I remember it. Their tour schedule for the middle of the year was light, as they knew they had to record their new album. By this time, the end of year tour would have been booked and there would have been no point in playing such a massive (sell-out) tour with no new album in the shops and with fans unfamiliar with their new repertoire. If the album had been postponed, it would have meant undertaking a second UK tour in the New Year to support its eventual release, which would have had an adverse affect on their plans for 1980. There's no doubt that as the deadlines got nearer, pressure was brought to bear on the band to finish the album, as by this time the music press were aware that a new album was due, and their tour had been confirmed.

In Graham Willmott's book, *The Sound Of The Jam*, Rick is quoted as saying: "At the time we (The Jam) were afforded the luxury of being able to afford studio time." Rick was always very down to earth; however, his statement is not quite correct. By now, The Jam's royalties were in the black, and as their recording costs were recoupable against future earnings, any money they spent was their own, and would eventually be deducted from their earnings on record sales. I can assure you, Polydor didn't give a monkey about how much The Jam spent, and were quite prepared to advance John money whenever he asked. The company knew they would get it back from sales of their back catalogue and the fourth album. Whilst they had the luxury of time to record their album, they had failed to prepare sufficiently, and at the death, Paul hadn't written enough songs to complete the album.

Setting Sons was supposed to be a concept album, but only enough tracks were demoed for about half the album before going into record masters at the Townhouse. 'Girl On The Phone' and 'Private Hell' were demoed on October 1, just six weeks before the album was released. The Jam had demoed 'Along The Grove' and Bruce's song, 'The Best Of Both Worlds' on September 11, and 'Hey Mister' was demoed at the same time as the acoustic versions of 'Burning Sky' and 'Thick As Thieves'. Paul was either unhappy or unsure about these tunes and didn't progress them further, which is why 'Heatwave' was included. I don't know why Bruce's song wasn't included, it ain't a great track, but with a bit of work and help from Paul, it could have been better, and at the very least, it was a Jam song.

As far as touring went, between May 24 and November 2, they played only one gig (Saddleworth Arts Festival on June 9). Prior to this, they played 34 dates over a five-month period (151 days), which included eight in February, one in March, ten in April, and 15 in May. They played just over 60 gigs during the whole year and other than promoting the singles, it left the rest of the time free. Nobody at Polydor was expecting a new album until the last quarter, when it would tie in with their massive autumn tour.

The release date had nothing to do with being in time for Christmas. The Jam were still not big enough to have any impact on this market, even with a top five record they hadn't crossed over into the bigger pop market. When *Setting Sons* came out Polydor weren't struggling for turnover as The Bee Gees had delivered a number one single and album, and in November, a *Greatest Hits* package was released to coincide with Christmas market. In addition, there could be no complaints about Vic, as he couldn't record the album any faster than Paul wrote the tunes. If Vic had a fault it was his laid-back approach, and I remember he once remarked that it didn't matter how long it took to record an album, or a single, as long as you got it right. This attitude is fine when you're shifting a million albums, but The Jam's albums never did. However, on *Setting Sons* Vic is not culpable, but should have learned from this experience. If I thought for one minute that Polydor were out of order, I wouldn't hesitate to have a go, but this time the pressure to release the album was due to a lack of planning and preparation at the beginning of the year.

No matter what was happening with the management, or their chart position, The Jam always had the support of the grass roots at Polydor, and it never waned. I was angry with the company when they wouldn't make an early single one of the three priority singles of the week. That night, I received a call at home from one of our strike force salesmen who told me: "Den, don't worry, the lads would take care of it privately, The Jam's single wouldn't get lost." The boys were always around Polydor's offices, and they chatted to everyone in the company, whether it was the MD, or the post boy Perry, which made them very popular.

If you want to talk about pressure, at the same time Siouxsie & The Banshees were really under the cosh. They began a large UK tour to support the release of their second album, but after a few gigs, Kenny Morris and John McKay decided to leave the group. Famously, they left resignation notes on the pillows in their hotel room, fleeing into the night like young nocturnal lovers. This was a crucial moment in the Banshees career, and many people, including myself, thought this would be the end of them. Robert Smith of The Cure stepped in to fill John McKay's shoes, which meant for the rest of the tour he played the opening set with his band and then went straight back on stage to play with the Banshees. Budgie, the only male member of The Slits, was brought in on drums, so not only was the tour saved, but the Banshees career as well. Siouxsie and Steve Severin overcame the trauma of losing half of their group, something I don't think many bands would have withstood.

Whatever has been said, everyone knew from the beginning of the year what the contract demanded, and all the advances would have been banked before they went into the studio. After the success of *All Mod Cons*, The Jam had moved on from being a niche band, and were fast becoming a big business, and needed to plan everything meticulously. They were under no more pressure than their rivals, or the other bands on Polydor, or any other record company, come to that.

When I took over The Jam, and became their product manager, it meant I co-ordinated the releases of their records and marketing, while Chris Parry took care of the A&R (music) side. When he left Polydor to set up Fiction, it left a void and Polydor brought in another A&R guy to take Chris's place, but he found it hard going, and through no fault of his own wasn't able to build a relationship with John and the boys. After a month or so, he told me he wasn't able to contribute and it would be better if I took over his role, as well as my own. I thought great, double bubble, but Polydor had other ideas, and although I worked both jobs, I still received the same salary. When I was the Jazz A&R manager, A&R was easier, as most albums took a day to record and in some cases only a few hours, and then it was down the pub for a pint. As far as pop music went, I wasn't sufficiently experienced, but had to learn fast. Given John's age and his abilities, it was probably too much to expect him to totally comprehend this aspect of the business. He had enough on his plate, what with everything else that went down with managing a successful band.

To make my life interesting, Sham 69's third, and Siouxsie & The Banshees second albums were scheduled for release at the same time as The Jam's fourth album. This gave me no end of problems as the bands were competing with each other, but any suggestions that Polydor had aligned themselves with either of these bands is unfair. To avoid any accusations of favouritism, each band were allocated £15,000 from the marketing budget, their marketing campaigns were identical and they received the same amount of advertising, fly posting and button badges. Even though there was a rift between The Jam and the company, when The Jam's album eventually came out, Polydor did the biz. All three albums were sold into the shops simultaneously, but as *Setting Sons* was held back until the last possible moment, it actually benefited The Jam as the sales team re-sold the album for a second time, on the back of a top five single, bringing in even more orders. There's no doubt that as the deadlines got nearer, pressure was brought to bear on the band to finish it, as by this time the music press were aware that a new album, and a large tour were due.

The running order of the album wasn't decided until the last minute and the first pressings had the track listing stickered on the back of the sleeves, an indication of how close we were to the release date. As far as the sleeve goes, Bill Smith once again did a great job and the packaging was superb. The front contained the striking image of the Benjamin Clemens sculpture of three St John Ambulance Bearers, whilst the inner bag, with the lyrics and photos of a very English bulldog and Union Jack deck chair on Brighton beach. The album sleeve won an award in 2002 when it was voted one of the best album covers of all time. As good as it is – I still think that *All Mod Cons* is the ultimate Jam sleeve and cannot understand why this didn't feature in the poll.

Paul's intention that the fourth album would be a concept album based on his left of centre politics didn't quite work, and only a few of the songs fit into this theme. It was an ambitious idea, and when they went in to record the album, there wasn't the time to carry it through. The album was released on November 16, and was much darker than *All Mod Cons.* Vic's production was slicker than the records that preceded it, something that Paul wasn't happy about, finding the sound a little dense, with too many overdubs, preferring the stripped down sound of his next album. Whatever his reservations were, the slick production certainly helped with 'Eton Rifles', which sounded great on the radio, and a step up from their previous recordings in terms of production values.

The album includes many tracks that became Jam classics. 'Private Hell' was a damming indictment on middle-class suburban life, and the desperation of middle-aged woman in crisis. I'd been through my own (but different) private hell with a member of my family and could readily associate with the sentiments of the song. When Paul wrote the lyrics, there was more than a grain a truth about them, and the song was about a real person, someone who was actually living the private hell. 'Thick As Thieves', a song about friends falling out, might have been an early signpost that all was not well within the group. By 1979, they each had their own circle of friends, and rarely socialised outside of when they were recording and touring. It's been said that this song is about Paul's changing relationship with his old school mates, Dave Waller and Steve Brookes, but I'm not sure about this. I had a (strange) conversation with Paul the following year, and looking back on the history of The Jam, it suggested to me that this song might also have also been about his relationship with Bruce and Rick.

'Saturday's Kids' was a tune that I could really relate too, as I grew up on a notorious council estate in Plumstead and many of my mates were Saturday kids. If I had been born in 1958 and not 1948, there's no doubt I would have been a Muppet at Jam gigs. Bruce clearly wasn't the songwriter that Paul is, but his revamped version of 'Smithers-Jones', which hearkened back to The Beatles 'Eleanor Rigby', is no embarrassment amongst the other tunes on the album. Although, I wonder if Paul had written enough songs to complete the album, would they have recorded this version?

'Little Boy Soldiers', an anti-war statement and an attack on the kind of naïve patriotism that leads to the unnecessary death of young men in the name of their Queen and country. Given what is going on in Iraq at this very moment, nothing seems to have changed and this song is as meaningful now as it was in 1979.

'Burning Sky' is about a man with bills to pay and mouths to feed who has lost the innocence of youth, and is making the most of the nine-to-five grind; something that happens to all of us, did any of us see our futures when we were teenagers, or want to? 'Wasteland' is one of the few tracks that isn't slickly produced, although it doesn't suffer. It's not quite up to the quality of some of the others; nevertheless, this melodic and wistful English song is a nice counterpoint to some of the more heavier tunes of this album.

'Girl On The Phone', which was knocked out during the recording session, is not quite up to the (very high) standards of many of the others. It is semi-autobiographical and about the problems artists face trying to retain their anonymity, something that Paul has struggled with most of his life. Too many artists have received undue attention from over obsessed fans stalking them. It's the price they pay for fame, and being in the public eye, and once you're up there, you can forget about privacy. Some fans think that because they've bought your album, they own a part of you.

There's no doubt that 'Heatwave' is out of place on this album, and it would have been better to have another original. Paul's mum, Anne, always harangued me about how much better The Jam's version was than the original, by Martha & The Vandellas, and no matter what I said, she just wouldn't accept that The Jam's version came second to the original. Ably assisting The Jam are Rudi on sax and a certain Michael Talbot on Hammond organ. Paul's vocals on this track are mannered and personally, I've always preferred the version on *Live Jam*, which has so much energy, something that is difficult to capture in recording studios. Although the version I recorded at The Jam party in 1980, by The Greyhound All Stars, takes some beating!

Given that the album was rushed, it has a very short running time at just over 32 minutes, and if you take off 'Heatwave' and 'Smithers-Jones' there's only just over 27 minutes of new original music. Nevertheless, and regardless of all the problems with the album, it was a success and went to number four in the charts, giving The Jam their highest album chart position yet. The success of 'Eton Rifles' and *Setting Sons* changed the attitude of the company towards the band, and the wounds caused by the earlier problems were healing, however a year later they were opened up again. I recall one of the execs finally getting the message about the band at the Bingley Hall gig. As we were leaving, he was waxing lyrically about how good The Jam were and what a great band they had become.

1978 saw the rise of the second Mod revival and by 1979 it was in full flow, and being a first generation Mod, I took a keen interest. I was looking after The Chords, who had signed to Jimmy Pursey's label, and as far as I was concerned they were streets ahead of their rivals. They had a decent songwriter in Chris Pope, and had they received the breaks, could have gone all the way. Their first record, 'Now It's Gone', with its target label, produced by Jimmy Pursey and Peter Wilson, should have been the Mod revival's first single. Prior to its release The Chords, perhaps stupidly, invited Pursey to Guildford Civic Hall where they were supporting The Undertones. Refused permission to get on stage for the Undertones encore [by their tour manager], Pursey, together with Paul Cook and Steve Jones, led a 200-strong skinhead invasion of the stage. Lighting rigs and amplifiers were smashed, a fracas erupted, and the gig was abandoned in total confusion and chaos.

The Chords witnessed the entire episode from the upstairs balcony, and were gutted at Pursey's behaviour. Buddy Ascott appeared in the office the next day, angry and upset over the brawl, and gave me an ultimatum: "If the Chords remained signed to Pursey's label, he would quit the band." Now I knew Buddy wore his heart on his sleeve, but he really meant it, he was upset and a meeting was organised with Pursey to discuss this incident.

Jimmy showed no remorse. By this time, his ego was so inflated by his own success that he couldn't see he'd done anything wrong. It was an angry meeting, but passed off with no blood being spilled, and it was agreed the band would sign directly to Polydor. They recorded, a new version of their debut single, and it came out on September 19 and went to 63 in the charts. Unfortunately for The Chords the Mod revival was snowballing, and the Merton Parka's single, 'You Need Wheels', claimed the title of "the Mod revival's first single". Released in August, it went to 40 in the charts. The band was led by brothers Steve and Mick Talbot, whom Paul had befriended.

Another Mod band Secret Affair had a top twenty hit (13) with their Mod anthem, 'Time For Action', but had no real substance. Ian Page mistook verbal diarrhoea for style, and whilst he talked himself up as being a leader, he never delivered the goods. Looking good wasn't the answer, you needed talent as well. Owing to a lack of genuine original talent, this revival was doomed, and petered out by the end of 1980. Most bands were merely mock imitations of The Jam, with little or no song writing skills and the vast majority drifted into obscurity. The Jam tried to distance themselves from this revival, but were seen as the band leading the pack. Whether Paul liked it or not, he was the leader; after all, he had championed the Mod look, which Jam fans and Mod revivalists emulated and replicated at Jam gigs.

Meanwhile, The Jam's stablemates Sham 69 and Siouxsie & The Banshees were enjoying mixed fortunes. Sham followed up their number six hit record 'Hersham Boys' with 'You're A Better Man Than I', but this unremarkable single just crept into the top fifty at 49. They released *The Adventures Of The Hersham Boys* in September, and it gave them their biggest chart album when it went to number eight in the charts. Siouxsie released three singles, all a bit pretentious, and nowhere near as good as their debut. Following 'The Staircase (Mystery)', their second single, 'Playground Twist', crept into the top thirty, and stuck at 28, whilst their third single, 'Mittageisen (Metal Postcard)', struggled to get into the top fifty, and died a swift death after reaching 47. Their second album contained the mind numbingly and monotonous performance of 'The Lords Prayer', but still managed to get to 13 in the charts.

The Jam's other main rivals, The Clash, had fallen slightly behind. They released three singles, 'English Civil War' (25), 'The Cost of Living' EP (22) and 'London Calling', which gave them their biggest hit single so far, and went to 11 in the charts, some eight places below The Jam's 'The Eton Rifles'. Their third album, *'London Calling'* went to nine in the album charts, five places below *Setting Sons.* Stiff Little Fingers made their first appearance in the album chart with their album *Inflammable Material* on Rough Trade. They preceded this with a brilliant single entitled 'Suspect Device', but given its risqué political lyrics, it had no chance on radio, or in the charts. They signed to Chrysalis Records and released 'Straw Dogs', which got to 44 in the singles chart. Many years down the line, Bruce would join the band and played with them for some time.

Elsewhere The Pistols, The Stranglers, The Damned were still in business and although 1979 was still a successful year for punk, only The Jam, The Clash, and Elvis Costello would go the distance. The year saw The Jam establish themselves as one of the top bands in the UK, and all they needed now was the big 'un. Regardless of the problems I had with them and Polydor, I was really looking forward to 1980, although the beginning of a new decade turned out to be another nightmare.

CHAPTER 4

Their Best Ever Single – But The Pressure Begins To Tell

Once again The Jam swept the *NME* readers poll, winning the best album, group and songwriter categories, and if their heads were swollen, it was deservedly so. The last quarter of 1979 established them as a major act in the UK and live they could fill up venues from John O'Groats to Lands End. The downside of this remarkable success was that anything less than a top five record would now be seen as a failure. The Jam had transcended punk and new wave, and were no longer seen as a niche band. This would pile on the pressure, not only for The Jam but also for Paul as their chief songwriter.

The record business is like a pressure cooker, and The Jam weren't the only ones under the cosh. Many fans and writers fail to realise that the very people who work with and for the artists are also under extreme pressure. Going into the New Year the pressure of working with Sham, Siouxsie, and The Jam got to me. As well as The Chords, I'd signed several other up and coming bands, and had a heavy workload, and whilst I enjoyed everything that went with the success, and the money I was pouching in, there didn't seem to be any spare time left to enjoy myself. If I wanted to have the vestige of a private life, I needed to offload one of my bands. No way was it going to be The Jam, as for Sham and Jimmy Pursey, they were on the way out, and no one else wanted them. I decided to part company with

Siouxsie. There was nothing personal about this; I needed some quality time for myself. My bosses had other ideas, though, and lumbered me with Godley & Creme and John Otway, which was the last thing I needed, given that both were in free fall, at the end of their careers.

The management at Polydor were also under pressure, no different from anyone else employed in the music business with wives, kids, and mortgages to pay. However, they also received large salaries and the perks that went with their position, so I am not altogether sympathetic with their plight. At the end of every year, I had to forecast what turnover I would generate for the company in the coming year, which went into millions, rather than thousands, of pounds. With the groups and the artists who were contractually committed, it was easy; most had to deliver three singles and an album a year. However, the company also wanted me to predict how much turnover would come from the unknown new groups that I might sign that year. Although, for me the greatest pressure was always being in the middle of The Jam and Polydor, which gave me many problems, taking Tony Bramwell off the case being one example. The company was aware that John Weller lacked the expertise that a manger of a top band should have, and expected me to fill the gaps when it came to getting their singles and albums released.

Everyone in the music business is under pressure, but it's considerably better than working in a factory, office, supermarket, or at the coalface digging out coal. After leaving school, I had several boring office jobs, and although I enjoyed working at the HMV record shop, it wasn't something I could have done for the rest of my life. Whatever the pressure, there's not many in the record business that would change their gig for eight hours at a checkout point at Tesco.

Going into 1980, I was genuinely excited about the approaching year, the band and Paul had risen to a new level, and it was only a matter of time before they fulfilled their talent. I was always single-minded about The Jam, although some of my colleagues would say bloody-minded and fought my corner fiercely. I was close to the band and enjoyed being a part of their success, regardless of the problems.

The band were back in the Townhouse Studios in early January to record their follow up to 'Eton Rifles' and the next single, 'Going Underground' b/w 'Dreams Of Children' was scheduled for release on March 7, but owing to a problem it came out a week later. There was now great anticipation and a terrific buzz within the company surrounding The Jam. Like 'David Watts', we released the single as a double A-side with 'The Dreams of Children' as the alternate. Polydor had 500 promo copies pressed with

'Underground' clearly marked as the A-side and I told the boys the factory had made an error but nothing could be done, and we would do everything to get 'The Dreams of Children' airplay. This was a little (white) lie, and one of the few times I wasn't honest with the band. It was a necessary deception as if you want to have a big hit you can't afford to split the airplay between two tracks, and no matter how good 'Dreams' was, 'Underground' was *the* big hit record. In addition, to the normal single a double pack was made available with the second single containing live versions of 'Away From The Numbers', 'The Modern World ' and 'Down In The Tube Station'.

It was decided to make the double pack a limited edition and press 100,000 copies, which would give us an excellent marketing and sale opportunity. Nigel Reveller or John Pearson, who ran our sales department, came up with the idea to ship the singles early. Although singles were released on a Friday, our factory shipped them out on the previous Monday and throughout the week, looking for big sales at the weekend, to give us a good chart position for *TOTP's* the following week. Nigel and John decided to get the packing department in over the weekend and do a bit of overtime, which enabled the warehouse to ship out the bulk of the orders first thing Monday morning and saturate the shops for a full week. Our strike force was primed to do the biz in the chart return shops, whose sales made up the national chart, and the demand for this single was truly amazing. As we approached the release date, the buzz was building up, and on the day of release, fans were queuing outside shops throughout the country, well before they were open.

For the first time, John Peel wasn't given the single for its debut airing on Radio 1. Clive Banks decided that after the success of 'Eton Rifles', Mike Reid, who'd now taken over the breakfast show, would be the first Radio 1 DJ to play 'Going Underground'. Although John had played a big part in launching The Jam's career, there was no time for sentiment, The Jam had moved into daytime radio, and John was given a second acetate to play that night.

'Going Underground' is one of the few songs that I have heard during my time in the music business that scores ten out of ten, with 'Dreams Of Children' not far behind. Paul, Bruce and Rick's playing is flawless and Paul delivers two of his finest vocals to date. Lyrically, both songs are incredibly strong, Vic's production is faultless, and even George Martin couldn't have done better.

I vividly recall the moment I was given the chart position. As I was entering my office, Tony Bramwell yelled out to me, "The Jam are number one," and on hearing this great news, I leapt up and punched the air.

Unfortunately, for me, I was standing in the doorway of my office and as I screamed "Yes", my head connected with the top of the doorframe, and I nearly knocked myself out, and for most of the morning, I was walking around Polydor in a daze. The boys cut short their USA tour to make an appearance on *TOTP*, and on their return, Bruce came in lunchtime and we went to a pub to celebrate, a little too hard as it happens. I arrived back at the office well pissed and carried on celebrating, ending up on top of my secretary's desk dancing. As I was throwing a few shapes, the Managing Director walked passed, gave me a polite nod, and went into his meeting with the head of A&R. I am not sure what his reaction would have been had the record only reached number 20.

There are many myths about the marketing of this record. It was said the single was deliberately put back a week to build up demand, which is a load of old bollocks. The real reason for the delay was the boys hadn't finished recording 'The Dreams of Children'. When I went to see the band at the Townhouse, Paul hadn't completed the lyrics and it was shy of two verses. It was clear we couldn't hit this deadline and I gave them an extra week, telling him: "The single must be finished by the end of next week, or all the hard work the sales guys are putting into the single will be wasted." I re-appeared the following Friday and Paul showed me the lyric sheet and it was still missing the two verses. I was more than a little worried and thought to myself, our sales manger is going to castrate me if I put the single back again. Paul noticed the worried look on my face and laughingly said: "Don't worry Den, I'll finish it now," and with that, filled in the missing verses! I'm certain he'd finished the lyrics long before I arrived, but felt this was a good opportunity to wind me up.

It was common practise at the time for record companies to manipulate the singles charts, with all sorts of bungs and free records given out in return for extra ticks on your record, and there was a lot of talk of Polydor hyping the single to number one. If you were one of the lucky shops chosen as a chart return shop, it was a license to print money. There were even independent sales companies that would guarantee you a top 75 position, even if the single only sold a few copies. Personally, this practice was something I didn't agree with: if a record wasn't good enough and the fans don't buy it, then so be it. Nevertheless, our sales boys went out armed to the teeth.

As far as this practice went, all the record companies were just negating the other company's efforts, and wasting a lot of money. If all the soddin' companies had refrained from this chicanery, it wouldn't have made any difference, and as far as I am concerned, 'Underground' would still have gone to number one. When I say this, I am not trying to put down my sales team, as they did a brilliant job and worked tirelessly during the first week. Jam mania was at its highest, and their large following rushed out to be the first to buy the single. I have to say, it was one of the few times the band and the company were in harmony, or at least singing from the same song sheet.

At the *Daily Mirror* Rock & Pop awards, 'Going Underground' won the best single of the year, and I attended the ceremony to watch the boys collect their prize. When it was announced, Bruce and Rick walked down to the podium, but Paul stayed firmly rooted in his seat. I leaned across and asked: "Are you going down to join the others." He replied, "No, I hate this bullshit, you go down for me", but there was no way that I was going to do this, and it was left to an embarrassed Bruce and Rick to collect the award.

Having a number one single must have given Paul, Bruce and Rick enormous satisfaction. Paul had wanted this kind of success from a very early age and had fulfilled his dreams, and perhaps even his destiny. He and The Jam were up there with the very artists and bands he'd idolised as a teenager. Even though Paul was always blasé about this kind of success, deep down he must have been ecstatic, and it must have been a heady time for all three members of The Jam. I was elated, anyone working in the record business dreams about this moment.

Following this, the company re-released all of their previous singles, and with the exception of, 'Tube Station', 'When You're Young' and 'Eton Rifles', they all charted. The so-called unprecedented demand for the back catalogue was a load of bollocks – it was just Polydor cashing in on The Jam's phenomenal success. They weren't going to miss out on milking a cash cow. I wasn't happy with this move, as it smacked of overkill. However, it did give The Jam the cache of having more singles in the top fifty than any other band since The Beatles.

With the success of a number one single, the band toured off and on and spent some time demoing songs for their eleventh single and fifth album. There was one track amongst these demos that was startlingly different, a nifty little tune entitled '2 Minutes', which later Paul re-titled 'Start!'. It incorporated the bass riff from George Harrison's tune 'Taxman', and at the time caused a commotion, quite unnecessary in my opinion. Since time immemorial, artists have been nicking bits of music from other writers and composers to make up new tunes and I couldn't understand what the fuss was about; after all, there's nothing new in music, and there are only so many chords you can play. Also, the bass line was used as the opening riff on 'Too Be Someone' in 1978 and nobody made a fuss then, but perhaps they weren't listening that closely.

Nevertheless, I was a little worried about the issue and decided to check out the track in Polydor's studio, playing the 24-track tape, dropping out the vocal and singing 'Taxman' to the backing track. It didn't fit, and it wasn't down to my crappy voice, the melody lines were different, and that's what counts. Like many other great tunesmiths, Paul has the creative genius to take a simple bass line and create a completely new tune. Also, unlike many artists, whenever interviewed, he is quick to admit which songs he might have nicked an idea from.

'Pretty Green', another good tune, was also in the frame and there was a big push for this to be the follow up single to 'Going Underground'. Vic Smith lobbied heavily for 'Pretty Green', as did the rest of the company. We had two sleeves designed to cover all eventualities, and the pressure to go with 'Pretty Green' was building, with only Paul and I wanting to go with 'Start!'. 'Pretty Green' is a great song, but I wasn't convinced, then or now, that it would have had the success that 'Start!' achieved.

There were no heated discussions or the stand-off that's been suggested elsewhere, although I was pushed very hard by the company to go with 'Pretty Green'. Paul just couldn't make up his mind as to which song to go with, and as we approached the deadline a decision had to be made. Still undecided, The Jam left for a tour of Japan and Paul was given extra time to consider, and I told him to phone when he'd arrived at a decision. *Melody Maker* had sent Paolo Hewitt to write a feature, and he called me from Tokyo with the news that Paul had made his mind up, and 'Start!' would be the next single. I informed the management of the news and it was met with a mixed reception. To this day, I am not sure why there was such a push to go with 'Pretty Green', perhaps because 'Start!' was so radically different to The Jam's previous singles and the fuss made over the 'Taxman' bass line.

The B-side of 'Start!' was 'Liza Radley', a song that should have been included on the next album and was the perfect match for the A-side, with its echoes of English psychedelia, and Bruce's understated accordion giving it an added dimension. I am not sure that this song came as a surprise to the fans given that they had released 'English Rose' on 'All Mod Cons'. Looking back, it's noticeable that after the second album how different every single and album is, and I have to admit by this time I was ready for anything. The single came out on my birthday, August 15, entered the charts at number three, climbing to the number one spot, and as for Radio 1, it was one of the most heavily played Jam singles ever. It was always going to be difficult to follow up on the success of 'Underground', but The Jam pulled it off. 'Start!' appealed to a much wider audience, and it was not only a stroke of brilliance but also a brave choice to go with this tune.

The video for this single was one of their best, and directed by Russell Mulcahy, who later went on to produce videos with many top artists, including Bowie, and eventually found fame in Hollywood. It was shot very quickly and cheaply at the Townhouse, with Russell doing a great job, and the quasi-psychedelic imagery he conjured up was fantastic. Up until then Jam videos weren't the greatest. 'Underground' wasn't bad, but Paul always came across as being self-conscious, and seemed uncomfortable acting and lip-syncing. It was even more noticeable on *TOTPs*, where Bruce and Rick would always make the effort and go for it, with Paul often looking wooden.

Many of the demo sessions for the forthcoming album were recorded with Pete Wilson in Polydor's studio, which just happened to be opposite my office. One evening, after listening to a playback, Paul and I were discussing the future. He was adamant in his views and said: "Whatever their achievements, I don't want The Jam to end up as a geriatric rock band (like the Stones or The Who) living off their early years. I want the band to mean something, and to stand for something. I'd rather finish at the top than end up touring, playing a set of our greatest hits." On the way home, I thought about his remarks, and what a strange conversation to have had, especially considering their momentum was on the up and they'd just scored two number one singles. Perhaps, Paul was unhappy with the kind of attention that was being paid to The Jam and himself, and saw a future that wasn't for him. It seems the seeds of doubt being were already being sown, and it was dawning on him just how high the expectancy was for him as a songwriter, and The Jam as a band.

Just after the release of 'Start!', *Melody Maker* featured on its front page a now famous photo taken in Soho of Paul with one of his heroes, Pete Townshend. It was an eventful meeting, arranged by Paolo Hewitt, but they didn't agree on much and ultimately it was a disappointing encounter for both parties. This didn't surprise me as they were from different generations with the only common denominator being that they were both in bands that represented the youth of their day. The photo appeared below the banner headline, The Punk And The Godfather, which Paul disliked, as he hated tags and labels. Strangely enough, A. J. Morris, the MD of Polydor, had this picture hanging in his office, perhaps to give him a bit of street cred.

It was time for the band to go into the Townhouse to record *Sound Affects,* which turned out to be a logistical nightmare, and the most problematic Jam album I worked on. Five of tracks were recorded in June and July, while the remainder were recorded between August and October. Halfway through the recordings, Paul came to see me and said he had a problem: there weren't enough songs to finish the album. As far as he was concerned, it could come out next year. There was no point arguing with Paul as he was in one of his ever-changing moods, and I resignedly told him: "Ok I'll tell my bosses, but they ain't going to like it. Everything is geared up for a September release. But, if you don't have the songs there's no point in carrying on recording and we will have to wait until the New Year."

I wasn't sure about this shortfall as I knew both Paul and the band had been in Polydor's studio throughout June, July and early August, and had recorded quite a few demo sessions prior to going into the Townhouse to record the album. While researching the box set I unearthed the following tapes:

PLDMC 0101 268 (24-track tape) – 11 April 1980
That's Entertainment, But I'm Different Now, Liza Radley, Rain, Bruce's demo, And Your Bird Can Sing, Bruce's 2nd

PLDMC 0103 890 (24-track tape) – June 1980
Boy About Town (First demo), Pretty Green, Dreamtime, But I'm Different Now, Start

PLDQC 0100 763 (2-track tape) – 18 June 1980.
Pretty Green (×2), Boy About Town (×2), Dreamtime (×2), Jungle Chant

PLDQB 0437 495 (2-track tape) – 30 June 1980
Supermarket, Boy About Town (demos)

PLDQC 0102 135 (2-track tape) – 31 July 1980
Pretty Green, Monday, Boy About Town, Start, Going Underground, Dream Time, Monday ('Live' two-track studio recording, which could have been a rehearsal for the Turku Festival on August 9)

PLDMC 0102 297 (24-track track tape) – 1 August 1980
Rick's demo, Bruce's demo, Paul's demo

PLDQC 0402 307 (2-track tape) – 7 August 1980
Paul's demo 1 & 2

PLDQC 0402 408 (2-track tape) – 11 August 1980
Paul's Accoustic demo, Bruce's demo, Paul's demo

PLDQC 0102 127 (2-track tape) – 14 August 1980
Paul's demo

PLDHC 0402 118 (2-track tape) – 18 August 1980
Jam demos (no titles)

PLDQC 0402 702 (2-track tape) – 27 August 1980
Jam demo, Paper Cup, Dingbat, Boy About Town, But I'm Different Now

NO NUMBER (24-track tape) – 8 September 1980
Boy About Town, Dream Time, Ablaze, Sweeney, Dead End Street, Scrape Away, Waterloo Sunset

PLDMC 0102 287 (24-track tape) – 1980
Paul's, T/Rolls, Ablaze demo.

PLDQB 0443 286 (2-track tape) – No date
Scrape Away, Go Native (×2), Dream Time, Pop Art Poem, Boy About Town (Flexi), Loop, No One In the World, I've Got My Mojo Working, You Don't Love Me

PLDQB 0437 496 (2-track tape) – No Date.
Boy About Town, Be-Bop-A-Lu-La, Summertime Blues, All I Know Is That I Love You, She's Not Good Lookin'

Finding out the exact recording date of a demo or a master is a difficult business as you have to rely on the tape op or the engineer filling in the label correctly and on the day the recording took place. Having said that it's unlikely that the dates are all incorrect, and with the Polydor sessions they are probably very accurate. Paul later admitted that instead of demoing songs for *Sound Affects*, he'd spent time fucking about with Peter Wilson recording covers of some of his favourite tunes.

'Start!', 'Pretty Green', 'Monday', 'But I'm Different Now', and 'Dream Time', five of the eleven songs used on the album, were recorded, in June and July, according to the dates on the multi-track masters (as on The Jam box set). It's possible that they weren't the final masters as many of the songs on this album were recorded more than once. 'That's Entertainment' and 'Boy About Town' were demoed in April and June respectively, leaving only four tracks to be written while the band were in the studio.

Several of the songs recorded as demos are untitled, or have working titles and could have gone on to become album tracks, and I cannot recall from memory the precise details of every track, and how they developed.

Vic would have been given copies of the demos before the boys went into record the album, and perhaps his biggest mistake was to book such a considerable amount of lock out studio time, which is expensive. Lock out means you have the studio at your convenience 24/7, and you pay for the time whether you use it or not, and the album ended up costing around £120,000 to record. In 1980, £40k would have been considered extravagant, never mind £120k, and ultimately this would prove expensive for Vic, although the excessive cost was not just down to his slowness in recording the tracks. Paul wanted the recordings to be spontaneous, an idea that rarely works. Also, you end up rehearsing on expensive studio time, which is what happened.

When I was archiving their tapes for the box set, I found a couple of 24-track tapes from these sessions, with nothing written on the labels to indicate what tracks had been recorded. Hoping to find covers or unreleased material, I played them. The whole of one tape was a recording of a conversation with a trumpet player, and on the second tape the boys – well pissed – attempted to play a song, which, after many false starts, they abandon, only to leave the tape running.

During an interview in the fanzine *All Mod Icon*, published in 2005, Rick stated (wrongly) that *Setting Sons* cost a hundred and twenty grand to record, and thirty grand went on taxis and takeaways. It was most definitely *Sound Affects*, as had The Jam's fourth album cost this much, Polydor would have given me my marching orders. Although, I have to say why the band ordered takeaways always mystified me, as the Town House had a kitchen that served nice grub.

Putting the album back was going to cause me problems and as much as I liked John, I was getting a little pissed off with him (and Paul at times). He was the manager of The Jam, and should have been the one to pass on the bad news to the company. This wasn't the first or the last time that John would dump one of his management problems on me. I had a good relationship with him and unlike most managers, he left me alone to get on with my job, but many times when it came to real problems, he would often pass the buck. On this one, John reckoned I could deal with the directors better than he could, and it was left to me to deliver the bad news.

At the time, Polydor were not having a great year financially and it looked like our yearly profit margin would be in the red, bringing inevitable pressure on the directors. I went up to see the MD and gave him the news, and he asked whether Paul was telling the truth. I replied: "Paul has never lied to me in the past and I have no reason to believe he is now. He is just going through a dry patch; a problem that all artists go through." He was pacing the floor concerned about what would happen if the album were not delivered and probably the affect it would have on his own career. His next comment astounded me: "What about getting Godley & Creme to write some songs for the album. They can do it you know, they're good songwriters." I choked and, almost lost for words, replied: "Kev and Lol are talented, but I don't think Paul would agree to this." I also couldn't imagine what the fans would think about this, and carried on: "It's not possible; there is nothing that can be done AJ. The album will have to wait until the New Year." I left his office knowing I hadn't heard the last of this problem.

There were more meetings, none of which went well, and for some reason the management thought I hadn't done enough to persuade Paul to complete the album. This was rubbish as I had tried my hardest, but at the time, there was no changing Paul's mind, and it culminated in my bosses not speaking to me for the next few weeks. At one meeting, it was put to me that business was so bad that year, if *I* couldn't get the album out, some of my colleagues might be laid off. I wasn't happy with this [implied] threat, there was enough pressure on me just doing the gig, and I really didn't need this kind of shit. I was beginning to understand why John had passed the buck to me on this problem. With the success The Jam had achieved so far, their profile was sky high and the album could have waited until the spring of the New Year. *Setting Sons* was a different story, as they were still consolidating their career; now, with two number one singles under their belt, their name was cast in stone.

After much persuading, particularly from John, Paul decided to finish the album, and it was given a release date of November 28, just in time to hit the Christmas market, and The Jam's extensive end of year tour and hopefully get the company out of the shit. I went to see Alan King, who liaised with our factory, and he informed me that owing to the (normal) Christmas demand for albums, there was no capacity, and what's more, no factory in the UK had any spare capacity to press *Sound Affects*. We needed to manufacture at least 200,000 copies and he told me: "There's no chance in getting the album pressed in the UK. You've got a big problem if you want get the album out this side of Christmas!" By now my bosses, desperate to get the album released, gave me carte blanc, so I decided to ask our French cousins for help. I telephoned the PolyGram factory on the outskirts of Paris. They informed me they had plenty of spare capacity and it would be no problem pressing the album.

The sleeve was another concern, as we would have to get them printed in France. I'd been recommended a printing company in St. Denis and the owner of the company assured me there would be no problème. "Providing you can get the films to me on time, I will deliver the sleeves to your factory". After arranging this, I went to see Alan, who told me: "Great news Den, I'm pleased for you but it's your baby and you will have to supervise the production, I'm too busy!" I wasn't pleased with this, as production wasn't a part of my brief, but there was nothing I could do and I went to see the MD and explained what I'd arranged. When I finished he nodded, and said: "Just get the record out before Christmas, I don't care how you do it, just get it out."

Over the next few weeks, I flew back and forwards to Paris and tied everything up. On the last day, I picked up the test pressings from the factory and headed for Charles De Gaulle airport and my flight back to London. By now, I was hacked off with the whole affair, my girlfriend was giving me gyp about being away from home, and I'd caught the flu. Arriving at the airport late, I raced through customs, and thankfully made the departure gate in time, and could clearly see the doors of the plane were still open. As I only had hand luggage it was just a matter of boarding the plane, or so I thought. I handed over my boarding pass to the flight attendant who told me: "You missed the last call and you're too late for the shuttle." I remonstrated with her to no avail and watched them close the door and the plane took off, sans me, which meant I had to wait an hour for the next shuttle, and I was lugging around my case together with a box of 50 test pressings. I was seething, as I'd arranged for a car to meet me at Heathrow to take me home, and turned to the girl and asked: "Does your mother have any children that lived", a remark she wasn't happy with! She gave me a stream of French abuse, ending with: "All you English are mad."

Although, The Jam and Vic were in the studio for several months, the album still needed more work and at least two or three tunes needed remixing, but there wasn't the time. I recall the problems Arun Chakraverty had in cutting the production masters for the album. Normally when cutting an album or single you very rarely go beyond a third cut. When this happens, it's indicative that there are problems with the final mixes. I can't remember how many cuts Arun made, but it went way into double figures, and it was asking too much of him to improve the album. When Roger Wake remastered *Sound Affects* for the box set, even utilising modern digital re-mastering techniques made no difference, and several tracks still needed to be remixed.

As much as I like this album, I didn't think it as good as *All Mod Cons* or *Setting Sons*, although it was a progression of sorts. My favourite track on this album is 'Boy About Town', and I recall that when Paul played me the demo, I couldn't believe my ears. He hadn't completed the verses and ad-libbed some strange lyrics, but it sounded great. The song, perhaps echoing The Kinks, was upbeat and had a joie de vivre unlike any other tune The Jam had recorded to date. A version was released on a flexi-disc given away with the magazine *Flexipop*, with the flip-side containing the very psychedelic 'Pop Art Poem', a tune recorded while Paul was fucking about in Polydor's studios. As well as recording covers, Paul and Peter Wilson played around with a track recorded by The Cockney Rejects, re-writing some of the lyrics and laying down a vocal on their track, 'England I Miss You'. Later, Paul distanced himself from this Oi band, who were also big Jam fans.

'Dream Time', originally titled 'Supermarket', was another great track and one that should have appeared on a best of compilation. 'That's Entertainment' is one of the finest songs in The Jam songbook, and a tune that I liked from the first time I heard the demo. I love the album version of 'Start!' with the brass section, which gives this great two-minute pop song an added edge. 'But I'm Different Now', 'Pretty Green', 'Set The House Ablaze', 'Man In The Corner Shop' and 'Monday', are great album tracks, and I received a lot of stick from the boys over 'Monday'. Bruce would often wind me up by singing this song when I entered the room. 'Music For The Last Couple' and 'Scrape Away' are not up to the standard of the other tunes on this album, and had there not been problems with the album, I suspect they wouldn't have appeared. I have to say, my view of this album is coloured by the shit that went down with my bosses and the struggle to get the bloody thing released on time.

The sleeve for this album was pastiche of a BBC Sound Effects record that Paul had found lying around Polydor's studios, and one of the photographs caused me problems. Above the heads of a group of people queuing for a bus was an estate agent's board, and you could clearly read their telephone number. During the first week of release, I received a phone call from the company complaining that Jam fans were swamping their switchboard with calls and if I didn't do something about it, they would set their lawyers on me.

As usual, sods law intervened and a major fuck up occurred with the inner bag. I received a call from the printers telling me the proofs were ready, could I hop on the shuttle to Paris and ok them, so they could commence printing over the weekend. That's how much spare time there was, getting the album ready to be released on November 28. My girlfriend had given me a yellow card and told me if I was away from home for another weekend, enjoying (sic) myself in Paris, I could forget about jollies for the next month. With this in mind, I delegated the task to our print buyer, Richard Fox, phoned my French cousins at Polydor, and told them to look after him while he was there. He arrived back on Monday, showed me the sleeve, which looked great, and when I enquired about the inner bag, he looked sheepish, produced a finished copy, and told me it was the best they could do.

The inner bag contained the lyrics on one side and a stunning photo of the lads by a lake at sunrise. It looked fucking dreadful, printed on paper that was marginally better than Delsey soft toilet paper. The photo looked appalling, and given the time factor, my sphincter started to pulsate. I phoned Paris only to be told they only use two kinds of paper for the printing of inner bags, and nobody had informed them which one to use. I asked Richard if they had started to print them, knowing his answer would be in the affirmative. There was no way we could use them, they were that bad. This meant we would have to destroy thousands of inner bags and it meant another trip upstairs to see the old man, something I wasn't looking forward to. I explained the situation and showed him the inner bag and to my surprise, he agreed that it was awful and it was ok to go ahead with a reprint and the company footed the bill for the bags that had to be destroyed.

The Jam always credited me on their albums, something I never asked for, or automatically expected. On 'Sound Affects', my credit appeared as 'Dennis *Heyward*', another wind up. The boys had found a picture of Nick Heyward and reckoned we looked alike and pinned it on the wall in the studio. For a considerable period, I received a lot of stick over this photo, but given what a handsome bastard I am, I couldn't see the resemblance.

All the hard graft paid off, and *Sound Affects* came out on time and everybody was happy. It went to number two in the album charts, with only Abba's *Super Trouper* album holding it off the number one slot. The company was saved and everybody got to keep their job. A couple of weeks later I got a phone call to go and see the MD, for a pat on the back and I thought a large bonus, but boy was I mistaken. I got the pat on the back all right, and at the end of the meeting I was given a brown envelope and the old man thanked me and said: "That's for you for all the hard work you have put in on getting *Sound Affects* out, you did a great job."

As I accepted the envelope I recalled a story that one of my colleagues, John Perou related when he worked on *Saturday Night Fever*. On this project, John worked long hours and well into the night for many months, and when the time came to receive his bonus, Polydor gave him fifty quid. I took the envelope, thanked the MD politely, and left the office. The weight of the envelope told me all I needed to know, and I knew it didn't contain anywhere near what I had been hoping for. As I passed by his secretary's desk, I thought, fuck 'em, and without opening it, threw it in the bin. To this day I have no idea how much was in the envelope, it could have been a big cheque, but then, why would they pay me a big bonus for *Sound Affects,* when *Fever* grossed millions, and all John received was a measly £50.

By this time, Sham 69 and Jimmy Pursey's star had waned and many fans that had a foot in both camps jumped Jimmy's sinking ship and became fully-fledged Jam fans. I recall talking to one called Seamus, who had converted, and asked why. He replied: "In the beginning we all thought Pursey was like us, but he wasn't. He told three different stories about why he was thrown out of school – which one do I believe? At least Weller is consistent, and tells the truth."

Many of these fans supported West Ham as did I, and were characters with extremely colourful names: Dickle, Binsy, H, as well as Vince Riordan and Grant Fleming, who were in The Cockney Rejects. Many belonged to the *unofficial* Hammers supporters club, the Inter City Firm, and carried business cards printed with the British Rail flying arrows and the words, "You have just been visited by the ICF." They would leave their marker on opposition fans after they'd given them a good hiding. These fans would often pop into my office, and my colleagues were forever asking me why I entertained them. I would tell them: "As long as they don't give me any trouble, and they behave themselves, there's no problem."

One day, Dickle, Seamus, Binsy, and a few of the lads dropped by, and we chatted, mostly about West Ham and The Jam. As I was busy, I had to ask them to leave so I could get on with my work. Dickle said, "No problem Den, we're on our way, can we have a few records"? I had a large cupboard that was stacked full of albums and singles, they helped themselves, and to their credit, they only took the records they liked, and departed. Dickle's head suddenly reappeared round the door and he said: "Den you're a real good bloke, you always treat us like human beings, if there's anything we can do for you, let us know. Word is you're having problems with the MD, do you want us to pay him a little visit and have a chat. He won't give you any trouble after we talk to him." I replied: "No, I can deal with him myself. He's not really a problem." For a second, I thought about taking up his offer, the

MD had given me an unnecessary hard time, and it would have been amusing to find the old man lying on his office floor, battered and bruised, with the ICF's calling card pinned to his suit!

These were real *hard* men, who could and would, mete out copious amounts of unconscionable violence at will. There was no thought of the consequences of their actions to the people on the receiving end, or themselves. Don't get me wrong I am not condoning them or, their violent way of life, but it struck me that if they were treated with a little respect, they gave respect back. I am by no means a hard man and even the smallest member of this group could have taken me without a problem. Nevertheless, whenever they came in to see me, I never had a problem.

1980 saw The Jam move ahead of their competition. By the end of the year, the Punk movement had imploded and given that it was based on anarchy, I suppose there was nowhere else for it to go. In 1980 the bands associated with this movement hardly penetrated the charts, and disappeared as quickly as they appeared. I was a little saddened by this, as I hoped more bands would make it and cross over into the mainstream market. When punk erupted in 1976 it shook the record business up, and certainly made a difference to my life. For sure, the biz didn't like this, as it curtailed their powers, the bands did what they liked, and were not easily manipulated. A new breed of management appeared on the horizon, and by the mid-eighties, the record companies became as bland as they were boring before punk arrived.

The Jam had well and truly seen off their rivals, and only Blondie (three number ones) and Abba (two number ones) matched them in the singles charts. They dominated the *NME* reader's poll, winning in ten categories, including Paul winning the ludicrous 'most wonderful human being' award. The Jam was successful, perhaps too successful, the pressure was escalating, and expectations were soaring even higher. However, I knew I hadn't heard the end of the recording problems with *Sound Affects*, but I was looking forward to 1981, although unsure as to what it would bring.

CHAPTER 5

No Album … Was This The Beginning Of The End?

In the New Year, the shit hit the fan regarding the exorbitant costs of recording *Sound Affects*. I was ordered to attend a meeting with my bosses and John Weller and by the time I arrived, it was a done deal. They'd laid the blame squarely at Vic's feet. Unfortunately for Vic, he'd lost the support of Paul, Bruce, and Rick, and *Sound Affects* turned out to be the last Jam record he would work on. However, Polydor were not without culpability either, as too much pressure was exerted to deliver the record to improve the company's financial position. Had Polydor's finances been healthier, the album could have been put back to the New Year. In addition, I must shoulder some of the blame, as it was my job to keep an eye on recording costs, although there wasn't much I could do given that everyone was leaning on me. There was also the large sold out (*Sound Affects*) tour, which eventually extended into 1981 that John had booked to coincide with the release of the album.

The recording costs were excessive, even by modern day standards, with each of the eleven titles costing over £10,000 to record, and *Sound Affects* ended up costing as much as the four previous albums put together. Rick, in the same interview with *All Mod Icon,* stated that they were spending Polydor's money, which is a mistake that many bands and managers make when it comes to recording costs. The studio time they racked up was recoupable against The Jam's future earnings. The company lent them the money, and when the next royalty payments were due, the recording costs were deducted from The Jam' s royalty cheques. At this time they were well and truly in the black, and it was the band who stumped up the £120,000, not Polydor. Had the album cost around £40,000 pounds, which is still a lot of money for a three-piece band in 1980, Paul, Bruce, Rick, and John would have each been £20,000 the richer. It's been stated the *Sound Affects* was their most experimental record, but these experiments came at a horrendous price.

This gave the company the excuse they'd been looking for to oust Vic as The Jam's producer. Perhaps, with the success of the previous two years, it went to his head, and his attitude towards Polydor did him no favours. Unfortunately for Vic he was spending someone else's money, and John was extremely *careful* when it came to The Jam's money. I'd supported Vic in the past, but this time the deal was done before I could present a case for his defence and whatever I would have said, it would have been overruled. It was decided that Peter Wilson would now produce The Jam's recordings; as far as John and Polydor were concerned, he was a safe pair of hands, and less expensive than Vic. Releasing what turned out to be a semi-finished album did The Jam no harm, as they were riding high and could do no wrong. However, it was still an error of judgement, and *Sound Affects* should have been put back until the spring of 1981, regardless of the problems.

Looking back, I can't help but feel that all the trouble with *Setting Sons* and *Sound Affects* date back to the second album, which was rushed out far too soon after their debut. If *The Modern World* had been released eight to nine months later, it would have given Paul plenty of time to write the songs and evolve as a songwriter. It's no wonder he had problems writing the third album. This created a domino effect, which carried through to their fifth album, and it would be interesting to speculate how the Jam's career would have developed had the second album been released in May 1978, and not November 1977. I fancy that things would look different, and who knows what would have happened? Nevertheless, with the problems that surfaced later, and Paul's increasing isolation, it wouldn't have changed the final chapter.

1981 bought a hiatus to The Jam's career and they were miserly with their output, releasing just two singles and no album. Given that Paul was creatively exhausted, I hoped this would take the pressure off, and give him the chance to recharge his batteries. They toured the UK, Europe, Japan, America and Canada during the early part of the year, and in the summer undertook a tour of seaside resorts, which included 'sunny' Birmingham. I was surprised, given that Paul was into George Orwell (and Northern Soul) that they didn't include Wigan; they could have done a gig at their famous pier. Following their gig at Guildford Civic Hall on July 8, they took the rest of the year off, save for playing seven dates in London during October and December. As far as I was concerned this pause took the pressure off me, and I was glad that there wasn't going to be the usual three singles and an end of year album and tour.

They now worked with Peter Wilson, which made my job easier, as I knew him well from his work on Sham, The Wall, and The Chords. Peter started at Polydor as an engineer in their (in-house) studio, which was used by Polydor A&R managers for demoing prospective talent. Pete had already had a stroke of good fortune when he became Sham 69's producer and worked on all of their big hits, but his appeal to Paul would have been that he worked with him on many Jam demos. They had a good working relationship, and Peter was a lot faster than Vic, and knew all the personalities involved so it was easy for him to take over the reins.

I remember when Peter started at Polydor, he dressed like a hippie, with long ginger hair, and homemade dessert boots with tyre tread for soles. Peter was well educated, and was a very introverted character, with a personality to match. He'd passed the very difficult Tonmeister engineering course, which included being able to read, write, play and arrange music, as well as fiddling with the knobs on a desk. Over the subsequent years, it has been disingenuously said that when Peter became producer he brought little to the table. I dispute this, as not only was Peter a first-rate engineer, he brought different production values to The Jam, and their records with him were every bit as good as the previous releases.

At the time, my German colleagues couldn't really handle The Jam and they were switched over to Metronome, a much smaller label that PolyGram owned. They couldn't do any worse than Polydor, and at least they were positive about working with the boys. They wanted 'That's Entertainment' as their first single, which was ok, as there were no plans to release it in the UK. During early January, I flew to the USA on business, and during the visit I phoned in and my secretary mentioned that 'That's Entertainment' was on the release schedule for January 30. This came as a surprise to me, considering I was responsible for scheduling their records and had no knowledge that we were going to release a new single. It was supposed to be a (very) limited edition German import with the B-side containing the live version of 'Tube Station', which had first appeared on 'Going Underground'.

Now, there's no doubting 'That's Entertainment' is a quality song and it would have made a great single, but the policy was always to release a new single after an album. They wanted to take a track of *Sound Affects*, to re-promote the album, and extract as many sales as they could and saw this release as an ideal opportunity. I was across the Atlantic and out of harm's way, so they slid it onto the schedule. This really pissed me off, given the shit that I went through with *Sound Affects,* and I decided to do something about it on my return to the office. I also found it a little strange that John and the boys had agreed to it, as it was against their philosophy, and wondered how the company had sold them this pup. I phoned John and asked what Paul thought about this, and he told me he was ok with the idea – something I wasn't sure of. Behind my back, the devious buggers at Polydor were treating 'That's Entertainment' like a full-blown single and imported it by the cartload. I went to see Polydor's marketing manger, had a few words and found out they'd coaxed John into agreeing to the import with an offer he couldn't refuse, that the band would make "loadsamoney" from this single. I spoke to John again and told him when Paul, Bruce, and Rick found out they'd been taken in, they would go berserk, and firmly told him: "I'm going to knock it on the head now before it goes too far."

My intervention brought the importing to an abrupt end and the single stalled at 21 in the charts. I had a meeting with Barry Griffiths who ran Polydor's import department, and explained why it was being pulled, and he agreed to halt it, not that he had any choice. He was extremely pissed off with me, but as far as I was concerned, he was interested only in his department's profit, rather than The Jam's career. This business amazed me. I couldn't believe that a major record company would behave like Del Boy out of *Only Fools And Horses* – mind you, the company certainly had its share of Rodney's working there! Stopping this single didn't make me popular, but I was single minded about The Jam and their career, although I was in the doghouse again, which was nothing new and to be honest, I didn't really give a toss.

Metronome requested a promo clip of the single, and because 'That's Entertainment' hit the top 30, *TOTPs* wanted to feature it on that week's show. This meant we had to knock out a quick video, and a shoot was hastily organised, and filmed in Old Compton Street in the heart of Soho. When we arrived, they'd just started setting up and we were told the boys wouldn't be needed for some time, so we retired to a pub opposite. It seemed to take forever to get the set ready and we were in the pub for a long time. Of course, by the time they were ready for filming we were four sheets to the wind. If you watch the video closely, you will see Paul visibly stumble on the stool that he was precariously perched on and his lip-syncing often slips.

The first Jam single recorded with Peter at the helm was 'Funeral Pyre', which featured The Who's 'Disguises' as the B-side, another nod to one their biggest influences. The writing credits read, Words Paul Weller, Music The Jam, and the single came out on May 29, some nine months after their second number one single 'Start!'. What really makes this single buzz is Rick's pulsating drums, and Peter Wilson's production, which is harder, and gives this song a real edge. Until now, their singles and albums took a step forward, but this song hearkens back, and sees the band standing still. Lyrically it was full of powerful images, reflecting Paul's political stance and his growing anti-right feelings.

Since 'Eton Rifles' all The Jam singles had received saturation airplay on Radio 1, and had been A listed and there hadn't been a problem, but it was noticeable that 'Funeral Pyre' wasn't receiving the airplay that their previous top five records received. Simon Bates complained about the line, "pissing themselves laughing", and I was sure the record was being censored and unhappy about this. I collared the MD and complained bitterly that the Beeb were censoring the record. To give AJ his due, he immediately phoned Doreen Davis, the head of Radio 1 and pleaded our case. He didn't get anywhere and she claimed they weren't censoring the single, treating it no differently from any other single.

What really annoyed me was you could regularly hear Lou Reed's 'Walk On The Wild Side' and Serge Gainsbourg & Jane Birkin's 'Je T'Aime', as well as other tracks that were far more risqué. 'The Eton Rifles' and 'Going Underground' spent 15 weeks in the charts, whilst 'Start!' spent ten weeks. Even 'Strange Town' stayed around for 18 weeks, and 'When You're Young' was in the charts for 11 weeks. 'Funeral Pyre' made a quick exit after only six weeks thanks to the lack of airplay, although it did sell in excess of 250,000 copies.

Like the music, the single powered its way to number four in the charts, but it dropped out quickly, By now, expectations of The Jam were high, with everyone getting [too] used to their singles going to number one, and because 'Pyre' didn't, it was deemed a failure. 'Going Underground' and 'Start!' started a phenomenon that lasted for the rest of The Jam's career and regardless of how high their singles charted, they only stayed in charts for a short time. Their vast and fanatical fan club would go out and buy their singles during the first two weeks, and more than half of their total sales were realised during this period. Their albums fared better, but there was the anomaly of their classic *All Mod Cons* album, which went to number six and stayed on the charts for 17 weeks, one week less than their debut *In The City*, which went to 20 and sold less copies. Many of their competitors' singles stayed in the charts longer, but this didn't mean they sold more records than The Jam; they just took longer to do so. The Police had five number one records, which stayed on the charts between 10 and 13 weeks, but their total single sales in the UK were not that much greater than The Jam's.

'Funeral Pyre' was The Jam, and particularly Paul, marking time, and this single could have been recorded at any time between 'David Watts' and 'Going Underground'. The original mix was a little flat and Peter added even more fizz when he re-mixed it for *Snap*, not that this would have made any difference to airplay situation. However, a number four single isn't to be sniffed at, given how hard it was for The Jam to break into the top ten prior to 'Eton Rifles'. 'Funeral Pyre' was also the last of what I call a 'typical' Jam single, from now on it would be all change.

As punk imploded, the music scene underwent a change and in 1980, the New Romantics arrived. The kilt-clad Spandau Ballet led the way, hitting the charts in November with 'To Cut A Long Story Short', which got to number five. Their album, *Journeys To Glory*, also made the number five spot in March 1981. During that year they released a further four singles, all of which made the charts, with 'Chant Number 1' going to number three. Steve Strange, who had worked as cloakroom attendant at the Blitz club, formed the band Visage, (I was their product manager!) with Midge Ure and Rusty Egan. In December 1980, they had a top 10 single with 'Fade To Grey' and their debut album *Visage* went to 13 in January. Adam Ant, who was loosely tied to this movement, was also very successful in the singles and album charts. During '80 and '81, he released nine singles, with seven hitting the top five, and two making the number one slot. Of the three albums released, one went to number 1 and another to number 2. Duran Duran's debut single, 'Planet Earth', charted in February '81, and went to number 12, and their debut album, *Duran Duran* went to number 3. Unlike punk, this musical revolution didn't implode but expanded at a fast rate, eventually spreading throughout Europe and dominating the Eighties. Although there were a few decent bands, the rest were more famous for wearing girl's clothes, Max Factor make up, and droning synthesised music.

With the exception of The Clash and the Pistol's, Paul's influences came from the sixties, with the likes of Ray Davies, Steve Marriott, Lennon & McCartney, and Pete Townshend prominent among them. Whatever else was happening didn't seem to have any impact on him, but that was about to change. He was influenced by the likes of Spandau Ballet, whose single, 'Chant Number 1', was released a couple of months prior to the Jam's single and Michael Jackson's *Off The Wall* album, which hit the number five spot, and spawned four top ten singles. Paul began to expand his horizons and was a regular at the Le Beat Route club on Greek Street in Soho, which would have opened his eyes not only to the New Romantics but also to jazz-fusion, soul and funk, which was very much a part of that scene. These broadening musical perspectives would have a decisive affect on The Jam whose next single would mystify even their staunchest fans.

On October 16, Polydor released 'Absolute Beginners' with 'Tales From The Riverbank' as the B-side. Both were recorded at Air (London) Studios, with 'Beginners' demoed under the title of 'Skirt'. I can still recall Paul coming into my office to play me the demo, and it wasn't what I had expected. He asked for my opinion and I said: "It sounds ok, it needs more work, and when it's finished, who knows." The song had many good ideas but nothing gelled, and it was a bit experimental. I gave him back the cassette and he promptly threw it in the waste bin. "It's a fucking load of old shit," he said and stormed out of my office. By now I'd become used to Paul's artistic temperament and I retrieved the tape knowing that eventually he'd finish the tune.

When I heard the finished master there was an improvement, but musically it was still a confusing fusion of The Jam and New Romantic, with a 'Penny Lane'-like trumpet thrown in for good measure. Whatever the shortcomings of the music, lyrically it was very strong, but even his words couldn't carry it alone. Perhaps Paul had already decided in his own mind that there would be no more singles like 'Funeral Pyre', and this was the first move away from The Jam sound. The B-side was altogether different, with its psychedelic overtones and there's no doubt that 'Riverbank' was in every respect the better song. Peter's use of reverb on the vocals adds to overall effect and to this day, I have no idea why we didn't go with this as the A-side. I don't even recall it being discussed. The drug references were far too subtle to be picked up by the boneheads at Radio 1 and it's more of a Jam song than the A-side. This was definitely an error of judgement as it went on to become one of Paul's most enduring songs: much later, he re-recorded it for a children's programme, altering the lyrics so as to make them more suitable for kids.

Even though it threw the fans a curve, they still rushed out to buy 'Absolute Beginners', and it went to number four with sales identical to 'Funeral Pyre', staying in the charts for the same amount of time, six weeks. Perhaps it is this single that marks the true beginning of the end for the band, as it highlights the gap that was opening between Paul and his two colleagues. It certainly needed to be played a tad slower and with more of a soulful feel if it was going to be (musically) successful. Bruce and Rick had by this time developed into fine musicians, but their style of playing doesn't sit right on this type of song. The single never worked on any level; perhaps if Trevor Horn, the guru of the re-mix, had been brought in to do the same kind of job he did on 'Chant Number 1', it might have been a different story, but I doubt it. They played this tune a handful of times live, and it only appeared on the Greatest Hits packages that Polydor subsequently released.

Jon Abnett, a huge Jam fan succinctly summed up the musical changes that commenced in 1981 when he stated: "A lot was said about the changing sound of The Jam, and 'Absolute Beginners' confirmed this. Nevertheless, it was The Jam and you had to buy it. The Jam could have released 'White Christmas' and it would have reached number one, such was the loyalty of the fans."

By this time Paul had began to tire of the laddish element that was following The Jam around and was starting to move away from their fan base. After 'Absolute Beginners' he wanted to change the direction of the band and the following they attracted but this was going to prove difficult and no matter how hard he tried, ultimately he would fail. This change of direction needed patience and time, and Paul came up short in both these departments. While the change was easy for him to embrace, it wasn't going to be that easy for Bruce, Rick and their fans, and the next year would prove a frustrating one for all concerned.

Around this time, Paul decided to start up his own record company and, typically, named it Respond. When we talked about it, he said he wanted the label to be an outlet for young bands and artists, and "like Tamla Motown", which was very optimistic of him as Tamla had more international hits than I care to remember. John Weller came into the office and sat down with the management, and Polydor bought into the idea and fronted up the cash for the venture, although I never felt there was anywhere near enough money on the table to do a proper job. I had mixed feelings about the label; generally, artists haven't a clue about A&R and rarely make good producers, and are dismissive about their competitors' music. Also, I couldn't see John having the time, as his workload with The Jam was more than enough to keep him busy. There was no doubt in my mind that the company made this deal as a sweetener, and I knew from day one that they weren't really behind the venture. My role in the scheme of things was as the sweeper, making sure things came together.

The first bands Paul signed up were The Dolly Mixtures and The Questions. It was too early in The Questions' career – they were still finding their feet – but The Dollys, on the other hand, were an interesting all girl pop band from Cambridge, and I have to admit to having a soft spot for them. When they supported The Jam they were barracked by the laddish element among their fans, with predictable cries of "show us your tits" and "get your knickers off" throughout their set, but they carried on gamely. The way Paul's fans treated the bands on Respond should have given him a clue as to how difficult it would be getting his fans to buy into his label.

One day the girls came into to see me and told me they'd spoken to Paul, and wanted Captain Sensible of The Damned to produce their next single. I was a little worried about this, as I didn't really know the Captain, and he never struck me as being a serious bloke. I arranged a meeting and I was more than a little offensive to him, saying something along the lines of "You'd better take this job seriously" and being generally unpleasant. When I visited Zomba studios where they were recording, I realised how wrong I'd been. He not only took the job seriously, but also did a fine job producing their single.

Paul also signed an amateurish rockabilly outfit called The Rimshots, of which I recall nothing. When he saw them play, he was under the influence of alcohol, and no doubt larging it. Rockabilly wasn't one of his favourite types of music and I couldn't imagine what made him take on this band. At the time, The Stray Cats had made it, and every wannabe rockabilly band came out of the woodwork, although none of the others would make it as big as the Cats, and the fad died quicker than it started.

The label eventually went to A&M records as Paul felt being tied to Polydor was too close for him and maybe it was having a negative effect on the bands. He got this bit right, but what he got wrong was they were too close to *him*, not Polydor. Only Chrissie Cremore, The Jam's press officer, and I took his label seriously and there was never enough money to do an effective marketing job. The execs at Polydor saw Respond as a *toy* for Paul, which, eventually would be thrown out of the pram, and they weren't going to invest big. It's fair to say that some of the bands may have faired better had they not been on Paul's label, if anything, being so closely linked with him and his success made it even harder for them to make it.

There's no doubt that Paul meant well with Respond, but ultimately he didn't have the time to put into developing a label, as his own career was flourishing. If you look at the great labels and the people who run them, they themselves are not artists: Berry Gordy at Motown, Chris Blackwell at Island, Ahmet & Nesui Ertegun at Atlantic, Andy McDonald at Go Disc and Independiente [Paul's old labels] are perfect examples. These guys are primarily music men, and whenever I hear artists saying they want to produce or start a label, I shake my head. Commit money to the project and get involved, but as far as A&R and producing goes, bring in the professionals.

Around this time, Polydor pulled another stroke with The Jam, which caused more friction. All record companies are capable of 'creative' accounting when it comes to paying out royalties and in the past have got up to all kinds of monkey business. After all, the fewer royalties you pay out, the better your bottom line looks. One morning I received an internal call from a mate in accounts, and he explained that a couple of guys working in the department had approached John Weller – and other managers – with a deal. If John paid over a certain sum of money, they would give him details of royalties they alleged were owed to The Jam that had not been paid. It was a stupid mistake for them to approach John, as the first thing he did was to call up the MD and demand to know what the fuck was going on. I had no business with The Jam's royalties. I always kept my beak out that kind of stuff, as it's more trouble than it's worth to get involved with that side of the business. My colleague in accounts suggested I make myself scarce, and I disappeared to some studio where one of my bands was recording and returned in the afternoon as the dust was settling. I kept quiet about this problem, as I didn't want to be tainted with any fall out, and to this day, I have no idea what happened, or what went down, but it must have been heavy. The two guys were dismissed on the spot and John's relationship with the higher echelon was strained for a while – well, until he went to collect The Jam's next advance!

With his support for CND, a movement I supported in the sixties, Paul was starting to dip his toes into political water. He'd always shown a healthy disrespect for the middle and ruling classes, and his anti-war feelings came over with songs like 'Little Boy Soldiers'. Now he was about to go down a road, which would eventually see him vociferously criticise one of Britain's most popular Prime Ministers and the ruling Tory party. However, with this came trouble which would frustrate him, as not only was Paul having problems getting everyone to accept a change in The Jam's musical direction, he would also struggle to get them on board his political manifesto.

The Jam didn't undertake a large tour in 1981 as they were busy in the studio demoing new songs. One thing was for sure, when they went into record their sixth album, they couldn't have been more prepared. They went into Air (London) studios and by the end of December, had laid down five tracks making sure they weren't going to repeat the expensive mistakes of *Sound Affects*.

1981 was a strange year, and in hindsight, one can clearly see the parting of the ways. The two singles released that year couldn't have been more different and 'Absolute Beginners' is a definite pointer to road that Paul wanted to take. As we went into 1982, there was an air of uncertainty. As ever no one could be sure just what the next 12 months would bring.

CHAPTER 6

A Number One Single And Album – But Even This Couldn't Save The Jam

1982 proved to be a decisive year for The Jam, and what followed would indelibly alter the futures of Paul, Bruce, and Rick. They spent January and February recording the final tracks for *The Gift*. Before going into the studios, Paul stated in the music press, he wanted the next Jam album, "to be the best ever", a comment I was never happy with, as it just isn't possible to set out and write a good tune or a good album. He was putting an incredible amount of pressure on himself at a time when he claimed the expectation of success for The Jam was getting to him.

On January 29, they released their 14th single. Paul had borrowed another bass line, this time from The Supremes classic, 'You Can't Hurry Love', and came up with 'Town Called Malice' but no one made a fuss made about this (fairly blatant) nick as they had done with 'Start!'. It was another double A-side with 'Precious', as the alternative and I had to get promo copies pressed [accidentally] showing 'Malice' as the A-side. I can't remember what I told the band, but by this time I'd run out of excuses as to why the factory fucked up every time The Jam had a double A-side. As well as the 7 inch version, for the first time The Jam released a 12 inch single, with a live version of 'Malice' and an extended version of 'Precious'. By now, the 12 inch had a market of its own and record companies expected all of their bands to release their singles in both formats.

There was no doubt that the previous two singles wobbled a little, but 'Malice' put things straight and The Jam back at the number one slot, where they stayed for three weeks. This was their third number one record and their second to go straight in at the top. They appeared and performed both tracks on *TOTPs*, which hadn't happened since 1965 when The Beatles performed 'Day Tripper' and 'We Can Work It Out'. While Bruce and Rick gave their all, as usual, Paul's performance was feeble. If they gave Oscars for the poorest performances on videos and mimed TV shows, nobody else would get a look in. The lyrics offered a stark portrayal of English urban life, and whether you lived in Woking or Wellingborough, or Paisley or Newcastle, you could identify with the sentiments. Unemployment was rife, and it wasn't a great time to be growing up in England. The B-side had more than a passing resemblance to Pigbag's, 'Papa's Got A Brand New Pigbag', which in itself was a nod to the James Brown's sixties classic, 'Papa's Got A Brand New Bag'.

Even though 'Malice' hit the top spot fans were still confused with the musical changes. Jam fan Jon Abnett's reaction when he heard the song reflects what many fans felt, about 'Precious': "What's happening? This is a disco number."

All through the Jam's career I had flashbacks to when I was a teenage Mod in the sixties, and it wasn't just the covers they recorded. Whenever I mixed with their fans in their Mod gear, it was like going back in time, and coming from the same working class background, I had an affinity. I'd done the nine-to-five and knew how lucky I was to be working in the music business, and although it went to my head, it only lasted a short while. At 23, I worked with some world famous jazz artists and it would have gone to anyone's head, but I soon realised that the world I worked in bore no resemblance to the one I inhabited. In many ways, working with The Jam brought me down to earth and back to my roots and I never had the problems many of my colleagues had with this generation or their music.

Paul was never happy with the pace of 'Malice', preferring to play it at a slower place, which he was able to do much later in his solo career. This also applied to 'Precious' but I always preferred the demo without the brass that appeared on the box set, as this seems more like a Jam song than the finished article. The problem isn't pace; it's the lack of feel that's missing. That's not to say Jam records didn't have a great feel – they did, but with many of the songs that Paul wrote from 'Absolute Beginners', a different kind of feel was required.

The change of pace was easy for Paul to achieve, but not so easy for Bruce and Rick and the fans. Adding a horn section gave The Jam another dimension, but also distanced them from their past. For any band to succeed and have a long career you need to progress musically, but very few established bands risk changing their style dramatically, and in many cases – the Stones being the best example – play the same formula for years. Whenever there is a change, to make it work all the band members must be in tune, which at this point The Jam clearly weren't. By 'The Gift', Paul must have realised that he was distancing himself from Bruce, Rick, and their fans, although with their audience it would have been a slower process, as live they were still playing many tunes from their golden period.

Although I'd popped into the studio many times and heard all the tracks, it's never the same as listening to the album in its entirety, and when it was completed I went to Air (London) for a playback of the finished album. The band, Kenny Wheeler, John Weller, Peter Wilson, and Renate the house engineer (who later married Elton John) settled back for the session. At the end one look at Paul's face told me that the album hadn't turned out as he wanted. Although he didn't overtly show his disappointment, it was plain to see that he wasn't happy with 'The Gift' and had to settle for a 'very' good album. There's no doubt that it was different to the other five albums The Jam had recorded, and more experimental. Paul had tried too hard to fuse all of his new influences with the old, and on this level, the album doesn't work. Core Jam fans must have wondered what was going on, and where Paul was taking them, as only a few songs had The Jam sound they were used to hearing.

Even if *The Gift* wasn't the greatest ever Jam album, alongside 'Malice' and 'Precious' were two other outstanding Weller compositions, 'Ghosts' and 'Carnation', for me two of the best tracks The Jam ever recorded. 'Carnation' was loosely based on Harry South's slower, bluesy arrangement of *The Sweeney,* which played over the end credits of this seminal TV cop series (later Paul would borrow from the music that opened the show for another song). Lyrically and musically, it stands out in The Jam songbook. 'Ghosts' is pared down to the bones with just the horn section playing a simple arrangement, scored by Peter Wilson, over autobiographical lyrics about the need to open up and reveal yourself. Paul always played his cards close to his chest, and there must have been a lot going through his head at this time. On 'Ghosts' he reveals just enough before closing the door quickly.

'Running On The Spot', 'Just Who Is Five O' Clock Hero?' and 'Happy Together' are songs that fans could readily recognise, and would have easily fitted on *Sound Affects*. Indeed, if you take the best tracks off *Sound Affects* and *The Gift*, you have one hell of an album. However, it is in the remaining four tracks where the problems lie. 'Trans-Global Express' is a messy cod funk parody that doesn't work. I have never thought that this type of funk suited Paul's voice or his song writing, and he wasn't much more successful when he tried this sort of thing in The Style Council. 'The Gift' itself isn't much better and although 'Circus' is an interesting instrumental, it doesn't go anywhere.

'The Planners Dream Goes Wrong' encapsulates exactly what is wrong with the album and, perhaps, why The Jam had run their course. It's one experiment too far, a failed attempt at fusing together The Jam's music with calypso overtones. Lyrically it's sound, with a strong message about re-development, but the music struggles along, with the backing track welded to the vocals, and even Paul's voice doesn't sound that great. Listening to it now, maybe Peter Wilson should have re-mixed this track, though I doubt it would have helped.

Regardless of its faults, the machine called The Jam fan club went out in their droves to buy this album and gave them their only number one album, if only for one week. It stayed on the charts for 24 weeks, five weeks longer than *Sound Affects* and while I applaud the commercial success of the album, on the musical front it was a little disappointing, although, 'Carnation' on its own is worth the price of the album.

I was a little disappointed with the sleeve, and didn't think it up to the standard of the previous five. By this time Bill Smith had left Polydor, the design & art direction was handled by Paul, and it seemed to mirror the music. Prior to its release Paul suddenly appeared in my office, which wasn't unusual, but it was a bit early in the morning for him. He was anxious about the sleeve and wanted to make a change, as he didn't like the frame that surround the three pictures on the front. This was a big problem as the sleeves were being printed as we spoke, but I could see that Paul was genuinely unhappy, and wasn't asking for the change on an artistic whim. I went to see Polydor's print buyer, Richard Fox, who informed me that 75,000 flats [un-made sleeves] had been printed and they would have to be destroyed, and he couldn't take the decision. Lionel Burdge who was his boss hadn't yet arrived and I had to take the responsibility, as Polydor would have to pay for the scrapped sleeves.

Paul was much relieved that this change took place, and for any lesser artist Polydor would have refused as the proofs had been around for quite a while. Whatever is said about Paul and his moods, I can't recall him making outrageous demands, and always asked politely for changes to be made. Most artists of his stature would make a phone call or send in one of their *gofers* and *demand* that changes be made. I'd worked with lesser artists who made ridiculous demands and expensive changes and didn't give a fuck about the cost. Much later the company wanted to charge The Jam for the cost of the destroyed sleeves, and at a meeting with John and Polydor's financial director, Ratnam Bala, I insisted the company bear the cost. They weren't happy, but begrudgingly accepted, and for once looked big and paid up.

When The Jam were recording at Air (London) studios, I was extremely fortunate to meet Paul McCartney and George Martin. I visited The Jam regularly, and on one occasion, I saw Paul talking to Paul McCartney. I wasn't going to miss an opportunity to meet one of the Fab Four, so Paul introduced me, and I listened in on the conversation. Macca was discussing his vocal for 'The Girl Is Mine', the duet he sang with Michael Jackson, and was incredibly self-effacing, claiming his vocal was nowhere near as good as Jackson's, and was gently putting himself down. A couple of days later I returned to the studio and bumped into Macca as he left the lift. He smiled, and asked how things were going. This impressed me no end as he could have just given me a nod, but he took the time to have a chat. Later on, Paul McCartney's wife Linda photographed the two Paul's together, a photo that must be a prize possession for Mr. Weller.

Peter Wilson was editing the soundtrack for the video of 'Trans-Global Express' at Air, and George Martin accidentally entered the control room while we were working. He apologised for the intrusion and asked what we were doing. We had a short conversation, but it was obvious that he didn't really like this kind of music, and he bade us farewell. I was tempted to ask him about the time Polydor wanted him to produce The Jam, but couldn't pluck up the courage. I was a little disappointed with him, after all, in the early sixties, at EMI he was considered a bit of an oddball.

On June 11, Polydor released 'Just Who Is The Five O'Clock Hero?' as yet another (Dutch) import single. It had the full weight of the company behind it, as we wanted to move some albums, and it reached number eight in the charts. The B-sides were 'The Great Depression', which was recorded during *The Gift* sessions, but never used on the album, and the Edwin Starr classic, 'War'. Both were co-produced by Tony Taverner who was filling in for an absent Peter Wilson and recorded at Maison Rouge studios. Until now, I'd always enjoyed the covers The Jam recorded, as they chose good songs and really did them justice. I was in the studios when they recorded 'War' and listening back, I couldn't believe it, they had completely mullah'd it. Someone asked if I wanted to help on the backing chants, but as far as I was concerned, it didn't need my dulcet tones to bugger it up any more than it already was!

During *The Gift* sessions, Paul cracked up, blaming the weight of expectation, and there was talk of mini-breakdown. Around this time, everyone was drinking heavily and there were many late night sessions, and I've often wondered how I managed to put in a full day at the office afterwards. Paul complained about the pressure of being in a successful band, but it was no different for the bands that influenced him as a youth, certainly not for The Beatles. They were under the cosh for their entire career, and this eventually caused their demise. In 1963, they released five singles and two albums, and in 1964, it was four singles and two albums. 'She Loves You', their best selling single, sold 1.8 million copies and I can't imagine what kind of pressure they were under trying to follow it, especially as this was at the start of their career when madness erupted all around them. The Who released three singles in 1965 and five in 1966, although they only released one album each year. The Kinks and the Stones were no slouches either, and somehow managed to maintain similar release schedules.

The ages of Paul's heroes when they scored their first hits weren't that much different to his. Lennon & McCartney were 22 and 20 respectively when 'Love Me Do' went too number four in the charts. Ray Davis was 20 when The Kinks' 'You Really Got Me' hit the number one slot. Pete Townshend was 19 when 'I Can't Explain' went to number eight, and Steve Marriott only 18 when The Small Faces recorded 'Watcha' Going to Do About it?' Steve Winwood was born in the same year that I was and when they released The Spencer Davis Group's debut single, he was only 16 years old. When they made the number one spot with 'Keep On Running' he was 17, and 21 when Blind Faith's only album went to number one.

In addition, there was no template for the bands of the sixties to look for guidance, so they had to write the book as they went along. Paul hadn't quite turned 19 when The Jam went to 40 in the charts with their first single, 'In The City', but the history of The Beatles and sixties bands had been well documented, along with the problems that come with being a pop star. The pressure on Paul was no different to The Beatles in the sixties, or Coldplay in 21st century; if anything less, as both The Beatles and Coldplay sold records on a worldwide basis, whereas the pressure on The Jam and Paul was just in the UK.

In 1981, The Jam played around 50 gigs and released only two singles, which should have taken the pressure off Paul. They were an established act, with number one hits and top five albums to their credit, and after

Paul Weller, photographed in 1978. *(Chris Walter/Wireimage)*

On October 16, 1976, The Jam – then largely unknown outside of Woking - set up their gear in Newport Court, just off Charing Cross Road in London's Soho, and were rewarded for their efforts with press reviews in *Melody Maker* and *Sounds*; top right; Paul on guitar; top left: Bruce Foxton on bass; below: the crowd gathers.
(Caroline Coon/Camera Press)

The Jam on stage at the London Royal College of Arts, March 25, 1977. *(Erica Echenberg/Redferns)*

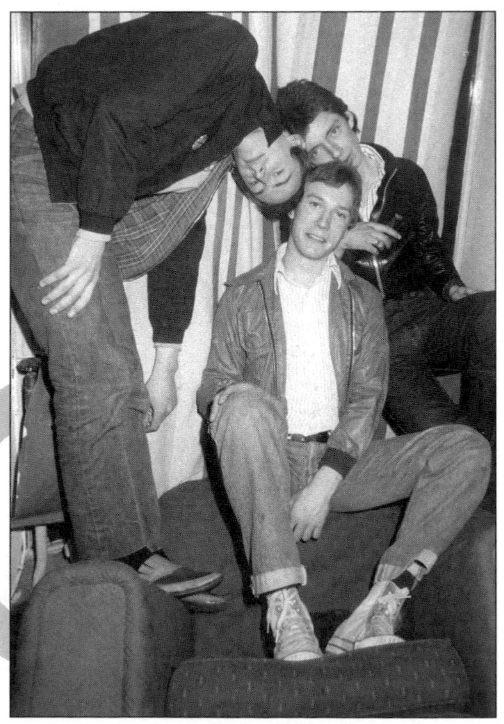

Paul, Rick and Bruce backstage at the Royal College. *(Erica Echenberg/Redferns)*

Hammersmith Odeon, London, July 24, 1977. *(Pictorial Press)*

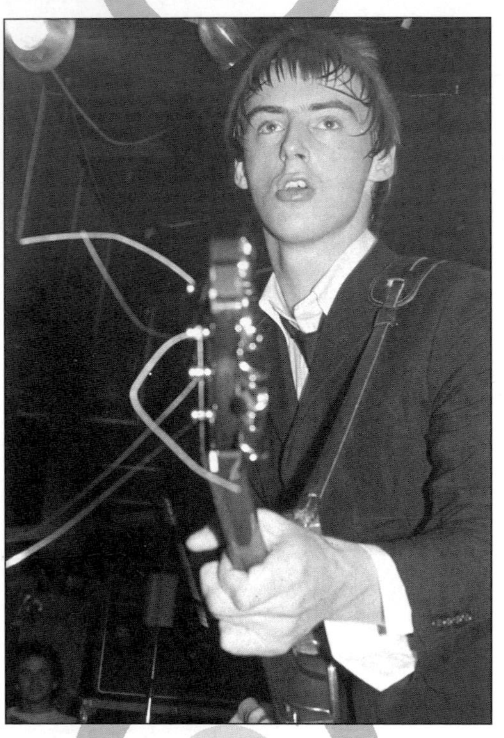

Paul at CBGBs in New York, October, 1977.
(Ebet Roberts/Redferns)

Sitting around in the dressing room, 1977.
(Ian Dickson/Redferns)

Bruce and Paul tuning up backstage, 1977. *(Ian Dickson/Redferns)*

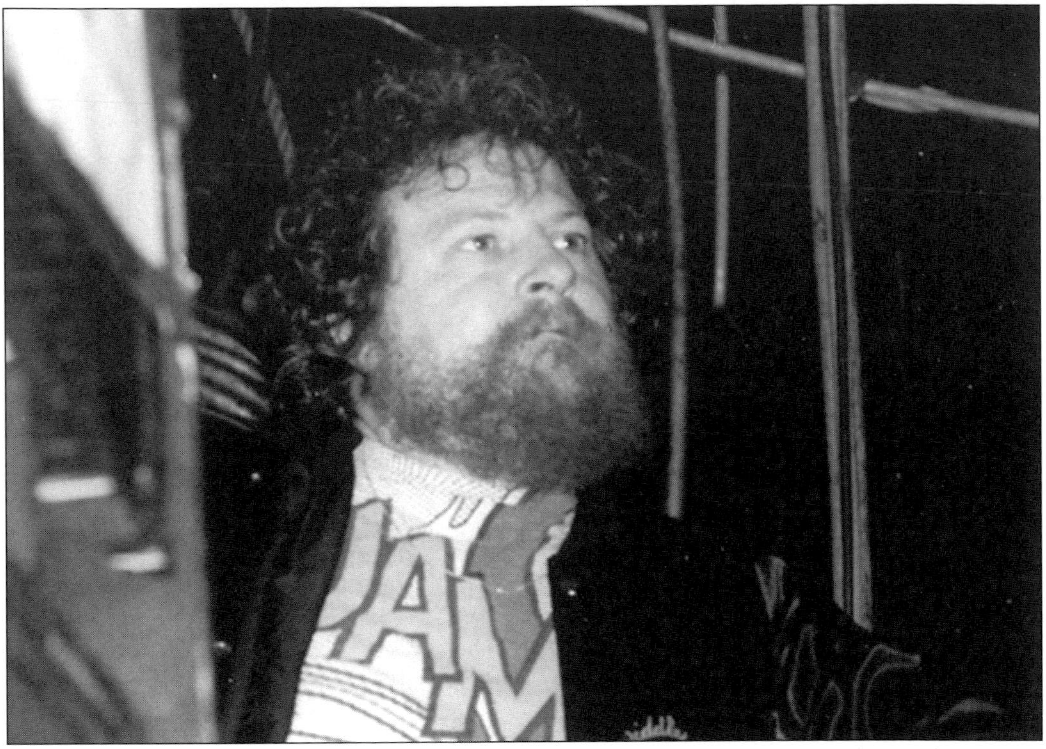

Dave Liddle, Paul's long serving guitar roadie, who died in May, 2003. *(Derek D'Souza)*

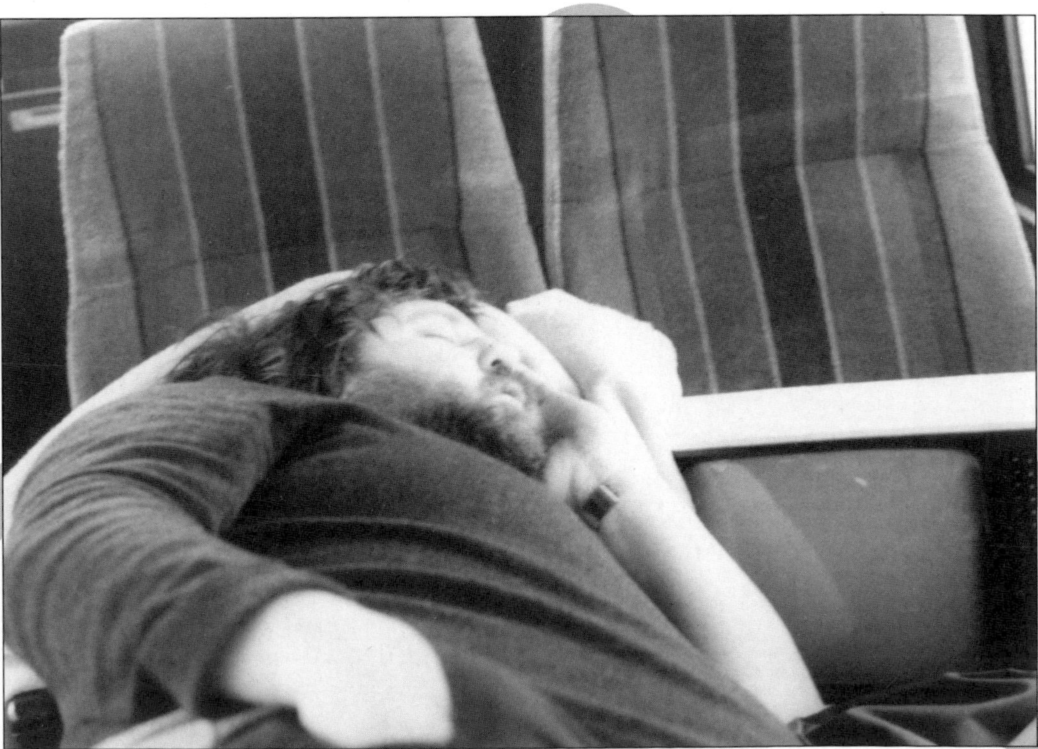

'Big' Kenny Wheeler, Paul's ever present security chief, nods off on the tour coach. *(Dennis Munday Collection)*

Rick and Paul in 1978. *(LFI)*

The band make a personal appearance at a record store in Philadelphia, promoting *This Is The Modern World*, March 1978. *(Scott Weiner/Retna)*

Paul, with Rickenbacker, on stage in 1979. *(Derek D'Souza)*

Being interviewed, 1978. *(Kevin Cummins/Idols)*

The band performing 'Eton Rifles' on *Top Of The Pops,* November 1979. *(BBC Photolibrary/Redferns)*

Paul performs 'That's Entertainment', 1981. *(Steve Rapport/Retna)*

the release of 'Going Underground' and 'Start!' were in the driving seat and should have been dictating to Polydor when to release their records. Instead, for most of their career they sat in the box seat, something I never understood. *Sound Affects* is a prime example: had John come in and *told* the company to put the album back six months they would have had to acquiesce. How could they say no – they needed The Jam more than The Jam needed Polydor. What could the company have threatened them with? They could hardly drop a prize asset, as another company would have picked them up faster than a rat up a drainpipe. In the beginning, Polydor certainly held sway, but once The Jam were up there the position should have reversed.

John was shrewd enough to employ a good legal team. John Cohen, who acted on The Jam's behalf, is one of the best lawyers in the business, and the deal with Polydor was very fair for both parties, which is unusual in the record industry. John Weller's no-nonsense approach was a welcoming change from the managers I dealt with on a day-to-day basis, and his bark was certainly worse than his bite. Having said that he never grasped the opportunity to gain the upper hand that two number one records afforded them, and should have banged Polydor over the head with 'Going Underground' and 'Start!'.

Following the two number ones, I took full advantage of my position, and from that moment, used the situation to my advantage. I went on the road with the band whether it was necessary or not, and did what I wanted to, and without asking permission. I was well aware that I was between the band and the company, and had my bosses by the short and curlies. When it came to dropping Tony Bramwell, and the fiasco trying to get *Sound Affects* out, I was dropped in it by the company. My bosses knew what was happening, but what could they do, when the shit hit the fan? It was call for Dennis – he'll sort it. If anything, I sold myself short and looking back, I didn't hammer the buggers enough.

The music press had dubbed Paul a spokesman for his generation, a tag that sat awkwardly on his shoulders. When researching the box set I spent a day at the British Library and went through all the music papers from 1977 to the demise of The Jam. I knew the band and Paul had done many interviews, but was staggered by the amount I came across, and to have read them all would have taken a month. The music press have tagged every kind of music, and artists and many suffered before Paul, so this kind of thing was nothing new. Tagging goes with the territory, and he only has himself to blame as he was very outspoken when it came to interviews and occasionally extremely vociferous. It was inevitable that the music press would put a handle on him. I have always felt this tag to be a slight exaggeration, given that at the time the sales of The Jam's singles were at best between 150,000 and 300,000 copies. While the music press was full of headlines and front-page pictures, it never transcended to the national papers at the level it did with The Beatles and the Stones at the height of their fame.

The record business exists in a world of its own, and when you compare it to other businesses, it is the size of a goldfish bowl. It currently has a worldwide annual turnover of about £24 billion but when you compare this to motor and the tobacco industries, it represents about a week's car buying and smoking. It is a world that has little to do with reality, and while music is significant, it is but a small part of life, and currently it's nothing like the business it was in the sixties. When The Jam started to make it big, it was during a low point in the business. After the boom of 1974 to 1978, (The Eagles were reputed to have sold one million albums a month in the USA for 15 months straight in '75 and '76) the disco bubble burst, and there was worldwide recession. The year Paul split The Jam up, there were three million unemployed in the UK. The comeback started around the time of the release of Michael Jackson's *Thriller* album, with global sales estimated at between 47 and 51.2 million, including 26 million in the States. This album on its own has outsold many artists' entire catalogue, and with this success, Jackson became part of the Holy Trinity of Pop, along side Elvis Presley and The Beatles. The introduction of CDs came about at the same time, allowing the record companies to re-release their entire catalogue and there was a revival in the industry's fortunes. This revival peaked in the mid eighties when the accountants started running the business and lasted until the early nineties. Since the arrival of the bean counters, the music business hasn't been such a fun place to work and they hold sway to this day. I'm glad that I worked in the business when it was about music!

When you're a teenager, music dominates your life, although with today's youth it has lost its authority and doesn't appear to be as relevant as it was to mine and Paul's generations. Reading the music paper articles on The Jam and Paul some twenty years later put the whole 'representative of a generation' into perspective for me. There's no doubt that Paul spoke for the teenagers who were marginalised, all those Saturdays Kids whose lives hung on the next Jam record or gig, but they represented only a part of that generation, and not all of it, as The Jam's record sales validate.

By the time The Jam recorded *The Gift*, the new romantics had swept all before them, eclipsing the punk and the Mod revival, and bands like Duran Duran and Culture Club had million selling singles and albums. The Mod revival itself was polarised around The Jam, and didn't capture the imagination of the bulk of the teenagers in the UK as The Beatles and their contemporaries did in my day. None of the bands in the vanguard of the Mod revival made any real impact, and disappeared quickly. I was born during the post-war baby boom, and for every teenager that supported The Jam, you can add another four to my generation. This was the determining factor in why sixties music boomed, and record sales were so high.

Paul's frustration and negative feelings for his fans at the time was unjust. Why should they follow him as he and his music matured into adulthood? Surely, he must have known that the vast majority were happy with the familiar and saw this as a comfort blanket, resisting change for the fear it might bring. Since releasing 'In The City', he had educated himself with poetry, literature, and become political conscious. Most of his fans didn't have the time for this kind of reflection: they were out there doing the nine-to-five, and the Jam gigs and their music was a welcoming respite. His lyrics ('Saturdays Kids') often reflected his fans, but unlike them, he went straight into The Jam when he left school, and was spared the daily grind. He has always had a tendency to view the world from the outside, with little or no experience of the inside.

To Paul, being a Mod was about self-expression and individualism, and he was often angry with the very audience that cloned themselves on their hero. I've always viewed him as a loner, rather than an individual, and if he didn't want to be a leader, why all the interviews. Recently I read *NME*'s magazine dedicated to 40 years of Mod and there was, the Modfather larging it with the Ordinary Boys, nearly thirty years after The Jam's flame expired. I have never met anyone who sells the Mod way of life better than Paul does, although his vision of being a Mod is very different to mine. In the sixties, we wanted to be different to the 'greasy' Teddy boy culture that preceded the Mod movement. There was a good deal of elitism and we proudly wore the uniform: mohair suits, Fred Perry's, Hush Puppies, Levis and parkas.

Paul was able to express himself as an individual; he was coining it in and could afford to be an ace-face. The ace-face in my team always looked sharper than the rest of us as he earned £20 a week whilst we were on £9 or £10. He had his suits made out of tonic by a local Jewish tailor, while the rest of us had to make do with mohair and wool mixture, and bought them from a high street chain of tailors, on tick. He wore expensive American *wash and wear* button down shirts, but all we could afford were imitation Ben Sherman's, made in Ireland, which were great, but not as good. What struck me more than anything, looking through *NME*'s wonderful feature, and at the photos of my generation, was how normal and ordinary we looked, just like The Jam fans.

If Paul thought my generation were any different to his fans he was very much mistaken, the bands we followed also influenced our dress code. When The Small Faces made it, every other Mod had a Steve Marriott bouffant, just as Paul did. Later, when The Beatles wore lapel less jackets, everybody had to have one. The Who provided many of the Mod images for my generation (and Paul), and just like all other fashion lemmings, the youth of the day followed blindly. We were a part of a new generation of teenagers who wanted change, just like previous generations. The sixties wasn't the first time that music and fashion had combined: in the forties Frank Sinatra had his zoot suit and a fanatical audience of teenage bob-bysoxers. The fifties gave us rock'n'roll, Teddy Boys, with their quiffs, drain-pipe trousers and crepe-soled brothel creeper shoes. The music and fashion of the sixties gave birth to the first real pop culture, and laid the foundations for successive generations.

The Jam's concerts were a musical experience, at least all the ones I attended were. I don't recall many gigs disintegrating into violent mayhem unlike Sham 69's. At the 1978 Reading Festival such was the violence meted out by their fans, they nearly bought the festival to a halt. The sixties Mods were also a laddish movement who went to see lads' bands, and football. We also got involved in the occasional punch up, and weren't that different from the fans I mixed with at Jam gigs. I recall the primitive football chanting that ended the Bingley Hall gig, with Paul vehemently insisting that this footage not be included in the final cut of the 'Trans-Global Express' video.

When The Jam went in to record *The Gift*, *he* had moved away from Bruce and Rick, both socially and musically. In retrospect, *Sound Affects* was the last Jam album, and only after this can it be said that it was Paul Weller & The Jam. Until the end of 1980, The Jam was a four-piece (I include John) and he would have had the support of both Bruce and Rick. Having his Dad as his manger must have been of great comfort for Paul but the downside for him was that he wasn't in complete control, and at times had to bow down to the democratic decisions taken by all four members.

Like all great artists, he'd had his moments of self-doubt, not only about The Jam but also his own talents, something I'd seen on several occasions. Paul also set himself high standards that weren't always achievable, and trying to make *The Gift,* the greatest Jam album ever was an example. As great a songwriter as he is, it's not possible to write a classic every time, and on occasions failed to meet his own lofty standards. 'Absolute Beginners' was a clear indication that all was not well, and by the time they went into

Air (London) studios, he must have had more than an inkling that Bruce, Rick, and the Jam's fans were going to have problems with his change of musical direction.

There's no doubt this period weighed heavy on Paul's shoulders, and although he was only 24, he had to make a crucial decision about his future. However talented he was, going solo didn't automatically guarantee him success. In addition, breaking up The Jam at the height of their fame could also backfire on him, as there were no guarantees that their loyal fan club would automatically follow. By the middle of 1981, it was clear that he had outdistanced himself from Bruce, Rick, and the Jam fans and there could be no turning back. To carry on with The Jam would bring upon himself even more frustration and pressure than before, and there was nowhere he could take The Jam without compromising his own musical agenda.

When word escaped that the band might split, seismic shock waves went through their fans and at Polydor. Within the company, there was general dismay about them breaking up at their peak. Like The Who, they were part of the fabric, and the company would have preferred Paul to carry on for at least another year. Going solo at this time wasn't what they expected or wanted. However, once the decision was made, there was no way he would reverse it and I was confident that Paul had the talent to carry off a solo career; you don't have four number one records with just luck.

After the announcement was made official, there were two final singles, 'The Bitterest Pill (I Ever Had To Swallow)' that mystified everyone except Paul, and 'Beat Surrender'. I remember a meeting with him and his dad where John was puzzled about the bracketed words in the title, and couldn't understand why he just didn't call it 'The Bitterest Pill'. Many of the forties and fifties songwriters often sub-titled their songs, but I can't think of many contemporary songwriters' that included bracketed lyrics in their titles. The string session took place on a Sunday, something I wasn't happy with as it meant paying the *gypsies* double bubble. Peter had written the string arrangement and when I popped in to see how the recording was going it was like entering a Derby & Joan club. I don't think one of the violinists was under 65, and I told Peter to finish the session quickly in case one or more of them passed away. A few days later Paul called me, said he wasn't happy with the recording, and wanted to do it again, and I thought he meant just the strings. No, he wanted to re-record the complete song, and the cost of scrapping this recording was around £9,000 of The Jam's money. On the second version, there were several changes, and I'm inclined to think that it wasn't the finished article when they went into the studios in the first place. The cod-sixties break was dropped, an extra verse added and Jenny McKeown of The Belle Stars came in to sing the backing vocals, thus becoming the first girl to sing with The Jam. The first version was slightly slower, and had a better feel about it, but both sounded well cheesy, and were about as far away from The Jam sound as you could get.

The single was released on September 10 and whatever its shortcomings, it reached number two in the charts and sold in excess of a quarter of a million copies. As far as the B-side, 'Alfie/Fever' goes, they'd go on to record a much better version during *The Gift* sessions, which came out on the box set. 'Alfie' leaned heavily on Harry South's (opening) theme from the TV show, *The Sweeney*. I knew Paul had diverse taste in music, but I am not sure why he picked the Peggy Lee classic to segue with 'Alfie' and for once over reached himself.

I've read and been told that the lyrics for 'The Bitterest Pill' were supposed to be ironic, but it was lost on me, and I am not sure that many fans understood it either. Paul has openly admitted that his own sense of humour was probably non-existent to some people, and his so-called humour permeated into the video for this single, which turned out to be elaborate and over the top. It was filmed over two very long days, and during Saturday evening's shoot they were taking an interminably long time to set up one scene, so Bruce and I decided to find a pub. He was a little on edge, as he'd only recently found out that Paul wanted to split the band up, and naturally wasn't in the greatest of moods. After we'd had a few, he told me: "I've had enough of this fucking about, I'm off home," and with that, stormed out of the pub. I could understand how he felt as the director was taking an unnecessary length of time over each scene, and kept disappearing back to his flat in Leicester Square for something or other. The slowness and the general poncing about would have tested the patience of Mother Theresa and the Pope, never mind Bruce.

Both day's shooting started early, finishing well after midnight, and the final sequence took place at about 2am Monday morning on the Thames embankment. The director had once again disappeared, leaving the crew, and cast waiting, and by now, everyone was tired and pissed off. We just wanted to go home and get some sleep – even Paul was fed up, and it was his sodding idea. I instructed the crew to get the set ready and if the director didn't return soon, I'd direct the bloody scene myself. As luck would have it, he returned just as they finished getting the lighting right. As Bruce and Rick had gone home, I was roped in to fill in for Bruce, but by this time, the lustre of appearing in a Jam video had worn off; fuck making my screen debut,

I wanted my bed! Mind you, all you see is the back of my head. The girl I was cuddling in the video was Lee Cavanaugh, who worked for Clive Banks and played the girl on the phone on Department S's single. 'Is Vic There?'

Now it was time for the final Jam single, and originally 'A Solid Bond In Your Heart' was chosen as their swan song. However, after a lot of soul searching Paul decided to go with 'Beat Surrender' b/w 'Shopping', even though their autumn tour was named after 'Solid Bond'. For radio we had to replace 'bullshit is bullshit' with bullfrogs are bullfrogs, and given the publicity and their fanatical fan club, there was no doubt where this single was heading – straight to the number one slot. At one time or anther it was mooted that The Jam would release an EP of covers and it was decided to manufacture 100,000 copies of a double pack with the second single featuring, 'Stoned Out of My Mind', 'Move On Up', and a re-recording of 'War'. The B-side, 'Shopping', was originally demoed under the title of 'This Flame' with different lyrics. The final version is laid back, with Paul giving a rather nasal vocal that wobbles a bit, and the track sounds like a good demo. The brass section consists of Steve Nichol on trumpet and Keith Thomas on flute, both of whom played on *The Gift* sessions as well as appearing on tour with the band.

On The Chi-Lites' 'Stoned Out of My Mind', a drum machine was used to underpin Rick's brushes, and later, when I discussed this track with Paul, he was scathing about the feel of the song. The rhythm section is too much on the beat, and they needed to be more laid-back to fit with the more soulful vocals and brass. Paul was never happy with the finished version and this tune perhaps epitomises why The Jam wasn't working for him, and where he wanted to go. 'Move On Up' is much better, drives along, and was one of the few pieces of baggage he took with him into The Style Council.

I'm not having a dig at Rick and Bruce with the above comments as they are fine rock musicians. During my career, I've been asked many times to recommend musicians for recording sessions or fill a vacant slot in a band and I worked with great jazz legends like Oscar Peterson, Ella Fitzgerald, and Count Basie. If they'd asked me to find them a rhythm section, Rat Scabies, Sid Vicious, John Entwhistle, Keith Moon, and Bruce & Rick wouldn't be the first names on my lips. It's a question of horses for courses and nothing to do with lacking talent. It is extremely difficult to find musicians who are versatile when it comes to playing all types of music, regardless of what instrument they play. Playing in a soul and jazz rhythm section requires a different technique to playing rock music, where the emphasis is on the beat and played with gauntlets and boots. To play soul and jazz you need to be wearing kid gloves and carpet slippers as it's about the feel and the mood of the track.

After the disappointing cover on *The Gift*, Pete Barrett, who at the time was a part of the Weller 'crew', was brought in to design the sleeve. Also making his debut appearance assisting Pete was Simon Halfon, who would go on to design all the future Style Council and Weller solo albums. The girl on the front is none other than Paul's girlfriend, Gill Price.

I was never happy with the production of 'Beat Surrender', and when I first heard the song, listening to it was like wrestling with an octopus. There is no space in the music, every gap has a fill, and it had everything on it, including the kitchen sink. I wished they'd gone with the original version of 'Solid Bond', which was definitely the better song. On this single, as well as a brass section, the band includes Afrodiziak, featuring Caron Wheeler & Claudia Fontaine, as well as Tracie Young, who would make her debut on Respond, and have a top 10 hit in March 1983. Caron Wheeler went on to have success with Soul II Soul in the late eighties, while Claudia would appear on Paul's solo covers album *Studio 150*. Their last single came out on November 26, and as well as the 7 inch version there was a double pack, and a 12 inch single released. Polydor was taking no chances. There was never any chance of this record not going to the top and it gave The Jam their fourth number one single and third to go straight in at number one.

Prior to releasing their final single, they appeared on Tyne Tees TV show *The Tube*. The sixties TV pop program *Ready Steady Go!* was the ultimate TV pop programme and there have been many attempts to reproduce and imitate the feel generated by this show. With the exception of *The Tube* and Jools Holland's great show *Later*, they all failed miserably. Malcolm Gerrie who produced and directed the shows in Newcastle did a great job, and there was always a vibrant atmosphere in the studio. I travelled up with the band and really enjoyed the show, and the augmented band delivered a dynamite performance. There was a little bit of sadness about this show, as it was their last appearance live on TV, but at least there was the farewell tour coming up.

The Jam still owed Polydor on their contract, and it was decided that their last album would be a live album, *Dig The New Breed*, which came out on December 10 and went to number two in the charts. As good as it is, it never did justice to their live performances, and with only 20 minutes a side many classics could not be included. I particularly like the cover of Eddie Floyd's 'Big Bird', where Peter Wilson overdubbed the organ when he was mixing the tracks. He told me, it was just crying out for organ, so I stuck it on, but other than that, it's The Jam live.

To cash in, Polydor once again re-released all 17 singles prior to 'Beat Surrender' in picture bags. All re-entered the top 75 with the exception of 'Funeral Pyre', 'Absolute Beginners', 'Just Who Is The 5 O' Clock Hero?' and 'The Bitterest Pill'.

There were no doubts in my mind that it was the right time for Paul to move on. Nevertheless, The Jam had become a part of me as it had with all their fans, and I still recall the strange, hollow feeling when reality kicked in with the realisation that there would be no more Jam albums and gigs. I would certainly miss the drinking sessions, although my renal system was quite happy about the split. It left me a little saddened, but life would go on, as it must do, but it wouldn't be quite the same.

The Jam's legacy is not about record sales, or their size and stature compared to other bands, both past and present. Between 1977 and 1982, they only released six studio albums, one live album, and 16 singles (plus two imports), and there's hardly a dud amongst them. Their music and Paul's songs meant something then and still does to this day, nearly 30 years after the release of 'In The City'. They were a quality band who sang and played quality songs and fostered one the finest songwriters of their generation. The fans that grew up with them were fuelled by the inspiration and perspiration they delivered with every chord and lyric.

There have been many calls for The Jam to re-unite, but I am not sure about this. My heart tends to want to hear them play live just one more time, but my head says no. Revivals rarely work and people tend think of the band as they were, not as they might sound and look now. Their music was of the time and they were a teenage band, which never quite progressed into adulthood. Paul, Bruce, and Rick are now approaching their fifties, and it's hard to reconcile this with the lads who were po-going about on stage at 100 Club, or turning it on at the Hammersmith Odeon, or Newcastle City Hall. No matter how good The Jam was, there's no guarantee that they could recapture the magic they had, and any kind of failure now would be unacceptable. Their image is one of burnished gold, their integrity and status are intact, and it must be left this way. Whatever they do now would only be an imitation of what they were, and whilst imitation is the highest form of flattery, it's not the real thing. The Jam was, and always will be, the real thing.

Given that current bands like Hard-Fi, the Arctic Monkeys, and the Ordinary Boys cite The Jam as an influence, makes them as inspiring, and relevant now, as they were when they launched their recording career in 1977, and they will never go away.

CHAPTER 7

The Bitterest Split?

Much has been said about the split, not least by the protagonists themselves, as well the authors and journalist who have written about The Jam and Paul Weller. I've been interviewed many times but have never felt able to tell the whole story, and always held back when it came to this part of the Jam's history. At the time of the split, I worked for Polydor and was looking forward to working with Paul on his next project and this prevented me from speaking out. No matter what I thought at the time, it wouldn't have been right for me to comment and not a very good career move. However, it's nearly thirty years since The Jam first released 'In The City', and whatever I write now isn't going to change history, or I hope, upset anyone. When author John Reed interviewed me about the split, it was necessary for me to be less than truthful which I wasn't happy about, but given the circumstances, I had no other option. I told John I was one of the first to hear the news, and although not the last, I was far from being one of the first to hear.

Since *Sound Affects* there had been problems, and even though *The Gift* went to number one, Paul wasn't happy. He went on holiday to Italy where he made the decision to leave The Jam and go solo, and it must have come as a shock to John, who wasn't expecting anything like this, particularly as they were riding high. Since working with The Jam, I'd watched closely how they had grown and matured as a band and how much Paul had come on as a songwriter. It was clear to me that Paul had moved on from Bruce and Rick and an open secret that they hadn't been mates for a long time. I recall after an appearance at *TOTPs*, we all went out for dinner with the people who worked on the show but Paul didn't show up, leaving Bruce and Rick to do the PR. This kind of thing happened many times, much to their annoyance. I had become part of the inner circle, and witnessed the deterioration in the relationship first hand. There was no way that John could change Paul's mind, and it was obvious that something was going to happen. After the Trans-Global Express tour, it all went very quiet in their camp and there was no real talk of recording and what the rest of year held for The Jam.

When the time came for John to discuss it with Polydor, I was kept in the dark. I am not sure why he did this, as I'd gone out on a limb for him on many occasions and supported them through thick and thin, even when I knew it wouldn't go down well with my superiors. I have to admit I was more than a little pissed with John and Paul that they didn't trust me enough to let me know what was going on, even though I suspected it. Shortly after their clandestine meeting, Clive Fisher, one of Polydor's legal eagles, gave me the news and I made out that John Weller had filled me in with the details. I was interested to see what explanation Clive would offer, but wasn't prepared for what came next. John Weller and his lawyer had met with Polydor's senior management and explained the situation and given there was no chance that Paul would change his mind, they stitched up Paul's solo deal. Polydor would get a live Jam album and a Greatest Hits package, which would see out The Jam's contract. Clive then dropped a bombshell: John and Paul hadn't told Bruce or Rick about the break up, and they were going to be kept in the dark until the end of the last tour. I was astound by this, and could only reply: "You're fucking joking!" He then explained that John was worried that Bruce and Rick would take the news badly and not play on the last tour, which would mean a huge financial loss. The plan was to give them the glad tidings on the ultimate date of the final tour, at Guildford Civic Hall on December 9.

Later on John came into to see me to give me the news personally, and explained what was happening, confirming what Clive had already told me. The news would be kept secret from Bruce and Rick until the Guildford gig, where they would receive their last big cheque, their P45s, and that would be the end of The Jam. If this were any other manager telling me this story I would have said it was a wind up, or checked the calendar to see if it was April 1. After he left, I tried to get my head round this idea. I was worried as the secret had to be kept quiet for a long period, and as far as I was concerned too many people knew already, and someone was bound to open their mouths. I mulled this over, and decided to go and confront my bosses. The whole idea of trying to keep the split a secret was ludicrous, and I couldn't believe they had agreed to it. I knew within days that there would be Chinese whispers throughout Polydor.

I'd known John Weller for a long time, and even though it was wrong, I could understand his reasoning as there was a lot of money at stake. What I couldn't understand was the attitude of Polydor's senior management. Whatever run-ins I'd had with them, they were professional businessmen with a wealth of experience behind them, and they must have seen the folly of announcing the split this way. I railed at them, pointing out this was not the best way to go about announcing the split, and if it ended in this manner, the fallout could seriously jeopardise Paul's credibility, and his future solo career. If the press got hold of this story, they would have a field day and not just the music papers; can you imagine the headlines in tabloids? Realising there was no way everyone in the know would keep their mouths shut, I insisted they talk to John and told them: "You've got to talk him out of this, Bruce and Rick have to be told as soon as possible." It would be impossible to keep the lid on this story, and certainly not until the end of the tour, which finished in December. What astounded me most was that nobody had thought this idea through, and the negative repercussions it might have on Paul's career.

John and Paul rescinded, and a meeting with Bruce and Rick took place at Marcus studios where they were recording the second version of 'War' and 'Stoned Out Of My Mind'. I decided to go along, but not attend the actual meeting, as I knew how much the band meant to Bruce and Rick, particularly Bruce, and it would come as a shock. Paul informed them that it was all going to end and although there was an effort to try to talk him out of it, he was never going to change his mind. They tried to persuade him to carry on with The Jam as well as recording his solo projects, but he wasn't up for the idea at all. There would have been no problems with Paul signing as a solo act to Polydor, and carrying on with The Jam. I'm sure John, and Polydor would have loved this, as it would have meant double bubble for both.

With the news sinking in, I took Bruce to a pub for a few beers and commiserated with him. By this time, Paul's solo career was a done deal, and Bruce asked if it was a shock to hear the news. I told him I'd found out the same time he had, and was surprised at Paul wanting to end The Jam as they were at the top. I felt incredibly guilty saying this, as I had known for a while, and to this day, I have no idea why John and Paul (and Polydor) didn't want to do the right thing. In the final analysis, regardless of the wobbler Bruce eventually threw, he would have completed the final tour. It was inconceivable to me that either Bruce or Rick would have done anything to damage the reputation of The Jam.

On October 30, 1982, an official handwritten statement, of a singular nature from Paul was given to the media, stating why the band was ending:

> *'Personal address to our fans – At the end of this year, The Jam will be officially splitting up as I feel we have achieved all we can together as a group. I mean this, both musically and commercially, I'd hate us to end up old and embarrassing like so many other groups do. I want us to finish with dignity. The longer a group continues, the more frightening the thought of ever ending it becomes and that's why so many of them carry on until it becomes meaningless. I've never wanted The Jam to get to that stage. What we (and you) have built up has meant something and for me that is honesty, passion, energy and youth. I want it to stay that way... Thank you for all the faith you have shown us and for building such a strong force of feeling that all three of us have felt and been touched by. Here's to the future, in love and friendship, Paul Weller.'*

Bruce found it extremely difficult to come to terms with the split. His emotions got the better of him, and after the video shoot for 'The Bitterest Pill' he quit, saying he didn't want to play on the last tour. His outburst was a knee-jerk reaction, and driven by sheer emotion. I didn't think for one minute that the [implied] threat of bringing in Glen Matlock made him change his mind. Had he not played the farewell tour he would have let himself down, and he knew deep down, no matter how much he was hurting, he couldn't let his fans down. Whatever is said about Bruce, and I know what he was like better than most, I knew he would never leave the band in the lurch, no matter what he felt. Rick took the split in his stride, and although it must have gutted him, he accepted the change, even though it was going to alter his life dramatically. I genuinely felt sorry for Bruce and Rick, as Paul's future was sewn up, while their lives were coming apart at the seams. I tried (naively?) to talk Polydor into giving both Bruce and Rick the opportunity to have a crack at recording a solo album each, but the company didn't want to know. They had Paul's moniker on the line, and told me candidly they were not interested in Bruce and Rick.

John's prime motivation has always been money, not that there is anything wrong with that, and no doubt worried about losing what would have been a bundle of dough on the last tour. The split up could have been handled more diplomatically, although diplomacy was never one of John's suits, and he wanted no personal or business interests in Bruce and Rick's future. Once the announcement of the end was made, it guaranteed that whatever records they released would go to number one and they would finish on a big high. Jam power was at its zenith.

Paul had lined up Mick Talbot quite a while before he told Bruce and Rick, so he must have been contemplating this move for quite some time. There hadn't been the mateyness with them for a long, long time, and Paul more often than not came into the office to see me on his own. Since moving in with Gill in 1978, Paul had separated himself from Bruce and Rick and with each passing year, he'd distanced himself further from them socially and musically. Paul was more introspective, while both Bruce and Rick were outgoing. There was always an element of Mr. Serious about Paul, while Bruce and Rick were happy to enjoy the trappings and fame that The Jam brought them, as any ordinary young man would. I know I lapped up the (miniscule) fame that working with The Jam brought me, even though the pressure got to me at times.

During the last tour, they hardly spoke to each other, but this didn't affect their performances, and all gave a 110%. Whatever the future held for Paul, he owed his fans a big debt, as they had put The Jam and Paul Weller at the top. For Bruce and Rick it must have been difficult to go on stage every night and give their all, knowing that it was all coming to an end. Their own futures were far from sewn up and the perceived view in the music business didn't give them much chance of surviving the split.

As The Style Council took off, Paul hardly saw or spoke to Bruce and Rick. Whatever friendship existed now rapidly expired. Much later, there was the acrimonious court case over money and demo tapes, and it became even more distasteful, tarnishing the name of The Jam. Even at this late stage, they still couldn't talk amicably about their problems, and had to do it through their lawyers. It was eventually settled out of court at the last minute, but no one came out of this fiasco with any credit.

In Bruce and Rick's book, *The Jam – Our Story*, the animosity came through, where they ended with the comment: "There were three people in The Jam and two weren't Paul Weller." The book and their comments saddened me a little, as every Jam fan knew how much Bruce and Rick contributed to the band. This statement was a riposte to Paolo Hewitt's rather biased account in *A Beat Concerto*, where they were virtually airbrushed out of the story. There was no need for them to explain or justify themselves, they were preaching to the converted. It would have been a much better book had they given the fans a slice of what it was like to be Bruce Foxton and Rick Buckler, and given a more personal insight into their life with The Jam. It would be nice if all concerned, including Paul, concentrated on the positive aspects of The Jam and their heritage, like five number one records. All three members and John should be proud of The Jam's achievements, and where they stand in the history of British music, and talk about their legacy, which after nearly thirty years, is all that matters.

In a recent, interview with *Uncut*, when asked how Bruce and Rick took the split Paul disingenuously said: "not well, the gravy train had pulled out of the station". I'm not sure why he has to make a comment like this, given that his solo success has eclipsed The Jam. I have never agreed with suggestions that Paul *was* The Jam, though he was the focal point in the same way as Pete Townshend, the Gallagher Brothers, Lennon & McCartney, Ray Davies, and Jagger & Richards were for their bands. Bruce and Rick suffered greatly from this, as would Mick Talbot in the Style Council. Unfortunately, it was the fate of Bruce and Rick, to play a secondary role, but to the people, who really count, the fans, they knew the score and in the end, that's all that matters.

When I first met Paul, he was close-minded when it came to music, and had narrow parameters; he knew what he liked and had a tendency to dismiss the rest. No one could have forecast the direction he would take The Jam in, and it certainly never crossed my mind that he would change musical directions and expand his musical tastes as he did. It seemed to me from *Sound Affects*, Paul was writing for a different band, and heard the tunes he wrote very different from the way they turned out. Many have been too quick to lay blame at Bruce and Rick's doorstep: maybe if Paul had taken the time to educate them into his musical changes, it might have been different, and Bruce and Rick aren't telepathic. On his own admission, he'd never sat down with them and discussed how the band was progressing and where they would go in the future, and it came to a head with *The Gift* album, which Paul wanted to be the 'best' ever Jam album.

Bruce and Rick were the linchpin of The Jam live, and I can't think of two other musicians that could fill their shoes. As Paul's horizon's broadened, he required a versatility to match his and they were unable provide this. In their book, *Our Story*, they admitted it wasn't their style and they didn't enjoy listening to the kind of music that Paul was getting into, and more important, what came next with The Style Council. The only way to keep The Jam going would have been to write songs that only suited The Jam sound, which meant taking a backward step and narrowing the parameters and the kind of songs that Paul was capable of writing. If I am going to be honest, many of the later Jam songs didn't come off, and it wasn't just the odd one or two. If you look at the music that both Bruce and Rick played after the split, (Time-UK & Stiff Little Fingers) it wasn't dissimilar to The Jam's, and nothing like what The Style Council released during their time.

Paul had a touch of the Victor Meldrews even in those days and whinged about Bruce and Rick not contributing to the Jam songbook. It was clear by *All Mod Cons* that he was going to have to shoulder the burden of writing the songs and it was no different from three of his biggest influences, The Beatles, The Kinks and The Who. By the time he got to *The Gift* he must have known that Bruce and Rick's contributions were going to be just the odd track or two. I know I did, and he would have baulked at the idea of sharing the song-writing spotlight with them, or anyone else come to that. However, that's no different from the majority of great songwriters, and as any chicken farmer will tell you, you can only have one cock in the hen house.

When discussing the demos for *The Gift,* Paul remarked they had a better feel than many of the later masters, and there is a kernel of truth in this statement. It wasn't the first time that this had happened: they recorded *That's Entertainment* three or four times, and Paul was never happy with any of the takes, even the final version. Perhaps he was more relaxed when recording demos, as there was no pressure to deliver the 'goods', and he could play them as he wanted to. The problem with this album and past recordings was that Paul failed to bring Bruce and Rick onside with the changes he was going through, both musically and as a songwriter. He had distanced himself from them and The Jam, and in hindsight, perhaps 'Absolute Beginners' was his first tentative step towards The (dreaded, as far as Jam fans are concerned) Style Council. It's been said that *The Gift* was the onset of the problems, but from my view, it was the climax, the writing had been on the wall for a long time.

Paul has always assiduously avoided becoming a big star and going down the celebrity path. He'd noted what happened to The Beatles and many of his other idols, and didn't want that kind of treatment. Even at the level The Jam were at, there were times on tour when he couldn't just take a walk, and was often stuck in his hotel room, which must have been frustrating. He loved it at first, but soon realised that the bigger he and The Jam became the more constricted his private life would be.

* * *

It's been said by many that the end ofThe Jam is the *classic* example of when a band should split up – at the top. It would be nice to believe in this altruistic idea, but it was mostly said after a topsy-turvy career with The Style Council and his 1.5 million selling solo album *Stanley Road*. Had he failed with The Style Council, I suspect that these very same writers would have had a right pop at him and told him what a wanker he was, and what a (big) mistake it was breaking up The Jam, many weren't that complimentary about his debut solo album. I don't remember statements like this at the time and quite a few people in the industry thought he might fail. The music business is always good at getting it right after the event. I doubt that Bruce and Rick thought it was the *classic* time for their careers to end, and we can only speculate where The Jam would have gone had Paul bottled out and kept them going. It's true to say that by breaking up The Jam at the top; he was running away from the super stardom that might have followed had the Jam become a football stadium band. But he was always a control freak and being in a band that was democratic meant he couldn't always get what he wanted, not without a scrap. If he wanted to be master of his own destiny, he would have to shed The Jam, move on up, and be in total control.

Was the split bitter? Not really, it was happy for some and unhappy for others and like any divorce, a messy affair at times. Paul turned his back on Bruce and Rick, and has never looked back, not for one minute. When Rick released a single with his band, Time UK, the Weller's refused access to The Jam's fan club. Why they took this step is a mystery, as Rick's band was never going to be in competition with The Style Council. There has always been an air of paranoia surrounding Paul, although he is not alone in music business in being a control freak. Every effort is made to control everything associated with him, and anyone who doesn't toe the line can expect a phone call. The people running Solid Bond were family, his sister Nicky ran the studio, Gill Price also worked there, and his Dad managed his career. By now, Big Kenny Wheeler was an intrinsic part of the set up and although not family, he was a clan member, and is still there to this day. There was a siege mentality about Paul, and the people he surrounded himself with, who always put him first, second and third. They wouldn't tolerate any criticism of him whatsoever, and when it came to The Jam, most were disingenuous, and Bruce and Rick were often referred to as those other wankers.

I had unlimited access to The Jam, and privy to conversations before, during, and after the split and from my vantage point watched it all unfold. Like most bands, The Jam had internal problems. The occasional punch up occurred, and there were many incidents of the artistic nature, where poor old teddy would be lobbed out the pram, or a cup of coffee thrown at someone in temper. By the time, they reached *The Gift,* being in the same band was the only common denominator, and there was no love lost, certainly in Paul's camp, which surfaced once they went their separate ways, and given his recent comments, nothing has changed.

There was a tinderbox atmosphere surrounding The Jam, and at times it was like waiting for a bomb to go off. From the time I started working closely with them, there was tenseness about The Jam that I hadn't experienced with any of the pervious artists I'd worked with. If the slightest thing went wrong, no matter how inconsequential, it could explode, and Paul fluctuated between Mr Serious and Mr Angry and occasionally threw in Mr Grumpy for good measure. I worked with some of the greats of the jazz world, who took their art very seriously, but they knew when and more importantly, how to relax.

When the split made the papers, one of The Chords let slip that Paul had signed to Polydor for a lot of money, which was quite true. He certainly wouldn't have received much less than we were paying for The Jam. A journalist phoned me and pressed me hard about his new deal, and I stonewalled, giving nothing away. It was more than my gig was worth to divulge privileged information. I should have known better than to have talked to the writer, as an article appeared about the deal, and the information ascribed to a 'senior member of Polydor's staff'. As I was the only member of the staff who talked to The Jam, it couldn't have been anyone else but me. They were touring at the time, and when I arrived at the hotel, I was warned that Paul and John were unhappy about the piece, and I should keep my head down. When we finally met up, they didn't give me a chance to defend myself. I was given a blasting, with Paul sending me to Coventry, for quite some time, even ignoring me on the tour bus.

I commented that Paul had taken The Jam as far as he could, and at the time The Style Council hadn't even been in the recording studio. Ultimately, it wasn't just a question of whether The Jam could go on, or whether they could play Paul's new material. He wanted to take control of his future, which was something he couldn't achieve staying as a member of The Jam. As well as being their A&R manager, I was a Jam fan, and could see Paul's problems from both angles and witnessed his frustrations first hand. I've always fancied that the Council would have made a better fist of 'Beat Surrender' and there is no doubt in my mind that The Jam's version of 'Solid Bond' that appeared on the box set, even though it was a rough demo, is far superior to the single that the Council released. But breaking up The Jam was never about this: The Jam and the Council were two different horses and whilst one went on the flat, the other went over the jumps, but both were thoroughbreds.

There were other, peripheral reasons for the split, but when Paul signed to Polydor as a solo artist, he would have been under the cosh to deliver the 'usual' three singles and an album every year, just like The Jam. Within five months of quitting the group, he lipped up and took on the Tory Government, and became the *leader of a generation*. This tough political stance couldn't have happened with The Jam as there was too much democracy for a start, and while he opposed the politics of the Tory government, his leadership of The Style Council wasn't that different from the way Thatcher ran her government, or Blair runs New Labour today. Everyone knows who's in charge, and from January 1983, he took control of his destiny and hasn't let go of the reins to this day.

Whatever the reasons were for ending The Jam, it was not only a big, brave, and bold decision, but also the right one at the time, and in hindsight Paul owes the heady success he has accomplished today to both The Jam and The Style Council. Leaving The Jam was a necessary step to fulfil his ambitions and talent, as history as now proved.

CHAPTER 8

The Last Jam Compilation Until The Next One!

Many fans have griped about the compilations released since the demise of The Jam. PolyGram (Polydor's parent company) was originally a part of the giant German conglomerate Siemens, and co-owned by the Dutch electronics giant, PSV. They were first bought out by Universal, and then Seagram's. Universal, as it is now known, is currently owned by the huge French media conglomerate Vivendi, whose only interest is that their record division makes as much money as it can. Since the early seventies Polydor have released around a dozen Best of/Greatest Hits compilations by The Who and it's now industry practice to release a hits compilation of their best selling artists every two years. As long as Paul is still at the top and whether we like it or not, the same will happen to The Jam and The Style Council, this is the nature of the modern record business – it's just a big money-go-round.

Since 1992, I have been responsible for the bulk of the compilations re-issued on The Jam, and for me this period probably gave me the greatest pleasure. There was no pressure or politics from the record company and both bands no longer existed. Paul, Bruce, and Rick had no control over their back catalogue, which gave Polydor the freedom to release compilations without having to acquire their approval. I was surprised by this, as it's common practice for successful bands when they re-sign to a label, to have a clause written into their contracts enabling them to control future releases from their back catalogues.

It all started when Polydor consulted me with regard to The Jam's *Greatest Hits* package that came out in 1991. I compiled a track listing, which naturally enough had all the hits on, and for some reason they rejected the running order and said they were going to bring in a market research company and would go with their findings. Later, I received a telephone call requesting me to attend a meeting to discuss this project, and when they presented their findings, the compilation was neither, a Greatest Hits or a Best Of, and it looked as if someone had pulled the titles out of a hat blindfold. The running order was dire and I argued against this proposal, but got nowhere and left the meeting more than a little disgruntled. Some weeks later, Carlos Olms, who was digitally re-mastering the album, phoned me and asked for help as he was having problems finding the original masters, and as the album was going to be TV advertised, he needed to supply the factory with a production master the next day.

When I arrived at the studios, Carlos gave me the running order, which was exactly the same as the one I'd provided in the first place. I noticed several of the tapes Carlos was about to copy weren't even the original masters and in some cases weren't the right version of the single. Not having the time, I located as many of the correct versions as I could, but in many cases we had to use the production masters for the records. These tapes had been specifically re-equalised for vinyl and as analogue and digital are not compatible, you don't get the best results for CD. It's necessary to go back to the original two-track master tape, which contains no analogue re-equalization. We got the job done, but the CD suffered and didn't sound as good as it should have. The compilation was released on July 1, 1991 and went to number two in the charts, proving just how popular The Jam were, even though they'd broken up nine years prior to the release of this compilation.

Following this success in 1992, I came up with idea of *Extras*, a rarities compilation that contained B-sides, out-takes, demos and covers hidden away in the vaults. Throughout The Jam's career, Paul had given me cassettes of demos that he'd recorded and because of the trust placed in me, I never played these tapes to my colleagues. Many of these tracks had never been heard before, and I knew what these recordings meant to the fans. At the time, it would have been nice to make a complete research of the archives, but the brief and the fee from Polydor didn't allow for this.

Although I knew many of the unreleased songs, I still found a few that were unknown to me. I hadn't heard 'Hey Mister', which was recorded at the same time as 'Thick As Thieves', and 'Burning Sky' which were not dated, but would have been recorded in the summer of 1979. Paul recorded two versions of 'Burning Sky', one on electric guitar, and the other on acoustic, which I chose for this compilation, as The Jam rarely recorded acoustic tracks. I am sure one day the alternate version will surface. There was an alternate version of 'Hey Mister', recorded on guitar but it wasn't good enough to be included.

The plaintive 'No One In The World' would have been recorded during a demo sessions for *Sound Affects*, in September 1980, at the same time as the very psychedelic 'Pop Art Poem' and 'Boy About Town', which is an early version and both released as a free flexi-disc with *Flexipop* magazine. The solo version of 'Saturday's Kids', come from a demo session recorded at Polydor's studio in July 1979, at the same time that 'The Eton Rifles' was recorded. When I played Paul the solo version he was dead against including it, and didn't think it was good enough to warrant inclusion, but I knew fans would want to hear it, and pressed him hard to keep it on. He was still a little reluctant, but after intense lobbying from me, he relented.

When Paul was at a loose end in the studios, he would often record covers of his favourite songs, and I included The Beatles 'And Your Bird Can Sing'. 'But I'm Different Now' and 'Liza Radley', which were recorded at the same time and come from the now infamous 'fucking around' session, and recorded on April 11, 1980. The Small Faces were a big influence on Paul and the compilation includes a dynamic version of 'Get Yourself Together', which was recorded on July 28, 1981 during a session that included an early version of 'Absolute Beginners', ('Skirt') and 'Not Far At All'. By chance when Peter Wilson went into Swanyard studios to re-mix this sixties classic, Paul just happened to be in the adjoining studio. As he didn't like the original vocal on the demo, he decided to record a new and much better vocal.

'I Got You (I Feel Good)' was recorded on February 5, 1982 around the time the swing version of 'Alfie' was laid down. An earlier version of this James Brown classic was recorded at the same time as 'No One In The World'. 'We've Only Started' (also known as 'Not Far At All') was demoed at Polydor's Studios in 1981 and an early experiment and eventually re-written as 'Tales From The Riverbank'. The version of 'A Solid Bond In Your Heart' was recorded in September 1982, and is a more professional recording than the one on the box set, and as this version has the bridge missing, it must have been recorded later.

Many of The Jam's B-sides had not been available on CD prior to this compilation, and it was great to see them available in this format. I included Bruce's 'Smithers-Jones' and the classic 'The Butterfly Collector', as well as

'The Great Depression', 'The Dreams Of Children', 'Tales From The Riverbank', 'Shopping', and 'Pity Poor Alfie/Fever'. Also included were the cover versions they recorded and included, Curtis Mayfield's 'Move On Up', The Who's 'So Sad About Us' and 'Disguises', and The Chi-Lites 'Stoned Out Of My Mind'.

Many of the demos were luckily recorded on multi-track so Peter Wilson was able to re-mix them, which enhanced the quality of the track. Polydor were not happy about this cost and to save money tried to fob me off with the excuse that fans want the rough mixes, something I didn't agree with. Paolo Hewitt came up with the title and his sleeve notes are excellent, as are the photos taken by Pennie Smith during the recording of *Sound Affects. Extras* was released on April 6, 1992 and went to number 15 in the album charts, which is a great chart position for an odds and sods compilation, some five places higher than The Jam's debut album and seven places higher than their second album.

When it comes to live albums, I hate it when the music is taken from one gig or compiled from one tour. Even worse is when the vocals or instruments are overdubbed into the studio. When you attend a concert, you hear the music, warts and all, which is how a live CD should be; it's the performance that matters. The Jam's first live album *Dig The New Breed* was released on vinyl and cassette in December 1982 and contained around 40 minutes of music, and as good as it was, it never did justice to their live show. It wasn't until the advent of CDs, where you could cram on nearly 80 minutes of music, that you heard the full force of The Jam live*.

The policy of recording The Jam throughout their career paid off, live recordings existed from the 100 Club to their last shows at Wembley Arena, and 20 gigs in all were recorded between 1977 and 1982. Peter Wilson did an amazing job and remixed all the tracks and with the exception of a couple of minor over-dubs and a bit of pitch twisting, the songs are exactly as you would hear them at the original concerts. I'd given him cassettes of all the gigs and a rough track listing, and from these he compiled a chart containing a box for each title and each instrument played. He then checked every version recorded, marking the performance and the recording quality to arrive at the best possible version. This live CD might not sound as polished as other bands, but the compilation perfectly captures the energy, the performances, and the atmosphere of the concerts.

* (Since writing this piece, many fans have chastised me about this, and said they would prefer whole concerts to be released in their entirety. I have noted this for the future!)

The compilation contains 24 tracks and features many ofThe Jam's classic songs, including some that sounded better live than they did on record. 'Billy Hunt', 'A' Bomb', 'Strange Town' and 'David Watts' are few that had another dimension when they were played live.'Tales From The Riverbank' was not included on this compilation, as there wasn't enough room to include this great B-side and there are no tracks from the gigs recorded in 1977 and '78. Although, the tracks chosen were from different concerts, Peter did a great job segueing the tunes to make the CD sound like one concert. Much later Peter mentioned that the applause loop used between tracks came from a Style Council concert, though nobody would have guessed this.

Instead of having some journalist banging on about bass riffs, drum rolls, and guitar solos I thought it would be a great idea to let the fans write the sleeve notes. After all, who knew the band better than the very people who paid to see them? Looking at their comments, what comes across more than anything else is the total respect the fans had for their idols, as well as how much the band meant to them. Lindsay Baker summed it up succinctly when he stated, "Their songs provided the soundtrack for the private, youthful epiphanies of a generation. The honesty and lyricism of the Jam's song encapsulated and transcended there time." And Gary Crowley wrote: "Most bands come and go. If they're lucky they leave a few good records behind, but very few touch people's lives. The Jam were one of those who did." These words come from the heart, not the pen, and only a true fan could write like this. *Live Jam* came out on October 25, 1983, and reached 28 in the album charts.

The Jam Collection, was the next compilation, and it consisted of the best album tracks and B-sides, with the bulk of the songs taken from their most fruitful period, *All Mod Cons* to *Sound Affects*. The Jam was renowned for their B-sides, which in many cases were almost as good as the A-sides. Indeed, many thought *The Butterfly Collector* and *Tales From The Riverbank* were actually better than the hit record they accompanied. I can't think of many bands that have the repertoire in their back catalogue to produce a CD, which contains no hit records, and no fillers. This compilation perhaps tells us more about the depth and the quality of The Jam and Paul's song writing abilities, than any other CD. The compilation came out on July 15, 1996 and went to 58 in the charts.

The next project turned out to be the big one and came about in a strange way. Prior to the release of Paul's 1995 solo album, *Stanley Road*, I unexpectedly received an invitation to the album launch party. I was looking forward to meeting Paul and John, but not the party, as I hated these affairs as they're always attended by liggers from the business and star fuckers. I was sitting drinking with Paul discussing *Stanley Road* and for some reason he wasn't in a great mood, and not enjoying his own party. He abruptly asked why Polydor hadn't released a box set on The Jam, after all, they'd released a Who box set. I replied: "My guess is that nobody had thought of it. If you want, I will go and discuss this with Polydor and see what they say." The next day I called up my old mate George McManus and discussed the possibility and although Polydor had considered the project, they hadn't decided on how to go about it. He was up for the idea, and said that providing the company accept my submissions, there shouldn't be a problem. It took a week or so to put the proposal together, and get the idea approved, and then it was full steam ahead.

By this time, The Jam had split into two corners, Bruce and Rick in one, with the Wellers in the other, and they were only talking to each other through their lawyers, which made it difficult for me. When it came to the final say on how the box set would look, and the running order, it kicked off with both camps and Polydor telling me they would have the last word. There was no way I was going to let the company have the last say, as this was going to be the definitive collection, and there was no room for error. No one was better placed to produce the box set and when it came to working on The Jam's back catalogue, I was neutral, a fan, and always did my best for all concerned. I decided that I would have the final say, keeping everyone informed with regular updates.

When I commenced work on the project, I realised the pressure would be immense, as the release of the set followed Paul's phenomenally successful platinum selling *Stanley Road*. The Jam by now had become a symbol of British music with such groups as Blur, Ocean Colour Scene, and Oasis quoting them as being influential in their careers. The majority of box sets are released when the artists' careers are over, or on the decline, whereas The Jam box set was going to follow the best selling record that Paul released during his entire career. Given The Jam and Paul's standing, if the music press panned it, the finger would be pointed firmly at me; not only that, Jam fans are train spotters, and I knew they and the whole of the music business would inspect my work closely.

Polydor gave me box sets by The Velvet Underground and The Who, and they asked for The Jam box to be produced along the lines of The Who. Writer and Who archivist Chris Charlesworth collated The Who box for them but was disappointed not to have been able to include a fifth CD of the live *Tommy* from Leeds University on February 14, 1970, from which the celebrated *Live At Leeds* came. Both Polydor and Pete Townshend evidently vetoed his idea which was a shame, as it would have made the box set perfect and a great buy for Who fans; not including this extra CD probably affected its sales. Since the demise of The Jam, their back catalogue had been regurgitated at regular intervals, and the fans would have collected these and the other compilations that were released over the years. The fifth CD, needed to offer something special to justify the price and give the fans a real bonus when they shelled out their hard-earned money.

I began the task with a thorough trawl through the archives, which was a laborious job and meant going through every master tape in the Wellers', and Polydor's tape libraries. Polydor's tapes were stored near Tottenham Court Road, at the Eisenhower Centre, which was constructed during WWII, and used to house troops in the advent of London being attacked. After a long descent in the lift, it took at least 10 minutes to walk to the area where Polydor's tapes were set aside. The vaults were deep underground, which I wasn't happy about, and in the labyrinth of corridors and rooms, you could actually here tube trains running above your head.

The Wellers' library was located at Boreham Wood and their tapes housed in large brick sheds, with no control over the climate, which was like an oven in the summer. Indeed, you couldn't enter until it had cooled off sufficiently, and in winter it was so cold it would have frozen the bollocks off an Eskimo. I was surprised and a little worried, as master tapes deteriorate with age and the extreme temperature conditions they were stored in would accelerate the ageing process. The tapes were still playable, but it was necessary to bake them in special ovens for two days prior to copying. Eventually, the Wellers moved their tapes to the Eisenhower Centre for if they had left their (valuable) tape library at Boreham Wood, their tapes would have deteriorated to a point where they are unusable, and the masters lost.

Jane Hitchen, who ran Polydor's tape library, supplied me with a computer print-out of all of The Jam's tapes, which was four inches thick and longer than *War And Peace*. It was a laborious job going through the print-out, which didn't contain all the information, which meant crosschecking each tape with the records stored on the computer. As well as the computer records the library kept photostat copies of the label on each tape box, and I was able to verify the details visually, to confirm the information on the computer print-out. As far as the recording dates go, they are working dates and I couldn't say categorically that they were the exact day the track was laid down. The tape op or the engineers are responsible for filling in the information as the session progresses, so you have to allow for human error.

Information such as the studio where the recording took place was accurate, and I double-checked the multi-track tape with the two-track master to be certain.

The time taken on the research was worthwhile. As well as locating all the original masters, I found many goodies that I knew would be of interest to Jam fans. One tape stood out for me: the first (8-track) demo session they recorded for Polydor at Anemone Studios on February 9, 1977. Included among the four tracks was the demo of their debut single, 'In The City', and I thought this version was more exciting than the actual single, and pleasantly surprised by how dynamic the band sounded at this early stage of their career. Certainly, the years of playing the pub and working-men's clubs circuit had paid off, and listening to these tracks put paid to any argument that they couldn't play. As well as 'Time For Truth' and 'Sounds From The Street', there was a version of 'Change My Address' and although I mixed this track, the recording wasn't as good as the other three, and I omitted it from the final running order. There were no over dubs, and it's possible Paul had only just written the song and the band hadn't worked on it sufficiently, or they were running out of studio time and just banged it down.

Although the guitar track of 'So Sad About Us' was a bit dodgy, Peter managed to get a decent mix of the original demo of this Who Classic. I knew Jam fans would be interested in 'Worlds Apart' as a part of this tune was used in 'Strange Town', and the version of 'Billy Hunt' is the original version that was going to be the follow up single to 'News Of The World'. This was included, as it is a piece of Jam history, even though it isn't that much different to the recording released on the album and single.

I included the demos of 'It's Too Bad' and 'To Be Someone,' and admit to picking these songs because they were big favourites of mine. The demo of 'David Watts' was included for commercial reasons. Polydor were paying my wages, and I had to please them. 'Best Of Both Worlds' wasn't included just to please Bruce, I felt it deserved a place on this CD, and was no worse than some of Paul's unreleased demos. As I have said, with a bit of work this song could have been included on an album, or at least used as a B-side.

Up to this point, I'd always believed the best version of 'That's Entertainment' was the demo that appeared on *Snap*. It had a more relaxed feel, but as I now found out, Peter Wilson originally recorded this song with Paul accompanying himself on guitar and overdubbed bass and drums later. The first version released on *Snap* featured Paul on bass and Peter on drums, while the version on the box features Bruce and Rick. 'Rain' came from the same demo session as 'And Your Bird Can Sing' and once again features Paul on bass, Peter on drums and Hammond organ and Paul's long serving guitar roadie, Dave Liddle on guitar. This Beatles cover was originally rejected for *Extras*, but Peter reckoned with a little pitch twisting, and good re-mix it would be good enough for the box set.

I came across a Townhouse tape that had many rough mixes of the songs that went on to make up *Sound Affects* and played through each one and was surprised when I played the very last track, 'Dream Time'. It was just Paul, accompanying himself on electric guitar, and it sounded great. On another tape, I found recordings of The Kink's 'Dead End Street' and 'Waterloo Sunset'. The first had to be included, but unfortunately, the playing and the singing on the second were well out of tune and must have been recorded after a session at the pub.

'Stand By Me', was a big problem. I'd had a copy of this for years, but during the original recording, there was a problem with an amplifier, and there was a lot of white noise on the recording. I paid a visit to the legendary Abbey Road studios, and with modern technology managed to eliminate the noise, and was able to include this classic Ben E. King tune.

It was no surprise to me that Paul covered the Brenda Holloway classic, 'Every Little Bit Hurts', although it's a blatant copy of The Small Faces' version, it's also a nod to Steve Winwood, who'd recorded this tune in the '60's with The Spencer Davis Group. The alternate version of 'Tales From The Riverbank' and the swing version of 'Pity Poor Alfie' were recorded during *The Gift* sessions, and are improved versions of songs released as B-sides. 'Walking In Heaven's Sunshine', is a demo recorded around the time of *The Gift*, and perhaps shows Paul caught between two stools. It ain't The Jam and it's not quite Style Council.

I included the demo of 'Precious', which is minus the brass, as I really liked this version, and for me it sounds more like The Jam than the final version.

The first version of 'The Bitterest Pill' makes an appearance and I had problems finding any multi-track tapes, which meant making another trip to Abbey Road, and mastered from a cassette copy. I know a multi-track tape existed, and when I collared Paul about this, he couldn't recall where the tape was. Even though it wasn't a great recording, I included the original and complete recording of 'Solid Bond In Your Heart', which included the bridge that Paul extracted and spliced into 'Beat Surrender'.

It was always going to be a tricky decision, picking the tracks, and difficult to please everyone. I passed on songs like, 'Along The Grove', 'Simon', as well as the alternate version of 'Hey Mister' and quite a few others. I know all the fans would have liked to hear these original tunes, but the quality just wasn't good enough for the box set and I had to draw the line somewhere. Paul and The Jam, recorded many covers and I found versions of Gene Vincent's 'Be-Bop-A-Lu-La', Eddie Cochran's 'Summertime Blues', Muddy Waters, 'I Got My 'Mojo Working', and 'You Don't Love Me', a song that most sixties blues band covered. During these sessions Paul's guitar roadie Dave Liddle would have been on hand, and in his youth had been in a rock band and tasted success with a hit record in Brazil. He would have known these tunes backwards and no doubt had a blow on these titles.

When it came to the photos and transparencies of The Jam, I was more than a bit surprised when I found Polydor's library was empty. During The Jam's career, they took part in many photo sessions and there should have been hundreds of photos on file, but there were only a few. I made enquires as to the whereabouts of the collection and was gob smacked when they told me they were either mislaid, or lost. I couldn't understand this, how could a major record company discard or lose valuable photographs of one of their major and most influential bands. This made my job even harder, as now I had to find the original photographers and it didn't please Polydor when they had to pay them repeat fees.*

Most photographers were still working and I was able to trace them, but we were talking twenty years or more down the line and many had moved on. I really wanted to contact Neil 'Twink' Tinning, who I knew had many unpublished photographs, but was unable to locate him, which was a pity, as I would have liked to include photos from his collection. Strangely enough, a year after the box came out he got in touch with me.

Paul Cairns and Neil Allen offered their collections of memorabilia free, which was great, as I knew Chris Charlesworth had been charged by Who fans for the use of their memorabilia. As they lived in Liverpool and the West Midlands, I asked Polydor to foot the bill for Paul and Neil's travel expenses, and a hotel for the night. The budget for the memorabilia shoot was around £2,000, and as I'd found a studio that could do everything, and supply transparencies for less than half of this, I couldn't believe it when Polydor refused to pay their expenses. I was insistent that they pay up, or else the session would be cancelled. After all, the sum was tiny in

* I received another shock in 2006, when I had a meeting at Universal, to discuss the forthcoming releases of The Jam. I mentioned that Polydor should have the large collection of photos that I unearthed, and was gob smacked when told that these too had gone missing.

comparison to the whole budget for the box, and they were getting the memorabilia free. This made no difference and they still refused to stump up the expenses. I knew Paul and Neil would pay their own way, and kip on a mate's sofa, but I wasn't having any of that. They were good lads, the record company were taking the piss, and I stood my ground. At the very last minute, Polydor caved in, and the session took place. After the session, we returned to the hotel and the lads and I hammered the bar for the rest of the night, charging all drinks to their room numbers. I kept mum, as I knew Polydor were only paying for bed and breakfast and in the morning Paul and Neil slipped out without signing their bill, leaving the company to pick up the tab.

Although Simon Halfon only worked on the tail end of The Jam's career, his design of the box set and book captured The Jam's imagery superbly and he did a fantastic job. The bulk of the material for the box was written by Pat Gilbert, John Reed, and Paolo Hewitt, and all credit must be given to the job they did, and the information on The Jam gigs, and the discography supplied by Neil Allen and John Devlin was first rate. As for the contents of the articles written, I issued no guidelines and left it to the journalists, knowing they would offer an objective opinion on the songs and The Jam's history. At no time did I feel it necessary to change, or censor any of their remarks, with the exception of having to ask Paolo to include Bruce and Rick in his foreword, as he had inexplicably failed to mention their names in the opening section.

In Graham Willmott's very good book, *Sounds From The Street*, he mentions there was a bit of an anti Foxton/Buckler campaign in some of the pieces. I can assure you this was not the case. Pat Gilbert's comment about the songs 'Carnaby Street' and 'London Traffic' "(coming perilously close to) cementing the band's reputation as blinkered little Englanders" is a valid comment and is aimed at The Jam as a band, and not just at Bruce and Rick. I can vouch for Pat's statement, as all through The Jam's career, this comment cropped up and many of my colleagues working around the world felt this way. I attended meetings at the various Polydor companies in the USA and Europe, but no matter what I said, they still viewed The Jam as a 'typical' English band, whose appeal never left the white cliffs of Dover. What gives credence to Pat's comments is The Jam never really sold records or CDs overseas, as they did in the UK.

The box set was *the* definitive collection and it was necessary to see all sides of The Jam and for the writers to be objective. Not everything The Jam recorded was great, and it would be disingenuous to the memory of The Jam to hold such a rose-tinted view. There was an up-front honesty about The Jam and their fans, and I know of very few who don't see all sides.

As The Jam no longer exists (except in our hearts) the biggest problem has always been that no one person represents The Jam and can speak for all three members, so at times I have made decisions on behalf of all the participating parties, including Polydor. I am sure I got it wrong occasionally, but for the most, I got it right, and no one can genuinely complain about the box set.

After I had delivered the parts for the box set, there was one more surprise in store for me. For reasons known only to Paul, at the last minute he decided he wanted the box to be released without the fifth CD, which caused me many problems. I received phone calls from the MDs of Polydor and Island (they had inherited Go! Discs at the time), as well as many other senior executives, including PolyGram's CEO, John Kennedy. Paul's decision baffled me, as to release the box set without the fifth CD, which contained all the unreleased material, would have been a mistake. The songs on the first four CDs, even though they were digitally re-mastered from the original masters for the first time, had been released many times before. I was against this, and argued for the fifth CD to be included, fortunately the company agreed, and overruled Paul. I couldn't understand why he wanted the fifth CD removed, as this material is exactly what the fans want, and a major factor in the success of The Jam's box set.

When the box set was released, I expected it to be a success; perhaps selling between 20 and 25,000 copies, but it genuinely surprised me when I was told it had sold in excess of 40,000 copies, and was one of the most successful five CD box sets released in the UK. A short while after the release, one of Polydor's press officers phoned me, and insisted I come in and read the cuttings, something I was reluctant to do. As far as I am concerned, a bad review is better than no review, and worth about the same as a good one. Whatever is said about fans, they are not as stupid as people in the biz assume, and I have never believed a rave review has as much influence as industry people imagine. I relented, and decided to check out the cuttings, and couldn't believe how generous the scribes were, with Alan McGee (who signed Oasis) particularly magnanimous in his five-star review.

I was fortunate to have a good team working alongside me, which made my job easier. Ultimately, this phenomenal success was totally down to the talents of Paul's songwriting, The Jam's credibility, and their dedicated fan base. I had the easy job of putting it all together. The box set was released on May 26, 1997, and went to number eight in the charts, some 20 years after the release ofThe Jam's first single. Statistics, never tell the full story, and can be easily manipulated. but in the case ofThe Jam Box Set, this stat says it all.

Following on, Polydor released all six-studio albums on August 4, 1997 with a new sleeve note, and re-mastered from the original master tapes. On October 13, 1997 PolyGram's TV division released *The Very Best OfThe Jam*, which made the top ten going to number nine. In 2001 during April, Polydor released two mini box sets containing CD versions of the original Jam singles in picture bags, and extra video tracks.

My last compilation, until the next one, was *The Sound Of The Jam* and when *Music Week* reviewed this CD, they reckoned it to be the best Jam record of all time. Originally, I wanted to call it *The Jam Legacy*, but Polydor overruled this and they went with their title, which is a bit *Asda*. This compilation contained a cross section of their hits and great album tracks and I included Paul's solo version of 'That's Entertainment'. When Peter remixed The Jam's version for the box set, utilising modern technology, he ironed out the flat spots and I now believe this to be the best version of this classic Weller/Jam song. The compilation came out during their 25th anniversary on May 6, 2002 and went to number three in the charts, and this chart position surprised everyone, including me. The majority of original fans would have skipped this CD as they had bought the box set and the compilation would have sold to a new generation of Jam fans, and there's no doubt Paul's continuing successful solo career has helped the Jam revival.

Since *The Sound Of The Jam* Universal has released many compilations, which some fans are unhappy about. Had I not worked in the record business myself, I too would probably feel the same way, but I know how difficult it is for the guys working there, who are music fans, but under pressure to make budget – something I know all too much about. When a record company's profits take a dive, or their A&R department isn't delivering, they put pressure on the catalogue department to fill the gap, so it's no good anyone moaning, including me. In addition, whoever works on the back catalogue has to deal with Paul, who we all know can be a little difficult at times.

The Jam At The BBC was a welcome release and featured the many sessions that were recorded by the boys at the Beeb's Maida Vale Studios. This came out on May 27, 2002, and included a bonus CD and LP of *In Concert*, recorded at the Rainbow Theatre on December 12, 1979. This made the album chart, and went to 33. On June 10, 2003, Universal released a Jam compilation as a part of their *Masters Series*.

Following this, on June 20, 2005, Polydor released the original version of *Snap,* and it went to number 39 in the charts. On February 13, 2006, to cash in on Paul's Brit award for his Outstanding Contribution To British Music, they released it again. This time it came with additional B-sides and the original four track live ep and went to number eight in the charts. Since its original release in 1983, this collection has now been released five times!

I played a walk on part with the deluxe edition of The Jam's *All Mod Cons,* which was released by Universal on June 5, 2006 as a 26-track compilation. The CD has the entire album plus additional demos from the box set, and the inclusion of 'News Of The World' with its B-sides, 'Aunties And Uncles', 'Innocent Man' and the single version of 'Tube Station' and the B-sides, 'So Sad About Us' and 'The Night'. I re-mixed 'Mr Clean', and 'Fly', a couple of demos previously unreleased, which were recorded at Polydor's studios on June 29, 1978. Accompanying the CD is a DVD telling *The Story Of All Mod Cons*, directed by Don Letts, which I found a little disappointing. It does feature Paul singing a new version of 'English Rose', but it's intermittently interrupted by snatches of dialogue, which spoils the song, and these comments should have been placed at the end or the beginning.

Paolo Hewitt narrates the rockumentary on screen, with interviews from Paul, Bruce, Rick and Gary Crowley. Incongruously, an interview with Glen Matlock of The Sex Pistols is included, although I can't recall him having anything to do with *All Mod Cons*. I looked into this, and it was planned to interview several *talking heads,* of which Mick Jones and Noel Gallagher were two. For one reason or another, the interviews never happened and although he sticks out like a pork chop at a bar mitzvah, it was decided to leave Glen in the video. I wasn't asked to appear, but this has no bearing on my criticism, as I was writing my book, and I really don't have much to add to how *All Mod Cons* came about, as I had just started working with the boys.

What I found unfathomable was that several key people who played an important role in the making of this classic album – namely Chris Parry, Vic Smith, and sleeve designer Bill Smith – weren't interviewed. Vic was asked to participate, but demanded an exorbitant fee, pricing himself out of the video. I am not sure why he demanded payment, as he will receive his producer's royalties from the re-issue. I've been interviewed many times, and it never occurred to me to ask for money, the Beeb paid me the princely sum of about £90 for my interview in *The Story of The Jam* on Radio 2, which just about covered my expenses. Regardless of this, I would have done it for nothing.

Noel Gallagher's views are well known, and it would have been better to hear comments on this album from more contemporary heads. Gary would have been better utilised doing a voice over, with Paolo making his usual Hitchcock like cameo appearance. The whole thing plays like the scene from *Casablanca*, where Capitaine Renault's Gendarmes burst into Rick's Bar – it's *round up the usual suspects*. Both Chris and Vic played a vital part in the making of the album, as did Bill Smith who designed the stunning sleeve. Given the shit that went down with The Jam's third album, this would have been the perfect opportunity to explain to the fans how this classic album came about.

Many Jam fans have complained to me about there dissatisfaction with the way the Jam story has been presented in the past. Here's what James Mayes had to say on the subject: "Am I the only fan that finds those Cappuccino cats (hangers on) the most annoying people on this planet. Anyone not knowing Weller's history would assume they were actually band members in both The Jam and The Style Council! The latest example being *The Story Of All Mod Cons* DVD, after all who needs Bill Smith, Chris Parry or Vic Smith when you can get the same old faces, who feature quite heavily in just about everything Weller does."

I am not having a go at the guys at Universal, I'm just as guilty as in the past I've followed this route just to have a quiet life. What was refreshing about this release were the sleeve notes by Lois Wilson, which for a change offered a fresh perspective on an album that is 28 years old.

Since starting to write this book, many fans have asked about releasing the Pre-Polydor demos, which they have acquired via bootlegs, and at a price. Karl Gonzalez is a devoted Jam fan and this is what he has to say on the matter: "I've always been bemused by Paul's reluctance to release any of the pre-Polydor recordings. Having heard around 20 or so tracks dating from 1973 up to 1976, the first thing that hits you is the quality of the songs that Weller and Brookes wrote at such an early age. Far from being an embarrassment that you'd want to keep hidden, the Weller/Brookes originals give a fascinating insight to the writing and influences of a 15 year old, whose later output we know oh so well. Paul has often spoken about being an avid collector of demos/out-takes etc by The Small Faces, The Who and The Kinks, so his reluctance to let these recordings be officially released is surprising. To let this large formative and important part of the band's history go unheard would be a shame. It would be a release that many fans would love to hear."

The release of this material is in Paul's hands, and only he can make this decision. Many other fans hold similar views to Karl's, and the fact that The

Jam (particularly Steve Brookes) are not earning income from these bootlegs, might sway Paul. There can be no excuse about the quality of the recordings, as the technology is now available to clean up these recordings, and I would hope that money doesn't become an issue when it comes to doing the deal. Releasing these demos would be a nice thank-you to the very people who put the band and Paul, where they are today, and the whole of The Jam's career in perspective.

The thirtieth anniversary would also be the right time to make a documentary of *The Story Of The Jam*, however, it will be wasted opportunity if the director isn't independent and given a free hand. The fans don't want the record put straight, and are clearly not happy with the staged managed stories that have come out in the past – they want the *real* story. As it's 30 years on, perhaps it's time to let go of the reins, and who knows, the lads might even start speaking to each other again!

CHAPTER 9

On The Road With The Jam

Having spent most of my life involved in the music business, I've seen quite a few gigs and bands in my time. Growing up in the sixties there was no technology to play with and all we had was TV, cinema and music, which played an important part in my generation's rites of passage into adulthood. We spent Fridays and Saturdays bombing around the pubs and clubs watching local artists, as well as bands that would eventually go on to become megastars. Nothing compares to the excitement of a live gig, and no matter how good an album is it's not the same as the adrenaline rush you get when your favourite band is turning up the wick playing live.

Live, The Jam was something else, and only their management, roadies, and a few fans attended more gigs than I did. I would go on tour every opportunity I could and enjoyed travelling with the boys, their concerts, and their fanatical following. The Jam was one of the most dynamic bands I have ever seen perform live, and there was an electric, supercharged atmosphere inside the halls, particularly when they got away from their home base in London. I definitely found the regional gigs more exciting, and I could relax and sink a few beers with the lads. Liverpool, Glasgow, Edinburgh, Manchester, and Newcastle were some of the places I enjoyed, and recall one gig at the Apollo in Glasgow. That night, the band was really going for it, the fans in the cantilevered balcony were jumping up and down with excitement, and you could actually see the balcony moving up and down beneath them.

Perhaps it was because they could only see the band once a year and the kids outside of London were genuinely thrilled about seeing their idols and gave their all, which often reflected in The Jam's playing. I also enjoyed the remote gigs like The Winter Gardens at Malvern and Guilford Civic Hall was a must for me to attend, and to this day, I cannot understand why we never recorded one of the hometown gigs. The Jam played the capital several times a year, and just because it was in London, the fans demanded a great gig, but the downside for me was many Polydor execs would turn up, wanting to go back stage to pose, and it was impossible to relax and enjoy the show. At one Hammersmith Odeon gig, John banned everybody from going back stage before the gig, and one senior executive didn't like this, turned nasty, and threatened me. I had to get a couple of the security guys to lean on him, and he went away cursing my name.

The only gigs I didn't enjoy were those that were recorded, as I would be in the sound truck or running back and forth making sure everything was ok. From 1979, at least two or three gigs a year were recorded, although the boys weren't sure about this. I had to swear an oath that none of the recordings would be used without The Jam's permission. When it came time to releasing a live album, I wanted plenty of material in the can, to do justice to The Jam's live performances.

When punk first burst on to the scene, it was said by many that the bands couldn't play, and live they just thrashed their gigs. In the case of The Jam, this wasn't true, as they had served a long apprenticeship between 1974 and 1975 playing in pubs and workingmen's clubs. Before signing to Polydor, with varying line-ups, The Jam played more than 150 gigs on this gruelling circuit, where you are sandwiched in between the bingo and the fish and chip suppers. I roadied for several of my mates' bands in the sixties and they played these kinds of clubs in Kent and South East London. Many times the bands were ordered to turn the volume down as they played too loud, and it interfered with conversation. Funnily enough, these bands played the contemporary sounds of the day, like Motown, soul, R&B, and blues covers, just as The Jam did a decade later. The clubs were better and you were able build up a following, and every band had a hometown 'club'. With The Beatles it was The Cavern, The Jam had Michael's club in Woking, where they played on more than 70 occasions.

They outgrew the cloth cap and beer circuit, and played their last gig at Michael's on September 26, 1975. Although not quite a premier league band, this didn't stop them being promoted to the London club scene where New Wave had arrived. In 1976, The Jam played around 20 gigs, but was now playing where the new in-crowd met: The 100 club, The Greyhound in Fulham, the Hope & Anchor in Islington, Upstairs at Ronnie Scott's, and the famous Marquee in Wardour Street, Soho. In the mid-seventies these venues were home to some really dreadful pub rock bands, who were ousted by a new generation uninterested in boogying on down. When the Pistols and punk took off, A&R men from every record company would make a beeline for these venues and could be seen standing at the back of the gig, looking dreadfully out of place, hoping to sign a winner.

In 1977, the year The Jam signed to Polydor, they must have been on speed as they played around 130 gigs in the UK, as well as their first gigs in Europe and America. This was their busiest year on the road, and for the rest of their career they never again went into triple figures. Between January and May, the bulk of the dates were in London and the Home Counties, and included names synonymous with New Wave: The Red Cow in Hammersmith, The Roxy in Covent Garden, The Nashville in West Kensington, The Rochester Castle in Stoke Newington, and the famous Roundhouse at Chalk Farm. They were building their fanatical support that would eventually see them play to SRO audiences all over the UK. They played a number of away gigs, like Leicester, Ipswich, Newport in Wales, and Edinburgh, but for most, they played home matches. The Jam pulled out of the White Riot tour, after a disagreement with The Clash, who were headlining. The under card included The Buzzcocks, The Slits and Subway Sect.

From June to the beginning of September, The Jam toured heavily and played their first headline tour of the UK. Paul boasted that The Jam was as big as the Pistols, but given their (Pistol's) reputation, it's unlikely that many venues would have taken them; otherwise, they would have been selling out much bigger venues than The Jam. It was a real mixture of gigs, and hardly a county missed, and at the end of September, they went to Europe for the first time. In Sweden, one gig was abandoned after punks rioted and smashed up the band's gear and the next date had to be cancelled. They also played The Paradiso in Amsterdam, a venue that Paul would visit many times during his career. October saw them making their first tour of the USA, where they played two dates at the Whiskey-A-Go-Go in Hollywood, The Rat's Kellar Boston, and the legendry CBGBs, situated in the Bowery area of New York.

On November 17, they commenced The Modern World Tour in support of their unjustly maligned second album. There were 24 dates in all, the majority at larger venues, ending at The Hammersmith Odeon. Looking at the list there were a few odd gigs, including The Village Bowl Discothèque in Bournemouth and The Greyhound in Croydon and it was on this tour that a punch-up occurred with an Australian rugby league team in The Jam's hotel in Leeds. Bruce, for his troubles, copped a hiding and ended up with heavily bruised and cracked ribs, and played the rest of the tour in severe pain.

As far as The Jam's early gigs go, I only caught a few. In 1977, I was still Polydor's jazz A&R manager, and working, and touring with the likes of Ella Fitzgerald, Oscar Peterson and Count Basie's big band, where I served my drinking apprenticeship. I recollect seeing one or two of the club dates, but can't remember which ones, but I do recall a Hammersmith Odeon gig, because Paul had a stack of Vox AC30s behind him. Although The Jam was excellent that night, they didn't quite have the repertoire for the size of the Hammersmith Odeon, and were reproducing their club act on a much bigger stage. However, when they did progress, nowhere was too big for The Jam to play.

That year The Nashville and 100 Club gigs were recorded for an aborted live album.

In 1978, they played nearly 70 concerts, and opened the year with a quick trip to Brussels and Paris for a brace of gigs, before they blitzed London, playing two at the Marquee and one at the 100 club, as well as The Music Machine. This gig stands out in my mind, as the support acts were Jab Jab, Gang Of Four and The Nips, led by the infamous Shane McGowan. Having finished their slot, Shane and the band went for a drink and propped up the bar for the remainder of the night. When it came to the encore, someone had the bright idea that Shane should accompany the Jam on, 'Heatwave'. When he arrived on stage, much to everyone's amusement, he was wearing a giant white nappy with a large safety pin holding it together. All through the number, the audience and the band was falling about laughing, and how the boys got through it is a mystery.

The band had brought in a co-manger to help them break into the American market and they undertook an ill-conceived tour of America supporting Blue Oyster Cult. This meant playing big arenas, some that held 20,000, and neither The Jam, nor their set list was ready for the type of audience they faced. When the American fans heard their music, they didn't like it one bit, and retaliated, bombarding the stage with missiles and jeering the band. It's common practice in the business for lesser-known bands to buy their way on to a major artist's tour, as it gives them the chance to play before huge audiences, and pick up new fans. On this tour, there was never a chance of this as the music The Jam played had nothing in common with BOC, or their audience. It would be easy to point the finger at John for this error of judgement, but at the time, he was finding his feet as a manager and had no doubt been talked into this move. Polydor must have known The Jam's music wouldn't go down well in America, and maybe agreed to this tour to please the American arm of the company. The band took a dislike to the States on this first trip, and this made them reticent about the USA. After one gig, they told the awaiting journalists to fuck-off, and gave their only (American) interview to an obscure fanzine. Their attitude did them no favours, and alienated them with the (mainstream) music press and for a while Polydor's American executives.

Following this, they undertook a mini tour of the UK in June, playing six gigs, with the last gig at The Lyceum in London. Late July and August saw them undertake another seaside tour, which – reflecting Paul's droll sense of humour – included the resort towns of Guildford, Swindon and Reading-by-the sea. They also had a paddle in European waters, playing on the bill at the Bilsen festival in Belgium and the Gronigen festival in Holland. On October 20 and 21, they played two gigs in southern Ireland, but never returned to the Emerald Isle again, north or south.

From this point, I went on every UK tour and many of the European jaunts as well. I remember The Friars at Aylesbury and the Reading Festival, which I had visited in 1964 and 1965 when it was an R&B festival. I had a band on each night, and while I enjoyed some of the shows, three days was a little too much. The festival was filmed and I went to see a preview and it was wonderful. The Jam, Sham 69, The Slits and The Pirates were all featured, but the highlight of the film (and festival for me) was the appearance of the original Ultravox band featuring John Foxx. I have no idea what happened to this film, which is shame as it's an excellent documentary of the festival and the period.

With the success of *All Mod Cons,* The Jam ended the year with The Apocalypse Tour, and all the dates were sold out. The support acts were The Dickies and the poet and singer/songwriter Patrick Fitzgerald, who by this time was signed to Polydor. They played 21 concerts, which started at the Liverpool Empire, and I cannot think of a better venue for The Jam to open a tour. They played all their strongholds in England and Scotland, and one date in Wales at Cardiff's University. I remember only a few dates as by now I was being led astray by the boys, John and Bruce in particular, and was getting into some heavy drinking sessions after the shows. The Music Machine was the only gig to be recorded in 1978.

In 1979, The Jam played over 60 gigs, starting the year off with a warm up date at Reading University before touring the USA, Canada and Europe, well… Germany and France. They played the Star Club in Hamburg, whose legendary status by this time had worn thin, and as the gig was poorly attended, Paul threatened to split up the band. By this time, the band was used to selling out gigs, and playing to a baying army of fans, and hadn't played to an empty house for some time. Punk (and The Jam) was a British innovation, and although popular throughout the UK and in some parts of Europe, it didn't travel. More than likely, the night before Paul had a few shandies and woke up with a bit of an artistic temperature, and poor old teddy hit the carpet. I've seen this happen on more than a few occasions, and I don't believe for one minute that Paul would have split the band up because of this. Danny Baker was at this gig and I remember him as being a soddin' nuisance, as he would turn up at the studios when they were recording and even made an appearance as one of the soldiers on *TOTP*, when The Jam played 'The Eton Rifles'.

Following this, in April they played ten dates in the USA and Canada and returned home for their Jam Pact Spring tour, which kicked off on May 4 with two nights at Sheffield University. There were two gigs at the Rainbow, where The Nips again supported them, sans nappies, and The Chords, a band from the new Mod revival favoured by Paul. On this tour, at the apocalyptic ending of 'A Bomb In Wardour Street', one of the roadies would let off a thunder flash, and at the Birmingham Odeon they slightly overdid it, and the noise was deafening. There was so much smoke you couldn't see the stage, never mind the band, and the manager of the theatre copped the hump and banned The Jam from appearing there again. As we were leaving the city, we passed a row of shops and someone noticed a couple in one of the doorways having a shag. We talked the driver into turning round, drove slowly past, and gave them a round of applause and hearing the noise the lad turned round, and saw twenty smiling faces, gave us a wolfish grin, and a quick wave before returning to his night's work.

In June, they played one solitary gig at Saddleworth's Art Festival, and in late August, they arranged to play three London club dates at the Moonlight Club Hampstead, The Bridgehouse at Canning Town, and the Nashville in West London, but all three were cancelled. Later in the year, during November, John arranged gigs at the Marquee and the Nashville, which were supposedly secret gigs, but the secret didn't last long and word got out. They were booked as John's Boys and The Eton Rifles, with some adverts using the pseudonym La Confiture, and you didn't need a degree in the bleedin' obvious to work out who was playing.

I went to the Marquee and the atmosphere was amazing, it was hot and sweaty, and my loafers stuck to the floor, as they did when I attended this club in the sixties. I met Gary Crowley, who was about 15 years old, who worked for the Jam's promotions manger Clive Banks. The day after the Marquee, he came into the office to show me the piece he had written for *NME*, and he must have talked about The Jam and the gig for twenty minutes before I could get a word in. I've have always liked Gary and found him to be a genuine person, as well as big, big Jam fan. I remember I attended this gig with Polydor's marketing manger, Nigel Reveler, who was from my generation and he asked if I ever felt out of place at a Jam gig because of the age difference. I replied no, but I don't go down the front where the kids are jumping up and down, as I would look pretty stupid po-going, and asked why the question. He then told me, as everyone in the club was 10, or more, years younger, he felt a little out of place. Many of my generation felt this way about the bands from this period, and were unable to come to terms with the music or the lifestyle of the youth of the day. I am glad to say that it wasn't a problem for me and I just enjoyed the atmosphere and the great music.

It was at this gig that I first met Big Kenny Wheeler, who is still by Paul's side to this day. After the show, I went back stage, but I couldn't go the normal way as fans were milling around the dressing room door. I vaulted the stage only to be confronted by Kenny, who I didn't really know, and he told me to fuck off, and get off the stage. I was about to explain to Kenny who I was, when John interrupted, and told him: "He's OK – he's one of us." Kenny at the time was doing the security for the band and it wasn't the greatest of jobs. Over the years, fans have made many comments about him, and not many were complimentary. To many he was known as the "fat bastard", due to his size and demeanour, particularly when he was chucking fans out of a gig. Kenny was indeed a big lad, with a heavy beard, who always wore a cheese-cutter cloth cap and braces. There were times when I wasn't happy with the way Kenny went about his job, as sometimes he seemed to go over the top. Mind you, I never saw him whack anybody, and if he told you to fuck off, nobody was stupid enough to ignore his advice.

With the possible exception of John, Kenny has spent more time with Paul than anyone else who's worked for the Wellers, and been subject to Paul's ever-changing moods. Many times John and Paul would shovel the shit his way, and he would end up on the receiving end of abuse. As The Jam became bigger (so did Kenny) and more popular (Kenny didn't) and when Paul became a big star, it was necessary for him to accompany him everywhere, including playing gooseberry, when Paul went out with his girlfriend Gill. I am certain he didn't enjoy these moments and would have rather been watching his beloved Spurs play football.

It's been said that he acted like he was the fourth (or fifth) member of The Jam, but as long as I have known him, he has never thought this way. He has always been extremely loyal, and does a good job for Paul. I found out what it was like to be a tour manager after I left Polydor, when I managed a band, and I can't say I enjoyed it, and this experience changed my opinion of Kenny. As far as Paul's music went, he came from The John Weller School of critique – everything was fucking great, but there's nothing wrong with that. He was a part of the inner circle that made Paul's life tick over more easily.

To support the release of *Setting Sons*, they booked a 29-date tour of the UK, which they probably could have sold out twice. They opened up at the Friars in Aylesbury, and played two nights at the Manchester Apollo, Southampton Gaumont, City Hall Newcastle, Leicester's De Montford Hall, and Bath Pavilion. They played three nights at the Rainbow, where were the support act was The Vapors, who just happened to be managed by John and Bruce. At the beginning of the tour, I was given my own tour jacket, something I didn't expect and it was big thrill for me to receive this present. Stitched on the front was a Union Jack with my name on, and wearing it allowed me to get into the venues and move about freely once inside. I made as many gigs on this tour as I could and remember being at both of the Manchester dates and Bingley Hall in Stafford, which they had to play as they were banned from the Odeon. Bingley Hall was a cavernous place, and the sound wasn't that great, but the atmosphere was terrific.

That year we recorded five gigs, Reading University, two at The Rainbow, Brighton Conference Centre, and the Guildhall Portsmouth.

It was a low-key opening for 1980 with gigs at Cambridge, Canterbury, Malvern, and a fund raising gig at the YMCA in Woking. They went on to play over 70 gigs, and by the end of the year, they had a repertoire and stage show that could match the best. They played their fourth tour of the states, but cut the trip short and returned to England to enjoy the success of their first number one record, 'Going Underground'. They played two gigs at the Rainbow, which were a part of the fiftieth anniversary of the venue, which was originally known as the Finsbury Park Astoria. It's been said that these two gigs were the best The Jam ever played. However, if you weren't there you wouldn't know and I am sure that every Jam fan has seen the best Jam gig ever – at least as far as they are concerned. My favourite came a little later in the year.

The American tour was the largest that The Jam undertook, but still not long enough for them to crack the US market. To make any kind of dent there, you need to play at least 30 to 40 cities and if you include Canada you can add another dozen to the schedule. With travelling time, you would be looking at spending at least two to three months on the road and the band went through a period where they wouldn't fly unless they had to. Due to the size of the continent, it's impossible to tour of the USA without flying, and the only way you can break America is to slog it out, playing gigs coast to coast, and you can't do this travelling around in a bus. The popularity of The Jam centred on the cities on both coasts, but they never penetrated middle America. If they had released an album every two years, it would have been possible to spread the touring over 24 months, and had this happened they could have engaged in longer tours of America, Europe and Japan. I visited my American cousins at Polydor many times to gee them up about The Jam, and although many of those working at the company were big fans, things never really took off for them.

The American market works much differently to the UK in every aspect, the way they promote, market and the way they sell their albums. Because The Jam didn't undertake large tours, and were popular only in a few urban areas, their records would have only been sold where Polydor knew there would be genuine sales. In America during the seventies, and up to the mid eighties, records were sold into the chains and record stores on a sale or return basis, which meant that all unsold records could be returned. One of the problems with selling records on this basis is the shipping figures rarely match the genuine sales figures, unless you are a name act. It's not unheard of for a record to ship vast quantities, only for the genuine sales to be a small percentage of the original figure quoted, and in a few cases, zero. Following the phenomenal success of *Saturday Night Fever* and *Grease,* in 1979, RSO records released the soundtrack to the *Sgt Pepper* movie and shipped a million copies. Unfortunately, for the record company, both the film and the album stiffed, and many unsold albums were returned to the record company for credit.

At the time of The Jam, royalties in the States were remunerated on an annual basis and a year in arrears. This meant that the true sales were not known until well after the album was released. Many managers often made the mistake of taking the shipping figures as genuine US sales, only to get a shock when their American royalties arrived. Following the colossal losses of *Sgt Pepper* soundtrack, and the *Thank God It's Friday* album, which Casablanca shipped out a million copies, only to see the bulk of them returned, the American record companies drastically changed their SOR policy. As far as royalties go, these days they have fallen in line with the rest of the world, paying out on a bi-annual basis.

They played sporadically over May and June, at the Pink pop festival in Holland, and on June 21 they headlined the Loch Lomond Festival, which stands out in my mind for many reasons, and none of 'em good. Whoever booked the bands must have been on serious drugs as the running order included The Jam and The Chords, (mod bands), Stiff Little Fingers, (punk), Bad Manners (skinhead) plus Punishment Of Luxury and The Tourists thrown in for good measure. What they were all doing on this bill is anyone's guess, but I suppose they thought that Annie Lennox being Scottish would put bums on the grass. The toxic mixture of fans was like pouring petrol on a blazing fire and there was trouble throughout the concert. When Fingers played, their fans would be at the front, whilst Bad Manners fans would collect behind them chucking stones, bricks, and (full) beer cans at their heads. This violence was repeated when each band played, with an assortment of missiles thrown back and forth. I spoke to one of the security guys, and he showed me a cut-throat razor that had been thrown into the crowd. How it missed is a miracle, and had it found a target it would have left a bloody mess. It was just mindless hooliganism, and not a pleasant sight.

When The Chords appeared, I was on stage as an unofficial roadie, but for The Jam I went out front and watched from the VIP area. As I was returning back stage, a 'nice' (Glaswegian) girl stopped me and asked me if I was from London. I clocked her reaching into a pocket of her leather jacket, and had no idea what she was searching for, but quickly scooted away to the relative security of the backstage area. It's possible she was only reaching for a tissue, but I wasn't about to hang around to find out. The band played well, but Loch Lomond was an ugly festival, and an experience I'd rather forget.

They played five dates in Japan, and a fundraising gig in Guilford. I recall Shane McGowan turned up at the gig, and as we left to get the bus home, he was gassed out of his head and comatose on the dressing room floor. Around this time, on Paul's recommendation, I'd demoed The Nips and, impressed with the tracks they'd laid down, wanted to sign them to Polydor. A couple of days after the gig, Shane's manager, a strange little man who was wearing the worse syrup (wig) I'd ever seen, came in to discuss terms. I was all for offering them a singles deal and about £10k advance, when he astonished me by asking for an album deal and £60k up front. I explained to him that when Polydor signed The Jam they only got a singles deal and six grand. I then asked if Shane was still drinking, and he swore blind that he was teetotal and completely off the booze. I pointed out to him that I'd seen him just a few days ago, backstage at a Jam gig unconscious and he said: "It was just a blip!" I didn't make the deal, which was a shame, as Shane is a talented and gifted songwriter. Once Shane came into my office, with his left arm stuffed inside his jacket and I enquired after his health, he replied: "I'm Napoleon Bonaparte!" Shane went on to great fame with The Pogues, whom I wanted to sign, but my bosses refused saying Polydor had enough of those kinds of bands already. Shane's problem with booze would haunt him all of his life and I hope he doesn't go the same way as George Best.

On August 9, The Jam played the Ruisrock Festival in Turku Finland, which also turned out to be violent, although I have some good memories from this event. The bands and road crews travelled on a charter flight arranged by Stiff Records from Southend (International) Airport. Wisely, the boys had decided to forgo this pleasure and travelled on a regular flight from Heathrow, which took half the time. Looking out of the airport bar window, I noticed the plane was a relic from the fifties, an old four-engine turbo-prop, and the flight took ages. The speed of the plane was nothing like a modern jet and it didn't seem to fly much higher than the Post Office tower. Halfway there, and to everyone's dismay, we were told there was no more alcohol left – we had drunk the plane dry. As the plane was only half-full, we were a little disappointed, even though the pilot explained he'd stocked the bar for a full flight!

We arrived at the festival in the afternoon and the site was nicely situated next to a large lake, but the crowd had been boozing all day on homemade hooch and were completely rat arsed. The gig itself was great, finishing early, and we were away by 10pm, which meant a few extra hours in the bar, but the crowd had other ideas and they rioted, throwing bottles and cans at the road crews breaking down the gear on stage. A mob raided the stage and pushed one side of the huge PA stack into the lake. Completely bemused, I watched as the large bass bins sailed off into the sunset across the lake, towards Russia. It was a bizarre sight, but then, it was a bizarre festival in a bizarre country.

Arriving back at our hotel, we went into top gear and got into a nice drinking session. On a trip to the toilet, I noticed John Weller playing poker with Nick Lowe's guitarist, Billy Bremner, and few roadies and I have to say, only mugs play poker with John, or come to that, Paul. John took them all, and I believe Billy lost all his money, which meant he played the gig for free. I saw many a roadie lose a month's wages to them, they were sharks circling for their next victim, and they always played for serious dough. Kenny was also a dab hand with the cards and at the end of a tour, he would have a grin on his face, contemplating whether he would buy a fridge freezer or a cooker, or a new TV with the money he'd skinned off Paul and John. At about 3am I'd drunk enough, it was time for bed and as I was leaving, I noticed the pilot and co-pilot were still there knocking back large ones and thought the flight back was going to be an interesting one! The Captain did at least stock the plane with enough booze for the return flight, and we all arrived home hung over, but safe. They followed this with a low-key charity gig at Bromley Tech where 540 tickets were sold through the Wings Shop in Bromley and three local colleges.

On October 26 The Jam began the Sound Affects Tour, which took in 22 dates with two nights at the Newcastle City Hall, Manchester Apollo, Brighton Conference Centre, Bracknell Sports Centre, Leicester's De Montford Hall, finishing with two nights at The Rainbow and the Hammersmith Odeon. The Piranhas were the support act, who at the time had a top ten hit with 'Tom Hark'. This was originally recorded in 1958 by the South African group Elias & The Zig Zag Jive Flutes, and went to number two in the UK charts. Georgie Fame featured this classic on his 'Rhythm And Blue Beat' EP released in 1964, and both the original and Fame's version were big favourites with us Mods. All I can recall about The Piranhas is the lead singer was the double of Gary Glitter, something I don't suppose he wants reminding of these days. Following the Hammersmith Odeon dates, they did a number of dates in Europe, and that well-known tax-haven Jersey.

I accompanied The Jam to Sweden, and as they wouldn't fly, we travelled by road, which took two days. We all met at the pick up point in Victoria, and as I boarded the bus, I met up with Joe Awome, who'd just been taken on as security. Joe was an ex-boxer and a Commonwealth Heavyweight gold medal winner, and this was his first tour. He asked me: "What's it like touring with The Jam?" I replied, "Different, I hope you like a drink!" We left at 10am, and as we wound our way down the Old Kent Road, Bruce suddenly piped up: "Time to get beer handed lads" and disappeared to the back of the bus, which had been turned, into a mini – well more a maxi than mini – bar. We drank all the way to Dover and carried on in the bar on the ferry. Late that evening we arrived in Hanover and checked into the hotel, had the three s'sss, and then headed for the in-house disco, and drank until the early hours.

At 6am, we headed for the port of Hamburg to catch the boat for the eight-hour sailing. Once the ship was in international waters, the bars opened, and we split into two drinking teams. During the session, a rather drunk Swede joined us and he was ok until a couple of girls joined us, and he couldn't keep his hands to himself, and was all over them, like a cheap suit. Out of nowhere two-armed security men appeared and carted him off, and on returning, they apologised for his behaviour. One of the officers explained that many Swedes used the ferry as a 24-hour pub, the fares were cheap, and they could drink on the trip over, and on the return voyage, with many not even leaving the boat when it docked in Hamburg. I asked what happened to the man and they explained the boat contained a brig (jail) to cater for this sort of behaviour, and he would be let out when the boat arrived back in Sweden.

When we were queuing up at passport control, Rick's drum roadie, Wally Miller, who hailed from Scotland, realised he had brought his wife's passport instead of his own, and was a bit worried that he wouldn't be let in. When he handed it over, the customs officer looked at Wally and then the photograph, and without batting an eyelid, told him to pass through. Either he had come across Scotsmen before, or possibly thought Wally had had a sex change! Mike Gardner, a music journalist joined us on this trip, and that night I took him out for an early supper. Now Sweden has quite a serious drink problem, although I am not sure why, as you need to take out a second mortgage to get drunk. It was early evening, and as we left the restaurant, the police were arresting a drunk, who stupidly took a swing at one of the officers. They grabbed hold of him, and in full view of everyone watching, unceremoniously bundled him into the car, something the old Bill in the UK wouldn't have got away with.

We returned to our hotel for what we thought would be a quiet drink and as we were entering the bar, a drunk walked into me. He was so smashed he couldn't see me, and I'm not exactly small. Most of the occupants of the bar were pissed, and I found a table at the back, far away from any potential trouble, and sure enough within twenty minutes a punch up started. Some wanker kept pestering a girl at the next table, and in the end her boyfriend, fed up with him, gave him slap. One of his mates came up to drag him away, and he turned on him and whacked him for his troubles. We couldn't believe it, these were not teenagers, they were grown up adults and probably ABBA fans! Sweden's liberal policy towards sex didn't extend to alcohol and the government had always had restrictive regulations concerning drinking, and there is no pub culture similar to the UK. They also have one of the highest suicide rates per capita in the world, which is strange considering how liberal and affluent they are as a society. This night certainly changed my views on Sweden, and whoever said Swedes were nice quiet people obviously hadn't seen this side of them.

On their return, the UK arm of the tour was extended and they played six concerts, and I attended the show at the Winter Gardens at Malvern, which was exciting, and both the band and the fans were on good form. After the concert, a huge drinking session took place and I didn't get to bed until the early hours of the morning. I checked out of the hotel feeling like shit, and instead of driving home to get some sleep, I decided to drive back to London and go into the office. When I arrived my hangover hadn't improved and by the afternoon I still had a king size headache. I received a call to attend a meeting with the MD, A J Morris, and John Weller and I trooped up the stairs entered his office, not in the greatest of moods. I'd done a good job on *Sound Affects*, was hoping for another pat on the back. The old man was in one of his Bruce Forsythe moods – "I'm in charge" – and went into some problem with The Jam that I was dealing with. Inside my head, it felt like Quasimodo was playing 'ding-dong merrily on high', and I wanted to be anywhere but in his office listening to him going on. When he finished his diatribe, without thinking, I told him: "If you're going to talk like that, then you can fuck off out of it," and left his office, not giving much thought to the consequences of my comments. After the meeting, John came to see me, worried about my outburst; and thought it might cost me my gig, but all I cared about was going home and getting some sleep. I heard no more about this outburst, and later AJ took me out for a spot of lunch. We discussed many topics, including The Jam's success, but he never mentioned the incident. I had a good relationship with him, and – with the exception of the *Sound Affects* album – he was always supportive, particularly, when it came to the Wellers. He knew the kind of pressure I was under, or perhaps just put the incident down to my drinking.

We only recorded one gig that year, which was on October 28 at Newcastle City Hall and Malcolm Gerrie, the producer and director of *The Tube* had decided to film the concert for Tyne Tees TV and supervise the recording. This was great news as I could watch from out front and was looking forward to the show. Peter Wilson accompanied me on this particular night, and we were behind the mixing desk, which gave us a blinding view of the stage. The atmosphere in the hall was crackling with anticipation as we waited for the band to appear, and when they came on stage, the noise was deafening. They opened up with 'Dream Time', and the audience went wild, the two girls sitting behind were so excited, they were jumping all over our backs. I have listened to the cassette of this recording many times, and although the playing and the recording are not technically perfect, the performance was great, and this is my all-time favourite Jam gig.

One evening I remember gong out for a drink with Bruce, Steve Smith (the bass player of The Vapors), and Chris Pope and Buddy Ascott of The Chords, a right nice little drinking team. As I was driving I couldn't keep up with them, but the rest went for it and around midnight Bruce decided that we would go to The Swiss Club in Wardour Street, and as he was a member, it would be no problem getting in. I wasn't sure about this, as everybody was really gassed up, and out of their brains. The manager of the club took one look at us and barred us, but Bruce and Steve were having none of this took and stormed the door. By this time, a bouncer had arrived, and a scuffle took place. I jumped in and tried to pull the two of them away and dodge the punches that were being thrown. I pulled them away from the door, and outside into the street. Buddy and Chris were no problem as by now they were out of their bonces, and were sitting on the pavement outside the club. There was no way they could get home under their own steam, so I escorted them to my car and drove them home. We left Bruce and Steve with their egos slightly dented, muttering oaths about not being let in. Still, you can't really blame the club, not many places would let in five blokes who were that drunk.

In December, Polydor threw a Christmas party for The Jam at the Greyhound Pub, a popular live venue on Fulham Palace Road, where they had previously played as an up and coming band. All their family and friends received an invite along with a sprinkling of company execs who decided to brave the festivities. The MD had decided to present the boys with their Polydor Christmas presents, video players and their silver and gold discs for *Sound Affects,* and not wishing to miss a good photo opportunity, a photographer was on hand to capture the occasion. Paul came up to me a few minutes before the presentation, and stated emphatically that he wanted to receive his present from Polydor's post boy Perry, a big Jam fan. He was well pissed by now, and I replied: "I can't ask the MD to step down for the post boy. It's more than my fucking job's worth." Paul replied: "He's never done anything for The Jam, fuck him, I want Perry to give me mine." I couldn't get through to him, and he eventually wandered off to get some more booze down his neck. When it came to the presentation, there was no problem and the old man went through the motions. A little later, the MD left for home, which meant, I could at last enjoy the party, and I hit the bar big time.

When I organised the party, as well as a DJ, I booked a covers band lead by my mate Jeff Martin as they played the sort of tunes that would go down well with this crowd. Even though I was well pissed, he dragged me up on stage to sing a number during the set, and I sang a very rude version of 'Old MacDonald Had A Farm'. Unfortunately, I'd forgotten that their mums, dads, aunties and uncles were attending the party, but it went down surprisingly well. I remember Rick and his girlfriend Lesley and few others gobbing at me!

As the party wore on, John came up and said: "Den, get the boys up on stage to play a couple of numbers, the families will love it." I wasn't too sure about this idea, but the boys surprisingly agreed and went on stage. The line up consisted of Paul on keyboards, Bruce and Rick on bass and drums, Staveley on guitar, and the Dolly Mixtures sang backing vocals. The lead vocals were handled by a rather drunk (no surprises there) Shane McGowan and I christened, the band The Greyhound All Stars.

I acted as MC and being out of my tree gave everybody abuse, specifically Shane and Vaughn Toulouse from Department S. After 10 minutes rehearsals, I charmingly announced, "Give it the big one for The Jam, The Dolly Mixtures and every other fucker in the place," not quite, what you'd hear at the Brit Awards, and they kicked off with the Motown classic 'Heatwave'. After this, wisely, The Dolly's returned to the bar, reducing the band to a five piece. Bruce took umbrage at something or another, left the stage, and my mate Jeff took his place on bass to finish the set. The next tune up, which came as a real surprise was the Rolf Harris classic, 'Sun Arise'. Unfortunately, Shane only knew the first verse and the chorus, and the song seemed to drone on forever! The third track was the Dusty Springfield's classic, 'I Just Don't Know What To Do With Myself', which they well and truly destroyed. The less said about it the better!

The party ended at about 1am and everybody returned home more than the worse for wear, but having enjoyed a good Moriarty. Around 10am the next morning, I was woken by a call from Jeff, and blasting down the phone was one of the tracks the band played at the party. Unbeknown to me, he had turned on his cassette machine and recorded the evening's entertainment, and with the aid of the latest digital software, I have transferred the three tracks to CD. What do they sound like now, the same as they did at the time of the party, bloody awful, but a good hoot!

In 1981, The Jam played around 50 dates, kicking off the year with some low-key gigs at Westfield Cricket Club (billed as The Jam Road Crew) and two fundraisers at the Woking YMCA and (the now infamous) Sheerwater

Youth Club. I remember arriving at Sheerwater early and everyone drank heavily, and when it came to the time to go on stage, Paul was drunk, he fell over during the performance, and the set was shambles. After the gig, he was incredibly pissed off, as he had not only let himself down, but also the fans that attended this local gig. I came in for a lot of stick as I'd bought many of the drinks, and my expense account had taken a bashing. Kenny went as far as to accuse me of loading the gun with the bullets, which pissed me off as Paul didn't have to take the drinks on offer. He could have refused. Bruce and Rick had drunk heavily, but they restrained themselves from going over the top. This comment riled me; after all, Paul knew he had to play a show that night, but perhaps thinking, it's not The Hammersmith Odeon, it doesn't matter. He wasn't under any (outside) pressure, and this gig was months after *Sound Affects*, and he'd had the Christmas and New Year period to wind down and recharge his batteries. It's a side of him I have never been able to fathom, as he is totally black and white in everything he does. I've never understood why he had to drink so heavily or not at all, there seems to be no room for moderation in all aspects of his life. After this episode, he embarked on yet another teetotal period.

After warm up dates in Norwich, Nottingham, and Crawley, they went on a short tour of Europe to support the release of *Sound Affects* and the European single 'That's Entertainment'. They played dates in France at the Pavilion Baltard in Paris before making their way north to Sweden, Denmark, and then Germany, Belgium, Holland, finishing off the tour where they started with the two more shows in France. The gig in Paris was one of the most unpleasant Jam concerts I attended. As usual, many of their English fans travelled the short distance from England, and there was a small army of Mods outside the gig. Unfortunately, a large gang of Parisian skinheads turned up and a riot ensued, and the police arrested more than a hundred people from both sides. The atmosphere inside the venue reeked of hostility and violence with skirmishes breaking out intermittently before the band went on. I was backstage and Kenny Wheeler came up to me and said: "We're going into the arena to calm the situation down. You're coming with us, they're only kids, they won't be any trouble". Some of these 'kids' were wearing crash helmets to protect themselves!

Kenny wasn't going to take no for answer so I meekly followed him and the other security guys out amongst the crowd. I am not sure how many went, but one of The Jam's security staff refused, fearing he would get beaten up. We strolled around, and I hid behind Kenny's huge frame, and as we walked among the fans, he gave any would be troublemakers his famous glare. As soon as they saw the ferocious look on his face, and that he meant business, they seemed to calm down. Much to my relief we returned to the dressing room in one piece. Whatever is said about Kenny, he never shirked his responsibilities, and although nothing happened, we could have all ended up tasting Parisian shoe leather. It wasn't in my brief with Polydor to go out and sort a ruck between The Jam's Mod fans and a bunch of skinheads. Although I didn't fancy this stroll around the audience one bit, I would have rather faced the mob than say no to 'Big' Kenny.

On April 27, they played a benefit concert at Liverpool's Royal Court Theatre in support of the 'March Against Unemployment', raising the tidy sum of £1,500 for this worthy cause. During May, they went on their second tour of Japan and played four dates, and then flew over the Pole to the East coast of Canada and the USA for their fifth tour and played four gigs in Canada, one in Montreal, and three in Toronto, with one gig apiece in Boston and New York. With the success of *Sound Affects* in the UK, my bosses dispatched me to America to sell the album, and get the Americans off their arses. I had a good relationship with the people who worked on The Jam in America and knew they were doing everything possible, but were handicapped by the short tours that the band undertook to support their albums. Without a large tour, the company would not invest their marketing money, and only concentrated their efforts in the cities where the Jam was popular.

In June, they went to Sweden for two shows and one night at the Rainbow to promote their latest single 'Funeral Pyre'. They followed this with a strange tour entitled, The Bucket and Spade Tour, which consisted of eleven gigs at some of the strangest seaside resorts I've ever come across. They included Leicester, Stafford, and Preston, and finished with two nights at that well-known costal town Guildford. In October, they performed six concerts in London in support of the CND movement and made a guest appearance at The Rainbow with Gang Of Four. They also appeared on a mobile platform on the embankment, opposite the House of Commons. Although the CND profile was now high, these concerts helped persuade a new generation to supporting the cause, one far removed from the duffle-coated brigade of the fifties and early sixties.

Paul and The Jam generously allowed CND a platform at their gigs and in December, they performed four more CND benefit dates in London at the Michael Sobell Sports Centre and Hammersmith Palais. I recall Anna Joy Martin addressing the audience, and being heckled throughout, with many obscenities thrown her way, but she was a plucky gal and never wavered, delivering her message with true conviction. Paul's laddish audience's lack of sympathy with his socio-political stance frustrated him greatly, but he was perhaps expecting too much from his listeners who simply wanted to get away from the day-to-day routine of their lives and be entertained. The bulk of the audience would have been in their late teens or early twenties, fans who wanted to get drunk on The Jam's music.

I recall the first night at the Palais very well, as Bananarama and Fun Boy Three, who along with TV21 and Rudi supported The Jam. When it came to the Bananas appearing there was a problem as The Jam's road crew wasn't interested in helping them out on stage and Siobhan came out front, found me, and had a right go about this. By now, I knew the Bananas well, having had the odd drink or two in their company, and I liked them. She wanted me to have a word with Paul and get him to straighten out his road crew. Knowing that he was busy, I had a word with Dave Liddle, and everything went off ok. I always joked about Paul being Mr Serious, or Mr Grumpy, but Terry Hall of Fun Boy Three made Paul look positively luminous. On December 9, they played their last show of the year at the Golders Green Hippodrome, which Radio 1 recorded for posterity, for their *In Concert* series.

Only the four gigs at The Michael Sobell Centre and the Hammersmith Palais in December were recorded that year. The Sobell Centre's acoustics were terrible and although the boys played well, the recording of these two gigs suffers badly.

1982 would be the final year that you could see The Jam live, although at the beginning, the majority of fans had little or no idea what the end of the year would bring. They played over 80 gigs that year and I suspect that had they not broken up, they wouldn't have played as many. They took most of January and February off to finish recording *The Gift,* and played only the one gig on February 24 at London's Central Polytechnic. They played a secret gig at Guildford to celebrate Paul's mum and dad's silver wedding anniversary, which was a warm up date for the forthcoming Trans-Global Express tour. This tour was to support their number one album *The Gift*, and 27 dates were booked. This was a big tour and they played two nights in Brighton, London, Birmingham, Leicester, Manchester, Newcastle, Glasgow and Edinburgh. They were so popular in Sheffield that they had to play three straight nights. In London, there were too many fans to accommodate and the Hammersmith Odeon wasn't big enough, so they played the famous Alexandra Pavilion.

The tours that took place in '82 all blur into one, it was hectic to say the least. I'm not sure if Paul was abstaining from alcohol, but I wasn't, and neither were John, Bruce, Rick, Kenny and the road crew. Make no mistake I had one rule about drinking – I didn't drink and work, but when the work was completed I would go for it. When they played Manchester, I went to see the lads in their hotel, The Piccadilly and I'd bunked in a couple of very young girls that wanted autographs from the boys. The night porter caught me and he was a real jobsworth, and told me he would have me thrown out of the hotel if I let any more in. I had to laugh at this tosser as I was staying at the Britannia Hotel across the road. The fans were always well behaved, and most were in awe when they came face to face with Paul, Bruce, and Rick.

On the road, John Weller had a habit of walking around with an aluminium briefcase full of cash to pay per diems and touring expenses. At one of the Brighton shows, he gave me the briefcase and said: "Den, it's full of money keep an eye on it for me, don't let go of it". After a while, I was fed up lugging this heavy case around, and I got The Jam's driver to open the tour bus and stashed it in the toilet. At the end of the gig, John came up to me frantic, asking: "Have you seen my case, I can't find it anywhere?" He'd obviously forgotten that he'd given it to me for safekeeping, so I told him: "No, the last time I saw it, you had it in the dressing room." Walking off with a worried look, he wandered around the venue in search of the case and when we met later, he was apoplectic. I decided to put him out of his misery and retrieved the case, and gave it back to him. His relief was immediate, and he called me every name under the sun and a few more for winding him up!

In April they followed up the UK shows with dates in Europe and in May and June went on their last tours of America, Canada, and Japan. That summer Paul took a holiday and on his return, surprised his dad with the news that it was the end of The Jam. The band had been booked to play the Solid Bond In Your Heart tour, which was due to start on September 20, with dates in the UK, Europe, and a couple of the Channel Islands. John knew The Jam could put bums on seats at all the big venues, and was making serious money playing live, and Paul's decision left John only four months to cash in on their success. Knowing that it was the end of The Jam Paul had decided to name this tour after what should have been their last single. However, as is his wont, he changed his mind at the last minute, as he wanted to save 'Solid Bond' for his next incarnation.

I had to go and see the boys when they played the gig in Jersey and was accompanied by Peter Barrett, who was brought in to design the final Jam single, 'Beat Surrender'. I liked Pete a lot; he was a good designer, and a real hoot, and always up to, and on, something. We boarded the plane and once we got airborne, Pete retrieved the artwork from the luggage rack and much to my chagrin, finished pasting up the typeface in mid-air. The look on my face amused him no end and with a large grin, he said:"Don't worry Den, the boys will love it!"The night after the gig a crowd of us, including Bruce decided to visit a local disco and as we were queuing up, I noticed a sign stating, *No one in jeans will be allowed in the club – smart wear only.* How Pete got in was beyond me, he was dressed in a Hawaiian shirt with the sleeves torn off at the shoulders and baggy brown cord strides that hadn't seen an iron since the day he'd bought them. Bruce followed, dressed immaculate as ever, but in [pristine] Levis jeans. The bouncer stopped him and gruffly said:"You can't come in with jeans on."We argued with him and asked, why he'd let Pete in dressed in a shirt that was [clearly] torn? The bouncer replied:"He had trousers on and that's all that matters, the rules are – no jeans." I tried to explain who Bruce was, but he wasn't having any of it, and refused him entry. Bruce departed, while the rest of us partied, with Pete keeping everyone in the disco amused for the rest of the night.

Following this tour, Bruce and Rick were given the news that the next Jam tour would be the last, and if there had been the time, they could have played five sold out nights at every venue in the UK. They only played 14 gigs on The Beat Surrender tour with a staggering five nights at the Wembley Arena. During the dates at Wembley, I was in a local pub having a drink with my girlfriend. My face was familiar with many of the Jam fans and they would often corner me to talk about their favourite band. I remember one young lad coming up to me desolate about The Jam breaking up, and woefully, told me: "It's the end of my life, after this tour there's nothing for me." I remonstrated with him and gently told him, "It's a big mistake to think like this, you have the rest of your life in front of you." Many of their supporters felt this way, and it was a clear demonstration of the affect his decision had on their loyal fans.

I attended all five nights at Wembley and the support group were Big Country, led by Stuart Adamson, who I knew from his days in The Skids, a favourite band of mine. I asked how things were going, as it was early days for his new band. He told me resignedly:"We're having a tough time of it, playing just about every night, and every (toilet) gig from John O' Groats to Lands End."They had recently signed a deal with Phonogram so it wasn't all doom and gloom, and I told him: "Look, after the gig we're all going back to the hotel for a drink, come back and join in the celebrations." Stuart replied a little embarrassed:"We don't have any money, we're skint Den." I replied, "I'm inviting you, don't worry, anyway Polydor's paying for it, you're more than welcome!" Much later, Stuart would sadly take his own life, which was a shame as he had worked hard to get to the top, and was a nice lad.

The final gig should have been Guildford. It was a fantastic concert, and would have been a fitting finale for The Jam, as they were a local band. Why they played Brighton was beyond me – money? It was a dour affair, with violence breaking out sporadically, the air was thick with disappointment, and the band was not on the greatest form. After the gig, there wasn't the usual drinking, and even the road crew were down and loaded up the gear in virtual silence and there were no end of tour high jinks. It's a shame, as they finished their recording career on such a high and yet ended their live career on a low note, and Brighton was definitely a gig too far.

Jon Abnett sums the mood of most Jam fans at the end: "I recall watching the band's final live appearance on the Tube in November, thinking that Paul seemed so up for it, maybe he'll change his mind? But all too soon, it was over. I caught the train up to London for five nights to see my heroes at Wembley, and each night for an hour or so the split was forgotten. Those last shows were in my opinion the best shows I ever saw (and I'd seen them hundreds of times). The last one at Brighton was a tense affair, tainted by the 'bottle' incident. I left the Brighton Centre on December 11, 1982, walked into the cold sea air and my head was just numb, I just couldn't come to terms with the fact that I would never witness one of the greatest live bands on stage again. Later, I read that after the final gig, Bruce Foxton was found wondering around the corridor that links the Centre to The Grand Hotel, in a daze. Bruce I know how you felt! The Jam was a big, big part of my teenage years and when they split, they left a big, big hole in my life . . . and I know I'm not alone when I say that".

One thing that always impressed me with The Jam was the amount of time the boys would give to their loyal following. They let their fans into the studio to watch them record and allowed them in at sound checks, no matter how many were outside waiting. After every gig, they would go out to the auditorium and talk to the many waiting fans and wouldn't leave the gig until they'd done their best to give autographs to everyone who waited.

Jon Abnett, one of the many fans who bunked in, had this to say about the band's generosity to their fans. "Sound checks were mini gigs in themselves, and if you hung around long enough 'Big' Kenny Wheeler or John Weller would let you in. Paul always had loads of fans surrounding him, and whereas Bruce and Rick always seemed to enjoy the adulation, Paul always looked uneasy, something that even to this day he has never quite come to terms with."

Many bigger artists and bands I worked with pissed off once the gig had finished. It was sod the fans – they wanted to get some drinking in.

Getting into Jam gigs was never a problem for me as I was part of the Jam machine, and my face well known to security men from Aberdeen to Shepton Mallet. One time I arrived backstage at the Hammersmith Odeon, and the security man on the door told me several fans had tried to get in giving my name. I always felt sorry for the fans that waited outside without tickets, and although it was frowned upon, I would often bunk them in after the show had started. I recall one gig at The Rainbow, when it was pouring down with rain and a security guy approached me, and said there were about 20 kids outside and they were soaked to the skin, and asked if he could let them in. I said no problem, and if anyone moans about it, blame me.

Often, I would have to man the backstage door to insure the right people on the guest lists gained entry. Jam fans were a cunning bunch, and would give you any story to get backstage. They would swear blind they were a friend of Paul, Rick, or Bruce, and do practically anything to get in to see the show. I recall one fan giving me my name, and when I told him he couldn't possibly be Dennis Munday, he swore an oath that was his name. Although I did fuck up at one of the Rainbow concerts, when a man and a woman came to the back stage door and attempted to walk in. I asked for their names and to my embarrassment, it turned out to be Ray Davies and his girlfriend who I hadn't recognised!

The Jam had a good road crew. At first, they were sceptical of me, and thought I was just another ligger from the record company. However, once they found out I wasn't that much different to them we got on famously, and I enjoyed many a beer with them. It would be difficult to write about the Jam road crew without mentioning their guitar roadie, Dave Liddle, and I recall a story when I had to travel on the crew bus, something I wouldn't recommend. The floor of the bus was littered with all sorts of debris, beer cans, cigarette packets, and stubs. You were literally ankle deep in garbage. The poor old driver's first job on arriving at the hotel would be to sweep out the bus. On the way to the venue Dave, who was the double of Jerry Garcia, was in full flow, and maintained he couldn't sleep on coaches no matter how tired he was. Within fifteen minutes, he'd nodded off and was snoring with his mouth wide open. Ray Salter noticed this and decided to play a prank on him, got his dick out, and placed it in his mouth while one of the other lads took a photo. Nothing was said when he woke up, but later on at a party, the road crew turned up wearing T-shirts with the photo plastered on the front and Dave to his credit took the jape well.

Dave died a few years ago, which was a real shame, as he was only in his mid-fifties, and what he didn't know about guitars wasn't worth knowing.

Ray Salter, who I have only just found out has also passed away, was a real hoot, and had a reputation for entertaining anything female, whether it moved or not. He married a Swedish stripper and at a party, being the good bloke he was, talked his missus into doing a turn for the lads. When Ray quit the road, he took up a new career as a postman in Basingstoke. An ideal occupation for a man of his calibre, and I imagine it was not only, lock up your wives and daughters, I bet a few grandma's were put to the sword!

The Jam's road crew worked hard at every performance, and were extremely helpful when I was recording their gigs. Recording any live performances is an arduous task and a road crew can make the difference between it being easy or problematical. The Jam crew always made it an easy ride for me and everything always went smoothly. They were a great bunch of lads and I made sure that Polydor kept them well supplied with booze.

Seven concerts were recorded during the last year of The Jam, Bingley Hall Birmingham, both nights at the Playhouse Edinburgh and the Apollo Glasgow, as well as two nights at the Wembley Arena.

I had a great time on the road with The Jam, met a lot of nice fans, and did some heavy drinking. Many times, I have been asked to sum up The Jam live, but I'll leave the last word on this to Tony Rounce. Tony DJ'd and announced the band on some of the last live dates. He came on stage and simply stated – "Put your hands together for the greatest thing on six legs – THE JAM" – Nuff said!

Part 2

THE STYLE COUNCIL

CHAPTER 10

Loafers, Blazers, Classic Tunes And A Few Dodgy Haircuts

It was a bold move to break up The Jam, and a risky one, as there was no guarantee that Paul could match their success. Going solo meant starting again and even though Paul was a face, he would have to prove himself again. The history of music is littered with artists who have broken away from successful bands and failed. By his own admission, he wasn't quite ready to go out as Paul Weller, and given his age – 24 – this was understandable. The Beatles were the only other band to end their career while still at the top, but they were on their twelfth album and Lennon and McCartney were 30 and 28 respectively the year *Let It Be* was released. Steve Marriott was around the same age as Paul when The Small Faces ended and he formed Humble Pie with the face of '65, Pete Frampton.

Whether The Jam would have become any bigger or sold records outside the UK is a moot point; they'd reached a plateau but weren't in the same bracket as bands who were selling albums by the millions world-wide. There's no doubt the easy option – and the best financially – was to continue with The Jam and record solo material as well. By ending The Jam, Paul chose the hardest option. There was never a doubt in my mind that he couldn't carry this move off, as the quality of all the records The Jam released showed Paul to be a songwriter of immense depth, which gave him a solid enough foundation to launch the next phase of his career. It's hard to explain how I felt at the time without sounding bigheaded, but from the end of 1978, I'd realised and believed that Paul had a special talent. I was determined to do everything I could to help make his next venture as successful, and to some extent the rest of the bands I handled suffered as I spent double the time with the Council as I did with The Jam.

Mindful of the outrageous recording cost of *Sound Affects*, Polydor changed the terms of his deal so that the large advance included recording costs, and should this ever happen again, any extra costs would be down to Paul and John. Once they signed the deal, it was the usual three singles and one album every year, which meant the pressure, would still be on Paul to come up with the songs. There's no doubt that the execs at Polydor were a little nervous about the move: major record companies are never happy with artists who change their image and musical style, and Polydor was no different. They would have preferred Paul to stick to a direct format that they could deal with, and no doubt saw this change as a risk. However, I've always believed that if you have real talent then you can go against the grain and succeed. Artists that come to mind who have adopted this policy are Bob Dylan, Tom Jones, Van Morrison, and Neil Young. All four have had long and very diverse musical careers, and have never been frightened to experiment, to try new directions, and explore different musical styles. Bob Dylan's country album *Nashville Skyline* was a perfect example. Neil Young has tried everything from punk to country, and all four are still going strong.

In the beginning, there was talk about calling the band The Torch Society, as it took the Mickey out of the New Romantics, but I was mortified as the name was pretentious to say the least. Fortunately, one of his mates came up with the name The Style Council, which was nowhere near as affected, and they named their fan club The Torch Society. Mick Talbot was recruited well before The Jam split was announced, although he was not a part of the Polydor deal and never received royalties from the record sales. Before joining the Council, he was on the dole and having a hard time, his previous band The Bureau having ended in failure, leaving Mick with his P45 and a large tax bill. When Paul phoned, it couldn't have come at a better time. I'd met him several times before when he played with The Jam, and appeared on The Chord's debut album and liked him a lot. During the early days of Wham!, it was said that Andrew Ridgeley was a crutch for George Michael, but this could not be said of Mick's role in the Council. At first, Mick found it nerve wracking, but he adapted quickly. His easygoing attitude had an affect on Paul, and I can recall him throwing only the occasional wobbler during the time I worked with him. While his contribution may not have had the same weight as Paul's, it was nonetheless crucial, certainly during the first two years, and he absorbed a lot of the flack that came the Council's way at the end, and was harshly criticised. Mick's loyalty has to be applauded, as many musicians would have jumped ship well before the Council's fourth album; even Steve White didn't hang around, when he saw what was coming.

It wasn't just that he was simpatico with Paul's musical tastes, and was able to deal with Paul's mood changes: he brought more to the table than he's generally credited with. It wasn't just music he had in common with Paul, his tastes in clothes were similar, but Mick was always subtly different, and he stamped his mark on the clothes he wore, like the Embassy coupon in the band of his *titfer.* Mick never set himself up to be a style guru, leaving this to Paul. Some Jam fans questioned his Mod credentials but this just wasn't true – he simply never wore the Mod tag on his sleeve. Some embittered Jam fans even accused him of being responsible for the break up of the band, which was absolute crap, as it was Paul who jettisoned Bruce and Rick, and Mick's part was no more than a cameo. After The Jam, the Council was always going to be Paul's band, and he decided the direction they were going in, whether it was music, clothes, politics, or videos. From the outset of the Council, Paul took charge of his destiny, and hasn't let go of the reins to this day.

In 1982, PolyGram decided it was time to sell off Phonogram's recording studio in Stanhope Place, where The Walker Brothers, Dusty Springfield, Rod Stewart, Status Quo, Thin Lizzy and many other famous artists had recorded. Running your own studio is an expensive business, specifically the need to replace (quickly) outdated equipment, but it would enable Paul to record whenever he wanted to without having to worry about watching the clock and retaining an office in the same building. When the deal to sell the Wellers the studio was going through, Mike Higgins, a senior accountant at Polydor popped in my office and asked a strange question: "Does John take drugs?" Mike was a down to earth geezer, who came from New Cross, and one of the few colleagues I enjoyed having a beer with. A little bewildered I replied no, he likes a drink, but he definitely doesn't touch drugs. Mike then explained that at a meeting to discuss the sale of the studio John had jumped the gun, and told the execs that he wouldn't pay PolyGram any more than the sum he was offering which was actually more than the studio was worth. PolyGram agreed and closed the deal instantly, and behind his back had a good laugh at his business acumen. Paul was one of the few talented artists on Polydor, and this move was typical of a large record company. However, it struck me as a stupid idea to rip the Wellers off.

Given that Paul was unhappy with the pressure exerted on him during The Jam's short but productive career, I for one fully expected him to take some time off before beginning recording with the Council. This was not to be and the dynamic duo went straight into Phonogram's studio, now re-named, Solid Bond. In January 1983, they made their first recordings and I wondered at the time whether Paul was conscious of leaving a gap between the end of The Jam and the first release of the Council. I know the company wanted a quick single to release and I attended a meeting with the MD and was ordered to give the Council top priority. They even offered me a bonus for every top ten hit single and album they released. A&R men at Polydor received this kind of bonus only on their new signings, as an incentive to bring in successful new acts. The irony of this offer wasn't lost on me, I recalled working my bollocks off on *Sound Affects*, and to this day, I don't know how much bonus was in the brown envelope that I chucked away.

Having unshackled himself from The Jam, Paul planned to have a floating line up that would embrace all the styles of music he was getting into including soul, funk, rap and jazz, which gave me a laugh. When I started working with The Jam, I mentioned to Paul that I'd worked with some great jazz artists. He said: "Den, jazz is fuckin' shit – all those long and boring solos, you can say everything in three minutes." To some extent, his analogy is right: Charlie Parker, one of the greatest innovators of modern jazz, rarely recorded tunes longer than three or four minutes. In this short space of time, he said more than many of his contemporaries who wailed on for twenty minutes or longer. However, I couldn't help chuckling at Paul's sudden conversion to jazz.

In early January 1983, Paul and Mick went into Solid Bond Studios to make their debut recordings, and Paul's idea of a loose assembly of guest musicians was given its first try out. The duo were accompanied by Orange Juice's drummer, Zeke Manyika and Jo Dworniak, who played bass with I-Level, and they were listed as Honorary Councillors, as all guest musicians were subsequently identified throughout the Council's career. The last recording sessions with The Jam were tense and torrid and it was noticeable that the first Council sessions were more relaxed. Paul could now choose the musicians he wanted to play with and tell them exactly what he wanted for his new songs. I took advantage of my new brief, and attended many of the sessions, and the songs they recorded were

'Headstart For Happiness', 'Solid Bond In Your Heart', and 'Party Chambers', 'Speak Like A Child' and 'Money-Go-Round'. The first three had been written prior to recording, but 'Money-Go-Round' was created in the studio when the band began an impromptu jam session. Peter Wilson, who was busy setting up for the next tune, suddenly sat up, and said: "This sounds great, I'd better record it," and switched on the tape machine, and recorded the remainder of the jam. As this tune was recorded half way through there was no beginning, and Annie Whitehead was brought in on trombone to add the front section.

'Speak' I missed out on, and I first heard it when I phoned the studio to see how things were going and was told that Paul was listening to a new track and the handset was laid down, but I could clearly hear the song. Even over the phone, it sounded great and when Paul finally picked up the phone, I'd forgotten what I wanted to discuss with him and asked: "What the fuck is that you were listening to?" He replied: "It's a new song; we've just laid it down." The version of 'Speak' I'd heard was without horns and when Paul augmented the tune with Martin Drover on trumpets, it gave the song an edge that the original lacked. Paul brought in Tracie Young, a 17-year-old who'd signed to Paul's Respond label, to sing backing vocals, and that completed the Council's debut single. I recall Tracie finished early in the evening, and was left to her own devices to get back home to Essex. Although a very independent, confident, and bubbly girl, I wasn't happy about her having to make her way across London, and drove her to the station.

With all the tracks recorded, it was a straight choice for the debut between 'Solid Bond' and 'Speak Like A Child'. For quite a while, Paul vacillated over which to pick, but as far as I was concerned 'Speak' had hit record written all over it, whereas 'Solid Bond' sounded one-dimensional, and carried to much baggage from the past. It reached a point where a decision had to be taken as a single had been scheduled for early March and Polydor was breathing down my neck with my bosses desperate to know what the first Council single was going to be. Everyone assembled in the control room of the studio and listened to rough mixes of both tunes, and there was much discussion about which one to go with. Peter Wilson mentioned the tracks would sound much better once they were mixed. John, thinking of the extra cost, asked why we couldn't release the rough mixes, so Peter explained to John that Paul's vocal would need re-verb (echo), and the multi-track needed to be e-qd and balanced. Painstakingly the decision was finally made with 'Speak Like A Child' becoming the A-side, but only as a 7 inch single, with a vocal version of 'Party Chambers' as the B-side. By this time every single released had to have a 12 inch single, which would include different mixes and additional bonus tracks. The idea of releasing two singles was a marketing ploy to get the fan base of successful bands to go out and buy both versions, doubling their income and the chances of getting a higher chart position. Polydor had noted the success of this ploy with 'Town Called Malice' and 'Beat Surrender', which meant there was going to be a problem, as I knew the company would demand the customary 12 inch version. When I informed my bosses, they weren't happy and I had to come up with a plausible explanation as to why there was only going to be a 7 inch version. I lied through my teeth, and told them: "'Speak' was just a three-minute pop song and it didn't lend itself to an extended version. And Paul and Mick haven't recorded enough tunes for any bonus tracks." Grudgingly, they accepted my explanation, but I have my doubts that they thought the single would do as well in the charts without a 12 inch version.

The first photo session in Boulogne, taken by Peter Anderson, caught the Council's new image superbly. Gone was the dour seriousness of post-punk Jam and in came the continental look, with white trench coats. Designer Simon Halfon was part of the new team, bought in to create picture bags, album sleeves and publicity material. Simon, along with Paul and Mick, decided there would be no photo on the front, just a plain black bag with The Style Council emblazoned across the sleeve, and the Keep On Burning torch logo. There would be no mention of the song title, although the rear of the sleeve featured a black and white photo of Paul and Mick and the credits. Polydor weren't happy, as this broke all the rules of marketing, particularly for a new band, which is how the Council were perceived. Although it was a critical time in Paul's and the Council's career, I couldn't see a problem and wasn't sure why they were so worried. Paul was a known quantity, The Jam had finished their career with a number one single and album, and he was a well-respected songwriter. One thing I knew, no matter what track the Council released as their debut single, it was going to do the business, regardless of what the company thought, and I didn't share their qualms.

There was freshness about 'Speak', a joie de vivre that The Jam captured only with 'Boy About Town', with the trademark sound of Mick's Hammond organ to the fore. It came out on March 11, stormed the charts, hitting the number four spot, and selling in excess of 250,000 copies; thus proving that no matter how many versions of a single are released, or how good the photos and packaging are, having a great tune is more than enough. For their debut performance on *TOTPs,* they had to re-record the backing track, as the MU didn't allow bands to mime to the original backing tape. To get round this you just copied the original and recorded a new vocal, and although a representative from the BBC turned up, they generally turned a blind eye, as they knew you couldn't record a new backing in such a short space of time. Tracie and Paul recorded new vocals, with Paul's superior to the one he had originally recorded for the single, and the brass was re-recorded as well. A quick mix was done and the tape handed over to the man from the Beeb for that night's mimed performance. Having just signed Tracie to Respond, when they performed the single on *TOTPs*, she was pushed up front and it looked like Tracie and The Style Council, not that it mattered as by now everyone knew who The Style Council were.

When it came to the promo video for 'Speak', I was a little worried as in the past there were always problems. I tried to get Russell Mulcahy who directed 'Start!', but by now, he was in the premier league and tied up finishing a Bowie video. In addition, the budget for 'Speak' was a miserly £15k, which was small change to make a pop video. Most major companies were spending anything from £25,000 upwards on their top artists. Tim Pope had been recommended to me as an alternative director – his CV included Soft Cell amongst others – and it couldn't have been easy working with Marc Almond. Impressed with this, I arranged a meeting with Tim, and his producer Gordon Lewis to discuss the possibilities. Tim arrived late and when he entered, I was taken aback by his clothes as he looked liked a refugee from a Charles Dickens story. I quickly changed my mind, as during the interview, he came across as a completely different character and had a very professional attitude, and I had no hesitation recommending him to Paul and Mick. Tim went on to become a legend as far as pop videos go and worked with, The Cure, Talk Talk, David Bowie, Neil Young, and Fatboy Slim.

Unfortunately, for all concerned Tim decided to film the video for 'Speak' on the Malvern Hills in the middle of winter, and it was bloody freezing throughout the shoot. During the day, it wasn't that bad and the temperature did at least get up to zero. However, one scene had to be shot at sunrise, and when we arrived at 5am it was pitch black. We climbed to the top and sat around in the freezing cold waiting for the sun to rise and it must have been around minus five. The M&S thermal underwear we'd been given to combat the cold was loosing the battle and if it got any colder, I was seriously worried it would jeopardise my future chances of having children. When the sun finally rose, the temperature went up a little, the filming took place, and after a gruelling day, we returned to the hotel for some anti-freeze. Tim did a great job on the video, the scenes were shot quickly, and he directed the filming with consummate skill.

Around the time of the Council's debut record Tracie also released her debut single on Respond, 'The House That Jack Built', which gave her a top ten record. There was no doubting her talent, but she was unable to match this chart success again, which had more to do with being linked to Paul than lacking the talent to go further. Had she been with another record company and a producer who could develop her potential, it's quite possible she could have gone all the way. Tracie's doing all right now and is the breakfast DJ on a local radio station.

Working closely with The Jam had caused many problems for me with my bosses at Polydor and if I thought it was going to change, I was much mistaken. I was about to get embroiled in another conflict. A photographer accompanied the film crew to take publicity shots, but owing to the extreme cold weather, his results were a disaster. Paul looked at the photos and made it clear he didn't want them used, and later they mysteriously disappeared. Cross-examined about this, Paul denied all knowledge of their whereabouts. Next door to Polydor, they were renovating a building. There was a large skip parked outside and I had my suspicions that most of them ended up in the bin. When Polydor received the photographer's invoice for £500, the company refused to pay, which left him no choice but to take Polydor to court. I spoke to one of our [so-called] legal experts, explained it was the weather, and not the fault of the photographer that the pictures were of no use commercially. Polydor were having none of this and by now the MD had got involved and insisted there was no way the company was going pay the photographer. I couldn't understand this decision. Polydor was a multi-national record company, and five hundred quid was nothing to them, probably a week's expenses for a director. The matter deteriorated further, and I ended up being interviewed by a silk. By now, the whole affair had pissed me off. The last thing I needed was to talk to a bloody barrister about such a trivial matter. As far as I was concerned, we should stop fucking about and pay up. Halfway through the interrogation I lost it completely, and went into one, stating: "The photographer had done his job and couldn't be expected to control the weather. What are we doing arguing about £500?" The matter was settled out of court and as well as his fee, we had to pay his and our legal expenses. I have no idea what all this cost the company but it must have been a lot more than £500. Strangely enough, when I was working on the Council's box set a number of these photos miraculously reappeared.

* * *

Shortly after 'Speak', Paul asked if I could find a drummer to augment the duo. He knew exactly what he wanted: talented, good-looking, and able to play all styles of music, including jazz. Whether I am in the studio or at a gig, I have always found drum sound checks boring, and didn't really fancy listening to twenty or thirty drummers. As it happened, another band signed to Polydor had been auditioning for a new drummer and I had a chat with their manager and asked whether he'd come across any young drummers who could play a bit of jazz, and luckily for me he recalled two. I phoned the first, but he didn't sound right, and called up the second, Steve White, who coincidentally lived in Eltham where I had grown up, and later found out we had both attended the same school, Crown Woods comprehensive. When he told me how old he was, I was little concerned, but the more we talked on the phone, the more he convinced me he had the talent and the diversification to give Paul and Mick what they wanted. I'd been around the music business long enough to recognise bullshit when I heard it, and working with some of the jazz greats helped. Steve's influences were all the great jazz drummers, particularly Art Blakey, and he told me he'd taken lessons with Bill Bruford, who played with Yes. Knowing Steve wouldn't have lasted five minutes with Bill if he didn't have real talent, I arranged an audition for him at Nomis Studios behind Olympia, and told him not to be late. About twenty minutes after I'd called him, his mum Kath phoned and asked whether the audition was a serious offer. I replied: "Yes I can't guarantee him getting the gig, but if he's as good as he says he is, they will give him a chance." She replied: "Good, I thought you might be taking the Mickey out of my son!"

The evening before Steve was due to audition, I received a call cancelling the try-out, and wasn't happy at having to pass on this news as I knew Steve would be incredibly disappointed. John had Steve's number, and he could have told him personally, or got Kenny Wheeler to cancel the audition. I gave it some thought, but couldn't bring myself to make the call and decided to let Steve go and let them give him the news personally. The audition took place, Steve was hired, and apart from one brief period, he has been Paul's anchorman since May 1983. Steve's first gig was a Radio 1 session for the Kid Jensen show a couple of weeks before his 18th birthday. His father dropped him off outside the BBC's Maida Vale studios, and as no one had arranged for a car to take Steve and his drums back home to Eltham, we ended up piling his kit into my Ford Capri (2.8i, I might add), which wasn't exactly built for carting around drums, and I dropped him off.

A lot of skin must be given to Paul and Mick for taking on Steve. Even though he was talented and had enormous ability, he was young, unproven and many other big bands would have gone for someone with more professional experience. After all, when they eventually played concerts, it was going to be big venues rather than pubs and clubs, and he would be thrown in at the deep end. I wasn't worried about Steve hacking it, even though he was starting at the top, as he had bags of confidence, and was very sure of his abilities, even at that young age. Steve eventually introduced me to all his family and I met his brother Allan, a cheeky little sod who followed in Steve's drumsticks, and became drummer and one of the longest surviving members of Oasis.

With the success of the first single, 'Speak Like A Child', whatever doubts there were about the Council were blown away, although there were still mutterings about The Jam, which would never be silenced. I half expected the second single to be 'Solid Bond', but I was in for a shock. Paul came into the office to discuss this and was very earnest, saying he wanted 'Money-Go-Round'. The lyrics to this tune were contentious to say the least, with Paul having a blast at one of the most popular Prime Ministers since Churchill. Nonetheless, Paul was desperate for it to be the next single and stated intently: "I want 'Money' out as the next single. I want to make a political statement. I don't care whether it's played on the radio, or gets in the charts. I want it as our next single!" I knew there would be problems with this record, radio would definitely give it a miss, and there was no real 7 inch version and the 12 inch faded half way through and was released as parts 1 & 2. All my bosses were rank and file Tories, and after such a great debut record, I wasn't looking forward to explaining the follow up to them.

As well as Annie Whitehead, the horn section for 'Money-Go-Round' was augmented with Guy Barker on trumpet, Spegos played percussion, and D.C. Lee made her first appearance on vocals. The 12 inch version featured the full-blown version with 'Headstart For Happiness' and 'Mick's Up' on the B-side. I liked 'Headstart' from the first time I heard this great tune and it's a song that links the Council to his solo career, as he often knocks it out during his live set. There's a nice simplicity about this tune, with just Mick's organ and a little percussion supporting Paul's acoustic guitar. Paul's always had a habit of putting in too many words ('Tube Station') for the meter and at times, he slows the tune down to get all the words in; nonetheless lyrically – this is a tune and a half. Paul hired Bert Bevans, who was virtually unknown, to do the 12 inch re-mixes, and when I went to the studios it was obvious to me that he wasn't experienced at re-mixing. With the Council

Paul took many chances, and often used inexperienced musicians rather than go for known names. Bert came up an assortment of club mixes for promo purposes, and Camelle Hinds made his first appearance with the Council playing bass on these mixes.

Even though the song was finished, I still wasn't sure how the company would view this single and decided to wait until the next marketing meeting, so they could hear it and brief the execs. I made it clear that it wouldn't be as successful as their debut single, and with its highly inflammable political content, radio stations might be reluctant to play it. I expected trouble, perhaps even a call for the single to be pulled from the schedule, but to my astonishment several execs raved about it. The single came out on May 20 and although on Radio 1 it received less than half the airplay that 'Speak' received, it reached a respectable number 11 in the charts. Like The Jam, the Council fans were a dedicated bunch and this chart position had more to do with Paul's following which was building steadily.

Looking at the lyrics now, Paul didn't hold back and 'Money' was not only a virulent attack on the Tories, but many of the other institutions that ran Britain including the Americans. It would be easy to write this song off as a piece of Britfunk with political overtones, but it's much more than that and it was a very courageous decision to go with 'Money-Go-Round' as the second single of his new career. If any other artists had released such a politically overt single at the beginning of their career, it's unlikely they would have lasted. Many other bands flew their flags for causes overseas, which had little fall out in the UK and on the sales of their records. The eighties was not the decade of agitprop and making such an overt political statement at the start of his career did make Paul unpopular with the Tory party and the right wing. It signalled his and the Council's future political direction and some of his royalties were donated to the Youth Campaign for Nuclear Disarmament.

The video for 'Money' was shot on a warm day in late spring in a large warehouse in Battersea, and after the filming we all decided to meet up at the WAG club in Wardour Street. Mick, Dee, and I arrived late and the bouncer on the door refused us entry, stating: "You can't come in here. You look too ordinary," and we were sent on our way. All we had to do was drop Paul's name, let him know that Mick was half of the Council, and Dee was singing with Wham! and he would have let us in. Mick was having none of this and said: "Fuck this Den lets go to a pub where normal people go."

* * *

With the Council, Paul wanted to lose that little England tag that followed The Jam and give the Council a European feel, so that his music was accepted outside the UK. The very first photo session in Boulogne, not one of the most exotic parts of France, firmly established the Council's image and moved away from The Jam's overt Mod look. For their third single, Paul decided he wanted to shoot the second photo session in Paris and it highlighted the difference between working with the Council and The Jam. On the last night of the last shoot, Peter Anderson and I went to an expensive bistro and enjoyed the meal so much that we were late for the session, which was taking place at midnight at the Arc de Triomphe. When we finally arrived, Kenny went into one, cursing us for keeping everybody waiting and had a real go. Paul turned to him and said: "For fuck's sake, Kenny give it a rest. This isn't The Jam – it doesn't matter." Paul was now more relaxed, and wasn't accepting unnecessary pressure on him, even from his own men. I have to say, Peter Anderson's photos for 'Long Hot Summer', are some of the best that he, or for that matter any photographer shot, and for me, the definitive image of the Council.

The next single turned out to be an EP and recorded at Studio Grand Aimée in Paris, and Solid Bond, and once the recordings were finished, I popped into the studio to hear them. Paul, Mick, and Peter Wilson had been in the studio all day listening to the finished mixes of 'Long Hot Summer'. Kenny warned me not go in the control room as Paul and Pete had been arguing about which take to go with. I ignored his sage advice, and entered the control room where the atmosphere was hostile. They'd been listening to eight or nine different versions and were bickering like a couple of kids. Paul would say: "I prefer the piano on mix 5," to which, Peter would retort: "The guitar on mix 3 is better." All it needed was for one of them to say: 'my Dad's bigger than your Dad', that's how stupid the argument was. Their ears must have been numb from listening to the different mixes, and it had got to them. I listened to a couple of mixes, but didn't fancy commenting, or staying in the studio with them in this mood, and said: "It's Friday, you don't have to make a decision now. It's coming up to the weekend, go home, come back next week when your ears are going to be fresh and you'll hear the mixes in a different light." They acquiesced, and I left the pair chuntering away like a couple of errant school kids. A few days later Peter came in and played me the finished mix and it sounded great.

The video was shot by Tim Pope and filmed on the River Cam in Cambridge, and as luck would have it, it was a hot summer's day. The filming was going well so Kenny and I decided to hire a punt, and floated up and down the river, spending an enjoyable couple of hours relaxing. When we returned they were filming the so-called 'gay' scene, where Paul and Mick are locked in a mock embrace and fondling each other. Paul had decided to do something *different* in each video (fairies in 'Speak') to lighten him or them up, and show everyone that he had a sense of humour. When this video was aired, I spent a lot of time fending off enquiries about Mick and Paul's sexuality, and the joke was taken too seriously. When the MD viewed the footage, he was apoplectic and really chewed my ear about this scene, even asking me if Paul and Mick were bent.

The EP entitled *'à Paris'* came out on August 5. The A-side contained 'Long Hot Summer' and the instrumental version of 'Party Chambers', whilst the B-side featured 'The Paris Match' and another of Mick's instrumentals, 'Le Depart'. 'Long Hot Summer' was one of the most accomplished pop songs that Paul had written, with the lyrics perhaps reflecting a cameo from his own life, something he was going through at the time? Credit has to be given to Mick for his keyboards, which along with the smooth production and Paul's wistful lyrics turned this tune into a classic summer song. Wherever you are in the world, when the sun is out, you will hear this tune radiating over the airwaves. As far as the other tracks go, 'The Paris Match' is the best version of this song, although I am not sure why 'Party Chambers' was included, as it doesn't add anything to the version on 'Speak Like A Child'. The single went to number three in the charts, and although one of the Council's most commercial, it was kept off the number one slot, by KC & The Sunshine Band's 'Give It Up' and UB 40's 'Red Red Wine'. Simon Halfon's sleeve design was exceptional and I recall there were two different fronts designed for the 12 inch version, but the one we went with was definitely the best.

To give the Council a lighter image and distance himself from The Jam's seriousness, there were sleeve notes written by the eponymous scribe, The Cappuccino Kid. The notes written in a very light-hearted manner, contained many in-jokes and witticisms and were a little pretentious, and if you weren't in on it, you wouldn't get the joke. For the *'à Paris'* EP, the kid wrote one of the few witty pieces about Mick's solo song, 'Le Depart', stating that the track would be used in a new French film called *The Golden Lama,* starring Alain Delon. It wasn't just the fans that were duped by this jape.

On September 2, they released a mini LP entitled *Introducing The Style Council*, and the Dutch copy was heavily imported into the UK. It would have sold enough to make the top twenty, but as it was an import, it wouldn't have been recognised by the album charts. The tracks were all the singles and a couple of club mixes of 'Money-Go-Round and 'Long Hot Summer', with two extra tracks on the cassette version.

Their fourth and final single for 1983 was 'A Solid Bond In Your Heart', which was released on November 11. As with 'Speak', there was no 12 inch single, but it was released in a limited edition (100,000) gatefold sleeve. I was never sure of the Council's version, as it was a hangover from The Jam days and although it has a nice Northern Soul feel, it wasn't a great single. When Paul nicked the bridge from 'Solid Bond' and inserted it into 'Beat Surrender', it substantially weakened the tune, and the song revs up, and takes off, but doesn't really go anywhere. Chris Hunter's soaring tenor adds to the feel but because of the missing bridge, the song is a bit one-paced. The video for this single was a pseudo Quadrophenia piece filmed at Woking Football Club. As there was a fuss made over the gay scene in 'LHS', to wind up the MD, Paul and Mick decided to include some hard core footage. I recall when I played AJ the video, he had a good chuckle, and didn't fall for the trick. Like 'Money-Go-Round', it reached number 11 in the charts, and its appeal never going beyond the Council fan club. The B-side was another great Weller track, 'It Just Came To Pieces in My Hand' that speaks of someone rising to the top and having it all. Live, the Council would do a doo-wop version of this tune.

They followed this single with a short tour of Europe and Paul's second appearance on Tyne Tees TV pop program, *The Tube*. I accompanied Nigel 'Spanner' Sweeney, who was part of the Council's promotion team, to the studio and when we entered, a bleached blonde girl yelled at 'Spanner', heaping abuse on him that you would normally hear on a building site. I innocently asked: "Who's that?" Spanner replied: "That's Paula Yates, take no notice of her, she's always like that"! I recall that during rehearsals Paul forgot the lyrics to 'Headstart' and smashed the white Fender Jazz guitar he was playing. They also performed 'Hanging On To A Memory' and aptly, 'My Ever Changing Moods'.

Unlike The Jam, the Council had no rivals as no other (name) band had such a flexible line up or played such diverse music. During the late eighties and early nineties bands like Massive Attack and Soul II Soul (featuring Caron Wheeler who sang with The Jam) would take this idea to its limit. If you look back to the sixties, there were the phenomenally successful soul packages, but they featured a backing band – like Booker T & The MG's – with known artists taking turns in the spotlight. In 1983, the Council was unconventional, risky and went against all the rules, and not enough credit has been given to Paul for this innovation.

They finished the year by going into Solid Bond to commence recording their debut album and postponed all tours until the New Year, with the exception of one show at the Apollo in Victoria and a Radio 1 session on New Year's Eve. This saw out the first year, the change of direction had worked for Paul, and everybody could look back with satisfaction on their achievements. In twelve months, he'd left The Jam behind, although they would never be totally out of his rear view mirror. Polydor could relax since one of their stars had failed to implode, and everyone was looking forward to the new album, and a bright and breezy 1984.

CHAPTER 11

The Debut Album And That Miners' Record

Paul had hoisted his political flag in The Jam but with the release of 'Money-Go-Round', he'd upped the ante. Over the next few years, he would go from being *spokesman* for a generation to becoming something of a *leader* of a generation and therefore a potential target. Other bands and artists had taken a political stance before him, but generally they paid lip service to the party they supported, appearing on election platforms and at photo opportunities. During 1983, Paul got the balancing act right between songs with political convictions and pure pop. With much of the country swinging to the right, left-wing politics were unfashionable; out dated, and for an artist of Paul's stature to offer unequivocal support for such an unfashionable cause was a brave move. Hindsight would suggest that his political stance was more than brave, given that the very party he supported would much later swing alarmingly to the right to make them more electable to the public.

The Council released their fifth single on February 10, 1984, the uplifting 'My Ever Changing Moods' and it turned out to be one of their finest songs. Mick came up with the idea of dropping all the instruments out bar the percussion and organ for the third verse, and for me this simple trick made the song. 'Moods' epitomises what the Council were about, with its light and airy backing track, underpinning lyrics that were a little too subtle for most people. It bounces along and is one the most refreshing songs the Council recorded, and one of the best pop records Paul has written. The B-side for the 7 inch was another instrumental, entitled 'Mick's Company', while the 12 inch version came with an extended version of 'Moods', plus an extra track, 'Spring, Summer, Autumn', which contained lyrics about not clinging to the past and having the courage to move on. Like The Jam, the Council's singles contained many gems on the B-sides, and although they were probably lost on the public at large, the fans never missed them. Once again, Mr Weller's simple but poetic lyrics shine through.

When it came to the video, I had mixed feelings about the idea. Gordon Lewis explained the storyboard and it sounded well over the top. Paul and Mick were going to be portrayed as two freewheeling spirits riding bikes around sunny open countryside, clad in spandex cycling gear. When I saw them in this lurid gear, I was beginning to think my idea of having donkey jackets stencilled with the Style Council across the back wasn't as bad as everyone said. Unfortunately, during the two days of shooting, the weather was overcast and grey, and the video turned out to be more Tour de Woking than Tour de France! The single went to number five in the charts and gave the Council their third top five single – not bad since they hadn't yet released their debut album.

As the recordings progressed for the Council debut album, *Café Bleu*, I realised there were going to be big problems when the company finally heard the tracks. They were expecting an album full of pop tunes like 'Speak', 'Long Hot Summer' and 'Moods', but Paul had made his mind up that it was going to be poles apart from anything that The Jam had released, and different it certainly was. Paul didn't even appear on *The Paris Match,* which featured Ben Watt and Tracey Thorn of Everything But The Girl, and there were five instrumentals and a rap song, I decided it would be better if the company were kept in the dark. With the success of five very different singles, there were no thoughts in my mind that the album wouldn't do well, but I wasn't looking forward to the day when the execs heard the album. I decided they could wait, until I held a playback of the finished album, and it would be a fait accompli for Polydor.

Paul and Mick re-recorded 'My Ever Changing Moods' as a duet, which was very different to the single version, ensuring the political message was clear. During the Council years, Paul would often record two versions of the same tune, sometimes with different or additional lyrics, or simply just a change of pace. In just over a year Paul's song writing skills had expanded greatly, and he was showing just what an exceptionally gifted and complete tunesmith he was becoming. With The Style Council, he had the platform to express himself, lyrically and musically and on whatever subject matter he wanted, be it politics, a love song, or just a great pop record.

However, the best song on the album is undoubtedly 'The Whole Point of No Return' and when Paul recorded this song the album was ostensibly finished, and he came into the office early one morning to make a passionate plea for this song to be included. The song, an acerbic comment on the middle and upper (ruling) classes is comparable to anything he wrote for The Jam, and showed he still had teeth. I explained that the sleeve had been finalised, so there was no way the title would appear on the credits, but it was nevertheless added at the last moment. Whatever is said about his ever-changing moods, and his ego, when I worked with him, he never made ridiculous demands, and would always *ask* if a change could be made. Even though the Council had yet to release their debut album, their success in the singles chart entitled Paul make serious demands on Polydor, and to his credit, he never abused his power to demand changes.

When they performed 'My Ever Changing Moods' for *TOTPs*, Joboxers were appearing performing their debut single, 'Boxerbeat', and during rehearsals Paul approached their bass player Chris Bostock to ask whether he could play the double bass. Sniffing an opportunity and being well Jack the buzz, he said yes. I turned up at the studio when they were recording 'The Paris Match', and Peter Wilson was fuming as it turned out that Chris only had a rudimentary knowledge of the instrument. Peering into the studio, I watched Peter china graphing small yellow crosses on the fret board where Chris was supposed to put his fingers to make up the chords. Peter returned to the control room, went into one, and had a right pop at me for allowing this. He moaned about having to work with amateurs: "I'm trying to make a serious album, and they're just playing about, you should have a word with them, you're their A&R manager." Unfortunately, once Paul makes his mind up, it's almost impossible to get him to change and he steamed ahead regardless of the consequences. They got the recording finished but it took an age; it would have been far easier and less time consuming for me to hire a good jazz bass player. I tried to mollify Peter, telling him Paul won't listen to reason, and nothing could be done. He carried on whingeing, and I decided to leave him to sort it out and left him fiddling with the controls, and shaking his head at what was going on. On the finished album, Paul also insisted they use the 7½ ips *rough* mix and not Peter's final production mix.

Also featured on the album was the cheery Joe Orton inspired 'Here's One That Got Away', which also features Chris Bostock on bass and that

Clark Gable look-a-like Bobby Valentino adding some nice swing violin. The album features a re-working of 'Headstart For Happiness' with D.C. Lee on vocals, and a new bridge. There isn't much to say about the jazz instrumentals, which were brave experiments, and could have backfired but luckily didn't. 'Dropping Bombs On The Whitehouse', a bop number in the Horace Silver tradition, was thinly disguised at the time to avoid confrontation with the American record company and the title seems even more relevant now after 9/11. 'Blue Café' is a little twee and saccharine sweet while 'Mick's Blessing' sees Mick pounding the ivories, whilst he gets his organ out on 'Council Meeting', one of his best outings, which fairly swings along. The *cod* jazz numbers at the time sounded quite amateurish, although I really admired Paul and Mick for trying to be different. The songs were as good as those recorded by the many other Acid Jazz bands during the early eighties. 'A Gospel', with a rap by Dizzy Hites, and 'Strength Of Your Nature' are ok, and Paul would dabble with this kind of music unsuccessfully throughout the Council's career. There's is no doubting he has soul, but it always came out better with his more traditional songs, like 'Speak', 'Long Hot Summer', or the next single, 'You're The Best Thing', one of the most commercial love songs he'd written to date, and one which would become the catalyst for the breakdown in his relationship with Polydor.

With the album finished, and the execs baying to hear Paul's new songs, I organised a playback meeting, which was packed, with half the company turning out. I should have charged an admission fee. I kept my speech short, and offered no real explanation as to what kind of music the album contained, only that the debut album of the Style Council was very different from the six previous Jam albums. As they sat there, munching their pop corn, I knew it wasn't what they expected and as the album played through it was interesting watching their faces. They couldn't make head or tail of what they were listening to and the instrumentals were just a little too much for them. To say it got a mixed reception was an understatement. There were some songs they could associate Paul with, but the album had no overall theme or thread running through it, and they were all slightly bemused. Afterwards the old man and my boss accosted me, explaining that they were worried about the fact that Paul wasn't singing on many tracks. Nonetheless, by now it was too late and whether they liked it or not, this was going to be the Council's debut album.

Paul and Mick decided to keep the French connection going and another photo session was booked in Paris. It went well, everybody was relaxed, and once again, Peter Anderson captured the mood perfectly. I have to say that lazing around in Paris was preferable to spending time in the office answering phones and attending boring meetings. However, when Simon Halfon delivered the artwork for the sleeve, it gave me more problems as Polydor was expecting the front to feature a colour photo in the same vein as 'Long Hot Summer' and there was a lot of huffing and puffing before they resignedly accepted the sleeve design.

Café Bleu came out on March 16 and went to number two in the album charts, selling in excess of a 200,000 copies. If I had given the management a chance to hear the album earlier I'm sure there would have been more than a bit of rucking and rolling over the instrumentals, and real aggro over the album version of 'Paris Match' that was sans Paul. The album received mixed reviews in the music press, with some hating it, whilst it was shock for others. In hindsight, it's very easy to have a pop at this album, as only a few of the songs have aged well, but at the time, it was a bold move to go with such a mix and match of music and personnel.

Throughout The Jam's career they had defied all the rules of marketing by always following up their albums with a new single, but that was about to change with the Council, as 'You're The Best Thing' was chosen as the next single. There was much discussion over this, but it was considered too good a song to be buried on the album. Paul wasn't totally convinced in the beginning, but decided to release the track as part of an EP entitled *Groovin'*, which would be a double A-side, with 'The Big Boss Groove' as the other A-side. This tune was a driving, upbeat number with a political message, you could listen to while steppin' out on the dance floor and a none-too-subtle dig at the Tory government. When it came to the video, Tim Pope directed a very moody number with Paul looking slick. We were set for a massive hit, or so I thought.

Musically, 'You're The Best Thing', was in a similar vein to 'Long Hot Summer', with a bass synth underpinning the tune, and I was confident that it would exceed the chart positions of the previous singles. The single came out on May 18 and although it was played to death on the radio, when it reached number five in the charts it stalled, which meant the company had to put its foot down hard on the gas pedal to get it moving again. I attended the weekly singles meeting where priorities were set for the singles sales force and promo department but when the Council's single wasn't even nominated as one of three priority singles of the week I was a little dismayed. The verdict was to wait and see what happens. They went as far as making a video for 'Big Boss Groove', but that wouldn't be enough: they needed to give it the welly in the chart return shops, where it counted, and I left the meeting praying the single would go up the next week. Without the company shoeing it, realistically I knew the single would drop down the charts, and when this happened, it would be left to me to give Paul the bad news, which I wasn't looking forward to.

Whenever I heard anyone say, "Let's wait and see what happens" it meant the death knell for my records. If the company wasn't going to *work* the record, how could it progress further up the charts. The next week the single dropped, and when I told Paul he asked pointedly, whether it was the record, or the company. There was no doubt in my mind that had this been CBS [Sony], EMI, Virgin, or RCA [BMG], they would have floored the gas pedal and done everything to get the record into the top three, perhaps even getting it to number one. I told him straight, Polydor didn't do the business; the company had let him down.

The video shoot for 'Big Boss' was hastily put together and had to be shot in one day to get it to *TOTPs* in time for the broadcast. Tim Pope wasn't available and his producer persuaded me to use his second director, which I wasn't happy with, as he seemed a bit flaky and, unlike Tim, didn't appear to have a strong enough character to handle Paul. The storyboard was simple, no corny ideas or dressing up, just the band playing live and when I arrived at the shoot, all was going well, but not for long. Paul decided to add a dance sequence, which was a problem – where could you find a troupe of dancers at this late moment? He then decided everybody attending the shoot would fill in, and be filmed dancing and I thought great, the video was going to turn into a Busby Berkeley number. Nothing I said could persuade him to change his mind, and everybody took their turn to strut their stuff, including me. At the end of the shoot, I collared the director and told him unequivocally not to include any of this footage in the final version and just to be certain, I went along to the studio where they were editing the film to see the final cut. As we got to the final sequence, I couldn't believe my eyes, towards the end of the video was a clip of me dancing, more Red Adair than Fred Astaire I might add, and we all had a good laugh at my hoofing. Paul and Mick explained the sequence would be cut from the final version and was only put in to wind me up. I was far from reassured by their comments, and more than a little anxious.

Later on, I met up with Mick and we headed for a pub to meet up with Paul and the rest of the team. I asked about the video and they told me my dancing debut was cut from the final version, although they were smiling when they told me and should have guessed something was up. We were at the bar and Mick asked: "How many drinks have you lot had?" Someone replied, "Four," and he ordered four large vodka and orange juices, and we got these down our necks sharpish. On downing the last one, Mick turned to me and said, "Your round Den, get 'em in," and we drank heavily for the rest of the night and when the pub turned out, we went to a Chinese restaurant for a meal, and then on to a club, and I arrived home in the early hours of the morning. When the alarm went off, I didn't feel like getting up, but duty called and I jumped in the car and weaved my way into the office. Around 10.30am I was forcing down another cup of coffee when my secretary told me Paul, Mick, John and Kenny were in the promotions office and wanted me to go down and view the final cut of 'The Big Boss Groove'. Still hung-over and not clear-headed I ambled down to the meeting and found them grinning from ear to ear, looking exceedingly slippery. As I looked around the promo office just about anyone that mattered in the company was there, even the MD and I had an uneasy feeling in my stomach, which had nothing to do with the previous night's intake of alcohol, and wondered what was going on.

Paul explained that they had come in personally to show the finished video to the company. I should have smelled a rat, as he rarely bothered to do this. The showing commenced and considering the video had been shot and edited quickly, it looked good. As we approach the end of the tune, suddenly I appear on the TV screen, dancing along. Not only had they not cut the original sequence, they'd added more footage, much to their amusement and my discomfort. Paul, Mick, John, and Kenny were laughing at my embarrassment, but their stunt didn't go down well with some of the execs as they thought I was in on it.

Smash Hits reproduced the lyrics of most hit singles, so you could sing along to your favourite tune. I received a call to help as they had a problem with lyrics they couldn't make out on the bridge of 'Best Thing'. Paul had a habit of mumbling lines he didn't particularly like, or perhaps wasn't happy with and I played the record through several times, but couldn't make out what Paul was singing either. I tried to get hold of him, but couldn't and decided to go into the studio and listen to the multi-track minus the backing. That way the lyrics might become clearer, but this didn't work, and after twenty minutes, I translated what I had thought he'd written and sung: *You're souled on me / You're the best for me / Come and rob my dreams / Take this chance from me.*

I phoned these lines through to *Smash Hits* and thought no more about this until the mag hit the streets and Paul phoned in. He said, "I've read the lyrics, where did the lines for the bridge come from? I'll be in to see you shortly." This worried me a little, as I knew how particular Paul was about his lyrics and was expecting to get a bit of a bollocking for getting them wrong. On his arrival, I explained how I'd come up with them and to my complete surprise he said: "They're better than the ones I wrote – I'm going to use them." I thought great, and envisaged seeing my name on the writer credits, Weller & Munday, and was looking forward to receiving a large royalty cheque. However, apart from Paul and a few others, nobody knew I wrote these lines. Mind you, as this tune has been on every *Love Songs* compilation for the last 20 years, perhaps I should ear 'ole John for some wonga!

There had always been a tenuous relationship with Paul since the early days of The Jam, and Polydor's failure to deliver the goods with this single didn't help. Releasing a single after the album did not increase the sales of the albums of *Café Bleu* to the extent that it should have, selling enough to go gold, but never recorded the sales to receive a platinum award. To support the album the Council undertook their first major tour of the UK, Europe, Japan, and the USA, which commenced in March and finished in May, but it was nowhere near as intensive as The Jam's touring schedule.

In every aspect *Café Bleu* was a success and people tend to forget that this was the Council's debut album and not Paul's seventh studio album. Even though it was a mixed bag, it established the Council's credentials, and was as far away from The Jam as Paul could get.

Now it was time for the sixth single 'Shout To The Top', and Paul decided to dispense with Peter Wilson's services and produce the record himself, which I wasn't happy about. I have always been of the opinion if bands like The Beatles, the Stones, and The Who required a producer, so did Paul. Producing yourself is a difficult task and very few artists are capable of it. The producer's job is to pull it all together and have the ability to step back to look at the songs objectively. Jay Mark, who worked out of Sigma Sounds Studio in New York, was seconded in to engineer the sessions and he had a good track record with credits that included working with artists on Gamble & Huff's Philadelphia label, as well as the legendary Thom Bell.

As the song required a string arrangement, Paul asked me to find an arranger and mentioned Fiachra Trench, who was hot at the time. I phoned his manager, Ian Levine, who said he wasn't free and he recommended Johnny Mealing as an alternative. Johnny was a jingles writer, who'd also written quite a few programme themes for BBC television, and on this recommendation, I arranged a meeting. When he arrived, he walked into my office and straight back out and had a good gander at the secretaries. Re-entering, he sat down and said: "How do you manage to get any work done with all these nice looking birds running about?" With this quip, I took an instant liking to Johnny, I also liked the idea that he'd worked on advertising jingles, as with this format you have to keep everything simple, but still say a lot in 30 seconds. At the end of the interview, I was more than happy to recommend him to Paul and Mick, although even with Jay and Johnny on board, I still wasn't happy about Paul producing the single. Just before going into the studio I had lunch with Mick in Covent Garden, and we discussed 'Shout' and he finally convinced me everything would be ok.

Jay was a nice lad, laid back with a good sense of humour and incredibly fast at getting the sounds that Paul and Mick wanted. Johnny's score, although very good and in the 'Philly' tradition, could have been better, but Paul wouldn't give him a free hand. He gave Johnny a cassette with a synth playing the arrangement, and told him to copy it. Johnny wanted to use violas and cellos, as counterpoint to the melody, but Paul was intransigent, and insisted that he copy *his* arrangement exactly. Kevin Miller, who was playing with Tracie's Soul Squad, played a much more funkier bass line on a previous version than the one used on the single, which just follows the melody. D. C. Lee and Alison Limerick provide the backing vocals, and in the nineties Alison would taste success under her own name.

Johnny hired Gavyn Wright as the leader and first violinist and he fixed the rest of the musicians for the session. He was extremely professional and thorough, right down to checking that Jay had the strings sounding right in the mix. Gavyn was one of the few classical musicians who were on the artist's side and had recorded many pop sessions during his career. He genuinely liked music and got the best out of his string players. You've no idea how snooty some classical players can be, with the majority looking down their Strads at pop music, putting nothing into the session other than the bare minimum. For them, pop music is an easy [and lucrative] way to earn extra dough when they're not playing in a symphony orchestra.

When the take was completed, Gavyn returned and listened to the finished track and decided to re-record certain bars that he considered not good enough. Johnny and Gavyn generously asked me what my thoughts were and I mentioned that one of the violinists had made an error during one part, and the playing on the tag (end) was too stiff, and the strings needed to play with the feel of the track, and swing out. Gavyn returned to the studio and explained all this to the musicians and they completed the session without any fuss. Before leaving Gavyn thanked me for pointing out the error and said: "I'm glad that it was noticed at this stage and not after the record had been released." When Jay returned to New York, he did a re-mix of 'Shout', but Paul wasn't happy, and commented: "It's too American for me," although I am not sure what he expected.

The single came out on October 5, went to number seven in the charts and I think that with a better arrangement and production it would have gone higher. The song pumps along, and the lyrics are excellent, with an uplifting message, but the finished tune ended up a carbon copy of Paul's original demo, and a bit one-dimensional. Nonetheless, to this day, it remains one of my favourite Council tunes. The B-side had a couple of quality songs, 'The Piccadilly Trail' and 'Ghosts Of Dachau'. The 'dilly was well known as a meat-rack rent boy's paradise, and Paul had visited Dachau concentration camp in 1978. It left a mark, and he later wrote some very haunting and evocative lyrics.

The video for 'Shout' was shot in an old school hall in North London, and during a break, I was chatting to Tim Pope about Paul's relationship with Polydor. Paul either misunderstood, or misheard what I'd said and stormed up to me saying: "Come outside if you got something to say about me. Why don't you say it to my face?" and went into one. There's no reasoning with Paul when he's like this, and for the rest of the filming I kept my distance. His attitude pissed me off a little, as I have always been upfront, and been very honest with him. Towards the end, and after he had spoken to Tim he magnanimously apologised and we kissed and made up. Well, we made up!

During his Jam days, Paul had shown his political credentials with his support of the working class, CND, and a number of other (not so trendy) causes close to his heart. With the Council, he aligned himself with many deserving causes, playing many free concerts for their benefit, and placed himself in the vanguard of the anti-Tory movement. He and Billy Bragg were seen as leading lights of left wing politics in the music business, and under the banner of The Style Council he was more up front and politically motivated. Paul wasn't just committed; he was determined to make an impact. Thatcherism was rampant, what was left of the manufacturing industries was sold off to foreign companies, or downsized, and even the family silver was sacrificed! Paul's generosity towards these causes could have held back his career, as at the time left wing politics were unpopular with the middle classes, and the Labour party unelectable.

Arthur Scargill had called on the miners to take industrial action and they were nearly a year into their now infamous strike. It reached a point where miners' families were suffering, and Paul boldly decided to rectify this. I was summoned to party HQ at Solid Bond studios for a cabinet meeting to discuss the next Council single and I could see he was clearly moved by the plight of the miners and their families. He decided that rather than just offer money, he would write and record a song about the dispute and donate the royalties to the suffering families. The title would be 'Soul

Deep', and when I read the lyrics, he certainly hadn't held anything back. His attack on the Tories and the Coal board was a damming indictment of what was happening to the coal industry and the miners. The only problem for me was explaining this single to the company. At least the politically motivated 'Money-Go-Round' was vaguely commercial, and it was bound to receive airplay. There was no question in my mind that 'Soul Deep', would be a big problem with radio, and only sell on the strength of Paul's reputation and credibility with his steadfast following.

The single was recorded quickly and a little rushed. Nonetheless, it captured Paul's mood and gave the striking miners a solid message of support. This single would be released under the name of The Council Collective and augmented with Junior Giscombe, Jimmy Ruffin, and D. C. Lee on vocals. Vaughn Toulouse and Dizzy Hites would handle the rapping end, with Animal Nightlife's Leonardo Chignoli providing the bass. The production credits read: produced by The Council Collective and re-mixed by Martin Ware (Heaven 17) and Solid Bond's engineer, Bryan Robson. Junior was the last to lay down his vocal part. He came in one evening, Paul handed him a set of lyrics and without rehearsing laid down a perfect vocal. I looked around at the rest of the crew who were looking sick. At a stroke, Junior had out sung the lot of them, including a Motown legend. However, once Junior had left the studio I believe several went back and re-recorded their vocals.

For the B-side Paolo Hewitt interviewed two striking miners. The younger of the two was a Scargill clone, bristling with political militancy, and was all for bringing the government down – an attitude that became Scargill's Achilles heel. The older miner was a nice bloke, down to earth, and said, resignedly: "I just want to go back to work and earn a decent wage that I can live on, and feed the family, that's all." His comments got to me as my wages were more than decent. I wouldn't have walked through the pit gate, never mind worked at the pithead, not for twice the money I was on. The miners earned their wages the hard way, and paid a heavy price with their health. At the time, I was puzzled as to why Jimmy Ruffin wanted to sing on this track and wrongly felt he was trying to enhance his own career as he was now reduced to playing the 'chicken-in-a-basket' cabaret circuit. When we met up, I asked him, and he simply replied: "My father had been a miner back in the States and I can empathise with the plight of the British miners. I know what it's like, coal mining is in my family."

From the outset, the company was unhappy about releasing 'Soul Deep'. They thought (wrongly) that the single would have an adverse affect on Paul's career and, most importantly, on his future record sales. Then the worst thing that could have happened did: the tragic killing of a mini cab driver by two miners, the consequences of which reverberated on 'Soul Deep' by bringing about immense pressure to withdraw it. The death of the cab driver wasn't a malicious act of wanton murder, just stupid albeit explainable, and the overall struggle was still worthy. My opinion never wavered; the record had to come out, even though Polydor's management made it clear they would prefer to see it pulled from the schedule. By now, there had been a considerable amount of publicity and I argued that not to release it would damage Paul's credibility and have an adverse affect on his integrity. The company wasn't happy, but I wouldn't budge, and left them with the comment: "If Paul wants it pulled, fine, but other than that 'Soul Deep' gets released."

The decision was made; we would run with 'Soul Deep', with Paul donating a portion of the royalties to the widow of the dead cab driver. The lyrics would appear on the reverse of the sleeve, but Paul had a change of mind as he thought some of his lines were inflammatory. On my way home, I paid a visit to the printer and made the necessary changes.

The single came out on December 14, and the airplay on Radio 1 was minimal. It reached 24 in the singles charts and a large wedge was paid out to deserving causes. The Council Collective appeared on *TOTP* and we all drove up to Newcastle to perform the single live on *The Tube*. When it came to the performance poor old Jimmy Puffin (as he was now known) had forgotten to memorise his part and Junior had to jump in and rescue him. We arrived back in London in the early hours of the morning, and I gave Mick a ride home to Merton Park, finally arriving home as the sun was rising, exhausted, but it was all worthwhile.

Of all the political records Paul recorded, this one could have damaged him more than any of the others he'd recorded to date. Given the circumstances, of the death of the taxi driver, and the fact that the cause was unpopular with the right-wing middle class, it was a difficult and brave decision to go with the record. He had the opportunity to duck out, but took the hard option, which could have really backfired, and lot of credit should be given to him for taking such a big risk with his career, as he did with 'Soul Deep'.

The record business has always been a mean moneymaking machine, and these days it's relentless in its pursuit of profit. It's unlikely that any modern company would allow an artist of Paul's stature to release records like 'Money-Go-Round' and 'Soul Deep'. Had Paul been managed by anyone other than John, I am certain they would have tried to talk him out of going down this road as it could have seriously damaged his career, not least because political records like this have no value outside the UK. It wasn't that John was taking the back seat, but it was noticeable that Paul was taking charge of his career, and there were times when he would take a decision, and tell John later. I doubt that this affected the relationship as John rarely interfered with this side of the business, but it was a different Paul Weller to the one who was a quarter of The Jam.

In December, Bob Geldof invited Paul to make an appearance on the Band Aid single and Paul asked if I wanted to attend the recording session. I dipped out as there were too many egos in one room for my liking, and I didn't fancy getting the first round in. The record itself wasn't that great but it was for a good cause and it was one of the few times where *style over content* mattered. The more big names meant a bigger hit, and more money to help the starving people in Africa.

Whenever I watch the promo, video I crack up, as Paul is never happy playing the star and he looks so uncomfortable amongst the star-studded group. In 2005, they reprised the idea with Live 8 Africa and held concerts in eight different countries around the world, although the event was spoiled by the appearance on stage by Bill Gates, one of the richest men in the world. The music industry is a rapacious business, but occasionally, it raises its head above the mire, and fair play to Sir Bob who upstaged himself the second time around, with a concert rivalled only by the games put on by the caesars in the Coliseum in Rome. I can't imagine the shit he went through organising these concerts, but he richly deserves any awards he receives for these two momentous occasions.

That was the end of a busy year for the Council; they released four singles and their debut album. While they hadn't had a number one single or album, 1984 cemented the foundation laid down the previous year, and with the heavy political stance that Mick and Paul were taking, 1985 was going to be an interesting year.

Although 1984 was a successful year, personally, I can't say I was happy working at Polydor. Since 1978, it was a running battle with the company, first with The Jam and although not as tough with the Council, there were very few easy records. I had planted my flag firmly in The Jam's camp first and then the Council, which many in the company weren't happy with, and I was never one to toe the line, or afraid to speak my mind. There were many Chinese whispers going around the company about my relationship with Paul and John, although no one was brave enough to front me out. Behind my back, it was said that I was in John's pocket and on the take, which was false. Since I have known Paul and John, I have never asked for, nor been given, cash or any other incentives whilst working on their records, nor would I take any if offered. All the extra hours I put in was for nix, why would the Wellers give me money; John wasn't stupid, he knew Polydor paid my wages.

By the mid-eighties Polydor's execs were past their sell-by date and there was a need for a change at the top. The indie labels that blossomed after punk had changed the face of the business, changes that had bypassed Polydor. I was used to the Machiavellian dealings of the music industry, but I knew that regardless of my relationship with Paul, if it came to it the company would shaft me as they shafted my boss Jim Cook. He'd worked for the company for more that 17 years and was callously given a couple of days notice, and told to clear his desk by the end of the week. There was a wind of change coming and if a director of the company could get the boot like this, what chance did I have of surviving. Fortunately, time was on my side, the Council was successful, and I was practically a member of the band and safe for the moment. I was earning more money than at any other time during my career and decided to put off the decision until 1985, hoping things might change. The Council was about to deliver their second album and everything looked bright on that front, and they would start the year at the top, although by the end the cracks began to show.

CHAPTER 12

The Walls Come Tumbling Down

1985 would see the Council release their most successful album, and along with Status Quo open the now historic Live Aid concert. There was a change of management at Polydor that would have a lasting affect on Paul and John, and result in big changes in my life. It also saw the end of his relationship with Gill Price, which was troubled, and perhaps came too early in both of their lives, as you mature into adulthood, everything changes, and you lose the naivety of youth. Both liked a drink, although Paul would often go on the wagon, leaving Gill to party on with the rest of the crowd. I know I found Paul difficult at times. I only had to work with him, and he couldn't have been the easiest person to live with, given his penchant for privacy and those ever-changing moods. Whatever the financial cost to Paul, it was a drop in the ocean compared to what Gill gave him, and I am sure he knows this better than most.

The beginning of the year was taken up with finishing the second album, which would be titled *Our Favourite Shop*, and preceded by the single, 'Walls Come Tumbling Down', which was released on the 3 May. The Tory party and Mrs Thatcher had gotten under Paul's skin with the result that the single and the forthcoming album was a clear statement of intent that he was going to take on both. I am sure that even the miniscule publicity inspired by the miners' record would have been drawn to the attention of

Thatcher and her cohorts, and there would be no let up during 1985. The content of 'Walls' was uncompromising and abrasive, and included the word 'crap' in the opening line, which had to be censored, as the BBC would deem it an offensive (yawn) word and might ban it. The lyrics call on the power of unity to fight unjust Tory policies, and I thought (wrongly) that following the miners' record such a strong political theme might harm sales and airplay on Radio 1. This wasn't a loss of confidence in Paul's abilities, but these were dark days politically, and it wasn't the time to challenge the Government's authority; the Tory party's popularity was sky high, and it would be long time before Thatcher's walls came tumbling down. However, my misgivings were proved mistaken and the single went to number six in the charts, but there is no doubt that it was Paul's talents as a great tunesmith that carried the Council's political songs. Had his song writing skills been ordinary, by now the Council would have sunk without a trace. Can you imagine the Thompson Twins, Howard Jones, Duran Duran, or Kajagoogoo making a political statement?

The B-side featured 'The Whole Point II', a reworking of 'The Whole Point Of No Return' from the *Café Bleu* album, and it was indicative of how far Paul had come as a songwriter. Although he had reworked two previous songs ('Ever Changing Moods' and 'Headstart'), neither were changed as radically as, 'The Whole Point II'. It's easy to alter a song by playing it either fast, or slow, or from a solo guitar/piano version to a band version – that's nothing new and has been done before. As well as having two very diverse storylines, with the exception of two lines both have completely different lyrics. I can't think of many songwriters from any decade who are capable of writing the same song twice, yet so different and of equal merit. If you look at the lyrics to both of these songs, it gives you an idea of just how innovative and innate Paul's song writing skills are. For many years he'd supported animal rights, in which Gill took an active part, and on the second track he took an uncompromising stand against the hunting community with 'Blood Sports', a head-on attack on this so-called (barbaric) sport. The 12 inch version had 'Spin' Drifting' as the extra track. Once again, this single bought into question the sexuality of the band, particularly Mick, as the photo on the front of the sleeve portrays him heavily made up, like an old silent movie actor. I thought he resembled Archie Rice, the character Laurence Olivier portrayed in the film, *The Comedian.* The promo video was shot in the only jazz club in Poland, The Akwarium, and the Council were one of the first European bands to be allowed to film in Poland.

Good song writing is about creating images as well as sound, and great songwriters have the ability to create images from ordinary, everyday occurrences that have passed by unnoticed until you hear the song. Paul is able to conjure up these images and his lyrics are often poetic. Listening to music is a form of relaxation and although you don't necessarily want to hear a message every time you play a CD, it is possible to write songs of conviction that entertain, and have a message, political or otherwise. After all, the whole purpose of love songs is to pass on the message of love, and both versions of 'Point' have very different messages. Many times, I've been told that it must be easier to write a simple song than a more complicated and protracted song, but this isn't the case. 'Money-Go-Round' is a good example of this, and while it's a good song, it isn't up to the standard of both versions of 'The Whole Point'. They are simple in their execution, but in every aspect well-crafted songs, and stand the test of time, which is the sign of not only a good song, but also a great songwriter. Both versions are a thread from Paul's past with 'That's Entertainment' and to his future with 'Wild Wood', and beyond ...

On May 31, 1985, Polydor released *Our Favourite Shop*, which gave the Council their only number one record during their turbulent career, although it didn't stay there long. Polydor released Bryan Ferry's solo album *Boys And Girls* shortly after, and they wanted that at the number one spot – know what I mean, nudge nudge, wink wink!

Following up on the theme of previous political songs this album contained many songs that once again openly attacked the Prime Minister and her government, and their anti social policies. 'Homebreakers', written by Paul & Mick opens side one, is a reaction to Norman Tebbitt's callous comment about the unemployed: "If you can't find a job in your town, you should get on your bike and move away", never mind about your family, friends and your community. Mick took the lead vocals, but by his own admission wasn't in Paul's league as a vocalist, nor did he try to be. The intention was to open up the album with a strong message, but as it was the first tune on the record, it was bound to draw attention and Mick received much unjust criticism for his vocal. It would have been better to open up with Mick's instrumental 'Our Favourite Shop', as it would have taken the heat off him.

'All Gone Away' has a laid-back bossa nova feel, with lyrics that attack monetarism, the very foundation of the Tory government. 'Come To Milton Keynes', Paul's trenchant criticism of the (many) 'artificial' new towns that had sprung up throughout Britain, caused a furore. Paul may not have visited this town, but he got it bang to rights. I remember seeing a John Otway gig there, and was decidedly unimpressed with the place – it was a faceless town, full of roundabouts, and metal cows. 'Internationalists', another song co-written with Mick, showed Paul had moved away from being a little Englander, that the world went beyond the shores of his England.

'A Stones Throw Away' is another highlight of the album and dealt with the harsh injustices that have been perpetrated throughout the world. John Mealing's string quartet arrangement adds poignantly to the story of man's abuse to humankind. At live gigs, Paul would perform this number solo on electric guitar, which gave the tune a real edge. 'The Stand Up Comics Instructions', rapped out by the comedian, Lenny Henry, was an attack on racist bigotry of the Northern and Southern club scene, which has since changed and there is now a new generation of comedians who do not need to use racist bigotry to get a laugh. Although strong on sentiment, the song would perhaps have been better suited to the B-side of a 12 inch single.

'The Lodgers (or She Was Only A Shopkeeper's Daughter)' features D.C Lee in a direct attack on Prime Minister Thatcher. Very few songwriters are prepared to assault a pre-eminent political figure at the apex of their power. In the Sixties, many songs attacked governments and their figureheads but these were heady and enlightening days when political comment through song was common. Strangely enough, this (my) generation would go on to elect the likes of Thatcher, Reagan, George Bush and (son of Thatcher) Tony Blair. When Paul recorded *Our Favourite Shop*, the times were neither heady nor enlightening, and political education was on the back-boiler. Steve White got his first chance as a songwriter and aired his own political thoughts on the Latin flavoured 'With Everything To Lose', with lyrics centring on the frustrations of the Saturday kids forced to work as cheap labour on Government schemes.

There were a few tunes on the album without a political flavour. 'A Man of Great Promise', dedicated to Dave Waller, one of Paul's old school chums who died tragically and far too young. I recall meeting Dave backstage after a Jam gig at the Rainbow; he was well pissed and he'd had a barney with Paul, and stormed out. It must have come as a shock to Paul to learn of the death of his friend at such an early age, and this fine tribute ensures Dave won't be totally forgotten. The church bells featured at the beginning seem to have been borrowed from The Small Faces' 'Lazy Sunday'. 'Luck', another song co-written with Mick, is a nice summery tune, while 'Down In The Seine' featured Paul singing rather self-consciously in French. Whenever he features this song nowadays, he leaves the French verse out! 'Boy Who Cried Wolf' was more or less in the same groove as 'Best Thing' although not quite of the same calibre. Many

Paul in the summer of 1981, at the photo shoot for 'Absolute Beginners'. *(Derek D'Souza)*

Rick, Bruce and Paul in 1981. *(Derek D'Souza)*

The band and some of the crew in Chiswick Park in 1981; left to right: photographer Derek D'Souza, Rick, Paul, Joe Awome, Dave Liddle and Derek's friends Suzanne and Melissa with Bruce. Kenny Wheeler can be seen dashing back from the bushes. *(Derek D'Souza)*

Paul and Bruce on stage, 1981. *(Derek D'Souza)*

John Weller addresses the crowd at The Jam's Christmas party at the Fulham Greyhound, 1980; left to right: Rick, Paul, author Dennis Munday, John Weller, Bruce and Polydor head AJ (Tony) Morris. *(Dennis Munday Collection)*

Bruce and Dennis Munday at John and Anne Weller's 25th Anniversary party, March 1982. *(Twink)*

In the dressing room on The Jam's final world tour, 1982. *(Twink)*

Paul swaps his Rickenbacker for a Fender Telecaster, 1982. *(Derek D'Souza)*

Bruce on stage, 1982. *(Twink)*

On stage at the Bingley Hall, Stafford, March 21, 1982. *(Twink)*

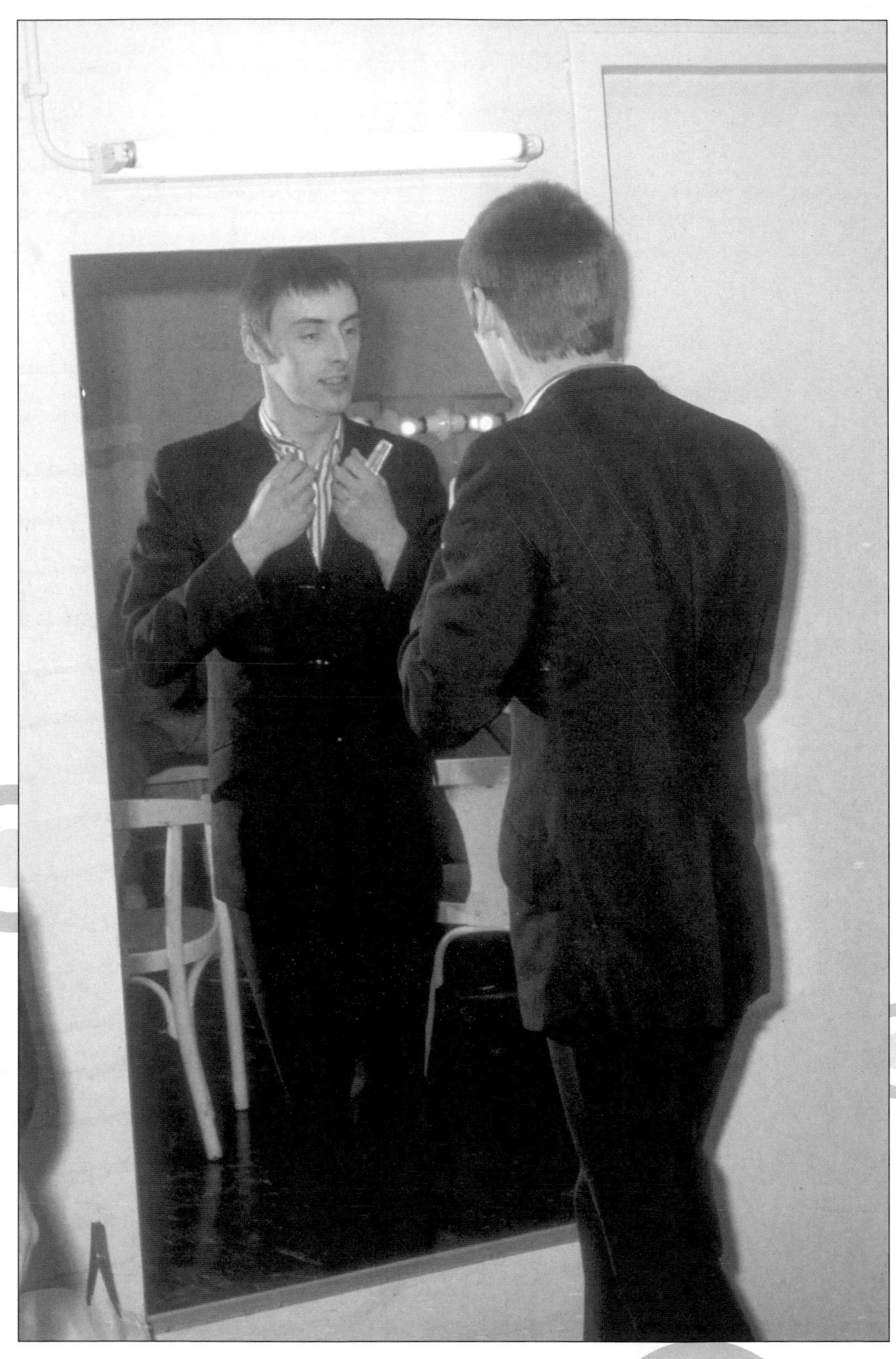

Paul checks the cut of his collar backstage, 1982. *(Twink)*

Paul with girlfriend Gill Price, Japan, 1982. *(Pictorial Press)*

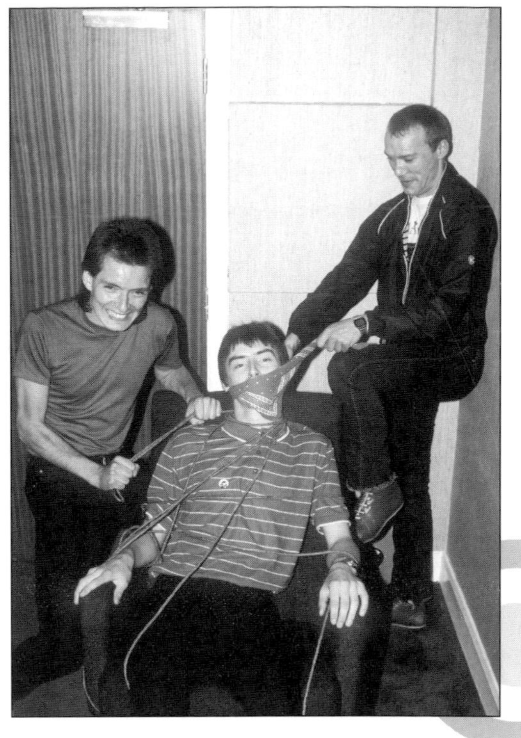

Bruce and Rick in a vain attempt at silencing their leader, 1982. *(Neil Matthews/Rex Features)*

Paul and John Weller, backstage at Wembley Empire Pool, December 5, 1982. *(Virginia Turbett/Redferns)*

The end of the road for the Jam. Paul on stage at their final concert at the Brighton Conference Centre, December 11, 1982. *(James Mayes)*

A thoughtful Weller immediately after he disbanded The Jam, December 1982. *(Virginia Turbett/Redferns)*

THE BRIGHTON CENTRE

SATURDAY, 11th DECEMBER, 1982
at 7.30 p.m.

M.C.P. PRESENT

THE JAM PLUS GUESTS

No 2562

STANDING TICKET
MAIN HALL ONLY £5.00

(Magnificent Sea View)
Open two hours prior to most performances
Reservations: Telephone 203130

Neither the Council or their officers accept any responsibility for any loss or damage (howsoever caused or sustained) to any property whatsoever brought on to these premises.

Tickets cannot be exchanged or refunded.

The taking of unauthorised photographs during the artiste's live performance is a breach of the Copyright Act 1956. Cameras being used in defiance of this regulation will be removed to the cloakroom for the duration of the performance. The Management may also exercise the right to expose film if so requested by the artiste.

An autographed ticket stub for The Jam's final show together. *(Courtesy of Derek D'Souza)* colleagues at Polydor wanted this as the next single, but it would have been treading water to release it.

There were no problems with the sleeve on this album and once again, Simon did a great job. The mocked up shop contained many personal artefacts of both Paul and Mick, and if you look carefully, hidden in there is a caricature of Paul and Mick by Pete Barrett in a homoerotic pose that was neatly censored. On the inside, there was a serious picture of Paul and Mick, and I have to say Paul's haircut is well dodgy. In the box set, Paul described it as a bit poofy and a little bit scally!

Our Favourite Shop was slicker and more confident than *Café Bleu*, but it was always going to be and it went on to become the best selling album the Council released during their career. It's been said that it sold a million copies worldwide, something I have doubts about. If you want to shift units, the Council would have had to undertaken large tours of the USA and other continents, and not just the two to three week *holiday* tours that took place.

While Paul and Mick were recording *Our Favourite Shop*, I'd made up my mind to quit Polydor. It wasn't a spur of the moment decision but something I'd been thinking over for the past year. When I started working at Polydor in the early Seventies, it was a fun place and the majority of those working there were music people who enjoyed talking about music. We worked long hours, but nobody minded, as you received recognition for a job well done. As Polydor's jazz A&R manager, I was shielded from the office politics, and left to my own devices, but I knew it wouldn't last, and when the job was made redundant and I moved into the pop/rock market I was exposed to the machinations of the company. I considered myself a good company employee, but not a yes man – if I didn't agree, I let the person, or meeting know, and in no uncertain terms. I didn't suffer fools gladly, which you need to do, if you want to get on, and it was always a matter of whether your face fitted. No matter how hard you worked, or whatever success you achieved, it didn't guarantee your job.

During the early eighties, the management that ran Polydor was out of date and there is no doubt that they needed to change, as the music scene had moved on. When the change came I was up for this, and looking forward to a more youthful and dynamic approach, but after a short period, I realised the changes weren't for the best, and overnight I didn't fit in. The new breed of executive that came in and dominated the industry was the very epitome of the 'yuppie' culture. It should have clicked with me by the way they dressed, and decorated their offices. It was all 'flash' Ryman furniture, Paul Smith suits in the drabbest colours imaginable, battleship grey – they even managed to make bank managers look interesting. The wife of one executive used to buy his clothes – and it showed. They lacked character, were humourless, and if they possessed charisma, they didn't bring it into the office.

Like Ali Ba-Ba, they whizzed in on their magic carpets, giving the impression they were young, gifted, and on the case and expected instant respect. When I began working at Polydor, you had to earn the respect of your colleagues, and the artists, whether you worked in the post room or on the top floor. Having a grand title was no guarantee, and no one gave a monkeys how successful you might have been with another record company; you had to earn your spurs working for the red label. Many of these execs came to Polydor just to further their careers and after a couple of years moved on to pastures new, leaving Polydor wallowing in the mire. The turnover of management went on for the next decade, causing much unrest for the artists signed to the label and the staff working there. I didn't care for their style of management and I now realised it was never going to work, they didn't like the way I worked, or my aggressive attitude. Perhaps I worked too closely with The Jam, the Council, and Paul for my own good. Throughout their career, I had a friendship that went beyond a business relationship, and as well as working with them, I would often go out drinking or go clubbing.

Unhappy with working there I took the MD, John Preston to lunch, and explained my grievances, but it came to nought. He told me that many of the senior execs were scared of me, and that I was aggressive at meetings, which was true. The fact that I put in long hours and got it right more times than wrong didn't come into it, and I was accused of being the voice of Paul. Well, somebody in the company had to talk to him. I concluded it would be better to fall on my sword rather than await the executioner's chopper, which was now looking inevitable. Although he generously said the company couldn't afford to lose a person with my experience, we were going round in circles and at the end of the lunch, I told him to make me an offer and I will go. Having concluded the discussion the MD departed, leaving me to pick up the tab for lunch.

It wasn't just that I couldn't work with these people; there were other reasons for me wanting to go. At the time the company needed to transform, it was stuck in a groove going nowhere, and had a poor reputation for breaking new bands. Many top producers wouldn't touch an artist on Polydor with a barge pole. Martin Rushent (Stranglers, Human League) produced a band for me as a favour, and did a great job, but as he predicted, their records disappeared. Managers were reluctant to place their bands with Polydor, and I remember when Deacon Blue's manger Peter Felsted approached me, when he was touting the band around, he said: "If I sign the band to CBS or Warner's they will put their foot down on the gas pedal. Polydor won't even get on their bike, they won't go balls out for a new band, unless it's a racing certainty," and depressing for me: "If you move to another company Den, I would be happy to sign a band with you"! This wasn't just a problem for me, as we had a couple of young Turks in our A&R department who had good ears who were signing bands that were relevant to the current music scene, and they had similar problems.

I'd also reached a point where I didn't enjoy going to work, I was burning out, and I'd had a gut full of the constant pressure. One morning on my way in, as I drove through Bermondsey an irate pedestrian gave me a V sign, and without a thought, I mounted the pavement, and tried to run him down. Further down the road I pulled over, and got out of the car shaking at what had happened. Not only was I losing it, I'd stopped listening to music, and rarely played records at home. This represented a major change, as music had been central to my life, since I was 14, and from 18 hardly a day went by when I didn't listen to music.

It might seem strange to some people that I would want to leave such a well-paid gig and I knew every Jam and Council fans would have cut a deal with the Devil to have the opportunity to work with both bands and Paul Weller. However, I had become disenchanted with the business, and I was tired of the unnecessary and constant grief of being in the middle, between Paul and Polydor. Having made the decision, I now had to tell Paul, Mick, and John I was leaving the company and the opportunity arose when they were recording a TV show on the Isle of Dogs. I told them of my decision and they didn't say much. I think it quite surprised them. It was a tough call as I had worked closely with John and Paul, since The Jam's 'David Watts' single and become good mates with Mick and Steve White since they joined the Council, friendships that last to this day. As I knew I was going to leave Polydor for some time, I'd run down my artist roster and for the last year, only worked on the Council. Having made the decision, all that was left was to see the month of June out, collect my money, and be on my way.

My leaving coincided with the Live Aid concert, and as well as the single a video album was going to be released for public consumption, with every band donating a promo clip, royalty free. Kate Koumis, my secretary rang through to tell me Bob Geldof was on the line and was extremely irate with John Weller. I picked up the phone and (stupidly) said: "Hi, what's the problem," and he went into one, ranting and raving about John. I had to wait until the end of his diatribe to repeat my original question. He explained he'd talked to John about donating a Council video clip for the compilation, which John agreed to and then asked for an advance. Bob pointed out thousands of children and adults were starving and dying in Africa, and it was for a good cause. I don't knock John for this stance, as prior to the news coverage of the people starving to death, not many people or governments took any real interest. The record business is not, despite what anyone thinks, a benevolent or altruistic industry. Many bands and artists flaunt their charitable acts supporting trendy causes, perhaps with a royal patronage attached as it raises their profile, and as my accountant once told me: "The Tax man gives you a nice tax break when you give to a 'worthwhile' charity." John was John, charity began at home, and make no mistake there are plenty of others far worse than him in the music biz. Many bands wanted to play on the Live Aid single and the concert, knowing it would be broadcast on TV worldwide, and saw this as a phenomenal opportunity to further their careers rather than aiding the starving millions.

I calmed the would-be Knight down and reassured him, there would be no problems, and I'd have a word with Paul and arrange for a video clip to be donated. I knew this video compilation would sell and be very popular, and decided to give them 'The Big Boss Groove'. The video had hardly been shown on British TV, and even better, I was featured dancing in it. I called Paul and explained what a great idea it was to donate this video for the compilation, and he agreed.

My first impressions of Bob Geldof's involvement with Band Aid and Live Aid were not very generous. Bob's career had been in free fall for some time, and the received opinion in the music biz was that he was using this to revitalise his own career. I wasn't the only one in the business who thought this way. The music industry is one of the most cynical businesses to work in, where nobody does anything for nowt, and it was hard to believe the sentiment behind his motives. When he was in The Boomtown Rats, he was a bit of a motor mouth and had an opinion on everything. However, we were all proved wrong, and what he (and Midge Ure) did with Live and Band Aid (and later Live 8 Africa) and the way he handled himself during the death of his ex-wife Paula Yates, proved us to be extremely cynical and very wrong.

At the end of June I quit Polydor not knowing what the future held, or really caring. I was given a substantial amount of money in lieu of service and had paid off my mortgage, so I didn't have to worry for a couple of years. Later I found out they would have shafted me anyway, and it's unlikely that I would have stayed at Polydor for more than a few more months. I wasn't entirely happy about leaving as The Style Council and Paul had been a big part of my life, and as I left the offices for the last time, although I had no regrets, there was a tinge of sadness.

For some reason 'Come To Milton Keynes' was chosen as the next single and released at the end of the month on June 28. The 12 inch had the customary remixes and there was a new track on the B-side, '(When You) Call Me', and an additional single in a gatefold bag. Even though there were three different version it went to 23 in the charts, the lowest placing so far for a Council single. The decision baffled me as it wasn't really a single, and even though it followed a number one album, it had no real chance of making the top 10. They would have been better going with 'Boy Who Cried Wolf', as other territories did, or go down the same path as The Jam who released a *new* single after every album. Shortly after its release, Paul distanced himself from the song, agreeing it was a mistake to go with it.

The point of releasing a second single from an album is to enhance sales, but in the case of the Council, this didn't really work. As good a song as 'You're The Best Thing' is, it didn't prolong the life of *Café Bleu* to any great extent. Although it went to number one, *Our Favourite Shop* only stayed in the charts 22 weeks, 16 weeks less than The Council's first album. To regenerate the album, Polydor needed to release a second single that was commercially viable. Although now signed to Geffen records in America, and the album re-titled, *Internationalists*, it had very little impact on the American market. I met the Geffen people before leaving Polydor and they were a good bunch, very enthusiastic, but the political tracks ensured that the record wasn't going to cross over. Paul refused to undertake big tours of this continent and this would have a negative effect on sales in America. At the time, Geffen was a hot company. David Geffen had the Midas touch when it came to picking bands, and their roster contained artists (notably The Eagles) who were shifting records by the millions. Unfortunately, like The Jam, the Council were unknown outside the large cities of the East and West coasts of America.

They undertook a short tour of the UK to support the album, ending at Glastonbury where they headlined. After a number one album, the Council's profile was high and there wasn't the need to undertake an extensive tour of the UK. Also, after the pressure of The Jam, Paul was keeping the tours to a manageable minimum.

On September 20, the Council released a re-recording of 'The Lodgers' although the political content would ensure that its appeal wouldn't leave the British shores and all their fans would have the original version of this track on the LP. It was suggested that the single was by public demand, but the public didn't rush out to buy it, and it only managed to get to 13 in the charts, two places lower than 'Money-Go-Round' and 'Solid Bond'. Polydor released the single as a 7 inch, 12 inch, and a limited edition double-pack single with different mixes, and the B-side had live versions of previous tracks, including 'Move On Up', one of Paul's favourite Curtis Mayfield tunes that he'd recorded with The Jam. Given the lower chart position of this single, and that it only stayed in the singles chart for six weeks, it would have given little impetus to the album, and made no real difference to overall sales. By the time they released 'The Lodgers', *Our Favourite Shop* had all but dropped out of top 75, and there was no way of reviving it, short of one of the band dying in public!

After *Our Favourite Shop,* the Council underwent a change with Dee becoming a permanent member of the band, which included Steve White, and the concept of the Council being a project band ended. This format certainly worked during the early period with various artists coming and going, and it gave their singles and albums variety. One of the main reasons Paul formed the Council was to get away from a rigid group line up. He wanted a band that was less predictable, so he didn't have to write to a format, and for every record to be different. However, the release of the singles 'Milton Keynes' and 'The Lodgers' started a downward slide, which they were unable to reverse for the rest of their career. During the first two and a half years, the Council could do no wrong, even the singles with political statements sold. The freewheeling attitude that pervaded during the early years gave way to some of the finest songs that Paul wrote.

It would have been far better to follow up their number one album with two fresh singles, or wait until the New Year and start 1986 with a new single.

From this moment on, the Council started to lose their way. I'm not sure what the execs at Polydor were playing at during the second half of the year, but they must have realised the folly of releasing 'The Lodgers' after 'Milton Keynes'. I never thought much of their man management skills, or their A&R abilities while I worked with them, but they should have talked Paul round and waited to see what the New Year would bring. The success of *Our Favourite Shop* going to number one bought them time, and it was unnecessary to release any more singles. A little later in the year, Dee released a single, 'See The Day', which went to number five, outperforming all three Council singles released in 1985.

That was it for '85 and the Council ended the year with a UK tour finishing off with three nights at Wembley. Live they were still doing the business, but with the failure of their last two singles, they needed a big 'un in '86 to regain their momentum.

The way the Council went about 1986 bears a striking resemblance to The Jam in 1981, when they too did not release a studio album. There were other things on Paul's mind, like the Red Wedge tours and making political points. His political convictions were as paramount as his song writing. During the first six months of the year, he placed his politics alongside his musical career, which in hindsight may have been a mistake. At the time, Neil Kinnock was trying to revolutionise the Labour Party whose ideas were clearly out of date. He wanted to make the party more acceptable to the middle class and the youth of the day. Eventually, Kinnock did re-shape the Labour party and although he was never elected Prime Minister, he paved the way for Tony Blair to serve three terms. The Labour Party had come a poor second to the Tory party for a long time and if things were going to change, it was at grass roots level. Gone were cloth caps, boots and pints of brown and mild, and in came designer suits, cocktails, and Buck's fizz. Kinnock set up a meeting with Paul's cohort Billy Bragg to try to find out what the youth wanted from a political party, and through this and Red Wedge, they were seen as leading political lights of music.

Billy was definitely the main voice behind Red Wedge, and was able to articulate politics much better than Paul, almost like a politician, and while Billy was seen as the mouthpiece, Paul was seen as the leader. As good an artist and songwriter as Billy is, he didn't have the success, credibility, or influence that Paul had. The Council's profile was high and they'd made an impact in the charts with political records. By 1986, Paul had charted at the number one slot six times and fans still espoused loudly about The Jam's credibility. People tend to forget that Paul was an established artist, who was in the second phase of his career, and had more to lose if his political stance went tits up. Of the other major artists who supported the cause, only Paul and Billy Bragg devoted the time, and while many others supported the cause, they didn't have the clout or the credibility.

The cause that Paul tied himself to was unfashionable, with even Labour party supporters finding it hard to come to terms with the changes that Kinnock had embarked on. Socialism was still a dirty word with the masses, who were caught up in Thatcher's I, me, myself society, while Paul wholeheartedly supported the working class cause. Live Aid would have had a big impact on their thinking, but they must have known deep down that politics are as far away from charity as you can get. Until Bob Geldof shoved Live Aid in the politicians' faces, they had conveniently ignored the problems but if liquid gold (oil) had been discovered in Africa, it might have been a different story. There was no doubting Paul and Billy's honesty and convictions, but it was always going to be difficult educating the masses. The tabloids, which were read by the bulk of the working class, were up Thatcher's arse, and were manifestly helpful in getting her elected and supporting her policies. It was impossible for a left-wing politician to get elected in the eighties and Paul and Billy were always fighting a losing battle.

On March 28, the Council released their next single, 'Have You Ever Had It Blue', which featured on the soundtrack of Julian Temple's film of Colin MacInnes' book, *Absolute Beginners*. The film was much hyped up and even though David Bowie starred in it, it was very pretentious and a bit of a flop. The single was released on 7 and 12 inch version and on music cassette. The B-sides contained an alternate version of the title track and another Mick Talbot's instrumental, 'Mr Cool's Dream', which was also featured in the film, and the title would later be hijacked by Iain Munn for his book on The Style Council.

The tune was a reworking of 'With Everything To Lose' with Paul writing the lyrics and a different title, and produced by Clive Langer & Allan Winstanley who had recorded with Madness, Dexy's Midnight Runners, Elvis Costello, Teardrop Explodes and Lloyd Cole & The Commotions. The renowned jazz giant Gil Evans was hired to write the score for the movie, and I went to meet him, and see him play, at Ronnie Scott's with Paul, Mick, and Steve. Gil's track record in jazz includes working with Miles Davis, Cannonball Adderley, Astrud Gilberto, and Kenny Burrell and many others. As far as pop music goes, he collaborated with Jimi Hendrix, but this was cut short by the guitarist's untimely death, and in the late eighties, he appeared in concert with Sting. Chris Hunter, who enlivened the Council's 'Solid Bond', single was fortunate to be selected to play in one Gil's big bands, playing second alto to Lee Konitz who was one of the great alto jazz saxophonists. The band playing on the single would have been made up of the cream of British jazz.

The arrangement wasn't as complex as I thought it would be, and it really swings. Billy Chapman from Animal Nightlife takes the tenor solo, and given the great players that Gil was associated with, I have often wondered what he made of his solo – if he heard it. I liked Billy a lot, but at the time he wasn't a great saxophonist and many of his solos bore no resemblance to the chord structure he was playing over. When they recorded 'Best Thing', I pulled Paul up about Billy's solo and told him the changes were wrong and I could get a session player in to take the solo. Paul rebuked me and wouldn't hear of it, saying: "Bill looks good, I don't care if the changes are wrong – it sounds ok and that's all that matters."

The single went to number 14, one place below 'The Lodgers' and although a great tune, it wasn't commercial enough for the top 10. Had the film been a big hit, there's no doubt the single would have sold and they would have scored a bigger hit. Perhaps if they had recorded in a more direct Style Council way, it would have crossed over, but it's a little too jazzy and subtle to appeal to a mass audience. I am surprised that no modern jazz singers have picked up on this tune, and couple of other early Council numbers. Although jazz was popular at the time, aside from Courtney Pine very little broke into the mainstream and the charts. Sade was massively popular, but she was more pseudo than jazz.

Following this single, they decided to release a live album, *Home And Abroad*, which as far as I am concerned was a big mistake. Had I still been at Polydor, I would have done everything I could to talk them out of releasing this album. After I left, the Council still recorded several gigs every year, but at this time, they had neither enough recordings nor tunes to do justice to a live album. When I was researching Paul's archives for a Style Council live compilation, released in 1998, I found out that most of the tracks were seriously overdubbed, particularly Dee's voice. Both live and on record, Paul chose keys that suited his range, but not always Dee and many of the songs they sang together suffered because of this. I doubt that Paul did this deliberately, as with Mick he would encourage everyone who played with the Council, and like Billy Chapman support their efforts wholeheartedly. The dates and venues were not even listed on the original releases, with hardly any taken from their early gigs. Unfortunately nobody copied the masters and the original recordings are now lost, and the overdubbed tracks are really of no value.

Home And Abroad came out on May 9, went to number eight, and stayed in the charts for eight weeks. The album has many of the best tracks of the Council's early period, but releasing a live album at this time was an error, and it would have been better to wait a few more years.

This album turned out to be the last that Peter Wilson produced for the Council. There were no doubts in my mind that Peter was a good producer and musician, and he did a fantastic job with both The Jam and the Council. In addition, Peter had to tolerate me sticking my nose in, which I did regularly, but he always listened and he was a good ally when there were problems. Paul perhaps wanted to move on to recording music that required different production values to what Peter could offer. Peter had a successful career and worked with The Blow Monkeys, who were led by Paul's pal Dr Robert.

Around this period, Polydor negotiated a new contract with Paul. Unbelievably, they gave him a golden handcuff deal worth one million quid an album. On hearing this, I did a Victor Meldrew and shouted I don't believe it. It staggered me and I wondered how Polydor could justify this deal. After all, they knew exactly what sales were needed to recoup such a large advance, and the bulk of the sales would have to come from the UK. Up to this time, *Snap* was the best selling record by either The Jam or the Council. This two LP set, released in 1983, featured the best of The Jam's singles and album tracks went platinum and sold over 300,000 copies in the UK.

When he signed to Polydor as a solo act, Paul received a sum not unadjacent to what The Jam would have received, which was easily recouped on the first two albums. I could have understood it if Polydor had upped the ante to a half a million pounds. This wouldn't have been that difficult to recoup, and at the worst, they would probably have broken even, thus avoiding going into the red. In addition, this huge advance would heap on Paul even more pressure than he had in The Jam, as he would have to deliver top five singles and albums from now on, and there would be no room for records like *Café Bleu*, or 'Money-Go-Round'. The Council were selling marginally better in foreign markets than The Jam, but still hadn't made the headway in the States, and with this kind of advance they would need to sell as many records there as they did in the UK. Even though they were now on Geffen, which was a credible label, they had cut back on touring worldwide, and by the end of 1985, they'd played less than a hundred gigs in total, which would have a negative affect on sales as well.

The Council's singles that followed their second album didn't even make the top ten. In handing out such a large advance for the Council's future recordings, Polydor were not only making a rod for their own back, but also one for Paul. When he formed the Council, Paul's message was clear and he wasn't going to be put under the same pressure as he was in The Jam with three singles, an album, and large tours every year. During the first two years, the Council's records, although successful, were of a mixed bag, and alongside the pop hits were political records and his commitment to unfashionable left-wing politics, meant it was never going to be easy for the Council to crossover outside the UK. He'd been frustrated with Jam fans and the fact that more often than not his political message was lost or misunderstood, and it was not that much different with Council. Like The Jam, the Council's not so commercial recordings sold because he had a large and committed following that was truly dedicated to the band and his music.

I am sure when it came time to re-negotiate John would have tried it on, but I bet this offer of a million quid surprised him, and John would have bit off more than Polydor's arm – he would have swallowed the company whole. Whenever John talked about the music business he would say, the King is dead, long live the new King. John would have been aware that no matter how popular you are today, the next week you could be at the bottom of the pile, the record business is that fickle and loyalty is not high up the agenda of most record companies, if it ever was in the first place. Had I gone to my (old) bosses with this kind of deal, they would have sent me to see the company shrink, or assumed I'd been on the nose powder. There's no doubt that Polydor wanted to tie Paul to the company, and would have used this enormous advance as golden handcuffs to keep him firmly tied to Polydor for the next three years. From now on, it meant that every album had to sell a minimum of 300,000 copies in the UK, which wasn't that tall an order, providing they had three big hit singles on them. To recoup, and make a profit on this deal the Council albums would have to go to number one in the charts and stay there for a month, as well as being accessible to the American and other foreign market.

In December, they released for the Japanese market a version of their next single, 'It Didn't Matter' before it went on sale in the UK. The B-side was a cover version of the Lionel Bart song, 'Who Will Buy', which was taken from his musical *Oliver*, based on the Charles Dickens novel *Oliver Twist*. Bart was one of the outstanding British songwriters of the fifties and sixties, and penned many hit records including, 'Fings Ain't What They Used to Be', which gave Max Bygraves a top five record in 1955. With his penchant for using cockney English, he was a precursor of Steve Marriot and Damon Albarn. Paul's vocals are underpinned by Mick's sparse Wurlitzer electric piano and although there are a few flat spots, he delivers a poignant rendering of this ballad.

In 1986, the Council hardly toured and for a workaholic musician like Steve White this would have been an anathema. Frustrated with this inactivity he formed his own jazz group, The Jazz Renegades, and I was roped into managing them. As well as supporting Art Blakey's Jazz Messengers for two weeks at Ronnie Scott's, in the New Year, we played a gig at the Palladium as part of the Soho Jazz Festival with, amongst others, Marc

Almond and Georgie Fame. Following this, they undertook their own small tour of Japan. The remainder of the band comprised Alan Barnes (tenor), Patrick Bettison (bass), and Steve Rose (piano & Hammond organ). Steve Rose had played double bass on a TSC tour and we later found out, bizarrely, that he was Max Bygraves' illegitimate love child. When this story broke in a tabloid it really disrupted his life and for a time he had to go into hiding. One of the journalists involved called me up and I declined to give him any information, or comment on the matter, although he'd done his homework and knew I'd worked with Paul, and told me: "There's an earner in it for you if you have any good stories." I told him where to stick his money and his paper.

In an effort to get even further away from The Jam, Paul decided to front the Council without his guitar and told *Record Mirror* that he wanted to sing more, and that playing the guitar got on his tits. This was a mistake as his guitar playing was part of the sound of the Council and his style had changed considerably when he moved on from The Jam. While he was no Eric Clapton, he wasn't half-bad and whenever he fronted the band without being attached to his guitar, Paul always looked self conscious, awkward, and danced marionette like. He wasn't a mover in the James Brown mould. However, this was the eighties, the age of the synthesiser, drum machines, and electronic dance music was the fad, and it wasn't hip to be seen as an axe man. The more melodic soul sounds of the sixties and the seventies were considered old and outdated, and during the next two years, he would not only move away from The Jam, but also the sources of his inspiration. Had he kept with the founding principles of the Council and kept the floating line up, perhaps he could have got away with this move.

As far as touring went, the Council spent the same amount of time on the road as they did in their inaugural year, which was next to nothing. During the latter half of the year, they went into Solid Bond to record the third Style Council album, and what a record this turned out to be. The Council moved into 1987, with money in the bank, and a millstone around Paul's neck, and whatever came next, needed to be big.

CHAPTER 13

The Council's Future Definitely Wasn't Orange

No matter how much money you give an artist, there's no guarantee that they will produce a great album. All bands go into the recording studio with this intention and do their utmost to succeed, but most great albums just happen. When Chris Parry turned down the original demos for the Jam's third album, they went back to square one, and after returning to the studios recorded what turned out to be their best album. It was well after the event and much later that it was hailed as 'the' classic Jam album. At the time, no one knew what was in store for The Jam, and as far as I was concerned, they would easily top *All Mod Cons*, it was a racing certainty. The Jam was soaring, and the sky was the limit. When they went into record what turned out to be the last album *The Gift,* Paul tried to make it a great album and failed. I have been in the studio when an album is really 'happening' and there is a buzz about the recordings, but rarely do you hear, or read of an album being talked up as being great before it's released. The Style Council now had to follow up their number one album and as far as Polydor were concerned, 1987 would see their chickens come home to roost.

With the advance safely banked, there was no choice; the next Council album had to be a classic. There was no room for an album as eclectic as *Café Bleu*, or as political as *Our Favourite Shop*. At the very least it would have to include three top five singles, with perhaps one going to number one and be every bit as commercial as 'Speak Like A Child', 'Long Hot Summer', 'My Ever Changing Moods', and 'You're The Best Thing'. If Paul delivered an album of this quality, it would make the Council bigger than The Jam. One question Polydor should have asked when they gave him such a large advance was whether Paul wanted the pressure that this kind of success would bring a second time?

Eighteen months after the release of the Council's second album, on January 9, Polydor released the first single from the new album and it didn't seem to me like the major change in direction that some people have said it was. The intention from day one was for the Council to record different styles of music with no two records alike. Even with The Jam, no two albums were the same, although there was thread running through them all. The Council had done the jazz, pop and the political stuff and it was time for a change. Although 'It Didn't Matter' went to number nine in the charts, the music press slated it. The B-side, 'All Year Round' wasn't that great, although this was down to the backing track, which tends to drag and sounds like it was recorded at the end of very long session. The lyrics are good, and if they had recorded this with a lighter, jazzier feel, it would have been better. Later on in his solo career he would re-record this and it would see the light of day on a rarities 3CD set.

In February, the long awaited film *JerUSAlem* was shown, and I can add nothing to the comments already made about this Tragical Mystery Tour (my thanks to Gary Crowley for this quote). It was pretentious and given that none of the four Councillors could act, it was always going to be poorly received and critically drubbed, although it was shown on one of Channel 4's more poncy programmes. The film contained more of Paul's irony and humour, which unfortunately got lost, and it gave his critics a late Christmas present. I have seen only a few clips, which is enough for me; as a songwriter Paul is one of the best, as an actor the least said the better.

During an interview for Dave Barber's BBC Radio 2 documentary on the Council, Paolo Hewitt commented on the *The Cost Of Loving* album, stating: "Paul should have made a sixties or seventies soul record and not an eighties soul record." In some ways, he his right, as Paul's songwriting lends itself better to the type of soul recorded during these decades. However, when Paul formed the Council, he wanted to get away from the retro style of The Jam and recording a sixties or seventies style soul record would have been seen as retrograde step, and had Paul done this, his critics would have slaughtered him.

The Cost Of Loving would be the first album that Paul produced on his own, and given that I was never happy with 'Shout To The Top' I was very sceptical about his ability to produce himself. The lack of 'production' values shines through, and although Robin Millar helped out, he really needed a co-producer. In the past Paul had successfully worked with Vic Smith and Peter Wilson, and if you fast-forward to his solo career, Brendan Lynch. There is no doubt that neither Vic nor Peter were the right kind of producer for the kind of music Paul now wanted to record, but rather than go in solo, it would have been better to go in with Peter. Many of the songs on the album suffer from the basic arrangements being leaden and a little sterile. Until now, all the Council records had a good feel about them, and their pop tunes had a real sparkle about them. Even the political songs felt good, but as far as 'It Didn't Matter' goes, they micro-waved it when it should have been simmered over an open flame! Although it reached number nine it spent less time on the charts than 'Money-Go-Round' and 'Solid Bond', two of the Council's less commercial records, and even the ultra political 'Soul Deep' hung around a week longer. It would also be the last top ten single that the Council would score for the rest of their career, as with the exception of their 14th single, the Council's records thereafter struggled to make the top thirty.

The debut single set the tone for the album and it must have sent shivers up the spines of Polydor's execs considering what they'd paid for it. The failure of the first single made it even more difficult for Polydor to sell the album into the shops and nothing short of a miracle would recoup their investment. The second and third singles would have to be out of the box. Polydor released *The Cost of Loving* as a double album on February 6, with each LP playing at 45 rpm, making them more user friendly for DJs. When it hit the streets, it was greeted with studious indifference by the music press, and although it went to number two, it only stayed in the charts for seven weeks, one week less than their previous live album.

Paul's rap songs were never that great and although The Dynamic Three do a good job on 'Right To Go', he should have left this style of music alone. Rap is a specialist area, requiring a different approach in every aspect, and Paul's songwriting doesn't lend itself to this automated style of music. 'Heavens Above' is almost in the (old) Council tradition and nowhere near as lumpy as some other tracks. 'Fairy Tales' is a thinly veiled attack on Mrs T, but lyrically not as strong, lacking the bite of 'The Lodgers'. Johnny Mealing, who I rated, came in to write the score, but even he couldn't save the day. The version of Anita Baker's 'Angel' is smooth but let down by a clunky drum machine and Dee's rather wafer-thin vocals. The drum programming lacks imagination and only Paul knows why Steve White's talents weren't put to better use. He is one of the few drummers who knows where the 2 and 4 are, even on a drum machine.

I rate 'Walking The Night' but, once again, it could have been so much better with the right production and arrangement. Lyrically this is a good song, but Paul's vocals are a little strange, as he tends to speak the lines, giving them a stuttering feel. 'Waiting' is altogether too dreary and needed to have the same feel as 'You're The Best Thing', or 'Boy Who Cried Wolf'. Recorded in this fashion, the song is really wasted as it has real potential, but then so do many of the other tracks on this album. It was released as the second single on March 6, with 'Francois' as the B-side, which was included in the film *JerUSAlem*. With another Johnny Mealing arrangement in a similar vein to 'A Stones Throw Away', it is a gem of track and maybe wasted as a B-side. John Valentine of the Valentine Brothers was brought in to do a re-mix on 'Waiting', but it didn't help the song which only reached 52, staying in the charts for three weeks. The title track, 'The Cost Of Loving', is a very good song, although it's a bit muddy and one of the few tracks on the album Mick plays organ. 'A Woman's Song' is a nice lullaby but Dee struggles and there are a few flat spots with an uncomfortable feel to her exposed vocals. Originally, they were going to go with a double A-side of 'Angel' and 'Walking The Night' and even though they pressed promo copies, the idea was scrapped.

As far as the production goes, Paul must shoulder the blame for the failure of this album. The credits show a number of people assisted with the mixing of the tracks, The Valentine Brothers, Curtis Mayfield and John Valentine, but it made no difference and the album is woefully short on production values. Producing records is a difficult and specialised art form, and above all, you need to be objective. Few artists are objective about their own music, and Paul isn't among them. 'Right To Go' and 'A Woman's Song' shouldn't have been considered, as they are simply not good enough. Maybe his ego got the better of him when he decided to take over the role as the sole producer, as even his vocals suffer in a way that hadn't happened on previous recordings. John left all the musical decisions to Paul but with this album, he needed someone on the inside who could constructively criticise the content. It's important from the start to get the backing track right; if you don't, everything else suffers, as many of the tracks on this album do.

Many were critical about his voice, but I don't remember anyone complaining about his voice on 'Long Hot Summer' or 'You're The Best Thing'. Around this time, there were quite a few blue-eyed soul boys who were shifting records and having big hit singles and albums. Paul Young and Mick Hucknall of Simply Red fame come to mind. Although both possess good voices, they are one-dimensional and tend to sound the same on every song they sing. The top soul boy at the time was George Michael, who at least wrote his own tunes and had a voice. Paul's response to the criticism was a knee-jerk reaction, angrily announcing that he would come back with a series of non-album singles and there would be two further Council albums. One would contain original material, while the second would be a covers album of favourite tunes, although this project wouldn't surface until 2004.

They undertook a 13-date UK tour in support of the album, which included three nights at the Albert Hall. It was dubbed The General Election tour and was the first gigs since 1983 that the Council played, without Steve White. Like the record, the new band floundered and the music press were highly critical. Indeed, they wouldn't let up until the Council turned up their toes.

On October 23, they released a new single, 'Wanted' (or 'Waiter There's Some Soup In My Flies') co-written and (now) co-produced with Mick Talbot. Paul tried this clever sub-titling with The Jam, but all he succeeded in doing by adding the pretentious additional words was to give his critics more ammunition. This single has a lively feel and treads more familiar ground, although it needed to be speeded up a notch and the unadventurous production lets down a very good pop song. If it had the zing of 'Speak Like A Child', or the bounce of 'My Ever Changing Moods', this could have been a big single, but at least it made the top twenty, just.

The B-side contained a re-working of 'The Cost Of Loving' and as far as I am concerned, it's the best thing the Council recorded in 1987. It's slower than the album version, and pared down, with the production of this track spot on and a great vocal. It was featured in the film *Business As Usual,* a story about unity winning over the system, something close to Paul's heart – although this could only happen in a film. They should have considered this as a single and they might have surprised themselves. It certainly wouldn't have faired any worse than previous singles.

As far as Polydor were concerned, *The Cost Of Loving* album was a very expensive failure. Looking at the statistics for it, the chart position indicates it was a success, but if you look at the weeks in the charts, the true indication of sales, the album was a failure. The Council's first two albums hung around for 38 weeks and 22 weeks respectively. The number two position was down to the Council's faithful fan club rushing out and buying the records in the first few weeks of release. When you look at the weeks in the chart, what is clear from this statistic, is the second single, 'Waiting' made no significant impact on the album's sales.

During the Council days, Paul tried to cover as many musical styles as he could, and while he might not have been as successful with some, at least he tried to be different. The next few years were dark days and this album was the beginning of the Council's slide. Polydor's investment of a million quid was now looking very shaky, and it was going to be interesting to see what excuses the execs would come up with to cover their arses.

The advance Polydor paid for this album magnifies the failure, and this aspect needs to be closely scrutinised. In Iain Munn's book, *Mr Cool's Dream* it was claimed (by Polydor) that the Council's best selling album, *Our Favourite Shop*, sold a million copies worldwide, something I have my doubts about. In the UK the album went straight to the number one spot and sold enough to receive a gold disc (100,000 copies) and it stayed in the charts 22 weeks. The last chart entry (in *Music Week*'s official chart) was on September 14, 1985 when it was at 84 and had still not sold enough copies needed to reach platinum status, (300,000).

As far as America goes, they were only popular in New York, Los Angeles, San Francisco, Chicago, Philadelphia, and a few other cities and if they managed 100,000 (genuine) sales, Geffen would have demanded they come over and undertake a large tour. In fact, the album hardly made a dent in the *Billboard* charts. If the album sold another 100,000 copies in the UK after it went to number two, it would have needed to sell 700,000 copies in countries like Belgium, Australia, Germany, France, Italy, Holland, Sweden, and Finland, where 25,000 sales will give you a gold album. Whichever way you look at it, the figure of a million sales doesn't add up.

I could be wrong as I have never been privy to the sales figures for this album, but I know the sales of all the other singles and the debut album, released prior to *Our Favourite Shop*. By the end of 1985, I doubt that *Café Bleu* sold more than 250,000 copies in the UK and stayed on the charts 16 weeks longer with only two singles taken from it. The three singles taken from *OFS* went to 3, 23, and 13 in the UK charts and had little chance of selling outside of the UK, given they were politically motivated songs. 'Boy Who Cried Wolf' was released as an alternative single, but would had to have been a top five record in every country to achieve the sales that are claimed. Whatever the sales were, advancing Paul a million quid for his next album at this time was at best naïve; a half a million pounds would have been more pragmatic, and taken the heat off both Paul and Polydor.

Polydor complained bitterly about the album, particularly the MD Richard Ogden, who stated that they had paid a million quid and then (Paul) he delivers this bloody album, with a terrible sleeve and an awful record. This remark has a very hollow ring, and the complaints seem to be an excuse to cover the companies' shortcomings with the regard to the deal they gave Paul, and their own involvement in the recording of the album. Ogden was the youngest ever MD and perhaps lacked the experience of running a major record label. Prior to this, he'd been Polydor's International manager and his previous experience was in management, where he'd co-managed Motorhead and managed The Motors, who had a hit with 'Airport' (4) in 1978, and 'Forget About You' (13). Their highest placed album was *The Motors,* which staggered to 46 in the album charts. Strangely enough, after I left Polydor one of the members of this band took over my old position.

When Ogden first heard the album, he summoned Sara Silver who'd worked with Paul for some time and asked her to talk him. I knew Sara as she was there when I left the company, but she had neither the influence nor the authority, and by this time was in no position to do anything about it. As the Managing Director he was paid a lot of money to make these kinds of decisions and should have confronted Paul personally, and told him to his face that he thought his album was bloody terrible. A.J Morris, who I worked for, wouldn't have hesitated to front up Paul, but he was a very experienced MD, with a wealth of executive experience behind him.

It was strange to offer Paul such a deal at this stage of his career and Polydor could have inserted a yearly option clause in the contract to pick up, or drop the artist just in case anything went wrong. Incorporated in the new contract was a clause that every album must include two singles, which this album clearly didn't. Polydor could have exercised this option and refused delivery and I can think of a million reasons why Polydor should have. More often than not, there is also a clause that allows the company to refuse delivery on an album, or single, if they don't believe it to be commercial viable. There was a precedent for this with The Jam when they delivered the first recordings for their third album *All Mod Cons*. Chris Parry sent them away and told them to come back when they had commercially viable tracks. When they finally finished the album, it turned out to be a classic.

Had Polydor had the courage to turn this album down, it might have changed the career of the Council as it did with The Jam – and who knows where they would have gone. There is no doubting the new management's admin skills and business acumen, which were first rate, but as far as dealing with an artist like Paul, they didn't have a clue. Their man-management and A&R skills were negligible, as this album proves and they took the easy option and shovelled all of the blame on Paul. I've no idea how I would have dealt with this situation had I still been there, but certainly would have had a word with Paul about producing himself.

As for the sleeve being awful, this too has a hollow ring to it, and it seems that Polydor was looking for additional excuses for its failure. I went through this shit with the company when 'Speak Like A Child' was released in a plain black sleeve with just the Council's name on the front and it sold in excess 250,000 copies and went to number four in the charts. The packaging for *Café Bleu* wasn't as good as *Our Favourite Shop*, but it still did the business. The reason these records sold well had nothing to do with the sleeve; it was because they were well-produced records containing some great Weller tunes. The sleeve was only a pastiche of The Beatles "white album" and by this time, the Council had scored six top ten singles, a number one album, and Paul wasn't an unknown quantity. No matter how you dress up *The Cost Of Loving*, it wouldn't have sold any more than it did, and what is clear about the third album, it wasn't as good as the first two albums. Regardless of the sleeve design, it was never going to shift sufficient albums to recoup the million pounds that Polydor had paid for it.

With *The Cost Of Loving* it appears that no one in the company had any idea what was going on until they'd completed and delivered the finished masters. There was no input when it really mattered, at the start and midway through the recording. It is hard to understand why no one at Polydor saw fit to check the progress of the recordings and what direction the album was going in. After all, he could have been recording anything, even a pretentious little classical number.

From the time I started working with The Jam, I was the only person in the company the Wellers would deal with, and this caused me many problems with the new team. Over a long period, I'd built up a relationship with John and Paul, and this trust was not only hard fought for – it was hard won. I spent a great deal of my time on the road and in studios with The Jam and the Council, and was able to see how each track was going, often from the demo stage. I honestly never found Paul difficult to deal with, but when there were problems, I went to see him on his own turf, and always dealt with him on a one-to-one basis. I was no yes man, for either Paul, or Polydor and had many an up and down with both the (my) company and the Wellers. It takes time to build a working relationship with Paul, and it's no good sitting behind your big desk with a nice fat title pontificating – you have to roll up your sleeves and get amongst it.

There's no doubt that Paul can be a formidable and difficult person to deal with, and at times a pain in the arse, but this was an important album, not just for him, but for Polydor as well, especially considering how much money was at stake. The execs at Polydor must accept their share of the blame for its failure, and the deal they gave Paul, which contributed greatly to the eventual demise of The Style Council.

Paul was going through one of his most arrogant periods, at the time listening only to the sound of his own voice and those that surrounded him. Mick would have backed him solidly, and although he was 50% of the Council, it was still Paul's band, which many people forget when they criticise Mick. The new execs at Polydor complained that Paul wouldn't listen to them, but why should he? By the time they arrived, he had racked up four number one singles and two number one albums, and how did their track record compare?

It would have been a different story had Paul recorded *The Cost Of Loving* in the same style as the first two Council albums. Perhaps, instead of harassing The Valentine Brothers to re-mix the tracks, it might have been better to bring them in from the beginning to co-produce both tracks. Listening back to the album now, there are lot of good ideas and songs, but no cohesion. Somewhere buried deep amongst the tracks could be a good album, although whether it would still be worth a million quid is open to debate.

Paul has never taken criticism well and his first response is to go on the attack and respond with a barrage of invective, finishing up with inviting the miscreant to step outside for handbags at ten paces. It's like the songs he writes are a part of him, like an arm or leg, and he would often explode at the tiniest criticism. Paul has always been aware of the quality of the songs he has written, and for the most, has always been honest about them. Whenever we were discussing the merits of a particular tune he was always truthful, and he knew when he had written a great one. His songwriting portfolio contains very few duff songs, which is something he should take immense pride in.

With this album, the Council lost the carefree spirit that permeated throughout the first two and half years. Even *Our Favourite Shop,* with its explicit political overtones, still had a diversity of songs and line-ups. True, it was not as varied as *Café Bleu*, but none the less, it was in the spirit of the Council, as Paul originally perceived the group. The 'Orange' album changed all this, and the Council was never the same band again. Now, Paul was shackled to the confinements of a normal band, exactly as he had been with The Jam. For my money, having to work with a fixed line-up affected all future recordings. Paul had boxed himself into a corner.

They saw out the year and on December 4, Polydor released three EPs featuring album tracks and B-sides. The only record to chart was 'Mick Talbot Is Agent 88', which got to 100 in the charts. There was no valid reason for releasing these EPs, and given the bad publicity that followed the 'Orange' album I am not sure why they were released.

The Council went into 1987 needing to re-establish their winning ways and failed comprehensively. Not only that, with the relatively poor sales of *The Cost Of Loving*, and the singles released that year, their royalty account would have slipped into the red. In a interview with *Uncut* magazine many years after the release of *The Cost of Loving* Paul talked about it, saying: "There wasn't enough passion in the performances, and the songs weren't up to scratch." As well as stating (by this time) the Council had become an anachronism and had lost their fire. As 1988, came in to view the Council needed to pull a chicken as well as rabbit out of the hat to retrieve the situation.

With the perceived failure of *The Cost Of Loving,* Paul and John lost the support of Polydor, as they did after *All Mod Cons*, but the problems this time were more serious. After I'd left no one came in to fill the gap between them and the company. I say this without a hint of ego, as had I stayed I doubt the story would have turned out any different. Now, there were no familiar faces around, and over the years, Chris Parry, Tim Chacksfield, Peter Schultz, Jim Cook, and A.J Morris had departed. Although there was the odd problem, there had been a reasonable working relationship throughout Paul's career and the first two years of Council. From 1986, the turnover of executives was high, even for the record business, and Polydor had to fit revolving doors to the execs offices to keep up with the personnel changes.

By the mid-eighties, the business was unrecognisable from the one I started in. Conglomeration and globalisation were the key words; music, what did that have to do with anything? Since the eighties PolyGram has been sold off several times, and with every sale came a change in corporate and local management. As well as the staff, the constant upheavals caused problems for the bands signed to the label, and these changes would affect an artist of Paul's stature. The first thing on any new management agenda is to cull the artist roster, with all the time and money put into these acts effectively wasted. After *The Cost Of Loving,* there needed to be a period of calm and a coming together with the company, but this wasn't going to happen. Stability and success wouldn't come Paul or Polydor's way for some time.

Whoever the new team were, they inherited a deal that was unsustainable and were in a position that was nigh on impossible to turn around. There was nothing they could do, short of renegotiating the deal downwards, which I doubt, John would have agreed to. For the moment, Polydor's back was against the wall, and they had to carry on as, after all, Paul was one of the few genuine stars amongst the crud on Polydor. Everyone was aware of just how talented a songwriter he was and that there was always a (slim) chance that he would be able to reverse the situation.

Since mid-1985 the Council started to spiral down, and for the first time in his career Paul was no longer flavour of the month with the music press that until *The Cost Of Loving* had lauded his every move. Many scribes wrote Paul's obituary, waiting for the moment they could seal his coffin. Along with acts like Spandau Ballet and Paul Young, he was written off. I remember one journalist stating: "Weller's best days were behind him and he should pack up now while the going was good and live off his past successes." There is no doubt his arrogant and self-righteous attitude did him no favours, and made more enemies than friends, and it would be difficult if not impossible to win them back. The failures of 1986 and 1987 meant that 1988 would be more important than any other year in the Council's career.

John and Paul always had a siege mentality, even when things were going well for them, and the failure of *The Cost Of Loving* meant that ranks were closed, the drawbridge raised. The next single was important for everyone concerned with Council and it needed to succeed at every level. The record company badly needed Paul to have a (very) successful year, as their credibility, like that of the Council, was at rock bottom and they were known throughout the business as a no-hope company. There was a ray of hope, Paul's re-working of 'The Cost of Loving' on the B-side of 'Wanted' showed that the magic hadn't left him and he was still capable of pulling it round. The first single was important and failure wasn't in the equation, as it would have a disastrous affect on the forthcoming album and question whether there was any validity in carrying on with the Council.

1988 commenced with Paul immersing himself in The Modern Jazz Quartet, the Swingle Singers, and Claude Debussy. These three disparate influences became Paul's world, while politics went on the back burner. I've never been keen on the idea of mixing classical and pop/rock music, all I can say is, it's not wise to mix these two very different types of music. This had been tried many times before and there was the odd tune that made the charts. Many progressive (sic) rock bands in the seventies utilised classical music, to varying degrees of success, Emerson Lake & Palmer had a number two single with *Fanfare For The Common Man* the same year The Jam were in the charts with *In The City*. Their LP *Pictures Of An Exhibition,* based on the work of Mussorgsky, was a turgid and dire affair, and one of the most pretentious and boring LPs you can hear!

Fed up with being unable to play live and miming to backing tracks, Steve White left the band, never to play with the Council again. As far as touring goes, during 1988 the Council didn't bother at all, making it doubly difficult for Polydor to shift albums. Polydor released their first single from the album on the 20 May, with yet another pretentious title, 'Spank (Life At The Top Peoples Health Farm)' b/w 'Sweet Loving Ways'. It came in every format available, but this made no difference, and it only reached number 28 in the charts. Paul stated that it was a modern version of Bob Dylan's 'Subterranean Homesick Blues'. Dylan excelled at this type of song and was able to pull it off many times. His lyrics on 'Subterranean Homesick Blues' are a seamless flow of searing images, with a strident backing track, and the song is superbly produced. In contrast, 'Life At The Top Peoples Health Farm' fails in every department, with a messy, average vocal and brass arrangement, and some truly dreadful drums.

Polydor wanted to bring in Norman Cook or Arthur Baker to sort out the problems, but I doubt that would have made any difference. Paul & Mick produced the single, although I don't hear much of Mick and as in previous recordings, the production suffers. The B-side 'Sweet Loving Ways' is a jazz/soul number that hearkens back to how the Council sounded at the beginning, and is a good tune, but by now only the fans were flipping the singles. Even *TOTPs'* interest waned and they cut short the video due to an offensive line in the second verse. Leaving this line in was risky as the Beeb rarely played records that contained even mildly offensive language, and in the past both The Jam and the Council censored their singles. Had the offensive line in 'Walls come Tumbling Down' not been changed it's unlikely that Radio 1 would have given it much daytime play and the chart position would have suffered.

Listening to the opening lines of the first two verses, I realised that I'd heard similar lyrics before. In 1962, Joe Brown & The Bruvvers had a number two hit record with the song 'What A Crazy World We're Living In' and included the lines, "Dad's gone down the dog track / mother's playing bingo". I know Paul had an eclectic taste in music, but Joe Brown? There was a tendency for Paul to abrogate his responsibilities when it came to the second half of the Council's career and the songs he wrote. After the release Paul tore the single to shreds, stating he didn't know where he was at the time he recorded this song. I doubt that anyone else did either, including many Council fans. I'm not sure why he took this attitude as in The Jam it was different story, and he ferociously protected even his weakest songs.

On June 24, Polydor released the Council's fourth album, *Confessions Of A Pop Group*, the longest album they released, and split into two separate sides. The first, entitled 'The Piano Paintings', featured jazz and classical numbers, which were illustrated in the accompanying booklet by Dan Davies' paintings. These illustrations described each track visually, and although they are quite striking they really only added to the pretentiousness of the album. The second side was titled 'Confessions Of A Pop Group' and contained the more jazzy soul numbers.

Featuring a sequence of songs under the collective title of 'The Gardener Of Eden Suite', I would have paid good money to see the face of the execs at Polydor when they first heard this cod classical music. After the failure of *The Cost Of Loving,* they needed Paul to deliver a commercial album full of pop hits, and on hearing this they must have reached for the valium. I have only played this track twice and I found it pretentious. I've never believed for one minute in the cockeyed theory that Paul "was being pretentious to take the Mickey out of being pretentious, whilst being perceived to be pretentious at the same time." This is bullshit – you are either pretentious or you're not! Like the Council's humour, this pretentiousness was over the top, and way off the mark. The small band of Cappuccino Kid followers may have understood all of this, but the bulk of the Council fans didn't, as the sales of this album showed, and 1987 saw the demise of their fan club, The Torch Society.

I felt sorry for Dee as she didn't have the voice to carry off this type of song, and it was unfair to place in her spotlight like this. Freddy Mercury got away with singing with Montserrat Caballé on 'Barcelona' because he had a great voice, and the technique and vocal range to do it justice. Dee just didn't have the range, or the technique for this kind of music, but then neither does Paul. John Mealing did a great job on the arrangement, but it remains one of the few pieces of music that Paul recorded which is utterly forgettable.

It's a real shame because elsewhere on the album there are some very good songs. 'The Story Of Someone's Shoe', where Paul re-creates the MJQ/Swingle Singer's sound, isn't a bad effort. Paul isn't a torch or jazz singer, but his vocals pass muster on this track. What nobody seemed to notice at the time was that Paul had written some keenly-observed lyrics reflecting the emotions that follow a one-night stand. Perhaps if it had a more conventional Council arrangement (if there is such a thing), the song would have been better received. 'Changing Of The Guard' is another good song, but once again Dee's vocals are exposed and the arrangement is a bit wishy-washy. Mick's solo pieces, 'The Little Boy In The Castle', 'A Dove Flew Down From The Elephant and Castle' are in the style of 'Le Depart', which was featured on the *À Paris* EP. After the demise of the Council, ill-informed critics saw Mick as a soft target and vilified him, knowing that he was unable to answer back. Mick, by his own admission, wasn't a great composer, and it was Paul who insisted his instrumentals appear on their records. He never tried to present himself as the new Jimmy Smith, or Rachmaninov, he just wrote a few nice tunes.

'Why I Went Missing' and 'How She Threw It all Away' are two tracks that really work, and Dee's vocal on the former compliments Paul. They're unpretentious, and what the Council were about when they set out – good music. 'Iwasadoledadstoyboy', apart from having a stupid title, should have been left off the album, or hidden away on a B-side. 'Confessions 1, 2 & 3', apart from the fake applause, is a solid track, but the production suffers, although Mick is featured on his mighty Hammond. I've left 'It's A Very Deep Sea' to the end, not only because it is the best song on the album but because it stands up alongside the best tunes that Paul has written throughout his career. The very poignant lyrics are delivered with a resigned vocal that sounds almost as if he is going under, and Mick's sympathetic piano is spot on. Even the sound effects (nicked from 'English Rose'?) add to atmospheric mood of the song.

As far as marketing goes, Polydor threw everything at the album, but it still bombed. With the aid of a walking frame, it went to 15, staying in the charts for just three weeks, 35 weeks less than *Café Bleu*. To get this album into the top five it needed big hit singles, which the Council hadn't had for a long time. As far as Style Council artwork goes, Simon Halfon got it right with the record sleeves he designed, always managing to capture the ever-changing moods of the band and the man. Looking back at these austere photos, they truly reflect the Council at this time. However, Polydor complained about the sterile packaging and the now familiar black and white photos, as they did with 'Speak Like A Child', and *Café Bleu*.

In one interview Paul admitted that the (*Confessions*) album bewildered Polydor, as did *Café Bleu*. The company had good reason for their bewilderment, as *Confessions* probably cost them three times as much as *Café Bleu,* and sold half the amount. Polydor released the Council's debut album on the back of five hit singles, including three top five records and fifteen months after The Jam's career had ended with a number one single and album. *Confessions* came out after a string of relatively unsuccessful singles.

Even though *Cost Of Loving* went to number two in the album charts, it didn't match the sales that the Council's first two albums achieved, or stay in the charts as long. If the Council's first five singles hadn't have made the top ten, *Café Bleu* would doubtless have suffered the same fate. Had this happened I am sure Polydor would have gone with a second album, but if this had failed in the same way as *Confessions* did, they would have dropped Paul from the label. Many bigger artists than Paul have been dropped when their album sales fell and they failed to recoup the advances paid (which are not returnable). The view would have been: why throw good money after bad, after all we have the back catalogue to milk, let some other company have a go.

When Paul signed to Polydor as a solo artist, the deal was reasonably structured for both sides and took into account the possible failure of some of the Council's records as well as not placing too much of a burden on Paul. There's no doubt that after *Our Favourite Shop* the contract needed to be renegotiated, and better terms offered for an extension, but the world-wide sales figures and the type of music the Council were recording didn't justify such a huge advance. A half a million pounds would have been more than fair and reduced the burden on both Paul and the record company, and going into 1989, they wouldn't have been looking down the barrel of gun.

On July 15 Polydor released the *1, 2, 3, 4,* EP featuring 'How She Threw It All Away' and 'In Love For The First Time' b/w 'Long Hot Summer' and 'I Do Like To Be B-side The A-side'. Things must have been desperate to include 'Long Hot Summer' on this single, even if the 12 inch version was a Tom mix, whoever Tom was. The single went to 41 in the charts, adding to the failure of the album, and it would have been better to have not released this and left the album to rest in piece. 'In Love For The First Time' is nice summery samba and a good pop song, although Mick's wittily-titled instrumental wasn't one of his best.

When Paul launched the Council, he refused to make records just to satisfy his fan club or the record company. However, if you're going to take a million quid from the record company they're going to look a little more closely at your records. This attitude only works when your royalty account is deep in the black and you are at the top end of the charts, or release a multi-million selling record like Michael Jackson's *Thriller* album. Polydor didn't complain at 'Money-Go-Round' or 'Soul Deep' because they weren't exposed and any losses would be made up by the more commercial records released by the Council. This balance suited both Paul and Polydor and the deal was fair to all sides. During a meeting with Paul, the subject of this advance came up, and laughingly he said: "How could I turn a million quid down, if they're [Polydor] stupid enough to pay me that kind of money – I'll take it!" He is right, of course, except that it placed an incredible burden on him, far heavier than anything he carried on his back with The Jam.

Towards the end of the year, many rumours were floating around, including one where Mick had caught a mysterious virus and might not be able to work for two years. Another was that Paul wanted to kill off the band so he could spend more time with his family. If there was a right time to kill off the band, then it was now. It's hard to see why they carried on, as the writing was on the wall at the end of 1987 – in capital letters. Paul's ego certainly had the better of him, he took his excesses to the limit, and was perhaps unable to look in the mirror and admit that he'd got it wrong.

1988 was a sad year for the Council: no tour, a couple of failed singles, and an album that in all honesty defies description. They went into the Townhouse Studios, to record their next single, a studio where many fine Jam tunes were recorded. No matter what the Council recorded next, it was unlikely to do the numbers to get them back to where they were when they started, and the next album would have to be massive, which, was a big ask, even for someone with Paul's talents.

CHAPTER 14

It Just Came To Pieces In His Hands

For more than a year scribes had been prematurely writing the obituary for both the Council and Paul, and heading into the New Year, they were sharpening their pencils for the final eulogy. For two years, the Council's appeal had been on the wane to all but a small nucleus of fans as their singles and albums failed to reach the top end of the chart. Polydor had gone through more changes and Dave Munns, who I knew from his EMI days, came in to run the company. Like the Council, Polydor was struggling to get back on track and if the Council could deliver the goods, the fortunes of the company as well the Council would change.

The eighties wasn't a great time for music and as the decade progressed, the music didn't, with the major innovations being technological. Drum machines and synthesisers were the order of the day and the music became formulaic and sanitised. Fashion has always gone hand in glove with music: in the forties, the hipsters were bopping to the big bands in their Zoot suits, and in the sixties, us Mods had our tonics. For me, the majority of eighties bands had the fashion sense of drunken clowns, their hair was cut by the local Council and Max Factor was more important than talent. As an A&R man, I *had* to go and see acts like Kajagoogoo, Howard Jones, Duran Duran and a lot worse, if that's possible. There were a few good bands and some good records, but the majority were tedious coat hangers. It was an era where producers would become as important and nearly as famous as the artists were, and every record had to be re-mixed, whether it needed it or not. The 12 inch single had to have extra tracks, and it didn't matter whether the tracks were throwaway songs, or late night mixes done under the influence of alcohol and drugs. It wasn't until the end of the decade, when house, acid, and garage came along that things brightened up. I liked much of this but as for working with it – no thanks. It wasn't that I was out of touch, or too old, as if this had been the case I couldn't have handled The Jam. Whether it was jazz, pop, or punk, I always stuck to the mainstream and rarely ventured outside. Although sceptical at first, Paul threw himself wholeheartedly into this scene, proclaiming this music as new form of Modernism.

Whatever Paul thinks, he is a mainstream artist and songwriter, and whenever he's stepped outside of this it was a lottery as to whether it worked. Even the cod jazz wasn't bad, but it was clear that his songwriting style sat uncomfortably with rap and the eighties soul funk scene. Even when he superglued his lyrics on, it didn't work. Going into 1989 the failures of *The Cost Of Loving* and *Confessions Of A Pop Group* were consigned to the bin, with Paul himself distancing himself from the failed records the Council released over the past three years. The big question was whether Polydor would invest another vast sum of money in another un-commercial album?

On February 10, 1989, the Council released a cover of Joe Smooth's 'Promised Land' b/w 'Can You Still Love Me', and the single came out on every format possible, with just as many re-mixes. This made no difference: it didn't even make the top twenty, stalling at 27, and selling only to the ever-diminishing fan club. The 'b' side was an indication of what lay ahead with the Council's fifth album, whether anyone at Polydor bothered to give this an airing is a moot point. If they had, they would have known what was coming. The single wasn't that bad, but like many of the later recordings, it lacks the feel of the Council's earlier recordings. Their version coincided with the release of Joe Smooth's original and some thought that Paul was cashing in to the detriment of Joe's chances of having a big hit. I don't buy this as the Council's version never crossed over and the airplay on Radio 1 wasn't that great. Joe's version peaked at 56 and I doubt that it had the potential to get into the top 20. Whatever his personal losses were, he made it up with the royalties on Paul's version, and as it's been on every *Greatest Hits* package, it's been a nice little earner for him

Around this time, the lads got up to a bit of skulduggery and recorded various mixes of 'Like A Gun' for release on Eddie Pillar's Acid Jazz label, under the name of King Truman. Polydor quickly rumbled the ruse and the single was withdrawn. If you want to buy a copy on eBay, it'll cost you £100. No doubt, the lads wanted to get their own back at Polydor, hoping the single would chart, showing up their own record company.

Polydor's next move – perhaps out of desperation – was to release a greatest hits package entitled *The Singular Adventures Of The Style Council Volume 1,* which for some reason, didn't include 'Milton Keynes'. At the time, Paul was at loggerheads with Polydor, not even speaking to them, and PolyGram's TV record division handled the compilation and the marketing. Released on March 10, the CD included a few extra alternate mixes and, boosted by an extensive TV advertising campaign, it went to number three, staying on the charts for 15 weeks. Releasing a greatest hits package at this time didn't bode well for the next album, as this was a stopgap, looking back on a career that was faltering.

This was followed by the Style Council's ultimate single 'Long Hot Summer '89' b/w 'Everybody's On The Run' and released on the 19 May. There was an extended version of 'LHS' and two different versions of the B-side for the 12 inch and a CD singles. Peter Wilson was surprisingly dusted down to assist with the re-mixing. Given how perfect the original was, I'm not sure why this single was proposed. The classic version has an atmospheric and haunting vocal from Paul, while on this version Paul's vocal is anything but, and adds nothing. The original went to number three in the charts but this re-mix only managed to creep into the top 50 going to 48. The B-side was yet another track taken from the Council's forthcoming album, which featured lead vocals, by Bryan Powell who had exactly the kind of voice for this style of music.

Now it was time for the new album, the infamous, *Modernism: A New Decade,* which ended Paul's career with Polydor. When the record was delivered, after hearing the content MD Dave Munns considered it uncommercial, but was unable to turn it down on this aspect alone. When Polydor renegotiated Paul's new deal, they gave him total artistic control. Munns, knowing the record wasn't going to do the business, activated a clause in the contract that stated every album must contain two singles, which this album clearly didn't, and turned it down. Following *The Cost Of Loving* and the *Confessions* albums, and the failure of their previous six singles to get beyond their ever-decreasing fan club, the Council hadn't been shifting records in large quantities for several years. This – and the fact that Polydor would have to shell out a million pounds – would have come into the equation. It's quite possible that by turning down the album, Munns was trying to provoke Paul into writing and recording better tunes that were more commercial as Chris Parry did with *All Mod Cons.* Another avenue he could have explored was to have offered a lower advance, but knowing John as I do, he would have refused this outright. The Wellers' relationship with Polydor at this time was unfriendly to say the least.

It was clear by the end of 1988 that the Council's tank was empty and they were running on fumes. Paul was on record stating: "I wouldn't like to be forced into a position where I have to compromise and make records just because that's what the public wants to hear. I would sooner do something else." However, having taken such huge advances, and whether he liked it or not, Polydor owned his ass, and as for doing something else; the only job he'd had since leaving school, was writing songs, and playing his music. What else could he do?

After Paul's successful platinum selling album, *Stanley Road,* Dave Munns received a lot of stick for his decision to turn the album down, with many industry figures putting the boot in. Richard Ogden was quoted as saying: "I would never have rejected the album. He was the most important artist on the label and they'd still have made money (*with what?*) out of The Style Council. It would be like EMI dropping Paul McCartney." This is rubbish, given that the Council hadn't sold records for several years and by the time *Modernism* was recorded their record sales had more than halved. When Paul was given a million pounds for *The Cost Of Loving*, (by Richard for that 'terrible album') in 1986, he didn't have the stature that the success of *Stanley Road* brought, and after the release many were convinced he was on the way out. Even Andy McDonald, who'd signed Paul to his Go! Discs label, agreed that it was a dreadful thing to do to someone with that much talent.

These opinions are fine, and spoken with the luxury of not having to make the crucial decision to shell out the money. Any record company handing out this kind of advance would be looking for a return on their investment, whether you're the biggest record company in the world or a small independent label. The record business isn't philanthropic, and stature alone is never enough to warrant paying out so much money. You have to be sure the records are going to sell. Paul McCartney has a huge back catalogue to fall back on, something the Council and Paul Weller didn't have. Perhaps Richard thought he was donating to a worthwhile cause when he gave Paul a million quid for *The Cost of Loving*. As far as John was concerned, charity starts at home!

Dave Munns was one of the few music men to run Polydor and I had a lot of respect for him. His confrontational attitude did him no favours with Paul, but what else could he do – he was in a corner. Polydor's artist roster was barer than Mother Hubbard's cupboard, and they could ill afford to lose such a potentially money-making artist who was one of the few genuine stars on the label with a long-term future. However, *Modernism* wasn't commercial and the losses were escalating, Munns had no option but to pass on the record. His view that *Modernism* wasn't a daring and innovative move is not far of the mark. Splitting up The Jam and forming the Council was brave and courageous, and required a great deal of bottle. The first two Council albums were daring and could have cost Paul dearly in career terms. However, by the time he got to *Modernism,* it was clear that Paul had lost his way. The two previous albums and singles highlighted the problems he was going through, and there was no way *Modernism* would halt the slide.

Munns' decision was certainly an affront to Paul's ego: he was astonished and angered by the decision and couldn't understand why they wouldn't release the album. He'd been signed to Polydor for more than ten years, and felt the company owed him for all the success he'd achieved in the past. In an interview with *Uncut,* he was ambivalent. Typical of the man, when he heard the news that Polydor weren't going to release *Modernism,* he went on the defensive, stating: "I've made all those fuckers millions of pounds," but made no mention of the large advances he received for commercially unsuccessful albums, now conveniently swept under the carpet. At the time, Paul delivered *Modernism,* his last, (and most) successful album was *Our Favourite Shop,* released in June 1985, three years prior to *Modernism.* The oldest adage in the record business is, *you're only as good as your last record,* and this applies to all artists, including Paul. His past successes will make no difference to his new label V2. If he's not at the top end of the charts, or selling records he will be dropped. Sorry mate, as you said, that's entertainment.

Other than a top 20 record in May 1988, the Council hadn't seen (real) success since 'It Didn't Matter', which went to number nine in January 1987.

When you're selling records everybody loves you, but by now the Council's sales and chart success had dropped off and the company would have had to hand over a huge advance for an album that clearly wasn't going to sell. The only time loyalty comes into play is when the artist and the record company are both successful. If another record company had offered Paul a bigger advance for his records, he would have dropped Polydor just as quick as they dropped him. This is the way the industry works, and you'd have to be naïve, or extremely arrogant, to believe any different.

Modernism was a flawed record with production values that suggest it's definitely not the finished article. The production credits read 'Produced by The Style Council', but I can't hear Mick's touch – he must have been wearing mittens when they recorded the tracks. Around the time of *All Mod Cons,* it was mooted that Martin Rushent should be brought in to produce

The Jam, which I was against, but he would have been an ideal candidate to produce this album. In the early eighties Martin produced Human League's *Dare* album which spawned the number one record, 'Don't You Want Me Baby'. One of the best producers of his generation, he excelled with electronic blue-eyed soul and was a wizard with drum machines. He had a background in punk and had he come on aboard, he might have saved this album.

The biggest problem with this kind of music is the unrelenting metronomic four-on-the-floor bass drum pattern, a seamless beat that really only lends itself to rapping and vocal chanting. Paul has always been a conventional lyricist, which has been the foundation of his writing and his principal strength during his long career, and tunes written in the standard pop format just don't fit the house/garage format. When he started as a teenager, he wanted to write songs where the words meant something, and were not just fashionable statements. Paul's writing style is neither in fashion, nor out of fashion, it is classical, which gives the majority of his songbook a timeless quality, and why he has had such a long career.

There is also no doubt that Paul's voice is far from suited to this type music, and if you go back and listen to 'Long Hot Summer', 'You're The Best Thing' and the 12 inch single version of 'The Cost Of Loving', Paul delivers a very soulful vocal. His vocals on songs like 'The Whole Point', 'My Ever Changing Moods', and 'It's A Very Deep Sea' are great and fit the track. Phil Oakey of the Human League doesn't have a great voice by any stretch of the imagination, but Rushent's production neatly glossed over this, whereas on Paul's later records his vocal problems were all too apparent. Listen to the two different versions of 'Everybody's On The Run', where Bryan Powell's vocal is strident and right out front, with the backing track supporting his vocal. Bryan came from the gospel circuit, which might have had something to do with it. Paul's vocals are at the back of the mix and sound tame in comparison. Paul never had that type of voice, which many of the tunes on this album cry out for.

Modernism also lacks the rush that was typical of this kind of music and is capricious and inconsistent. The opening 'A New Decade' is virtually an instrumental with some rapping by Jimmy Ruffin, which was recorded for the 'Soul Deep' single but never used, whilst 'The World Must Come Together' sounds unfinished. With the box set, the lyrics of all the songs were in the booklet and on this tune, there were many lines where I couldn't work out what Paul was singing. I phoned and asked what they were, but he couldn't remember what the missing lines were. 'That Spiritual Feeling' is probably the best track on the album, but it's an instrumental. 'Love Of

The World' is interesting, but tends to drone on. On 'Sure Is Sure', Paul's falsetto vocal just doesn't work and sounds forced and a little thin, although his lead vocal is better. Had Polydor accepted *Modernism*, this track would have been a single, and a picture bag was designed to go with it, but they didn't and there would be no more singles.

NME's Steve Dalton summed up this period and the album concisely when he wrote: "Weller was 'swallowed up and suffocated' by modern dance trends, with the Council aiming at Prince-like Technicolor funk, but settling for Shakatak shoddiness," though this comment was a little hard on Shakatak, who were neither pretentious, nor shoddy, and never pretended to be anything other that what they were. The price tag for the album was Saville Row, but the music turned out to be Man at C&A.

Apart from the B-sides of the last two singles, I didn't get to hear this album properly until the mid-nineties when I was putting the *Council* box set together and on hearing it, I was mightily surprised. All I knew was what had been said at the time it was delivered and I wasn't sure what to expect. While going through the Council's demos and covers for their box set, the studio copied *Modernism* for me. When I went to collect the tape, a black guy who was in another studio recording, asked, "Who's this band?" I replied, "Paul Weller, it's the last Style Council album, it was recorded at the end of the eighties." He gave me a sideways look, shook his head, and said, "Man, it sounds great. It could have been recorded today."

Although, the album was up to date, and maybe a little ahead of the current trends, the style suited neither Paul's voice nor his songwriting. Maybe if they had given the tracks to a garage re-mixer, he could have done something with them. By now, his fans had given up, and it was only out of pure loyalty that the staunchest were still buying his records. Had he gone beyond this album he would probably have lost them too. At this point Paul's relationship with Polydor had soured to a point where there was nowhere for the Council to go, and it was left to the lawyers sort out redundancy terms. One thing was for sure: with the massive investment made in Paul, Polydor wouldn't let him walk away that easily.

It was a sad end to the Council's career. To some extent, no matter what he did, it was going to pale beside The Jam and there were many who had still not forgiven Paul for breaking up the group. It wasn't until the success of *Stanley Road* that he was able to unload this burden and be seen as Paul Weller, a great songwriter and artist in his own right, and not Paul Weller of The Jam and that funny band he had in the eighties.

After the intenseness of The Jam, there was a light-headiness and exuberance about the Council, their records, albums sleeves and even their promo videos. They had a bright and breezy outlook and the odd laugh. With a wider horizon, Paul's songwriting talents developed and progressed quickly and he was able to hear and play his songs exactly as he wanted. The floating line up was an innovation and well ahead of the times. No other bands were willing to take a risk like this, and it's hard to imagine any group from the past five decades releasing an album where their leader doesn't appear on one of the tunes on their debut album.

The Council's career was a tale of two halves. The first half was unbridled success, where even the politically motivated tunes made the charts, but the second half of the Council's career is a different story, a bit like watching a Technicolor film that half way through, and without warning, changes to black and white. The single 'Milton Keynes' was the start of the rot and a big mistake, which Paul acknowledged after the event. After *Our Favourite Shop*, for the first time since signing to Polydor, John and Paul were no longer among friendly faces and instead found themselves surrounded by some very smooth talking executives with oversized egos. The golden handcuff deal that Polydor gave him was a mistake, and not just in hindsight. Even after the success of *'Beat Surrender'* and *'The Gift'*, it's unlikely that Polydor would have offered more than £500,000 an album. If they'd broken into the American market and sold more in Europe, then a million quid wouldn't have been unreasonable. The bulk of The Jam's sales were in the UK, and even though the Council were more successful in Europe, they didn't penetrate the big American market any more than The Jam.

When I discussed the deal with Paul, he said it was an offer he couldn't refuse, which is quite true, as you would have had to be a fool to walk away from this kind of money. I left the meeting wondering if Paul had realised that he was handcuffing himself to Polydor and would be under even more pressure than he was when he broke up The Jam. The monies paid for the first two Council albums were acceptable and their sales, along with the singles, recouped the advances. In the mid-eighties, no record company would have handed out a million pounds an album, unless they were certain of recouping this amount and making a profit. If the first album failed, the burden placed on the next would be enormous. £500,000, would have halved the expectation and the pressure. Whether this deal had any affect on Paul only he knows, but he'd been around long enough to know that there was a price to pay for walking with the devil.

Many years after the event, the execs who no longer worked at Polydor complained that John didn't see the bigger picture, which is not strictly true. When I started working with The Jam, I recall John telling me that his biggest wish was to see the band play Madison Square Garden and you don't get much bigger than that. I realised quite quickly that as far the music side of Paul went, John would have little influence, and I rarely discussed this aspect with him. When it came to discussing the Council's music, I went to Paul, as I knew he had the last word. With no disrespect to John, he wasn't qualified to involve himself with the complicated procedure of recording and production, and the execs at Polydor were well aware of John's shortcomings in this area. Paul called all the shots as far the musical decisions went, and it is unfair to lay the blame on John.

I worked at Polydor for a long time, and comprehended the way a major record company works, and I can't understand their role in all of this. They advanced him a titanic amount of money and then spent the majority of the time hiding behind their desks, complaining about the Council's records. The question I have to ask is: "What was their input and why wasn't there an A&R man assigned to take care of Polydor's interest?" I have to say, if my bosses had given Paul a million quid an album, they would have expected me to be around him 24/7, and when he woke up in the morning, he'd have found me cuddling up to him and not Dee!

No one at Polydor believed in his talent more than I did, and even though his well showed no sign of drying up, and he was still writing well-crafted songs, in 1986 he simply wasn't worth a million pounds. No one knew what direction he would take the Council in, and what effect his overt political stance would have on the future of the band. If it was done as sign of support, it was done blindly. It's fair to say that no other major record company would have offered this kind of deal at this point of his career.

The success that followed *Our Favourite Shop* was inconsistent, paling in comparison to the first half of their career. After each perceived failure, Paul distanced himself from his records, and found excuses for their failure, like: "I don't know where my head was when I recorded that stuff." On *The Cost of Loving*, it was suggested he'd used the wrong drum machines and synthesisers, which is crap – the album would have turned out the same whatever machines he used. Since when have machines made music? Maybe the programmer was at fault; after all these machines would only play what you tell them, they can't think for themselves.

It seems Paul's ego got the better of him, as on the later records, he was the writer, producer, singer, arranger, guitarist, and probably made the tea as well. I have never doubted his songwriting ability for one moment, but as far back as 'Shout To The Top', I had deep reservations about whether he was capable of producing the Council's records. In one way or another I have been there since 1978 and witnessed how stubborn and egotistical he could be. When I commenced working with The Jam, I was given a soddin' hard time and it took a long time to gain their confidence to get to point where I was trusted. Even so, had I failed to deliver the goods for Polydor, my bosses would have taken me off the case and replaced me with another A&R man. There's no way they would have advanced, even a quarter of million pounds without having their man in there, looking after their interest.

Paul was focused throughout the first half of the Council's career and although there were a few fuzzy moments, the images, and music, although eclectic and varied, were sharply defined. Paul seemed to know where he was going, and even the political songs made sense and were a part of the Council's development. During the second half of the Council's career, it was the opposite with the music becoming blurred and he became even more difficult and egotistical. There is no doubt that his father's total devotion to him and the people surrounding him gave him a (false) sense of security. However, this only worked while Paul was having hits and selling records. From 1986 the Council's sales and hits declined, and the criticism of the *Cost Of Loving a*nd the subsequent singles and album bit deep, and many of his old insecurities resurfaced and perhaps a few new ones. There was no one in the camp who was prepared to confront him about these excesses, although I doubt he would have listened anyway.

In the beginning the posturing and the humour, had a naive appeal, and the excessiveness was acceptable. Later on Paul pushed this excessiveness way beyond the limits, and gave his critics the ammunition they'd been seeking. Like Paul's invective, their criticism was disproportionate, and over the top, but it was God sent, and they weren't going to miss out on crucifying him with his own words. His arrogance increased and it was Weller against the world, or so it seemed. Every artist has an arrogant streak about them, it would be impossible to survive the vicissitudes of the music business if their egos were normal. I've had the dubious pleasure of working with artists with the same amount of arrogance as Paul, but half the talent. This arrogance is part of their defence mechanism and is seen at its worse when things go wrong, and when the very foundation of their existence is threatened. After all, to be someone must be a wonderful thing, but only when you are someone.

Any artist needs to be inspired and the eighties were un-inspirational, with very few artists and bands having any real substance. In his formative years, Paul was motivated by Motown, The Beatles, The Kinks, The Small Faces, and The Who and from his own generation, The Sex Pistols and The Clash. When he formed the Council, he genuinely opened his mind to a diverse range of music, including some he couldn't play, and propelled the band forwards. By the middle of the decade, there wasn't much decent music to encourage or motivate. Great artists – and I count Paul as one – are like sharks swimming amongst a shoal of much smaller fish, and they feed off of them, borrowing a riff here, a line there, and through hard work and talent turn this into a new tune. During the eighties, the only thing Paul could have borrowed from his competitors were their make-up bags, it was that bad.

Throughout the early nineties, the critics maligned this part of his career, as they did Mick's role in the Council. When *Stanley Road* came along, suddenly the Council's name was no longer mud: they were an important stepping-stone to Paul's new (sic) found success, something that every TSC fans knew. Mick, particularly, came in for a lot of stick and without exaggeration, 99% of it was rubbish. Once the Council folded, Mick returned to being a jobbing musician and an easy target for the scribes to have a pop at.

Throughout the Council's career, the use of the royal We was used to good effect by Paul when it suited him, particularly towards the end, when the shit was hitting the fan. To this day Mick, steadfastly refuses to discuss his part in the Council with most authors, (including me) telling them he'll speak when and if an official biography of the Council (or Paul) is written. In the music business, this kind of loyalty is hard found and perhaps Paul chose Mick for this as well as his musical abilities. When the (inevitable) demise of the Council came, Mick was left out in the cold to fend for himself, but he's done all right, and hasn't changed and is still the same person I met in 1983. He ain't the millionaire some people think and he doesn't reside in a wealthy suburb, and whilst his address might read Blackheath, it's more Kidbrooke. I know, because in the sixties I used to have the occasional ruck in the pub just around the corner from where he lives.

The Council was always going to be different and Paul went out of his way to make sure of this. The music was different challenging and daring at times, allowing Paul the widest possible parameters to write within, as well as catering to his excesses. The Council never enjoyed the vociferous support that The Jam received, and their spectre haunted Paul and would do so until *Stanley Road* exorcised the problem. It's been argued that even if the

Council had made a great record, it wouldn't have been recognised, and although there is a grain of truth in that statement, it is a slight exaggeration. What's more, they did make some great records, but everyone seems to focus on the end, and the shit that went down with Paul's excessiveness, what was said in the music press, and the problems with Polydor.

Here are the thoughts of a few Council fans regarding the end, and their favourite band.

Paula Cuccurullo, an American fan, writes: "The Style Council's music was a breath of fresh air for a would-be 14 year old mod girl who grew up 3000 miles and an ocean west of where she felt she belonged. The Council opened my mind to the fact that music could be beautiful and romantic, yet still mean something greater to the world. I may not have known what miners were striking about or why, but I knew passion when I heard it and could transfer Weller's hatred of Thatcher to how I felt about our doddering old chimp in charge of the White House. Over two decades later, who I am – musical taste, political leanings, sense of style, sense of humour! – owes much to Paul, Mick, Steve and Dee, and yes even the Cappuccino Kid... no matter how much else changes in the world and in my life, for me TSC will always be the band who says 'yes!'"

Iain Munn, who has written his own book about the Council, writes: "Looking back at early 1989 there was no real indication to the fans that the band would split. We had the 'Promised Land' single, which came out in five flavours, Paul & Mick were back on TV, the well-received *Greatest Hits* package nearly topped the charts, and the first live show in 20 months was booked at the prestigious Royal Albert Hall. Things couldn't be better?

"Little did we know that an underground track by an 'unknown' band King Truman was released and that negotiations behind the scene were focused on Polydor refusing to release their new album. In the end TSC didn't split, they just faded away and it only warranted a few sentences in the music press. It wasn't a shock but luckily, I didn't know then, that I'd need to wait nine years to hear the 'lost' album. In a way the split was a good thing – the rejection of the LP kept the band at the front of many people's minds to ensure that in 2006 we are still discussing this fine musical experiment."

Dave Lodge, who edited *Boys About Town*, one of the best Jam/TSC/Weller fanzines, encapsulates what this period meant to him: "Perfect pop singles – so many of them, almost seemed like a new classic every month or two in the early years! The politics – so of the time, so real, so honest, so intense, so right (or rather left!). Different musical styles, no boundaries – guest vocalists, classical, rap, jazz, soul, pop, house, piano, funk, sometimes no guitar! European laid back, cool! Every album different –

from eclectic jazz/soul/pop to mainstream soulful pop to modern soul to classical/pop to house. Ever changing moods. '83–'85 the glory years, not a step wrong. '86 – '89 slightly off track, mistakes made but still great, brave music. You're the best thing that ever happened!"

In many ways I'm glad I was on the outside looking in, and not experiencing first hand the Council's fall from grace as their now small but loyal fan club did. After the first three years it would have hurt, and bad. Whatever else is said about this period of Paul's career, The Style Council didn't fail – they just failed to live up to an expectancy that at the time, and in hindsight, was undeliverable.

CHAPTER 15

The Last Style Council Compilation Until The Next One

When it came to the Council's back catalogue, I realised Polydor would never put the same amount of weight behind it as they did The Jam. In the beginning, it was too soon after the acrimonious ending and there were many people employed there who remembered *The Cost of Loving, Confessions of A Pop Group*, and the final album. It wasn't until the mid-nineties that the Council were seen in a better light, but even with this renaissance, they would always come second at Polydor. Even though I have a foot in both camps, and am a fan of both bands, I have always resisted the temptation to make comparisons, as both bands are the opposite of each other and significantly different. It was never the case that The Jam was better than the Council, or vice versa. Each had something singular to offer that the other didn't, and both were of equal importance to me, and more importantly, to Paul Weller's overall career.

There is a tendency for both sets of fans to dig in and defend their lines, although Council fans are not as polarised as some Jam fans. There's no doubt that Paul's attitude and invective at the time of the split didn't help, and perhaps sent a confusing message to Jam fans. Council fans are equally as defensive when it comes to the second half of the Council's career, defending their man to the hilt, even to the point where the argument is indefensible. However, this is what being a fan is all about, and I am certain the Weller (solo) fans feel the same. I have always considered myself lucky, as I can appreciate all three aspects of his career, and what all the fans should appreciate is the equal part that The Jam and the Council played in making Paul an icon of the British music industry. He wouldn't be where he is now if it wasn't for The Jam, but equally as important, he metamorphosed through the Council into his solo career, and throughout the Council's influence can be heard.

I derived great personal enjoyment from working on the back catalogue of both the Jam and the Council, as I was able to indulge my fantasies as well as earn a few bob for my endeavours. The most interesting part is the research, which is a little bit tedious, but even I learned something new about each band. Although I worked with both bands, there was never enough time to keep up with everything that went on and once I left Polydor I was an outsider looking in, which made researching the Council's back catalogue even more interesting. I have to give Paul a lot of skin, as I had virtually a free hand and he never interfered with the projects I worked on. Regardless of my relationship with the Jam, the Council and Paul, not many artists of his stature would have given anyone that kind of scope. When it came to the Council, I had unlimited access to his tape library, and could visit his vault whenever it suited me, but he never gave me access to his personal collection of tapes, which he has stashed away in a cupboard.

The very first Council compilation contained the demos, out takes and covers and was entitled, *Here's Some That Got Away*. Very few artists are prepared to release CDs containing this kind of material, but Paul was all in favour of making these tracks available. He himself collected rarities and knew what these recordings meant to his fans. On many other compilations, he took a passive involvement, but with this compilation, he was genuinely interested in the project.

The Wellers' filing system contained limited information and was nowhere as good as the one at Polydor, where the details are programmed onto a mainframe computer. When it came to the Wellers' archives I had a problem as all I had was a listing of their tapes, which meant I had to go through every tape and inspect the information. Unfortunately, there wasn't the time to check and listen to all the tapes, and I relied heavily on the cassettes in my archives. Paul and Mick were very helpful and suggested many titles, which would have been difficult to locate.

All told, nine titles were previously unreleased and included the covers of Willie Clayton's 'Love Pains', and David Sea's 'Night After Night'. These were recorded in 1986 around the time of the *Cost of Loving* album, and although good were unused. Six of the remaining songs are

Weller originals. 'My Very Good Friend', 'April's Fool' (Weller/Talbot) and 'I Ain't Goin' Under' were recorded in 1986. 'A Casual Affair' was demoed in 1985, whilst 'Waiting On A Connection' and 'I Am Leaving', with Dee on vocals, was recorded in 1988. There were few Weller originals not released during his Jam days but with the Council, there seemed to be more that never saw the light of day. The ninth song was a cover of Lionel Bart's 'Who Will Buy?', which had only been released in Japan as the B-side of 'It Didn't Matter'.

Similar to The Jam, the Council's B-sides were of the highest standard and this compilation includes 'Ghost Of Dachau', 'The Big Boss Groove', 'The Whole Point II', 'Blood Sports' as well as 'Party Chambers' from the debut single, the Latin tinged 'Sweet Loving Ways' and 'In Love For The First Time'. Three of Paul's demos, were also included, his version of 'A Woman's Song'. '(When You) Call Me' and 'A Stones Throw Away', which should have been mastered and released as they are significantly different from the originals, and could have been included as a B-side similar to both 'Headstart' and 'The Whole Point'. I included a couple of Mick's instrumentals, as a Council album wouldn't be right if his organ didn't make an appearance. This CD is indicative of just how versatile the Council were, and reflects how Paul's songwriting skills matured and developed. The tunes on this album are certainly a cut above those that are generally included on this type of compilation, and if every track had been finished, it would have made for a great Council album.

Polydor released the compilation on July 2, 1993, but it only managed to get to 39 in the charts. Paul's second solo *Wild Wood*, came out a few months later in September, and went to number two and this compilation may have fared better, if they'd waited until after the release of this album.

With *The Style Council Collection,* it was my intention to make it a best of the album tracks and B-sides as I did with The Jam. However, as the sales on previous compilations weren't that good I decided against this and compiled a 'Best Of' instead. The compilation was released by Polydor on February 23, 1996, some nine months after *Stanley Road*, which was still in the album charts. However, even though I included four of their biggest selling singles, the compilation didn't make the top fifty, which surprised me, as the track listing contained many of their finest songs. There was no doubt in my mind that Polydor were only going through the motions and did very little to aggressively market the Council compilations.

The next compilation was *The Style Council In Concert* and I had to awaken Peter Wilson out of hibernation. I gave him a track listing to listen to and he went away and chose the best versions from the 16 gigs recorded from 1984 to 1987. As with The Jam, Peter drew up a chart, which contained each song and a box for each instrument and vocal and marked each performance out of ten. I have no idea how long this took, but as there 20 tracks on the CD and it must have taken Peter an age to go through every version.

The first big band was always my favourite line up and I wanted to squeeze on as many tracks from this period as I could, as well as the early cover versions that were in the can. Curtis Mayfield's group The Impressions was a favourite of mine and I knew 'Meeting (Over Up) Yonder' and 'Move On Up' from my days as a soul boy in the sixties. I really liked, 'One Nation Under A Groove' and 'Hanging On To A Memory', and both versions were excellent with Jayne Williams playing the female chanteuse. Paul had recorded 'Move On Up' with his alter ego The Jam, but by the time this version was recorded by the Council, Paul had dispensed with the brass section and although he delivers a great vocal, it doesn't sound as good without horns.

When I discussed this project with Steve White, he reckoned The Melbourne Leisure Centre concert on August 18, 1985, was the best live recording and I included 'Man Of Great Promise' and 'Boy Who Cried Wolf' from this show. 'Up For Grabs', 'Long Hot Summer', ' Here's One That Got Away', 'Speak Like A Child', and 'Mick's Up' (one of Mick's finest organ piece) are more or less as they were originally recorded. 'It Just came To Pieces in My Hands' is virtually accapella, apart for Mick's Hammond and a spot of percussion. The medley of 'Money Go Round'/ 'Soul Deep' /'Strength Of Your Nature' came from their 1985 Wembley concerts and feature a cameo appearance from Junior Giscombe.

There are three duets, two feature Paul and Mick, on 'My Ever Changing Moods' and 'Spring Summer Autumn' with the third featuring Mick playing 'Lé Depart' accompanied by Stewart Prosser on trumpet. I've always liked this song and Stewart's playing gives it an extra edge, and the feel of Mexican Mariachi music, often heard in spaghetti western. Although there was a slightly better version of 'My Ever Changing Moods', I chose this one because of the tag where Paul ends the song with a quote from Curtis Mayfield's 'People Get Ready'.

There are two solo efforts from Paul, 'A Stones Throw Away', and 'Down In The Seine'. On the studio version of 'Down In the Seine' he sounded self-conscious on the French verse, as if he was reading the lines from a song sheet. On this version, his delivery doesn't sound anywhere near as uncomfortable. When picking the gigs to record on the various tours it was always going to be a lottery and you couldn't be certain which gigs would turn out great. I made a point of recording both The Jam and the Council in Scotland, as the gigs there were always good. I was at the Edinburgh Playhouse the night they recorded 'Stones Throw' and Paul gave a fiery performance, and I can still see him playing his cherry red Gibson guitar. Anyone who thought he'd lost his edge should listen to this version. His voice isn't at its best – it's a bit croaky in places – but this takes nothing away from the performances and you feel the real emotion of the lyrics coming through. Many artists would have overdubbed their voice in a studio but had Paul done this the magic of his performance would have been lost.

The bulk of the songs come from the Council's first half of their career, as after 1985 only three gigs were recorded which meant only two tracks on the compilation were taken from the later half of their career. On *'Heavens Above',* Dee struggles a little, and the cod funk break is a bit passé, but lyrically this is a sound tune. I've already waxed lyrically about the album version of 'It's A Very Deep Sea' and this live version is every bit as good, with a slightly jagged vocal giving this version an added poignancy. I was disappointed not to have come across a worthy version of 'The Whole Point II', but there was only one recording which was awful, so I was unable to include this wonderful song.

When it came to the sleeve notes, the fans had their say and the contributions came from many countries including Germany, USA, and Holland. What comes across from their comments is the sheer joy of attending a Council concert. You just didn't go to a Council gig to fill in the evening. It was an event, something of a celebration. Scot Moskowitz from the USA, wrote: "What so many other bands lacked The Style Council had, be it on record or in concert." And Graham Atkins from Sheffield: "Whether or not their importance will ever be fully recognised and valued remains to be seen. For me though, The Style Council was, and always will be, the best pop group in the world." The CD was released on February 14, 1998, but didn't sell enough to chart, which is a shame, as it is a great compilation.

During the second half of their career, the Council didn't play many gigs but even so, more should have been recorded. Also, the very last gig should have been captured for posterity. They must have known at the time that it was the end and it didn't matter how it turned out. I know bootlegs exist of the Albert Hall show, but it's not the same and a vital part of the Council's history is lost.

Following the success of The Jam's box set, Polydor decided the time was right for a Council box set. By this time, Paul's solo career was at its zenith and people were talking about the Council more positively. I also hoped, mistakenly, that Polydor would do a similar job with the Council as they did on The Jam. I assembled the same team of John Reed, Pat Gilbert, and Paolo Hewitt to write the essays for the accompanying book, with Iain Munn taking care of the discography and gig listing. It was also decided to include an interview with Paul, talking about the Council's career, something I wished we'd done on The Jam, though I'm not sure he would have been up for it.

It was decided that the rejected final album, *Modernism: A New Decade*, would be the extra CD and the irony of selling this album back to Polydor must have given Paul and John a good laugh. The rejected album had a mystique about it, mostly because very few people had heard it in full; however, it's no forgotten masterpiece. I spent a considerable amount of time searching for a tape of 'Harvest To The World', which was recorded for the Lenny Henry Show and featured Tracie Young & The Questions. I'd lost my cassette, and unable to unearth a copy anywhere, I even got on to the TV company, but they hadn't retained a copy of the show. After the box came out, I was visiting Paul and John at their office at Nomis, and I happened to be looking through a rack of tapes, and found a cassette with this tune on. With modern technology, I was able to master the alternate version of The Jam's 'The Bitterest Pill' from cassette, and could have used this tape. Paul was never happy about this track being included, although I'm not sure why as it's a knock out version of this classic Isley Brothers song.

The Style Council photos had met the same fate as The Jam's, and Polydor's files were empty, which meant another painstaking search unearthing the original photographers. Simon Halfon did a fantastic job on the box and the book and the finished packaging looked every bit as good as their albums and single. It was Simon's idea to include a booklet containing all the lyrics of the Council songs as an added bonus, something that we didn't do with The Jam, another error. I went to see Paul at his office to obtain copies of the lyric sheets, and was given a folder, which contained about twenty songs, and told there were no more, and to get in touch with the publishing company. Unfortunately, EMI never received lyrics sheets from Paul's previous publishers and they couldn't help out, which meant listening to each song individually and typing out the lyrics for the remaining songs, and although it took an age, it was worthwhile.

As far as the fifth CD goes, if I am going to be honest, it would have been better to select three or four of the better tracks of *Modernism*, and mix them in with demos, out takes, and covers hidden away in the Wellers' archives.

The fifth CD was undoubtedly the reason why The Jam's box set was so successful and I think the Council may have done better had their fifth CD contained more of the hidden gems. The box set was released on October 23, 1998, but Polydor didn't really get behind the Council's as they did with the Jam, and it didn't help when they released it at full price. The initial copies of The Jam's box sets were sold as a limited edition at half the price, but when it came to the Council, Polydor were not feeling so charitable and the Council fans had to pay the full whack from day one. They also held a big launch party at the WAG club for the Jam, but as far as the Council were concerned, it wasn't even tea and biscuits in the bothy! I was a little disappointed. Nonetheless, sales were more than respectable and it ended up selling around 25,000 copies.

My very last Council compilation, until the next one turned out to be *The Greatest Hits* package, which Polydor released on August 14, 2000, and although TV advertised, only reached 28 in the charts. I included 'Milton Keynes' on the compilation, as it was genuine hit. I didn't know at the time this would be my last compilation, as I had one last idea up my sleeve and wanted to go out with *The Sound Of The Style Council.* This job was given to Paul and Paolo, which miffed me a little as it would have rounded off my career with the Council nicely. This compilation was always going to be a difficult task as the majority of the tracks used were on a *The Style Council Collection* and even with Paul being involved in the project, it didn't sell that well. A TV advertising campaign might have helped, but I doubt that Polydor would have gone for this idea, given that the *Greatest Hits* was only a top thirty CD.

I always tried my best with these compilations. The Council's credibility was at the forefront of my thinking, together with the fans. One thing for sure is I never made the balls up that occurred on a recent Council CD. In the late eighties Paul's publishing company put together a compilation of his songs, using the original backing tracks, but overdubbing his vocals with a session singer. The publishing company felt that this might encourage other artists to cover his songs. 'Waiting' was one of the songs they chose to cover and Polydor included this version on the compilation. It's quite unbelievable that no one noticed Paul wasn't singing!

Many Council fans have complained about the lack of availability of Council demos, out takes and covers lurking in Paul's archives. Hidden away are many rarities that collectors would like to possess, but whether they will ever see the light of day is down to Paul. It's nearly twenty years since the band passed away, but perhaps in the near future he will be generous and allow these rarities to be released, which I know will please his many fans.

In the autumn of 2006, Polydor will be releasing the double CD deluxe edition of *Our Favourite Shop*, although at the time of writing there's nothing new going to be added. After this, I'm not sure what will happen. March 11, 2008 sees the 25th anniversary of the Council's debut single, and it would be nice if this birthday were celebrated in style.

CHAPTER 16

On The Road With The Council

With the Council Paul refused to take on the arduous tours that the Jam undertook and during the second half of the Council's career, they all but disappeared. The biggest problem that artists face when touring is boredom and the endless motorway journeys with a stop for brunch at a service area. All this travelling wears you down. The days and weeks meld into each other. There's no doubt that when you're young touring has an appeal, you have the energy of youth and everything is new. Many artists see their own country, as well as the world, when they go on tour, but once the novelty wears off, the travelling becomes monotonous. This monotony can drive you crazy, as there's only so many books to read, and DVDs you can watch. As for playing the tourist and seeing the sights, this was ok for the first few trips, but after visiting the same cities thirty or forty times, you run out of sites to see.

The record business has never been part of the real world, and when you're on the road life takes on an even more surreal feel since everything revolves around the needs of the tour and everything else is inconsequential. It's a strange goldfish bowl existence, with all energies devoted towards the two hours or so when you're on stage, and that's all that matters. The rest is tedious to say the least, and living in hotels doesn't help, as there is no substitute for your own home. Even when you can afford to stay at a five star hotel, it makes no difference, as it's not your own, and you are only keeping the bed warm for the next occupant. After years on the road, the view from the hotel window doesn't change wherever you are. Unfortunately, for all musicians and whatever music they play, the road will play a big part in their life if they want to stay at the top.

In the beginning, it would have been difficult for the Council to tour as there was no real band, and Paul and Mick didn't have enough tunes to do more than a half hour spot. In January 1983, Paul guested with Everything But The Girl at the London ICA and in May, the Council played charity gigs at the Liverpool Empire and Brockwell Park Brixton, as well as a show at the Paris Theatre in London for the BBC. The Liverpool and Brixton gigs were in support of the Merseyside Unemployment Centre and CND, and performed with a very makeshift line-up. At Brixton, the band spent most of the time dodging mud balls thrown by the crowd, but it was very light hearted and enjoyable and a signpost to how life would be on the road with the Council.

October saw the Council undertake a short European tour, which was more EUFA Cup than Champions League, with Tracie as the support act. From the outset, Paul and Mick had a youth policy and wanted the line-up to contain young musicians to give the band energy and drive. Alongside Steve White, there was the 17-year-old Anthony 'Bert' Harty from Coventry on bass. When Paul mentioned he'd found a great 17-year-old bass player, I was extremely doubtful, until I heard him play. The band included Barbara Snow on trumpet, and Hilary Seabrook on tenor saxophone.

I joined the band in Paris and we stayed at the Le Fonetenac, or the Front & Neck as Kenny called the hotel. We spent the first night in the bar and during the drinking session, I kept referring to the French barman as 'Powerful Pierre' and talking to him in a pseudo French accent. I waved my arm in the general direction of our crowd, and explained to Powerful: "All their drinks are on me, stick them on my room number." The bar was packed and later, as the other guests were leaving, many waved and said good night. I thought this odd at the time and we continued drinking into the early hours of the morning. At the end of the session, well pissed, I signed the bill, said goodnight to the barman, who I thought had taken my Mickey taking well, and gave him a tip. Appearing at the cashier's desk the morning after the gig, I received a shock, as the bill came to nearly 6,000 francs. The cost of the room for the two nights was only 1,600 francs, and I immediately thought the hotel was trying to rip me off. I demanded to see the manager, and when he arrived, had a right pop at him. After I finished my tirade he explained the bill included the previous night's drinking session, which took me aback, and I explained it couldn't have been anywhere near this much, there's no way we drunk that much alcohol. The manager produced my bar bill, and it was just over 4,000 francs. Then it dawned on me that the barman had exacted his revenge for my piss taking, and why everyone leaving the bar said good night – I'd paid for all their drinks. I apologised immediately and signed the bill; it didn't particularly worry me, and I gave Powerful Pierre a nod of admiration. He'd well and truly turned me over!

In Brussels, we stayed at a five star hotel, where the bar had a high ceiling, a massive chandelier, and a large grand piano, where Tracie's keyboard player Toby Chapman, entertained us. On our night off, my Belgian colleagues treated us to supper, and after the meal, Mick, Gill Price, Kevin Miller, and I went for it big time on the cocktails. The last two or three we drank were called volcanos, and when the waiter appeared, smoke was pouring out of the glasses. They actually tasted awful, but we somehow got them down our necks. After the restaurant closed, I found a jazz club and smooth talked the maître d' into letting us in for a nightcap. We carried on drinking and everything was ok until Gill fell off her stool, and we had to make a hasty return to the hotel. By now, it was after three in the morning, and we were all well pissed, and as we exited the lift on the floor where Paul was sleeping, Gill couldn't stop laughing, and making a lot of noise. Kevin had to walk her up and down the corridor until she stopped, and somehow we got her into the room without waking Paul up. As there was no gig the next night, we knew we could go for it. When the bars closed, we returned to my hotel room where Mick, Kevin Miller and I carried on drinking and talking until seven o'clock. As we had to catch the bus at eight thirty, Mick and Kevin returned to their rooms, and I took a shower, changed clothes, and went for breakfast, returning to pick up my bags before heading for the bus. The strange thing was that I never used the bed, and considering the room must have cost something like £60 or £70 for the night, it might have been cheaper to get a room with just a shower and a mini-bar.

The gig in Amsterdam was broadcast live on Hilversum Radio and although it sounded a little rough, the band performed well. As this was the first Council gig to be recorded, I wanted to use at least one track on the *In Concert* CD. Unfortunately, the concert was only recorded on to two-track stereo and no multi-track tapes exist of the show. In Amsterdam, we always stayed at the (Japanese) Okura hotel, and on this trip Martin Hopewell, Paul's agent since the early days of The Jam, made an appearance. Although not a heavy drinker, he joined in the late night revelry, and when the bar closed, he was silly enough to invite everyone back to his room and we drank his mini bar dry. I still remember the astonished expression on his face as every drop of alcohol was rapidly consumed. It was my turn next, and the mini bar in my room went the same way. I called up room service and we carried on partying. I was lying on my bed supping a beer when someone set fire to the counterpane, fortunately, it was extinguished before any real damage was done. The rest of the night and early morning carried on in much the same vein and we ended up in Mick's room. Paul's girlfriend Gill was well lit up and disappeared into the bathroom where she found a giant can of shaving cream, and sprayed foam everywhere. She then turned the can on me, and I made a hasty exit with Gill not far behind. As I got to the lifts, the doors miraculously opened, I dived in, hit a button, and waited before returning. When I returned there was a line of shaving foam along the corridor walls and when I entered Mick's room and it looked like an elephant had shot his lot – Gill had emptied the can!

Following the gig in Amsterdam, we drove to Hamburg, where we were booked into the five star Four Seasons hotel, not just the band, but the road crew as well. After a shower, I ambled downstairs to find a bar and as I was about to enter, I noticed a large ballroom where a posh do was taking place. Looking in to see what was happening, I spied the road crew helping themselves to the lavish selection of food and drink. Watching on was a group of bemused, well-coiffured Germans in monkey suits and ball gowns. They were none too happy with the lads, and I had to intervene and extract them before World War III started. Normally road crews are booked into smaller hotels or motels on the outskirts of the town, where they can get up to mischief without causing the band problems. A good road crew is invaluable to a successful band, and their job is extremely arduous and they work long hours. When doing back-to-back gigs, after breaking down the vast amounts of stage equipment, they have to sleep on their bus on the way to the next gig. The Jam and the Council were extremely lucky their road crews were good lads, dedicated to their work, and I don't remember too many problems occurring on either band's tours.

As we had a night off, the young lads in the band were eager to go out for a drink. The bar in Four Seasons was too expensive, even for my expense account and we went to a bar just around the corner. After a few beers, they tried to persuade me to take them on a visit to Hamburg's infamous red light district, the Reeperbahn. Most of the group were teenagers, or in their early twenties, and this was a notoriously rough area. On my first visit to Hamburg in 1969, I witnessed a mugging at nine o'clock in the morning, and as Polydor's HQ was based there, I'd visited this city many times. Parts of this seaport would frighten real hard men, never mind the Council's crew, and we stayed in the bar!

The first UK Council tour was supposed to take place at the end of the year and six dates were booked. However, these had to be cancelled so that Paul and Mick could finish recording the debut album. Although the early shows weren't that great musically, it allowed Paul to see how the songs and the band sounded live and what changes to the personnel would be needed when they played the big venues the next year.

In December, the Council made an appearance on *The Big One*, a theatrical show for peace at the Victoria Apollo, although peace and theatrical are words that have no real business occupying the same sentence. I remember Susanna York was part of the organising committee and Ken Livingstone made an appearance accompanied by his main squeeze. The venue was loaded with the leading lights from the left, CND, and the peace movement. The line up included U2, Ian Dury, Elvis Costello and many others. Paul dueted with Elvis on, 'My Ever Changing Moods' and it's a shame this version has never appeared on a CD, as it was superb.

The first full-blown UK tour was *The Council Meetings Part 1*, and prior to this Paul and Mick asked me to find musicians for the big band they were putting together. Helen Turner, a nice Northern lass, turned up in my office with a good pedigree and I sent her to Solid Bond to audition for the second keyboard gig. One evening I was in the studio when the trumpet player, Stewart Prosser, arrived for his try-out, and Paul delegated the task to Mick and me saying: "He looks all right; if he can play, give him the job." Stewart brought in his pal Chris Lawrence on trombone and Billy Chapman who played tenor with Animal Nightlife made up the horn section. Jayne Williamson was the female chanteuse, with Anthony 'Bert' Harty still on bass, and Steve Sidelnyk on percussion. Steve White underpinned the band and by now had become a permanent fixture alongside Paul and Mick. During the auditions, a funny thing happened when a guy turned up, sat at the piano, and calmly announced he couldn't play a note but was a fast learner. He was that desperate to be in The Council!

With so many youngsters in the band, there was a lot of enthusiasm for the gigs and the tour that lay ahead, which opened up on March 10 at the Chippenham Golddiggers club, and was broadcast live on Radio 1. Before the show, there was an air of nervousness in the dressing room, which affected even Paul and Mick. By the time the band went on stage, the atmosphere was tense and the whole band were shitting themselves. After a shaky start, they settled down and played a good gig, which boded well for the rest of the tour.

The Council opened and closed the show with support acts Billy Bragg and The Questions sandwiched in between. This concept was a complete success, making the Council's gigs different to all other artists touring at the time. It was brave of The Questions and Billy to play in front of such a partisan crowd, as in the past Paul's fans were not known for going along with his musical tastes. Billy Bragg was a real hoot and kept us all amused on the bus, playing his guitar and singing everything from blues to folk songs. We'd left Newcastle and were heading towards Glasgow when the coach was pulled over by the police. The tour took place in the middle of the miners strike and a couple of 'Plods' came aboard to check us out, thinking we might be flying picket. At the time the vocal group The Flying Pickets were in the charts and much to the amusement of everyone, Billy started crooning 'When You're Young And In Love' as the police officers were getting off the coach.

With a band this size, the bus was packed and inevitably split into two teams. At the front, you had the 'Cynic Clinic' lead by Paul. At various times during his life he'd stop drinking, or become a vegetarian, and was surrounded by his acolytes, who had miraculously seen the light and overnight became veggies. Mick ably captained the 'A' team who were the 'drinkers', and we were entrenched at the back of the bus. There was none of this 'woosy' food for us, we liked our meat raw, and a drink or three, and as for sleep, that was for wimps. We would party all night, and try to get some kip on the bus. Kenny Wheeler, Paul's tour manager, wasn't always happy with our boozing and would wait until we dropped off, and shout loudly, "Are you asleep", and keep us awake for the remainder of the journey. Whatever Kenny, or come to that Paul, thought about our drinking, it never affected the band's performance, and everyone was on time for the gigs. As young as the band was, they were very professional and their performances never suffered.

When we recorded the Council at Newcastle City Hall, and the Glasgow Apollo, I asked the engineer in the sound truck to record Billy's set. As he was playing solo it was no big deal, and it would only cost Polydor a couple of reels of quarter-inch tape. Afterwards, I gave Bill the tape and told him too keep it to himself, as I wasn't sure the company would be pleased at paying for his recordings. After the show, I asked Bill for one of his promotional T-shirts and he sorted one out, and it surprised me when he asked me to pay for it. That's socialism for you!

There were many good piss ups on this tour and the session at Glasgow was memorable as Mick threw a wobbler, which was a rare sight. We were staying at the Embassy Hotel and three of Polydor's directors turned up for a pose and apart from talking to Paul, they generally ignored the rest of the band. Mick, who'd drunk a lot, came up to me and aggressively asked why the execs were ignoring the rest of the band, and just starfucking with Paul. I quietened him down, gave him a large Pernod & OJ, and explained that these executives were long on ego, but extremely short on charm and personality, and they didn't have the ability to mix freely with the lads.

The European arm of the tour kicked off in Brussels and I joined the band in Paris for the third gig and was looking forward to staying at The George Cinq hotel. This hotel had a reputation as being one of the best in the world, and I'd dreamed of staying here for years. The rooms were furnished with antiques and original paintings, and the cost of one night was way beyond my wages. As the Council were booked in for a couple of nights, and Polydor were paying, my ship came in.

Hotels of this quality don't mind rock bands staying, and generally have a wing where they can stash unruly people out of the way from their regular (rich) guests. I'd booked separately knowing what would occur if the hotel realised I was with a band, and was looking forward to being treated like a millionaire. As I checked in, a couple of the roadies, Robbie Glandfield and Ray 'Rat' Salter spied me, and Robbie yelled out: "See you in the bar Den, don't forget your wallet." On hearing this, the girl on reception asked, "Are you with the pop group"? I could hardly lie, and replied: "Yes I am," and I ended up in the annexe, which had its own entrance in a side street. I don't recall how much the hotel charged but the breakfast – orange juice, toast, coffee and a piece of Haddock with poached egg – cost about £25, and that was in 1984.

With no gig that night, Mick and I decided to make a day of it and wandered from one Parisian watering hole to another. As we passed a shoe shop I spied a nifty pair of red, green, and yellow boat shoes and considering where we were, they weren't that expensive. We entered the shop, I removed my American Bass Weejun loafers, and tried them on, and as they looked the business (remember I was pissed), I purchased them. I told the girl not to bag them up, I'd wear them, and we left the shop and carried on with our drinking tour. After the night's session, Mick once again crashed in my room and when I awoke the next morning, I was unable locate my loafers. When he finally awoke, I asked if he had seen them and he mumbled: "No the last time I saw them was in the shop where you bought your new shoes." I suddenly realised, when I left the shop, I hadn't picked them up, and as the Weejun's were brand new, I was gutted. I'd bought them at Simon's in Covent Garden, and they cost around £75! Turning to Mick I asked, "Where the fuck did I buy those boat shoes, where was the shop"? Mick helpfully replied, "I don't remember Den, somewhere in Paris, I think?" We spent the whole morning walking round the area visiting every shoe shop, but were unable to locate the missing loafers, and the boat shoes turned out to be anything but cheap!

On the way to the gig in Bochum, which many English squaddies attended, we stopped over in Düsseldorf to shoot a promo clip of 'My Ever Changing Moods' for German TV. Paul had everyone appear in the film, even though many weren't in the band. Following this, they played a concert in Berlin, before making the long drive back to Utrecht for the last gig of the European leg. On April 8, they played a warm up gig at the 100 club prior to flying to Japan for two gigs, where they filmed the video *Far East & Far Out*. The next stop was the USA, where they played two gigs in Los Angeles and New York, and on their return home, they played a benefit gig for YCND, in Anthony Harty's hometown of Coventry.

On July 7, along with Madness and Bronski Beat, the Council played a miners' benefit in Liverpool. Madness made their own way while everybody else travelled up on the Council bus. The appearance itself went well and I recall everybody on stage for the encore, the Smokey Robinson classic, 'Shop Around'. Kenny Wheeler was a great tour manager but would always insist on doing a head count before giving the nod to the driver for us to be on our way. Bronski Beat sat at the rear of the bus and the driver had turned the lights down so we could get some kip. Kenny walked up the aisle counting aloud, and when he got to the rear, he let out an almighty groan – he'd caught Jimmy Somerville locked in a heavy embrace with his boyfriend. Kenny quickly returned to his seat and spent the remainder of the journey with his flat cap pulled over his eyes drinking beer and muttering to himself, "I don't believe it," à la Victor Meldrew.

On September 7, they and Wham! played another miners benefit at the Royal Festival Hall, which was attended by Arthur Scargill. When he showed up back stage he was flanked by a couple of goons, and looked more like a Mafia Don than the leader of the miners.

In October, they were back on the road in the UK, for *The Council Meetings Part 2* and performed another ten concerts. For this tour, Paul and Mick decided on a change of format for the show. The original, somewhat pretentious idea was to have a short play between sets, which never happened as the leading actor thankfully broke his leg (sic) and Tracie stepped into the breach. The Edinburgh show was great and when we arrived back at the King James Hotel the band was in high spirits. We hit the bar for a big party and I recall having to bung the manager and the barmaids quite a few quid to keep it open for an extra couple of hours. When they finally closed, the boys wanted to carry on, so I bought a couple of bottles of Pernod and enough orange juice to mix with it. We polished this off and before going to bed, at about 5am, I told Mick: "Whatever you do, don't drink any liquid when you wake up." There was more Pernod in our system than blood, and a glass of water would have kicked it off again. When Mick boarded the bus next morning, I could see he was still steaming and hadn't heeded my advice, and drank orange juice and coffee at breakfast. As he entered the coach, he gave Kenny some real abuse, telling him to have a go at Paul for being late for the bus and he was a pain in the arse for the next hour. We were all nursing hangovers and just wanted to get our heads down, and it wasn't until he passed out and went to sleep that we could get some kip. Mick had a canny sense of humour, although you never knew with him, he could have been putting on the whole thing and it was just an act. I also remember we stopped at a motorway service area for refreshments and we drove off thinking Mick was in the [bus] toilet. A little later, everyone realised that he hadn't boarded the bus and we'd left him stranded at the service area.

The Council returned to Europe on October 22, playing gigs in Italy, Germany, Holland, and Austria. The night before the gig in Amsterdam, my Polydor colleagues took the band to a restaurant for dinner and quite a few European bigwigs attended. This was something I hated as I had to be on my toes and lay off the alcohol. During the meal, the waiter tapped me on the shoulder and said there were three girls outside asking for me, but he couldn't let them in as they were very drunk. I went outside and lo and behold, there stood Sarah, Keren and Siobhan of Bananarama, well pissed and demanding to be let in the restaurant to see their mate Paul. I tried to reason with them, but they wouldn't listen and they gave me some serious abuse, shouting out they would have a word with their mate Paul when he got back to London. As much as I liked the girls, and I've had some great times drinking with them, I have to say they were that gassed up it was more than my job was worth to let them in!

Following the dinner, we had to return to the hotel by cab, as the old Bill had nicked the tour bus for parking on double yellow lines. We hit the bar and ended up drinking made-up cocktails well into the early hours. Brian Hawkins, who handled the merchandising, ordered a round and told the barman: "Make the next cocktail up from the brown, blue, and green bottles." I have no idea how many we drank or, whether we enjoyed them, and at about 3am, Mick fell asleep on one of the sofas. I saw an ideal opportunity for a wind up. I collared Helen Turner, borrowed her make-up bag, and made up his face like an Aunt Sally, with large red rouged cheeks and plenty of lipstick. Helen looked at my make over and decided it wasn't quite right, and spent the next 20 minutes finishing him off, and Mick looked a treat. A little later, Mick woke up, and said, "I'm going to bed lads, see you in the morning, goodnight" and it was difficult not to laugh. Once he left, we fell about and wondered how he would take the joke when he looked in his bathroom mirror. The next morning Mick entered the breakfast room dressed in the same clothes, and still made up, but by now the cosmetics was smudged all over his face. We erupted with laughter, as did the rest of the diners in the room. Mick, with an innocent look on his face, asked, "What's the joke lads?" One of the roadies told him to look in a mirror, and on seeing himself he feigned surprise and said, "Which one of you bastards is responsible for this?" There was nothing precious about Mick; he could laugh at himself the same as if the joke was on someone else, he was that good a bloke.

The band finished off the year with a benefit for Animal Rights at the Winter Garden in Margate, an organisation that Gill Price whole-heartedly supported, and two nights at the Royal Albert Hall in London.

That year we recorded six concerts at The London Dominion (March 15), Newcastle City Hall (19), The Apollo Glasgow (20), Tokyo Nakano Sun Plaza Hall, Japan (May 4), The Apollo Manchester (June 14) and The Liverpool Empire (15).

The personnel in the band was Paul Weller (vocals & guitar), Mick Talbot (Hammond organ, piano & vocals) and Steve White (drums), with honorary Councillors Jayne Williamson (vocals), Billy Chapman (tenor saxophone), Chris Lawrence (trombone), Stewart Prosser (trumpet), Helen Turner (keyboards and backing vocals), Anthony Harty (bass and backing vocals), Steve Sidelnyk (percussion).

When you go on the road everything becomes a blur, you lose track of time and never mind what day is it, what week is it? During one tour, we'd been drinking non-stop for a few days and after a very heavy night, Mick crashed in my room. I awoke after a couple of hours of kip in a cold sweat, and thought we'd slept through our early morning call and were going to be late for the bus. I looked out of the window, to see what city (country) we were in and couldn't see any recognisable sites. Panicking, I rang Kenny, only to find out it was a day off. He was more than a little pissed off with me for waking him up early. I knew we were somewhere in Europe but didn't dare ask him where. When you're pissed, it all looks the same.

When Paul wasn't flying, we travelled everywhere by coach, which meant we had a lot of free time on our hands. During one tour, I'd been on the road for a week and was partying 24 hours a day and my heavy drinking caught up with me. I can't even remember where we were, but after one heavy all nighter, I awoke feeling dreadful, hung-over, dehydrated and I couldn't stop drinking water. I'd lost my appetite and couldn't face the thought of eating solids, and decided to fly home early. I went into Polydor the next day and sat at my desk faking it, when the 'old man' stuck his head in and asked why I was in the office. I muttered something about having some important work to do, but he was having none of this and told me to go and see Dr Drexler, the company MD in Harley Street. I told him I would make an appointment that day, but didn't bother, I thought, "I'll have the hair of the dog," that should do the trick. The old man must have known I wasn't going make the call, so he got his secretary to book the appointment, and ordered me to attend the clinic.

The doctor gave me the once over, did a blood test and told me to return to his office that evening and he would let me know the results. I returned still feeling rough and I hadn't eaten for nearly 48 hours. He asked if I was a heavy drinker (silly question), and I explained that in the music business drink and drugs are de rigueur, it went with the job. He quizzed me on how much I was drinking, and I lied through my teeth. Looking at me seriously, he replied, "The blood test shows otherwise," and then lectured me on the dangers of binge drinking and overindulging, and then said, "You don't have a problem at this moment but in ten years you will, and it will be serious." He was then very perceptive and told me, "You don't have to give up drinking, just stop trying to drink every pub dry. Cut back now, or later on in life you will suffer." I took his advice and took a month off the booze, went to the gym three times a week and only drank water and soft drinks. On finishing my Ramadan, I returned to drinking though I'd made my mind up, from now on it would only be beer and wine, with only the occasional drink for the top shelf, and it's been that way ever since.

1985 arrived, the Council was busy recording their second album, which went on to be their best seller, and the tour that supported this album would be my last. There was a major change in the line-up and it no longer featured a horn section. Steve White has always maintained the best Council line-up he played in featured Paul, Mick, Dee, Camelle Hinds, Helen Turner and Steve Sidelnyk. In terms of musicianship, I have to agree but still preferred the Council as a 'big band' and really enjoyed the early tours, where

Paul had successfully gotten away from a guitar-lead band to a group of rotating musicians where anything could happen on stage.

As I knew my days at Polydor were numbered I went for it on the tour, which commenced on June 5, and I've only a vague recollection of the concerts I attended. My last gig turned out to be the Glastonbury Festival and the weather was filthy, it rained all day, and when we arrived at the site, it was a sea of mud. The Council was headlining the festival but John and Kenny decided to let Ian Dury top the bill, which meant we got away quickly, and weren't caught up with 60,000 people trying to leave at the same time. The VIP area was no different from the site; it resembled the trenches from WWI, and we had no choice but to stay on the bus, which was (too) well stocked up with booze. Paul was drinking with the lads again, and by the time the Council went on everybody was well and truly oiled. The only other band I caught that day was the Australian band Midnight Oil, whose line up was similar to the first Council band and featured a brass section.

I was on stage for the Council's set, and looking out at the sea of people was a fantastic sight. The show went well, with Paul and Dee spending most of their time dodging mud balls thrown by his fans. Towards the end, and unknown to me, Steve White left his drum kit to make an announcement, and told the vast crowd that I was leaving Polydor at the end of next week, and this was my last gig with the Council. Steve then informed the multitude that I was having a leaving party the following Friday at the Lamb & Flag in James Street, London and you're all invited. A big cheer went up and for a moment I felt faint, and a vision passed in front of me of having to get in the biggest round of my life. Funny enough a couple of fans did turn up and I was well chuffed as they lived quite a distance from London. The return journey home was a sombre affair as it would be the last time I travelled with the Council and I had mixed feelings. I knew leaving Polydor was the right thing, but it was a big wrench to leave the Council. The band was in high spirits and I joined in, but it was half-hearted. Paul and Dee disappeared to the back of the bus to discuss their harmonies and from that moment became an item.

Following Glastonbury, they played a number of European festivals, including the massive Wercher Festival in Belgium, where an estimated 120,000 fans attended and the bill included U2, Depeche Mode and Joe Cocker. On July 13, they appeared at Live Aid, following Status Quo who opened the proceedings. The two bands were lucky, as they were first on they got a sound check, something no other band was afforded, not even Queen. Although I'd left Polydor, Kenny phoned and invited me to come along and said there was a backstage pass for me. I declined, as on that day I'd moved into my new house, which was some distance from London and Wembley, and like the many other millions of fans watched the phenomenal event unfold on the box.

During August and September, they toured Japan, Australia, Italy, and October saw them return to Germany for four shows, finishing off this trip with a single date in Belgium. In December, they toured the UK for the second time that year, playing seven dates including three nights at the Wembley Arena. For these shows, the band augmented the brass section and added a 12-piece string section. I popped in to see one of the performances but the out front sound wasn't great, and the vocals were swimming in reverb. This was a shame as the band were in good form. The three nights at Wembley were the last time the Council would appear as a big band.

In 1985, seven concerts were recorded, at The Apollo Glasgow★ August (16) – a Radio Clyde Broadcast), The Melbourne Entertainment Centre, Australia★ (18), The Phillipshalle, Düsseldorf Germany★ October (17), The Leisure Centre Gloucester★ (December 5), The Playhouse Edinburgh★ (6), and The Wembley Arena ★★ (9 & 10).

The Personnel on the ★gigs was Paul Weller (vocals and guitar), Mick Talbot (Hammond organ, piano and vocals), Steve White (drums), and Dee C. Lee (vocals) with honorary Councillors Helen Turner (keyboards and backing vocals), Camelle Hinds (bass) and Steve Sidelnyk (percussion), while the personnel on ★★gigs was Paul Weller (vocals and guitar), Mick Talbot (Hammond organ, piano and vocals), Steve White (drums) and Dee C. Lee (vocals) with honorary Councillors Billy Chapman (tenor saxophone), Chris Lawrence (trombone), Guy Barker (trumpet), Stewart Prosser (trumpet), Helen Turner (keyboards and backing vocals), Camelle Hinds (bass), Steve Sidelnyk (percussion) and guest vocalist Junior Giscombe. The string orchestra's 1st violinist was Anne Stephenson and the band was conducted by John Mealing.

By the end of 1985, the Council had racked up nearly a 100 shows and concerts, and played all over the world, but in 1986 that changed, and their gigs didn't even go into double figures. In January, the Red Wedge tour went on the road, supported by the Council's road crew and security, with Paul generously picking up the tab for this. The line-up was different at every gig and featured among others Jerry Dammers, Tom Robinson, Madness, The Smiths and The Communards. The majority of the bands supported the aims wholeheartedly, but at least one name act didn't want their name plastered on the posters. While it looked good to be aligned with Red Wedge, they didn't want their name emblazoned outside the venues, as it may have affected their career. The concerts were two hours long and it cost only £1 to see the show, which considering the bill was excellent value.

The Council appeared at the GLC farewell gig at the Hammersmith Odeon on March 2 along with The Flying Pickets, Lindisfarne, Billy Bragg and others. Once again, ticket prices were kept low, at £2.50 and £3.50, although the concert would still have sold out if the prices were doubled.

On June 28 the Communards dropped out of the Artists Against Apartheid concert on Clapham Common and at the last moment the Council filled the gap. They played a short set, which included 'Johannesburg', a song they never played again. Spandau Ballet, Sade, Sting, Elvis Costello and Gil Scott-Heron appeared on the bill, guaranteeing a large turn out.

In July, there were three nights at the Shaw Theatre and on the 20th, the Council made a 'secret' appearance, billed as The Party Chambers and played an acoustic set, which included songs they rarely played live. As far as touring goes, the Council's own career took a back seat with Paul and Mick focusing their live performances on the political and the other causes they genuinely supported. Not many groups could afford to take a year out, and one can only admire this stance. The causes they supported were unfashionable to say the least, and insured they would never appear on the Queen's honours lists, not even when New Labour came to power.

As they only played a handful of gigs in 1986, no concerts were recorded.

At the start of 1987, to support the release of *The Cost Of Loving,* the Council undertook a major tour of the UK, entitled *The General Election Tour.* Apart from Dee and Steve Sidelnyk, the band featured a new line up. By now, Steve White who was genuinely disillusioned with the band's inactivity the previous year had quit the band and moved on. The tour included four nights at the Royal Albert Hall, and other large venues and considering they hadn't played a tour since December 1985 and their singles weren't doing that well in the charts, it showed the Council could still hack it live. In March, and April they toured Europe before flying to Japan for five concerts. On April 25, at Hyde Park, they played yet another benefit gig for the anniversary of the Chernobyl nuclear disaster. During May, they played three dates in Italy, one in Belgium, and on July 19 a show at The Brixton Academy celebrating the eighth anniversary of the Nicaraguan revolution.

September saw the band back in Italy for two dates, and in October and November, they embarked on what turned out to be their last tour of the UK. This tour featured even more changes to the band, but also saw the return of Steve White. Ten concerts were booked, but two in Scotland were cancelled and the tour ended with two nights at the Hammersmith Odeon.

Three concerts were recorded in 1987, at the Apollo Manchester October (17) and Hammersmith Odeon November (24 & 25). The personnel was Paul Weller (vocals and guitar), Mick Talbot (Hammond organ, piano and vocals), Steve White (drums) and Dee C. Lee (vocals), with honorary Councillor Mark Edwards (keyboards), Simon Eyre (guitar) and Paul Powell (bass).

They entered 1988 without a settled line up and didn't undertake any tours, perhaps indicative that things were not going well. In 1989, on March 6, they played a benefit gig at the Hackney Empire, and in June flew to Japan for three concerts. Their final concert took place on July 4 at The Royal Albert Hall, a show that has now become infamous. Dee, Dr. Robert, Brian Powell and Camelle Hinds handled the majority of the vocals, with Paul looning about dressed in dayglow Bermuda shorts! The bulk of the concert featured the garage/house songs that were recorded for their ill-fated *Modernism: A New Decade* album. The music was a change too far for even the most loyal of Council fans. Many were unable to come to terms with what they heard and jeered the band constantly, with the fans in the upper tiers, tearing up their over priced programmes, and raining them down on the people below. The scenes were reminiscent of Bob Dylan's first 'electric' UK tour with The Band in May 1966, where during the two shows he played at the Royal Albert Hall (and the tour) he was barracked throughout, with some fans calling him a traitor and Judas. Dylan's change of musical direction led to a cataclysmic change in rock music, whilst The Style Council's appearance at the Royal Albert Hall only bought about the end of the group.

Julie Kershaw, a big Council, fan sums up their live concerts perfectly: "Lord knows they played some lacklustre concerts – the General Election Tour springs to mind and don't even get me started on the infamous Style Council Review – and there were some well dodgy haircuts – the blond Aryan look anyone? But there's no escaping the fact that when they were good, they were *very, very* good. Think back to the grey, deeply depressing days of Thatcher when liberties were being steadily eroded and a whole generation consigned to the scrap heap. Then remember the group that bought us the hope that things could change. Yes, ladies and gents, I give you The Style Council – when they were on top form, they were unbeatable. I remember the sheer energy and excitement of the Nicaraguan Solidarity Concert at Brixton Academy in 1987 – Paul prowling the stage spitting out an electrifying version of 'Money-Go-Round' – far superior to anything we'd ever heard on disc – and as the song reached its biting crescendo, Dee was dancing as if her life depended on it, and all the while the most serious topics of the day such as the miners' strike were married to some of the most up-beat classy pop melodies that you're ever likely to hear. The sheer joyous sound of flutes, strings, and organ and sweet harmonies would momentarily make you forget that you were singing along to lyrics that could make you cry if you ever sat down and thought about them. Their lyrics summed up the reality of the eighties, but the beautiful music means these songs will never lose their appeal. Time may fade the ravages of Thatcherism but not The Style Council at their best."

When the Councils live career began, it was like a giant fifth of November firework party, but at the end it went out like a damp squib, which was a shame. From 1986, the floating line up disappeared and a more conventional Council took the stage, and although the line up changed several times, the early magic wasn't there. When they started I never envisaged an end like this, and perhaps had Paul stuck to the (original) floating line up, things may have turned out differently. Nonetheless, there were some great concerts and the Council remembered for these and not just for the final show at The Albert Hall.

Part 3

ALONE AGAIN NATURALLY

CHAPTER 17

From Zero To Hero

There is no doubt that the Council went on for a year too long. After *Confessions Of A Pop Group,* they should have been dealt the coup de grace, but this could also be said of The Jam. When both bands' careers came to a halt the fans were left a little dazed and confused with the direction and the music that Paul was writing and playing. With the Council, there's no doubt that he got as far away from The Jam as he could, but he also put a lot of distance between himself and Paul Weller. His character has always been black and white and there was never room for moderation, or compromise, whether it was music, politics, drinking, or becoming a vegetarian. Paul was always full tilt on, often refusing to accept he could be wrong, even when he patently was. He gave his detractors short shrift, and plenty of ammo, and as far he was concerned, attack was the best form of defence – get your retaliation in first.

Nobody likes criticism, not even a plasterer in the building trade, and although Paul deserved some, the critics of the Council went way over the top; after all, he was only making records. No matter how great an artist you are, this criticism has an affect, whether you are a painter, actor, sculptor, or a poet, genuinely talented artists need their egos boosted and massaged. Gifted artists are never satisfied, and constantly strive to improve on their best work, subconsciously knowing that this is not always possible. They set themselves high standards and no matter how much talent they have, it isn't possible to maintain and make every song, every picture, and every performance great. Was every song that Lennon & McCartney wrote a classic, I doubt it, there were the classic tunes, and many of them, but some were just plain good. Artists might laugh off their critic's words, or show disdain, but they file away the critique in a deep and dark place, often pointedly reminding the offender at a later date when they are back on top.

Talented artists practically demand accolades for a job well done, and recognition for what they have painted, or written, as well as the price paid. And not just to boost their over sized egos. When Paul commented that he wouldn't make records to satisfy his fans or his record company, he was talking about the quality of his songs and not the quantity. This is why every record company wants an artist like Paul Weller, because they know, no matter what excesses he goes through, that innate talent will always come up with the goods. All through his career, he made records that his fans liked and bought, even the last Council recordings, which tested the most loyal of Council fans. I still laugh at Paul's criticism of his own song 'Absolute Beginners' – "Its fucking shit" – and he is as acerbic with his own songs as he is when criticising other artist's efforts, and shows no mercy.

Paul's ego is huge, but no bigger than many artists I've worked with and perhaps his verbal invective was a defensive mechanism to cover up the fact that he was struggling internally. When artists go through a difficult stage in their career it's difficult for them to see where they are going wrong or even admit that there's a problem. As their confidence goes into melt down, the ego steps in and bridges the gap, giving the artists a veneer of self-confidence to feed off. Paul is no different from any other artist in this respect, it's their fragile egos that drive them, and throughout their careers, it is this fragility that is the difference between success and failure. Success in any vocation is easy to deal with, when you're on the up everything is fine, but the crunch comes when the going gets tough, and it's how you deal with the failures of life that truly define your character.

In many ways the demise of the Council was inevitable; trying to weld his songs to music that was alien to his natural talents was a mistake, whether it was eighties soul, the MJQ, Debussy, or House, although they were as far away from The Jam as you could get. Can you imagine Michelangelo painting the Sistine chapel in the style of Picasso, or Pollock, and towards the end of the Council's career, that's how far away he got from The Jam. The eighties should have been a bridge between The Jam and his future, but by the end of the decade, the bridge had all but collapsed, and only held up by sheer will power, and a (very) loyal fan club. If Paul was trying to find himself during this period, he was looking in some strange places.

Paul went through a period of crisis, which affected his self-confidence, and when Polydor refused the last album, it took lumps out of his ego, but they were right. The album wasn't the finished article by a long way and he must have been well aware of this when he delivered it. All through his career, he has surrounded himself with yes men and it created a vacuum around him, where he knows he's safe from criticism. This is nothing unusual; every artist in the entertainment world surrounds himself with passive employees. This has a positive effect when you are successful, but negative when things start to go wrong, and when this happens, you need to have someone close to you who can offer constructive criticism, show you where you're failing, and point you in the right direction. Paul has never had anyone in his camp that was capable of taking on this mantle. John is a great nuts and bolts manager but even after 25 years in the music business, when it comes to marketing and the music side of Paul's career he is unable to contribute.

During the latter half of the eighties, when Paul had clearly lost direction, what he needed was someone who could take him aside and point out his failings, and suggest an alternative direction. Prior to David Munns' stand, no one at Polydor had the courage to rein in Paul's extremes and I have no doubt that John would have been worried about this period of his career. He would have seen the sales of Paul's records and CDs going down every year and would have realised that eventually Polydor were going to call it a day, as they were paying out seven figure advances for an artist whose sales were declining into infinity.

As he entered a new decade, Paul was unemployed, but John had made sure that by this time Paul was financially secure and wouldn't have to sign on the dole. Even allowing for this, Paul still had to find something to occupy his time, and although he now had a family, and could throw himself into playing husband and father full time, it would never be enough. He still had a burning desire to make music. He might have lost the plot but he still had the talent.

It was time now to take a stroll down memory lane, and Paul returned to his roots, listening to the music that captivated him as a teenager, as well as bands like Free, Spooky Tooth, Traffic, Van Morrison, and Crosby Stills, Nash & Neil Young. I'd followed these artists as a teenager and into my early twenties and have always been a huge Neil Young fan since his days in Buffalo Springfield. I recall going to a solo performance at the Festival Hall in the early seventies, not that I ever admitted this to Paul when he was in the Jam.

Paul renewed his friendship with Steve Brookes who was more than amused at Paul's newfound interest in this genre of music. He raved about Free's *Fire & Water*, an album that had been a favourite of Steve's for a long time. When Paul first heard the album, he said it was shit. I had a little chuckle on hearing this, recalling the conversation during the early Jam days, when I told him of my interest in modern jazz. He replied: "Den, it's a load of old shit!" Like most artists, Paul has always had a blinkered view on other artist's music; if the music doesn't have his approval, it's no good. I recall working with Joe Pass, one of the all time great jazz guitarists, and he was scathing about musicians who lacked his exceptional skills and talent. Writing and playing comes much easier to the talented few, with the rest relying on 50% perspiration and 50% talent to come up with a good song. Around the time of 'You're The Best Thing', Paul told me he could easily repeat this formula and write an album full of tunes like this. "I'm never going to do it, though," he added. This wasn't some idle boast, and neither was he massaging his ego. Paul knew that to be acclaimed as a great songwriter you had to transcend your own songs and move on; that it's no good repeating the same formula endlessly. Had he followed this path, he would never have been anything other than an ordinary songwriter, and whatever is said about the man, ordinary he ain't.

After a period of deep soul searching, Paul started to get his act together and consider the next phase of his career. Although he'd left Polydor, his divorce from them hadn't yet taken place, and though he was without a publishing deal, this wouldn't have been a problem as his Jam and Council catalogue were still worth a mint. However, it would be better to wait until he got a record deal, which was inevitable. Even at the lowest point of his career, as Polydor's MD, David Munns succinctly put it, "Every record company wants an act like Paul Weller on their label", and it was just a matter of time before he would bounce back. Whatever suffering Paul went through, it must be said it's no different from what many people go through during their (mundane) lives. What of the miners he supported wholeheartedly, where many lost their livelihood and although they received compensation, their lives were wrecked. They had to start again and didn't have a back catalogue worth thousands to help them over a rough patch. The music press and journalists have always tended to over exaggerate the importance of music and often write about the significance of this artist, or that song, as if it's life or death, which it clearly isn't. There's no doubt that music plays an important role in people's lives, but when reality kicks in, it's about paying the mortgage, putting food on the table, and clothing the kids. Most artists who whine about a need to find themselves and their loss of direction don't inhabit the real world. If they did, they would do what every normal person does when their lives are turned over, you knuckle down and get on with life as best as you can.

I am not just having a go at Paul, as many other artists I've worked with have the same attitude. Whenever there is a crisis, they feel the need to bare their soul. During my career, I have done my fair share of pandering and have made excuses for artists who behaved like spoiled children, which many are. I've seen expensive guitars smashed up for no reason, and teddy slung out of the pram more times than I care to remember. I recall at one gig, a musician threw a cup of tea over a roadie, and what did he do to deserve this treatment. He had the temerity to hand the artist his guitar the wrong way round. This brattish behaviour is passed off as artistic temperament, and is considered part of the artist suffering for his art. This tends to increase when the artist has a six or seven figure bank account and they can afford these fits of artistic temperament, where the cost to them is the equivalent of the average person buying a new shirt. What about the working stiffs who do the nine-to-five thing in an office, or a factory, or a labourer on a building site, who spend their hard-earned cash on their CDs and concert tickets who turn the artist into millionaires. If they really don't like it, they can walk away from the music business any time they want. When he'd had enough of the business, Rick Astley did just that, although for some reason he has now decided to make a comeback. There aren't that many people who don't go through a period of self-doubt and suffer a loss of confidence during their lifetime, but they don't need to inform the world of their anguish, or be pampered like a poodle. Whenever I hear any artist, including Paul, whingeing, about their lives, many times I felt like telling them to shut up and go look in their bank accounts.

After the Council, Paul felt unleashed and free for the first time, although the prison he was in and the problems endured in the Council were of his own making. Mick never gave him the problems he had working with Bruce and Rick. To some extent, he was behind bars with The Jam, but he couldn't make the same complaint about the Council, and he didn't have to pander to any musical whim other than his own, as their recordings show. As for being at the bottom, no way, he just bottomed out after diving in too deep, and it was always a question of when he would come to the surface, and what lessons he'd learned. He was always a man on a mission and a househusband was no more of a job for Paul than working in the local supermarket. His interest in garage faded, but then most musical fads, particularly teenage fads, do and quickly, and as far as his music went, it was more a question of where he was going to lay his hat.

The answer to that question was playing live, something he tired of in The Jam and hardly did at all during the Council's final years. Although he'd signed to Polydor as a solo act, for the first time Paul went out under his own name and formed The Paul Weller Movement, with Steve White on drums. Bringing Steve back into the fold was a shrewd move, as Steve is not only multi-dimensional as a drummer, he knows what to expect of Paul's ever-changing musical moods. It's said the best drummers are those you only notice when they stop playing, and Steve typifies this. When he joined the Council, he was a talented lad, and developed his skill through hard work, and putting in endless hours of practicing. Steve was astute enough to listen to and study many different styles of drumming, and developed into one of the great all round drummers. He is as immersed in drumming as Paul is with songwriting and is equally as driven, with an intenseness they both share. Drumming is an art form, and because you have a good technique to play rock music, it doesn't mean this will transpose other types of music. Steve is a part of a rare breed of drummer, able to play all kinds of music equally well. If Paul ever needs to replace Steve, it will be no good knocking on my door, as I don't know another drummer than can slip so effortless from one style to another.

Around this time, Paul gave up being a veggie and returned to being a meat and potatoes man, and was back on the booze, something he should have considered earlier, as during the Council days he could be a pain in the arse with his fads. During 1990, he played just over 20 gigs with a makeshift line up at low-key venues like Dingwalls, plus several universities and colleges in the UK, as well as gigs in Italy, Germany and Holland. He sold out the two Town & Country Club dates in London in December, where the audience would have been packed with die-hard fans, but outside of the capital, they played to half-empty houses. It must have been tough going back to the beginning and a bit of a catharsis for him, but he is tenacious, and has always had a strong belief in himself from day one, and after the final year of the Council, he needed a strong dose of both of these attributes. On his first solo tour, he played his newer material and songs from his Council days, and after shunning The Jam for such a long period, he introduced a few oldies from their catalogue. I went to see a couple of dates on this tour and although there were cracks, which is to be expected when you start again, the gigs weren't that bad.

Shortly after the Council expired, their old plugger Clive Banks, who was now the MD at Island Records, approached John about signing Paul. However, the legendary owner of the company, Chris Blackwell, wasn't impressed, and knew Paul wouldn't sell (big numbers) outside of the UK, let alone become as big as their top act U2. The terms they were demanding were a little over the top, given that Paul hadn't been successful for several years, and the music industry, regardless of what people think, is a small business. The Council's failures over their last years were an open secret, and whoever signed him would eventually have to talk to Polydor to straighten out the old deal. The companies at the time weren't taking the piss – as John stated – but were just being practical, and it would have been bad business to sign Paul for a fortune, given that his last album (*Confessions*) probably didn't sell more than 50 to 60,000 copies. No one was going to bankroll Paul to the tune that John was demanding, and there was no back catalogue to include in the deal, which would have helped recoup a large advance.

John has always been quick to ask for a big advance. It's not that he lives in the dark ages; John's a shrewd operator. While his knowledge of marketing and producing records is zilch, he was a great wheeler and dealer and knew the record business often, and stupidly, handed out vast sums of money to artists far less talented than Paul. However, as far as Paul was concerned it was a buyer's market, and no one was going to give them a million quid, or anywhere near this sum. Also, the demand for total control over his recordings would have been considered over the top, given what had happened with the Council's last albums. Although it amused me no end to hear the record business having a pop at John's impudence, as when a record company feels it's being ripped off, it cries foul and hands out a red card, but when a record company rips an artist off, it's fair play ref, even though they are offside by a mile! Every A&R man worth his salt knew Paul wasn't out of the game, and saw the opportunity to acquire him on the cheap, and in this case, John was right to hold out for a big advance, although perhaps not quite as big as he was demanding.

In 1991, he spent just three months on the road, playing just over 30 gigs. During April, he visited some old haunts, which included the Rock City, a club in Nottingham, Brixton Academy, Guildford Civic Hall, and The Royal Court in Liverpool. Having gotten back into touring, it was now time to go in and record a single and Paul decided on the prophetic 'Into Tomorrow'. The legendary Jimmy Miller, who'd worked with the Stones and Traffic in the sixties, was brought on board to produce it, but this didn't work out as he was past his best and too fond of a drop of the hard stuff.

Paul started working with Solid Bond's in-house engineer Brendan Lynch. Brendan was in the same mould as Peter Wilson and Vic Smith, although younger and more hip to the current music scene, and had a lot more to offer Paul than established producers. They went into Solid Bond's editing room and co-produced a new version of 'Into Tomorrow', and it was the beginning of a fruitful partnership. Throughout the time, I worked with Paul I was pressurised to bring in a name producer, but knew this would never work, although I have never believed that he was capable of producing himself. However, when he finds the right partner like Peter, Vic, or Brendan the combination not only works but the success transfers to the charts, and it's no coincidence that all his best selling records are co-produced. Bringing Brendan on board was a good move and the successes that this partnership went on to achieve would eventually eclipse The Jam and the Council.

With a good single under his belt and his confidence growing it was time to kick-start his record career. Given Paul's attitude towards a deal, no major record company would sign him up, well not on his terms, and Paul had to release his first solo effort on his own interdependent label, Freedom High, which sounded like a hangover from his *Modernism* period with the Council. After the failure of Respond, I have my doubts that he saw this move as his long-term future. There was no way he was going to put his own career on the line – neither he nor John was that stupid. Nevertheless, if he could achieve a modicum of success and a hit record with 'Into Tomorrow' b/w 'Here's A New Thing', it would open the doors and prove he was still a force to be reckoned with. They brought in Pedro Romanyi to produce a video at a cost of £10,000, just £5,000 less than Polydor put up for the Council's debut single. Pedro had been around for years and was a big fan of Paul's, even appearing in the crowd scenes in the video shoot for 'Solid Bond In Your Heart'.

Their next move was to bring in Nigel 'Spanner' Sweeny to promote the single. Nigel had previously worked on The Jam and the Council with Clive Banks. They asked if he could help market the single as well, but he couldn't help them out and pulled a favour from a mate who happened to work at Go! Discs. Independently distributed, the single was released on May 6, 1991, and despite the DIY approach, it went to 36 in the charts some two years after the Council's last hit single ('Long Hot Summer '89'), and 12 places higher. I can imagine what disgruntled Jam fans thought when they first heard it; it not only hearkened back to the sixties, but also to his alter ego. The 12 inch and CD featured three extra tracks, the first, 'Here's A New Thing', is reminiscent of the early Latin touches that permeated many

Council tunes, while 'That Spiritual Thing' came from the *Modernism* album, which Polydor roundly rejected. The third track was the original 8-track demo of the A-side. Given that his critics had written him off, this chart position must have given him a lot of satisfaction. A top 40 record may not have measured up to his chart record with The Jam, or the first half of the Council's career, but this could be seen as a giant stride, compared to the erratic steps that occurred during the final years of the Council.

There was also talk of a deal with Talkin' Loud records, but this was never really going to happen as John was going to stick to his guns and get the best possible deal he could for Paul. They also made a decision to rid themselves of Solid Bond Studios, which had been something of an albatross for them and as they only leased the property, their only return would be on the studio equipment. Paul's sister Nicky was working there and they had a big bust-up, swapping blows of a brother and sisterly kind with the rift lasting several years before they finally kissed and made up. After the demise of Solid Bond, Paul and John relocated to one of their old haunts, Nomis studios. In November, they played a warm-up gig in Brighton before embarking on a tour of Japan, where they played eight gigs. December saw Paul playing five shows in Los Angeles and one in New York, ending the year at The Guildhall, Portsmouth, and the Kilburn National.

The Jam and the Council were always popular in Japan and Paul's popularity hadn't waned there, not even during the turbulent last years of the Council. After Europe and the USA, Japan is the most important market for an artist or band, no matter what music they play. In Japan, pop music is taken seriously, and they welcomed Paul back like the prodigal son. Paul's over-the-top persona of the late eighties would have passed them by, and his inscrutable humour is similar to that of the Japanese. It was at this time that Pony Canyon offered him a solo deal for Japan, as they did his mate Robert Howard from The Blow Monkeys and Dee C. Lee. At the time, he said the Japanese had the bucks and they advanced him the money to complete his first solo album. This was no brave or bold decision to sign Paul, but a calculating business decision. In Japan, the Council's records, like the rest of the world, had dipped during their last years and the guys at Pony Canyon would have been aware of this. However, they were a bunch of shrewddies, who knew Paul would come through and deliver the goods and this deal was a sound investment in blue chip stock.

It's debateable just how far Paul's stock had fallen. Certainly, his profile in the charts had slipped and the music press had fallen out with him, with many hoping they could rub salt into the wound. However many record companies were hovering with their chequebooks, waiting to see what happened next. They knew Paul wasn't finished. I have no doubts that the Paul and John could have funded the recording of an album themselves and even though Paul went through a shallow period as far as record sales go, he and John were unlikely to be struggling. There's an old adage in the record business that applies when it comes to the business side: "Never spend your own money, always spend someone else's." No matter how talented you are, there is no guarantee that you are going to make it, and it's always wise to get a third party to front up the money. Had Paul and John been under the cosh financially it would have been a different matter, and perhaps they would have had to swallow their pride and take what was on offer. For two years his stock hadn't fallen – it had just remained stationary, but as the next decade proved, he was still as sound as a pound.

During 1992, he played nearly 50 shows including a spot at the Yello Club in Tokyo, and in April, his debut solo album was released in Japan. During June, he played half a dozen gigs, mostly in the London area, before returning to Japan. Following this, they flew over the pole and played four dates America and a solo effort in Toronto, Canada, and in August, he was the guest of his mate Dr Robert at the Mean Fiddler in Harlesden.

Having got off to a good start in land of the rising sun, all that was required was a deal with a UK label and with a top forty hit in the bag, John had some ammunition, but who would he sign with? Around this time, I had a meeting with Paul about *Extras,* the Jam out takes album, and he was in great shape, more bullish than when I'd previously seen him, and we discussed the next phase of his career and his thoughts on what record label he would go with. I knew there was no way he would go with a major, not after his final experience with Polydor, and he confided that one of the big companies, CBS I think, had made a serious offer, but for the money they were offering, he would have to sell his soul. I suspect the terms of the contract were the problem rather than the money, as no major label would give him the kind of artistic freedom he demanded.

Fortunately, the indie scene was thriving, and bands could now circumvent the majors' vice-like grip on the industry as many small labels were having serious success and breaking bands into the big time. Finally, Paul chose to sign with Go! Discs, an independent label based in Chiswick, which had been around since the early eighties and featured artists like Billy Bragg, Gabrielle, The Housemartins, which became The Beautiful South, and Portishead. Andy McDonald founded the label and was very much a music man. Before the label took off, he and his wife Juliet sold their records out the back of a van. The culture at Go! Discs was similar to Paul's own musical culture, and they were a company staffed with good people who not only had a head for business, but were also music heads. Andy would have been one of the few music men in the business who could deal directly with Paul, and would have his respect. If you look at the names of the other bands signed to the label, Paul Weller's name fits seamlessly alongside, and in Andy McDonald and Go! Discs Paul had found a natural home.

Throughout Paul's career on Polydor there always seemed to be problems with their management, and he left under a cloud. Andy was simpatico with his artists and gave them their head, allowing them the freedom to record their music, a freedom that Paul wouldn't have found with a major. Emerging from a personal wilderness, starting his career for a third time, must have been a little daunting, and he needed time to find himself. There is enough pressure on an artist from outside of the record company, the fans, the baying media, and a need for the company to absorb some of this pressure. Nowadays record companies and their A&R mangers like to interfere with everything, and meddle for the sake of it, with some execs having egos bigger than the artists they sign. At Go! Discs Paul was given a lot of latitude, which allowed him to come back not only on his terms, but also at a pace that allowed him to find himself gradually without the pressure to deliver big selling albums.

I never had any doubt that he would return after the Council, but with a major label it would have been harder, and the last thing he needed, as he was kick starting his career was an unsympathetic record company. The set up was ideal for Paul as he could make the records he wanted. Go! Discs had the muscle of PolyGram's conglomerate machine behind them, who were capable of selling and marketing records worldwide. Paul was with a record company that would get behind him and had total faith in his talents, and Andy's part in Paul's rejuvenation cannot be understated.

There were a couple of problems: firstly Go! Discs were tied to PolyGram, the Wellers' nemesis, and secondly, Paul's contract with Polydor needed to be straightened out. No matter what you think, you can't just walk away from a record contract as easy as that – as they say, marry in haste, repent at leisure. As far as Polydor was concerned it was payback time, and leaving them would prove costly. They were not stupid, and knew Paul was too talented to remain on the shelf. They knew that when he returned, they could recoup any losses and so took an override on the royalties of his solo albums for quite a chunk of his Go! Discs career, as well as cross collateralising his Jam and Council royalties. Not only that, Paul had to relinquish control over his back catalogue, which meant Polydor could release whatever compilations on The Jam and the Council they liked. Having dealt with Polydor, the deal was finally tied up and on August 3, Go! Discs released their first single, the lead in track to the forthcoming album, 'Uh Huh Oh Yeh' b/w 'Fly On The Wall', with the 12 inch and CD containing the extra track, 'Always There To Fool You', a quasi-jazz version of the A-side, and the acoustic 'Fly On The Wall'. It went to 18 and stayed in the charts five weeks, giving him his first top twenty record since 'Wanted' in October 1987.

Paul's first solo album came out on August 31, 1992, titled simply *Paul Weller* and showed him taking his first tentative step on part three of his turbulent career. Now known as The Players, the line-up of musicians had a familiar feel from the Council days with Steve White, Dee C. Lee, and Camelle Hinds. The only one missing was Mick Talbot; well not quite, as he co-wrote 'Strange Museum'. Jacko Peake played the horns and Paul's mate Dr Robert makes an appearance, as well as Carlene Anderson and Marco Nelson from The Young Disciples. I visited the studio several times when they were recording the album and Paul took me aside and asked me to listen to a track. He'd lifted a chord sequence from Spooky Tooth's version of The Band song 'The Weight', and was a little worried someone would spot the nick. I've always been good at spotting nicks and not just Paul's, but couldn't hear it, even when I played it against the original record. There's not many artists who don't nick bits from other tunes, but very few actually own up and I've always admired Paul, as he always puts his hands up, which could have cost him.

All good songwriters write about their own experiences, and the great ones are able to inhabit the skins of others and write about experiences they have never been through, and Paul excels in both. In The Jam he was never a Saturday Kid, and never knew what it was like to be on the dole, or down a pit, but was able to take the experience of others and translate this through his songs. He has always had the ability to write in the first person and as a voyeur of life. Whether it was The Jam, the Council, or solo, when you listen to him singing, there is a belief in the lyrics he writes, which is the key to his success and why he has never lost the support of his fans.

Packaging has always been an important to Paul throughout his career, although with CDs, many of the images are lost because of the size, and he has always given value for money. In every artists' contract, tucked away in the small print, there is a clause that refers to packaging deductions, which mean the artists contributes to his own sleeve and inlay design. For normal packaging, i.e. just a four-page insert, it's small, but when it comes to the type of packaging Paul demands, it will be double. The packaging on his first solo album is elaborate, containing many photos and a booklet, with his beloved lyrics faithfully reproduced. Simon Halfon had done a great job with the Council, where even at the end he captured perfectly both the tone of the band and Paul's austere image. Photographers Lawrence Watson and Nick Knight were also a throwback from the Council days as they took the pictures on the third and fourth Council albums respectively. Looking through the photos you will notice one of Paul casually strumming one of his many Rickenbacker guitars, which would have been locked away when The Jam finished their last gig at Brighton.

Gone was the four-on-the-floor mesmerising beat and above all, the lack of real *soul* that permeated the Council's final recordings, and there's an air of freshness about the album and Paul. Whether 'I Didn't Mean To Hurt' is autobiographical or not I don't know. Paul is one of the great borrowers, and not just of lyrics and the odd bar or two, but he's also good at nicking the odd emotion, and a bit of someone else's life as well. This song could be about him, but equally it could be about someone else. Paul is underrated when it comes to playing the keyboards, and I particularly like his keyboard work on this track, which is nicely understated. 'Bull-Rush' is very Traffic-like, and the better for it and Brendan's production work on this is excellent. Paul's never one to let us forget his past, and chips in The Who's 'Magic Bus' at the coda. 'Round And Round' and 'Remember How We Started' are very good, both lyrically and musically. Jacko Peak's tidy tenor work on both songs is a nice touch, and Paul's pseudo jazz guitar is very reminiscent of the kind of style he embodied during the early years of the Council. 'Above The Clouds' for me is the best tune on the album, with spot-on vocals, although when he sings, "Will I Last", it's well tongue in cheek. Of course he will – it's been his destiny!

'Clues' has a late sixties feel, not just the Traffic-like flute but the opening guitar is very reminiscent of the likes of Gordon Lightfoot and other singer-song writers of that period. Towards the end of the Council, Paul was never able to meld the current sounds to his own talents, and his songs suffered, but when he gets in his time machine and goes back, it's a very different story. 'Clues' has the feel of something old, but with a dash of today, as do many of Paul's songs, both present and past. 'Amongst Butterflies' shows just how a good a drummer Steve White is, as the song starts off as standard rock tune with Steve driving a solid beat. Just when you think the tune is over, they break into a funky jazz rhythm with Steve playing a very syncopated and funky beat. 'The Strange Museum' sees Paul singing in falsetto, something that hadn't always worked in the past, but it's ok on this track, though I prefer him when he's singing in his natural voice. Curtis Mayfield made an appearance in The Jam and the Council and 'Bitterness Rising' has his influences stamped on it, particularly the high falsetto swoops, and 'Kosmos' rounds things off nicely.

On the last recordings by the Council, his vocals were not always that great and many times were back in the mix, and quite frankly, to my ears they weren't always well recorded or produced. On this album, his vocals are strident and where they belong, on top of the mix. Paul sings with a confidence that I hadn't heard since *Our Favourite Shop* and the odd occasion during the final years of the Council. On this album, he plays to his strengths; listen to the Weller soulfulness, which is a far cry from the leaden performances on *The Cost of Loving*.

There's an upbeat feel to the tunes on this album, but then so was Paul. The songs on this album are an amalgamation of his newfound musical tastes mixed in with his old influences. He'd toyed with psychedelia in The Jam as early as 1977 with 'Away From The Numbers' as well as 'Pop Art Poem' in 1980 and 'Tales Of The Riverbank' in 1981. The combination of styles and music contain the best elements of both The Jam and the Council and was perhaps what Paul was looking for when he ended The Jam in 1982, and never quite found in the Council. It's certainly more convincing, and overall has a better feel than many of the last recordings released by the Council. What Paul's first solo outing indisputably shows was that at last he was coming to terms with his past, and had not lost his flair for songwriting.

Gone was the politicking and the verbal diarrhoea that tainted the Council's career. Overall, the album fell short of being a masterpiece, although in hindsight it stands up well alongside the albums he's recorded during his solo career.

The two-year gap between the end of the Council and this debut album gave him enough time to find himself and a new direction, and the album shows he still had a future, and at this time that's all you could have asked of Paul.

The music press still weren't happy and thought his debut single, 'Into Tomorrow', sounded redundant. Negative reviews suggested it was out of step with current trends. Whoever wrote this didn't listen to either The Jam or the Council's debut albums. When The Jam released *In The City*, it too was out of step with the punk scene, very R&B, and I have my doubts that anyone saw a 30-year career for Paul, when it was first released. The Council's *Café Bleu* threw everyone a curve and although it contained some very good tracks it was different to every other album released that year, or come to that any other year. Adam Sweeting (a huge Jam fan) wrote, "The songs are devoid of shape and content and if you play any of these songs against 'A Town Called Malice' or 'That's Entertainment', you'll wonder where the real Paul Weller went", a comment that could be made about the latter half of the Council's career, but not his debut solo album. A much fairer analogy would have been to compare the tracks with 'Wasteland', 'Man In The Corner Shop', 'Man Of Great Promise, or 'Shout To The Top'. It wasn't just Jam fans that never forgave him for walking away, many journalists who grew up with The Jam also clung to the band as if they were a safety blanket, and like many fans were unable to embrace his newfound openness with the Council. This is true more than twenty years after the event. After the Council ended, did anyone really think he would get back together with Bruce and Rick? On another planet maybe, but not here on earth.

The music press from the late seventies wielded enormous power and could make or break a band. This permeated down to the record companies, where a new band's profile in the music press was sometimes more important than their talent. I know of one A&R man at Polydor who wouldn't sign a band unless they had a profile in the press well before they put pen to paper. The music press was no more an arbiter of talent and good music than the record companies they often criticised, and it was an unhealthy power. However, by the nineties, their power waned and the record companies had grown into colossal powers, with marketing machines that were awesome.

Whether the press liked his new material or not, he was back and proved many wrong, and for a second time. The album went to number eight in the charts, some seven places higher than the Council's *Confessions Of A Pop Group*, and stayed in the charts four weeks longer. There's no doubt that Paul had only taken a small step forward, but given the last few years of the Council, it was of Neil Armstrong proportions, and this is no exaggeration. I speak now as an A&R man: no one seems to realise how difficult it is to get on the ladder in the first place, and regardless of a (new) artist's talents, they have less than a 5% chance of making the first rung. When you fall off the ladder, as Paul did, you can halve this equation.

What is astonishing is that during his lay-off, Paul never attempted to produce the get-out-of-jail card that was hidden in the back pocket of his pristine white Levis 501s – namely, re-form The Jam. This would have pleased many, including the sniping journalists, who would have written in capital letters, 'I TOLD YOU SO'! However, this wasn't an option for our man, and credit must be given to him for not taking the obvious, and easiest way out. Instead, he set himself up for a third time and led with his chin, knowing full well if he failed again, Madame Le Guillotine awaited, and no quarter would be given.

With this newfound success, he'd established himself for a third time, and was one of the few figures to emerge from the seventies punk scene as a meaningful force. On September 28, Go! Discs released a third single, 'Above The Clouds', b/w 'Everything Has A Price', with the CD containing two extra tracks, a live version of 'All Year Round' and Traffic's 'Feeling Alright', which got to 47 in the charts, and hung around for two weeks. The first track was originally the B-side of the Council single, 'It Didn't Matter', which co-incidentally was his last top 10 single in January 1987. The addition of the Dave Mason song is a tasteful version of the original song that was also covered by Joe Cocker in the late sixties. The acid jazz producer Chris Bangs co-produced the A-side and received a credit on the album, which thanked him "for getting that one out of him".

During October, Paul toured Europe and the UK. Gone were the clubs and the remote gigs, it was return to the big time. Shows were played at Barrowlands in Glasgow, Newcastle City Hall, Manchester Apollo, and London's Royal Albert Hall. In November, he went to America and on these dates he included some old Jam and Council numbers, another indication that he'd come to terms with his past.

As much he wanted to be European with the Council, Paul is English through and through and his music has reflected the English sound of bands like The Who, The Small Faces, The Kinks, The Beatles, and now the quintessential British band Traffic. It's been said by pundits, who weren't around in the sixties, that Traffic were a bit messy and that Paul's solo material was of a similar nature. I remember when Traffic's first LP was released in 1967, it was a real breath of fresh air, and the words that was bandied about to describe the album were eclectic and different, and although very English, travelled well. Paul's first solo album is diverse rather than messy and shows his old influences and the new ones that were now shaping his playing and songwriting. Paul's own career does mirror that of Winwood, who went from Spencer Davis to Blind Faith and then Traffic, before pursuing a solo career, but it's more by accident than design.

He'd also learned his lesson about taking on the press, a war you can't win, and his lack of interest in political and social issues was an about turn, but no surprise. The support he gave to the miners, CND, and the other left-wing causes could have ended his career, and there would be no point in kick-starting his career in the same vein as the Council. It wasn't a case of playing safe – there was simply no point fighting another loosing battle; he'd been there and done that. What's more, although he valiantly defended his principles in the eighties, the early nineties would see the right root itself so deep in Britain that even the Labour party had to swing to the right so that Blair and New Labour would appeal to the tabloids and the middle class. There is no doubt that his innate songwriting talent carried the political issues, but his best songs were always the others. There were a few exceptions, but his prosaic lyric writing was always far superior to his political polemic, as the next years would prove. In two years, Paul had hauled himself slowly back, and defied pop history making it for a third time – what would 1993 hold for the boy wonder?

CHAPTER 18
Woking Class Wonder

The comparative success of Paul's first solo album should not be taken for granted. Although he was unable to penetrate the top five, it was a successful outing, and in hindsight more successful than was perhaps seen at the time. With The Jam, everyone quickly got used to their singles going to number one, and after this even a top five single was seen as some kind of failure. This kind of expectancy put Paul and the band under unnecessary pressure and given the implosion of the Council, at the start of his solo career he was under the cosh to match his previous success. We remember The Jam for what they were, and everyone tends to forget that they never really transcended from a teenage band into a fully-fledged adult band. This is one of the most difficult changes a band has to face, and it is by no means certain they would have made the transformation, or that their fans would follow, given their bewilderment with the musical path Paul trod during the final releases.

Paul can be a bit of a whinge bucket at times, but he should be given a lot of skin for this come back and making an album of this quality, and at this time of his career. He was in his thirties, an age when many artists' best days are behind them, and most banished to the leisure centre circuit, or touring as part of a revival package. The debut album showed all of his influences past and present, and were not only a pointer from where he came from, but where he was going.

For his second solo album, Paul went into The Manor, a residential studio in Oxfordshire where many famous rock bands had worked. Paul has always been insular about the people he surrounded himself with, and it was the same when it came to his backing band. It had to be a line up of musicians that Paul could rely on and trust. The players were Marco Nelson, Steve White on drums and percussion, Jacko Peake on horns, and Helen Turner, who is not only a fine keyboard player, but also a good songwriter in her own right. Max Beesley added his vocals and played the Wurlitzer, and Paul's mate Robert Howard added to the mix. Steve Craddock made his first appearance, as did Simon Fowler from Ocean Colour Scene. Craddock was a big Jam fan, who hailed from the Midlands and first came to Paul's attention when he was in a Mod band called The Boys. Mick Talbot played a bit of organ, and Paul's partner, Dee C. Lee made an appearance. Dave Liddle who'd been Paul's guitar roadie since 1978, guested on guitar, and as well as his co-producing duties, Brendan Lynch played on many tracks. This mafia type set up is common to most artists, as there's no point in recording with musicians you are uncomfortable with. The recording studio is a small space, where the longer the recording goes on, the closer the walls come. The strengths of Paul's albums are the songs he writes, not who played the bass or keyboards, although Steve White is the exception.

Paul has always been a bit of a hoarder and collector, with a wonderful collection of guitars and other instruments. What makes the album interesting is the use of antiquated synthesisers, like the Moog and mini Moog as well as a Mellotron, which I first saw Graham Bond play in 1965. In the sixties and the seventies, these keyboards were on the cutting edge of a new sound, but as the synthesiser became digital and more advanced, they became out of date and confined to the attic, practically worthless. However, no matter how much they refined the digital keyboard, they still couldn't quite replicate the sounds of these old analogue polyphonic synths, and once again, they became fashionable. If you want to buy one now, you will need to part with some serious cash.

On July 5, 1993, *Sunflower* was released as the first single, b/w live versions of 'Bull Rush' and 'Magic Bus' segued together, which were recorded at the Royal Albert Hall in 1992. The 12 inch and CD single contained the extra track 'Kosmos SXDub 2000', one of Brendan's re-mixes, and a new mix of 'That Spiritual Thing'. In the past, Paul was always reluctant to give his producers a free hand, when it came to remixing his songs, and this was a sign of him loosening up, and trusting in Brendan's abilities. The single went to number 16 in the charts, not great by previous standards, but as the nineties progressed, the single was fast becoming redundant anyway.

Preceding the album, on August 23, came the second single, 'Wild Wood', which proved conclusively that Paul's creative juices hadn't run dry. This tune is as good as anything he recorded with The Jam and the Council. Paul's vocals are not as smooth as the other songs, but this adds to the song rather than subtracts, as does the slightly woolly production. The B-side, 'Ends Of The Earth' could easily have been added to the album, and features a nice flute solo by Jacko Peake.

Paul's second album *Wild Wood* came out on September 6, lyrically he was back to his best and the songs were an amalgam of his old influences fused with newfound interest, like Traffic, as well as the Canadian maverick Neil Young. Although *Wild Wood* talks of all things rustic, there is still a grittiness about Paul and his music that you don't find walking up country lanes. 'Foot Of The Mountain' is a great tune, which Paul sings accompanied only by his acoustic guitar. There's no doubting that Neil Young was influencing him, as there are echoes of 'Heart Of Gold' in this tune, not that it matters, as it is a fine song in its own right and one of the best on the album. There is an elegiac edge to the lyrics, although the third line of the third verse is sung slightly differently to what appears on the CD insert.

Introspective as ever, Paul asks the rhetorical question, 'Has My Fire Gone Out?' to which the answer is no, though occasionally in the past he's managed to piss on his own fire! The anger that burns inside is never far from the surface and there's much talk of raging inside his head. On '5th Season', he sings of the changing seasons, like the man himself. 'All The Pictures On The Wall' and 'Country' are simplicity itself, on the former Paul plays all the instruments with just Steve White accompanying him, whilst on the latter he is accompanied by Robert Howard on guitar, with Brendan Lynch on stylophone, an instrument made famous by Rolf Harris. At seven and a half minutes, 'Shadow Of The Sun' is long by Paul's previous standards and is full of childhood reminiscences. It is difficult to write lullaby that isn't mawkish or mushy, but Paul manages to do this with 'Moon On Your Pyjamas', a song about his love for his children which, although sentimental, retains a lyrical poetry that takes it out of the ordinary.

A second single, 'The Weaver', was taken off the album and released as an EP on November 1, and went to 18 in the charts. The other tracks were 'This Is Not Time', co-written by Marco Nelson, and 'Another New Day', which was developed from two of the instrumentals on the album. The fourth track was a live version of Neil Young's 'Ohio', a song about the state terrorism America inflicted on (its own) students at Kent State University. Neil Young's polemic would have a struck a chord with Paul. Some critics had suggested his new songs lacked commitment and drive, which was not true. As far as making statements go, he'd been there, and done that in The Jam and the Council and had moved on. *Wild Wood* contains plenty of drive, but of a different kind, with statements that are musical rather than political.

Wild Wood went to number two and stayed in the charts for a year bar one week, cementing Paul's comeback. The richly deserved acclaim it received was a welcome relief after the bone crunching comments passed on him personally during Council's final years, and gave his confidence a huge boost. This album doesn't just show a return to form, but also demonstrates what he does best: writing, recording, and singing good tunes.

Flushed with *Wild Wood*'s success, Paul spent much of 1994 on the road, and along with Steve White the new band, including Steve Craddock on guitar, Helen Turner on keyboards, and bassist Yolanda Charles. A new single, came out on March 28, entitled 'Hung Up' b/w 'Foot Of The Mountain' recorded live at the Royal Albert Hall on November 23, 1993 and 'The Loved' plus another Brendan Lynch re-mix of 'Kosmos', and almost made the top 10, but stalled when it got to number 11. This was the first time since 'The Bitterest Pill' that Paul had released a ballad as a single. Simon Fowler sang backing vocals on this angst ridden tune. 'The Loved' is an acoustic ballad overlaid with some nice flute. The A-side was slapped on the *Wild Wood* album and re-promoted by Go! Discs and it climbed back up the charts for a second time, making the top five and eventually going on to sell over a half million copies.

On September 12, 1994, *Live Wood* was released, which I believe was too early in his solo career. The recordings could have stayed in the vault until they had built up a sufficient amount of live recordings over the next four or five years. This would have given them more songs to choose from, as at this time there weren't enough songs to do his solo live career justice. It reminded me of the Council's first live album, which was also too early in their career, although on this outing there are no overdubs. The tracks were taken from four gigs; one of The Royal Albert Hall gigs in November 1993, one in March 1994 at the Wolverhampton Civic Hall, and two in April at the Paradiso in Amsterdam and La Lune in Brussels.

Live Wood didn't fare that well, reaching only number 13, and staying in the charts for five weeks, which suggests it only appealed to Paul's fan club.

Curiously, *Live Wood* mirrored Neil Young in the seventies, when in 1979, after releasing the studio album *Rust Never Sleeps;* he followed it up six months later with *Live Rust.* Neil's studio album went to 13, stayed in the UK charts for 13 weeks, whilst the live album went to 55 and managed only a three-week stay in the chart.

Many of the songs feature extended jams and are different to the studio takes. 'Bull Rush' is longer and like the studio version breaks into The Who's 'Magic Bus'. 'Can You Hear Us Holy Man' ends with the Edwin Star song, 'War', which he recorded with The Jam. 'Remember How We Started' goes into Donald Byrd's '(Falling Like) Dominoes'. Many of the songs are band workouts, something he wouldn't have considered with either The Jam or the Council. At over ten minutes, 'Shadow Of The Sun' is slightly overcooked though the singles featured are kept to the same length as the originals. 'Into Tomorrow' is more interesting with its harder edge while 'Wild Wood' is filled out with synth and Hammond organ, giving this great tune a fuller sound, and 'Above The Clouds' is very reminiscent of the Council. The CD is a snap shot of Paul Weller at that moment in time but it would have been better to wait until the solo songbook had a few more tunes.

On October 24, Paul's eighth solo single, 'Out Of The Sinking' b/w 'Sexy Sadie' and 'Sunflower (Lynch Mob Beat)', was released. This laid-back love song is chock full of soul with a pulsating rhythm section and it went to 20 in the charts. The flip is a Beatles cover, with Damon Minchella from OCS making an appearance on bass. During the past two years, Paul had clawed his way back playing many concerts throughout the world, something he hadn't done since the Jam days, and with the genuine compliments paid to *Wild Wood,* his confidence was buoyed by this and the success of his comeback. In the beginning, there was no band as such, just Steve White, and Paul was finding his feet with no set list to play from, as he'd only written a few new and original numbers which he mixed up with covers and the odd tune from his Jam and Council songbook. There was no way he could delve too deeply into his past as this would have given the journalist more ammunition to have a go at him, given their critical mauling of his 'Into Tomorrow' single. By the end of 1994, his solo songbook was filling up and he was able to put together a set list of great tunes, with the bulk of them made up from his new songbook, and a few classics from his past.

In his youth, Paul Weller would have cringed to be likened to Neil Young, Steve Winwood, and Van Morrison, all artists from a generation that had little in common with seventies teenagers. In the same way that Frank Sinatra, Bing Crosby and other crooners were an anathema to the sixties generation, the seventies punks and new wavers wanted to sweep aside the past and the music of their fathers. However, like all teenagers, as they matured so did their musical tastes, and as the music scene moved on and developed so did they. The close-mindedness that goes with the territory of being young developed in an open-mindedness that meant Paul – and those of his peers who had the aptitude to do so – could draw from a much deeper well than Ray Davies, Pete Townshend, or Steve Marriott.

The nineties saw a resurgence in British pop with Bands like Oasis, Blur, Suede, Dodgy, and Supergrass offering a welcome blast after the dirge of the eighties. Many of these groups were influenced by the sixties heroes that once influenced Paul, with several quoting The Jam too as a major influence. The nineties also saw the emergence of grunge, the sound of Seattle, with the likes of Nirvana and Kurt Cobain in the roles that The Sex Pistols and Johnny Rotten played in the seventies. Like punk, it would quickly implode, with even the premature death of Cobain mimicking the death of Sid Vicious. In the UK, the new music was christened Britpop and many of these young artists, whose records actually outsold his, venerated Paul, now dubbed The Modfather. He became very pally with Noel Gallagher from Oasis, and they played on each other's albums, as well as playing live together. I recall Noel opening for Paul at one of his solo concerts, which says much about the respect that Noel has for Paul. Both know their own worth, are very opinionated and given to spouting off. When they appeared together on the channel 4 TV show *The White Room* it was said that Paul's legacy was assured. However, it's not who you've played with, it's your songbook that matters, and if Britpop never happened, Paul's legacy of songs would still be written in stone. Nevertheless, Noel gave me a big laugh when he said Paul was the Victor Meldrew of pop music; whenever I catch a re-run of *One Foot In The Grave*, after one of his tirades I expect Victor to burst out singing 'This Is The Modern World'.

Having felt the backlash of the critics at the end of the Council's career, Paul was back in fashion. Not that he would ever forget, or forgive, the writers. Indeed, he would nurse a lifelong grudge against many. Writing in *Melody Maker*, Alan Jones referred to Mick and Paul as the Don Estelle and Windsor Davis of supine albino funk. During an interview more than a decade and half later with *Uncut*, of which Jones is now editor, Paul recalled this quip and was abusive towards Jones, calling him a cunt. There doesn't seem to be any chance of Paul growing old gracefully. The barbed comments aimed at the Council's records and Paul were replaced with plaudits and both he and *Wild Wood* were showered with compliments. In

1994, Paul won a Brit for best British Male Solo Artist, but as he dislikes these kinds of ceremonies, chose not to pick it up. He also won the Lifetime Achievement Song Writing Award at the more prestigious Ivor Novello Awards, which meant a lot to Paul, and he attended the ceremony. A Novello is one of the few music business awards of any real value and is awarded to songwriters who have *outstanding talent*, as judged by a panel of their peers. The Brits on the other hand is just the music business massaging its over sized ego and slapping themselves on the back for doing their job. It wasn't always like this. I recall having to attend the awards ceremony when it first started when it went by the name of The Britannia Awards. There was nothing fancy about the do: it was just a good piss up with artists and industry folk mixing freely. The awards were given for talent, rather than how many tattoos an artist has, and – thank God – they weren't televised.

In August 1994 a documentary covering Paul's career was released by Go! Discs. Pedro Romhanyi was the producer and Paolo Hewitt took care of the narration. Bruce and Rick refused to participate and I wasn't asked to appear either. Paul has always been a control freak; the documentary is a perceived view of his career rather than being even-handed. It was shown at the National Film Theatre on the opening night of the NME's series of rock films entitled Punk – Before And Beyond.

With his first solo album, writers still harped on about a band that had long ago ceased to exist, although this showed the mark The Jam made on the psyche, and the benchmark they set. There's no doubt the success of *Wild Wood* went some of the way towards banishing the spectre of The Jam, and although it outsold every Jam album there were still murmurings of dissent. The only way to slay the beast was to record an album that would put The Jam part of his career into perspective.

On April 24, 1995 Paul released, 'The Changing Man', and it was said he nicked the title from a band with the same name, managed by his old mate Terry Rawlings. A fuss was made about this, but I doubt that it made any difference to the outcome of the band's future. The A-side, which has a taste of The Beatles' 'I Am The Walrus' about it, sees Paul deliver a very convincing, but gruff vocal. The B-side featured 'It's A New Day' with Paul on acoustic guitar and another cut from his Royal Albert Hall concert in 1993, 'I Didn't Mean to Hurt You'. The single also included a cover of the Etta James classic, 'I Would Rather Go Blind'. Paul's version is in keeping with the original, and he made a point of stating this on the CD insert. Rod Stewart had covered this in the early seventies and in 1969 Chicken Shack, part of the British blues boom, released a version that went to 14 in the charts. This featured Christine Perfect on lead vocals, and is the version that most are familiar with. Paul's ninth single went to number seven in the charts, giving him his highest chart placing of his solo career so far.

Now came the time for his third album, and it was a walk down memory lane with large dollops of nostalgia. It was named after the road he and his parents lived in when he was growing up, though the house itself was long gone. Woking isn't what you call a country town, and as a youth, he couldn't wait to get away from the claustrophobic suburban atmosphere to the vibrancy of London. Throughout his life, nostalgia has been a big influence, whether in music, fashion, poetry, or literature, and it's hard to think of another artist who delves as deeply into the past as Paul does. There's nothing wrong with this, as to understand the present you need to appreciate the past. All the great jazz artists I worked with knew the history of jazz, and they too borrowed heavily from their predecessors, and like Paul came up with something new. The reason all these artists and Paul had long careers is because they understood the history of music, and they were a new link in a never ending, but very old chain.

Paul has always been fastidious about the visual images that accompany his recordings and has been so since the first single The Jam released. For Paul's fourth solo album, Peter Blake, one of the leading pop art designers of the sixties whose most notable work was The Beatles' *Sgt Pepper* album design, came up with a concept for the sleeve. Coming from Dartford, Blake's background was similar to Paul's, as this suburban town on the outskirts of South East London isn't that unlike Woking. Mick Jagger came from there and they named the local theatre after him. The sleeve was typical Weller and contained many of his favourite images from his musical past, as well as combining other interests of his. It was an idea he's used with both The Jam and the Council. *All Mod Cons* included many of his favourite Mod images and icons that influenced The Jam's music, and the photo on the gatefold sleeve on *Our Favourite Shop* showed Paul and Mick rummaging around a shop filled with books, records, magazines and photos, all reflecting their tastes, most of them supplied by Paul and Mick. All three albums have a common feel to their design, and although the imagery is nostalgic, the music on all three albums was very much of their decade. Nevertheless, no matter how well the record or CD is packaged, or who designed it, if the music isn't there, it ain't going to sell. The history of music is littered with albums that have well-designed sleeves that only sold a few thousand copies.

Stanley Road came out on May 15, 1995, and went straight to number one, giving Paul his biggest selling album, and eventually going on to sell in excess of 1.5 million copies. With this success, he finally stepped out of the shadow of The Jam, and became one of the few artists who've had number one albums with two very different bands and as a solo artist. Unlike his first two solo albums, *Stanley Road* has a band feel about it, and is more mainstream rock. The line-ups on the first two albums were more mixed and less fixed, with Paul playing the odd acoustic number, which gave them a rambling feel. With the exception of one track, all the songs were recorded with a conventional guitar, bass and drums back line. The first single opened up the album, and followed by 'Porcelain Gods', which has lyrics that comment on the plastic nature of the record industry and the effects of fame, themes Paul wrote about in The Jam on *All Mod Cons*. This segues into Dr John's 'Walk On Gilded Splinters', with its late sixties/early seventies feel, and which reminds me of bands like Iron Butterfly, Quicksilver and all those American psychedelic outfits. Noel Gallagher plays acoustic guitar on this track, although it gets lost in the mix. On July 10, Go! Discs released a second single from the album, 'You Do Something To Me', which went to number nine in the charts. Paul has always had a laddish following, and he's very bloke-ish himself, but this heart-rending ballad showed a tender side to his psyche, and undoubtedly appealed to the girls in his fan base. Many were critical of him for following up *Wild Wood* so quickly with *Live Wood'* and 'Woodcutter's Son', which features Steve Winwood on piano, is a gentle reminder to his critics, that he doesn't care what they say.

Bob Dylan is one of the few songwriters who could write polemic political songs, as well as tunes relating to the fragility of human relationships. Paul's political songs were no match for his other songs. His main strengths as a songwriter is his ability to communicate passion, and feelings of love lost, found, and unrequited, and is something he has in common with all great songwriters, whatever genre of music they come from.

In 'Time Passes' Paul sings of a love lost, while 'Stanley Road' hearkens back to the sixties. 'Out Of The Sinking' has a great hook, another of Paul's many talents, and 'Pink On White Walls' sees Steve Winwood back on keyboards with Paul singing about being defiant, proud and loud, perhaps summing himself up. 'Whirlpool's End', with its sha la la la la, looks back to The Jam and 'Man In The Corner Shop'. 'Wings Of Speed' closes the album, and is Beatlish, but that is to be expected and gets better the more you listen to it. Its angelic gospel chorus is a nice touch, and gives this track a different feel to the rest of the album.

'Broken Stones', a third single from the album came out on September 18 but by this time *Stanley Road* had been in the charts for four months, and its release was intended to kick start sales again. The song is a bit one paced, pleasant rather than spectacular, and although the album had sold well, the new single still managed to get to number 20 in the charts.

The success of this album made no difference to the critics who still found fault, suggesting that the production suffered, and it was a bit leaden. The production on his later Council recordings deserved to be criticised, but not *Stanley Road*, and Brendan Lynch did a great job producing the album. Many were also baffled by the unadulterated success of *Stanley Road* including Paul, and thought *Wild Wood* to be a better album, which artistically it probably is. The phenomenal success certainly owed a lot to Paul's prodigious songwriting talent, but it's also the most straightforward album he'd released to date. Gone was the quirkiness, and whimsy that permeated his previous albums, which is perhaps why *Stanley Road*'s appeal went beyond his fan club. It's a CD you'll find in the collections of people who previously hadn't bought a Paul Weller recording. For the first time in his career, he'd really crossed over into the mainstream market, although he hasn't managed to emulate this success to this day.

On May 30, 2005, Universal released the Deluxe edition double CD + DVD of *Stanley Road*. The second CD contained the demos that went on to make up this album, and many of the songs have different arrangements. 'You Do Something To Me' is at the same pace, but features a churchy organ, and is more bluesy, with very little guitar than the pared down album version. The demo of the third single 'Broken Stones' is different to the final version, as are several of the others. Although listening to these earlier versions, doesn't offer up any clues as to why this album made such an impact.

Stanley Road was unashamedly dedicated to Paul's parents, who have supported him and been by his side since the day he was born. In their eyes, their son can do no wrong, and they have a fierce pride in all his achievements, not just his best selling album. The only dark cloud that year came with the failure of his relationship with his wife Dee C. Lee. The music business is anathema as far as marriage goes; the lifestyle is simply not conducive for a normal relationship. While Dee was in the Council it would have been ok, and during the hiatus between the Council and his first solo album, it must have been hard for her to have Paul under her feet all day. The long hours away from home, touring and recording place impossible demands on a relationship and it would take a saint to be able to resist the many temptations. This business is always referred to as sex, drugs, and rock 'n' roll – and it ain't for nothing!

Paul guesting with Everything But The Girl at the ICA in central London, January 5, 1983.
(Leon Morris/Hulton Archive/Getty Images)

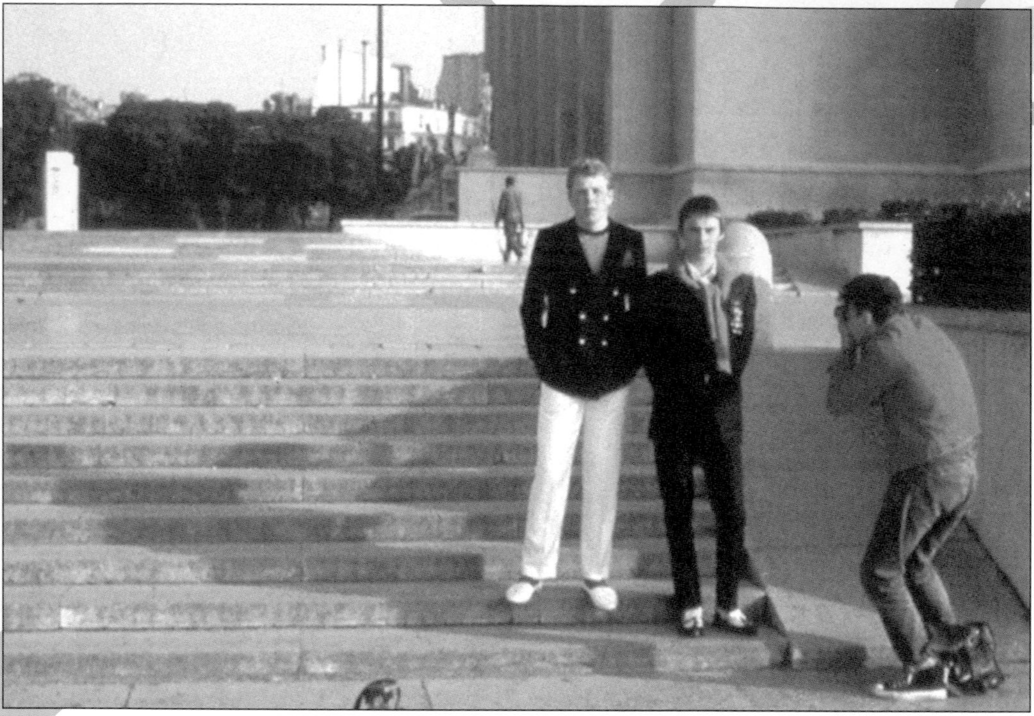

Peter Anderson photographs the two-man Style Council, Mick Talbot and Paul, in Boulogne, 1983.
(Dennis Munday Collection)

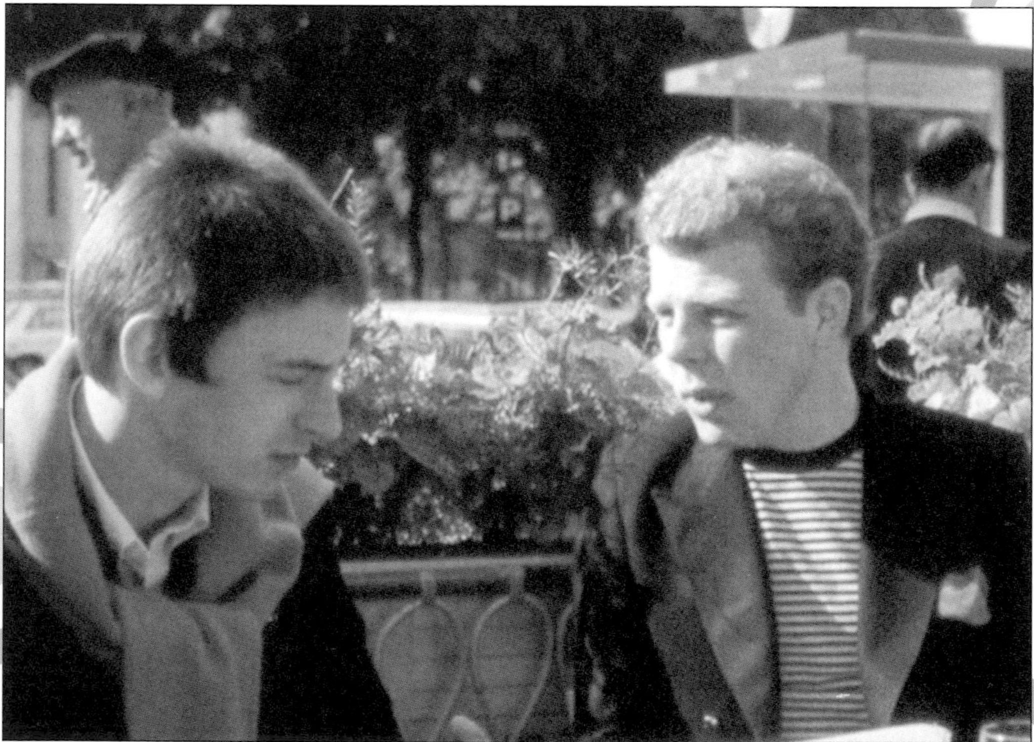

Councillors Paul and Mick in Paris, 1983. *(Dennis Munday Collection)*

Dennis Munday with Paul and Mick, in 1983. *(Dennis Munday Collection)*

Paul, freezing on the Malvern Hills for the Tim Pope directed video for 'Speak', February 1983.
(Eugene Adebari/Rex Features)

Paul with Bob Geldof at the Band Aid recording of 'Do They Know It's Christmas', November 24, 1984. *(Steve Hurrell/Redferns)*

Paul's future partner, DC Lee, flanked by Paul and Mick. *(Kerstin Rodgers/Redferns)*

The Council shoot the video for 'The Lodgers', summer, 1985; left to right: Mick Talbot, DC Lee, Paul and Steve White. *(LFI)*

Paul on stage with the Council at the Artists Against Apartheid gig on Clapham Common, June 28, 1986.
(Adrian Boot/Retna)

The final Style Council photo, July 10, 1989.
(George Chin/Redferns)

Mick and Paul at London's Royal Albert Hall, July 4, 1989 – the infamous final Council concert.
(George Chin/WireImage)

Paul fronts the Paul Weller Movement, 1990.
(Ian Macauley/Retna)

Going acoustic for ***Wild Wood,*** 1994.
(Steve Double/Retna)

Paul playing with Pete Townshend at the Royal Albert Hall, November 27, 2000, for The Who's charity show on behalf of Teenage Cancer Trust. They performed 'So Sad About Us', a 1966 Who song. *(Dave Hogan/Getty Images)*

Paul on stage with Ocean Colour Scene's Damon Minchella on bass, 2004. *(LFI)*

Paul at Cargo, London, February 11, 2005. *(Allan Jones)*

Never one to favour awards, Paul surprised many fans by accepting a Lifetime Achievement Award at the 2006 Brits. After accepting his award from actor Ray Winstone, he and his band played a storming set. *(Patrick Joyce)*

Paul in Amsterdam in 2005. "The acerbic criticisms, his quick temper, and those ever-changing moods are a part of his character. I know that whenever I talk to him I'm never sure whether to wear a T-shirt or a flak jacket… If Paul didn't have real talent he'd have been found out a long time ago." *(Peter Pakvis/Redferns)*

Given the immense success of this album and the fact that Paul was now writing and playing music that was accessible outside of the UK, there was a chance it might even cross over into America. Unfortunately it didn't. The only way that you can crack the States is to undertake long and gruelling tours, and while Paul toured there regularly and appeared on big TV shows, he still refused to play the kind of long tours that turned U2 into superstars there. If you don't play the game in America, you don't sell records. Perhaps his fear of flying, which still manifests itself today, makes him reluctant to undertake two to three month tours. There was talk that PolyGram screwed up the international release of *Stanley Road*, but I hardly think this made much difference. During the seventies and eighties, PolyGram was struggling against the likes of Warners, RCA (now BMG), Capitol and CBS (now Sony). However, by the mid-nineties they were a well-oiled machine and a force to be reckoned with anywhere in the world. If they made the decision and pushed the button, Paul's records would have happened. Go! Discs profile was high within PolyGram, as *The Best Of The Beautiful South* was one of their best selling albums, selling throughout the world.

Both John and Paul are fond of blaming the record companies for their inadequacies when it came to overseas sales, but the fault lies squarely with them and their attitude towards touring and selling records overseas. There was nothing Polydor could do in the seventies and eighties, or Go! Discs in the nineties and I certainly wouldn't fancy working as Paul's International Manager at his new record company. Even here in Italy where I now live and where the Council were popular, when I say I worked with Paul Weller, nine times out of ten the reply is, Paul who?

Paul joined up with Paul McCartney and Noel Gallagher to record a version of The Beatles' 'Come Together' under the name of The Smokin' Mojo Filters. This track was for inclusion on the compilation album *Help*, which was co-ordinated by Go! Discs as part of a fund raising album for Brian Eno's War Child charity, which went to help children in war torn Bosnia. Many sniped at this, but Paul has never supported a charity he didn't believe in, regardless whom he plays alongside. The single went to number 19, while the album went to the number one slot and I am sure there was a lot of mutual backslapping and ego massaging from this trio that spanned three generations. If the album only helped one child, it was worth it. Looking at the promo photos, I wondered whether Macca asked his two scally mates about them borrowing the odd bar or two from his (and John Lennon's) songbook.

Paul suffered a tragedy of his own when John suffered a stroke and while in hospital underwent triple bypass surgery. John loved a drink or three, especially if Polydor was paying, and was a heavy smoker. Unlike Paul, he was never tempted by a healthy diet, so the ravages of the road and record business eventually caught up with him. Throughout his career, Paul was extremely tight with his dad; it wasn't just father and son – they were mates! John never left Paul's side, and I can't recall a time when he wasn't there. No matter how bad things went, when Paul turned around his father would be there for him. Whatever his management weaknesses were, his support was total, 200%, and he did his best for his son, and played an immeasurable part in his success. John was soon back on his feet and back to his old self and ten years later is still doing the wheeling and dealing for Paul. It's quite hard to believe that one day John won't be there, he's like Paul's shadow.

As far as playing live went, in 1993 they played just over thirty gigs, and in 1994 with the success of *Wild Wood* behind him the number of shows doubled, and they played almost 70 concerts. At the end of 1994, there was special benefit concert at the Shepherds Bush Empire on December 4 for Joe Awome, the former boxer who worked as a minder for Paul, who'd died suddenly. I knew Joe, and he was a nice bloke who didn't drink, something unusual in the music business. Paul could have just binned Joe's family some money, but as this concert will be in every Weller gig listing, it insures his name won't be forgotten.

In 1995, it was a similar amount as the previous year, and he played concerts every month from June until the end of the year. Not forgetting his roots, he played the 100 Club, as he'd done with The Jam and the Council. Throughout July and August, he played just about every outdoor festival in Europe, and on August 26, he made a return to the Reading Festival, where he played 16 years previously with The Jam, almost to the day. He ended the year with a massive UK tour, and such was his popularity that he played two concerts at the Aston Villa Leisure Centre in Birmingham, The Apollo Manchester, and the Barrowlands in Glasgow, finishing the tour with four nights at the Brixton Academy.

The success of *Stanley Road* eclipsed everything Paul achieved previously, and he was now bigger than The Jam and the Council put together. There was still the odd criticism here and there, but it wouldn't be a Weller album if someone wasn't carping on about something or other. It was a long and hard road to arrive at this point, with more than a few rocks in the road, many put there by Paul himself, but it must have given him great satisfaction. It's some achievement to have this kind of success in your teens and twenties, but it's an even greater achievement in your thirties, especially as it was Paul's second coming.

CHAPTER 19

Everything Has A Price To Pay

The record business has changed so much that it is unrecognisable from when I started in the late sixties. When The Jam signed to Polydor in 1977, there was still a multitude of record companies, from the big labels to the medium and small. Now four companies, EMI/Virgin, Sony/BMG, Warner Music, and Universal, control 80% of the output of music in the world. This is not the first time this has happened, as in the early sixties when The Beatles signed to Parlophone, EMI, Decca, Pye and Philips controlled the record industry in the UK. The big difference between today's multinational companies and the large record companies of yesteryear is the advent of the computer and the internet highway, which make communications simpler, quicker, and more efficient. You can now set up a meeting with colleagues in different countries and there is no need to leave the office. The advent of CD in the early eighties bought a big change to the manufacturing and distribution side of the business. With vinyl discs, it was necessary to manufacture the discs in each individual country and have huge warehouse facilities for storage and delivery. Now the multinationals have a small number of factories, which manufacture CDs for each different continent, cutting their overhead costs drastically. Nevertheless, this saving isn't passed on to the consumer, with CDs kept at an artificially high price; certainly, this is so in the UK.

The leisure pound is much sought after, and there is stiff competition in the market place and having a product that is over priced doesn't help, particularly now that every computer comes with a CD burner. For the last few years, sales of CDs and records have dropped for the first time since the industry began, although they did recover a little in 2005. For the voracious majors, the only way they can increase their turnover and their profit margins is to gobble up the smaller record companies. Many famous marques, like Chrysalis, Island and A&M, have now disappeared, and although CDs still appear on a few of these labels, they exist in name only and the music men who founded these very individual companies have moved on. With these mega-sized companies, there is no room for individuality and everything, including the artist, must fit in with company's uniform policies, marketing, and packaging. When I started out at Polydor the business was about people selling people to people, now a record company is no different from a company that sells dog food, and it's all about shifting product. Don't get me wrong, I knew the importance of making a profit, but it was about the music, the artists, and although the hours were long it was a fun place to work.

There is now no place for the maverick artists such as Paul Weller who have to ply their trade through smaller independent companies which allow them to keep their individualism and to record the albums they want, with whom they want. Paul had serious problems with Polydor at the back end of the Council's career and although Go! Discs were part owned and distributed by PolyGram, Andy McDonald had the final say. He shaped the musical policy of the company and many of the artists that he signed were like Paul, difficult but successful; well, difficult for the big companies and their A&R departments to get their heads round. Given Paul's attitude towards the majors, recording music for Go! Discs was a home from home.

The rampant success of *Stanley Road* allowed Paul to keep his head down during the early part of 1996. There was no need to think about a follow-up album, or singles, as the album was selling, and stayed in the charts for most of the year. On February 26, Go! Discs released a single of a re-recorded version of 'Out Of The Sinking' as a tribute to Paul. The A-side was backed with, 'I Shall Be Released', one of Bob Dylan's finest songs, which The Hollies, Scott Walker, and The Band had recorded several decades earlier. Although only available for a week it went to number 16 in the charts and was a neat idea by Go! Discs.

As far as taking a break from recording, he'd done this twice before with The Jam and the Council and I am not sure how much of a coincidence these breaks are. It's strange that with The Jam, the Council and during his solo career, as soon as Paul has become ultra successful he takes a break. Most artists, having done all the hard work, would have consolidated their success.

Although there would be no album this year, there was a new single, released on August 5, and was a foretaste of what was to come. 'Peacock Suite' b/w 'Eye Of The Storm' gave Paul his highest chart position as a solo artist, reaching number five in the charts. The track is very much a band jam, with Marco Nelson on bass, and Steve White on drums. Marco, along with Steve White, had been a part of Paul's engine room since his first solo album, and contributed greatly to Paul's comeback. Steve Craddock plays second guitar, and the track is a balls out rock number, with the intro guitar licks reminiscent of Creedence Clearwater Revival, while the guitar interplay has shades of Danny Whitten and Neil Young all over them. It was Paul's most straightforward single to date, and very reminiscent of the late sixties and seventies rock music. The B-side, arranged and edited by Brendan Lynch, features Paul on mouth harp, but the tune doesn't really go anywhere, not that it's meant too. It's the kind of jam all rock bands get into when recording; Jimi Hendrix recorded many jams in a similar vein.

At the Brits, Paul once again won the Best Male Solo Artist award, but didn't show for the ceremony, sending along a pre-recorded message and leaving his dad to pick up the award, another special moment for John. Jools Holland subsequently devoted the whole of his show to Paul, who was backed by the usual suspects, including Guy Barker who played with the Council and is one of the UK's finest trumpet players and a Mercury award winner. I'd met Guy previously as a 14-year-old prodigy, playing with NYJO in the mid seventies. Alongside Guy was the veteran reggae trombonist Rico Rodriguez.

With the fantastic success of *Stanley Road*, you would have thought all the ghosts from his past had been exorcised – but had they? Things were about to change, and Paul's career would go full circle, and once again, he would have to face his old nemesis, those wankers and PolyGram. 1997 started out quietly; there was the odd gig or two but nothing to strenuous. On June 23, Go! Discs released his fourth solo album *Heavy Soul,* and there was much anticipation, with everyone anxious to hear his new songs. Paul was on a run and there was no way the next album wouldn't be successful, but whether it would match the surprise success of *Stanley Road* was another matter. He was fired up and even though approaching forty, his song writing had improved during his thirties and he was more successful than he'd been in his teenage years and twenties. This was unusual insofar as most artists peak by the time they are thirty. By then they are more than likely trundling out formulaic music that owes more to their (own) past than their present, or their future.

Heavy Soul turned out to be less innovative than the first two albums, lacking the instant crossover appeal of *Stanley Road*. The songs were pared down, and there's a rougher, angry edge to the music. The feel on this album is heavier and blacker than on previous records, and as the man himself said, "It's not the kind of album you want to play everyday". There's always a charged atmosphere around Paul when he records, which is normally positive, but on this album it all sounds a bit dark and a little negative. There are a few subtle moments but not many, which is strange as subtlety had always been one of Paul's strong suites. This would have been deliberate, as when he enters a studio, Paul knows how he wants to record his songs. I have no doubts that he could have repeated the formula of *Stanley Road*, but that's not how he works.

The songs hearken back to sixties psychedelia and seventies R&B and rock. The vocals are deliberately on the gruff side, and influenced by the likes of Steve Marriott, Joe Cocker, Chris Farlowe, Paul Rogers and Roger Chapman. It kicks off with *Heavy Soul (Pt 1),* with opening chords that recall Neil Young's 'Cowgirl In The Sand', although this changes when Paul comes in for the verse. Steve Craddock swaps guitar licks with Paul during the middle eight, with vocals that move from the gruff to a near falsetto, and segues neatly into the first single, 'Peacock Suite'. The delightful 'Up In Suzes' Rooms' is one of the few lighter moments, although the emphasis is more rock than soul, with Paul playing acoustic guitar and a string arrangement by Rosie Watters. The looping lead guitar break is reminiscent of the American band, Quicksilver and their guitar solos on 'Fresh Air' and 'Gone Again'. 'Brushed' hearkens back to seventies psychedelia and reminds me of bands like The Youngbloods and Buffalo Springfield. 'Driving Nowhere' plods along nicely, and is the kind of song Paul can write in his sleep.

'I Should Have Been There To Inspire You' is sung with an apologetic passion, which is appropriate for lyrics that talk of lost time with somebody close, and are possibly autobiographical, given the time Paul spends away from those that are close to him. The instrumental 'Heavy Soul (pt2)' is another nod towards Neil Young, although when the guitar comes in it loses the weirdness the Young stamped on his records and breaks into a more trad rock jam. 'Friday Street' is very sixties, particularly the lyrics and the title, and reminds me of The Jam in the eighties. With 'Science', Paul asks questions, which is something he's made a science of during his long songwriting career. 'Golden Sands' is the weakest tune on the album, and just a little bit too much rock 'n' rolly, while 'As You Lean In To The Light' meanders along nicely. 'Mermaids' is the best track on the album, and should have been the lead single. The 'Sha la la las' hearken back to The Small Faces 'Sha-La-La-La-Lee', and it's The Beatles meets Neil Young, but who cares, it's a great tune.

Heavy Soul went to number two and stayed in the charts for 13 weeks, some 74 weeks less than *Stanley Road,* and failed to crossover into the mainstream market. When it was released, it actually outsold Radiohead's critically acclaimed *OK Computer* and hit the number one spot, but the chart compilers marked it down to number two as the record company had screwed up the release by giving away too many freebie postcards. This move was considered a heinous violation of chart procedure and the album punished. I'm surprised they didn't ask for the death penalty!

It's not a difficult album to get your head around; in fact, it's very direct and more traditional. Lyrically Paul has rarely sold himself short, always maintaining a high standard, and the songs on *Heavy Soul* are no exception. To be a consistently good tunesmith you need talent, and the will to grind away and not accept second best. As you age, this becomes harder and harder to maintain, and many artists run out of steam and churn out banal lyrics. Paul's well appears to be bottomless, either that, or like Robert Johnson he went down to the crossroads and did a deal with devil! While Neil Young's music borders on suffering, Paul seems to enjoy the anguish he puts himself and his fans through, although he can occasionally raise a smile amid all the seriousness. Both artists rail against the unfairness of the world and in particular, the record business, although for all their angst, both have done well and carved out very long, successful, and lucrative careers.

The graphics are up to the usual high standard with many sixties psychedelic icons and the usual smattering of pictures taken of the lads while they were recording, plus all the lyrics. Simon Halfon by this time had moved to Los Angeles and was responsible for putting together the Jam tribute album, *Fire And Skill,* which took a long time and tested his patience to the limit. Working with one band is difficult enough, but trying to get different bands to record on both sides of the Atlantic was an almost impossible task. There were many problems with PolyGram (nothing new there) and Simon did well, and pulled it all together. Among those paying homage were The Beastie Boys, Everything But The Girl, Reef, Noel Gallagher, Ben Harper, Silver Sun, Gene, Heavy Stereo, Liam Gallagher, and Steve Craddock. I am not entirely convinced of the merit of tribute albums, some work, some don't, and most excel at ego-massaging, although I must say I really like

Liam Gallagher and Steve Craddock's version of 'Carnation', one of The Jam's finest.

There was now a new line up, including Matt Deighton, and Yolande Charles returned to play bass after Paul fell out with Marco Nelson. This was a shame as Marco had formed a great relationship with Whitey, and they were a dependable rhythm section.

Shortly after the release of his fourth studio solo album, PolyGram decided to implement a buy out of Go! Discs. When Andy formed the label PolyGram held a 49% stake in the company, while Andy retained 51% and control. When the original contract was drawn up between Go! Discs and PolyGram, there would have been a clause inserted where after a certain period either party could buy the other out, and own the label outright. PolyGram's asking price for Andy to buy them out was £26 million, an outrageous price, making it virtually impossible for him to find backers. They also offered him £20 million to stay on, but at a given point in the future, he would still have to sell his own label and start again. By asking such a high price, PolyGram knew Andy had no option but to accept their deal and sell the company, knowing he would have to start up all over again.

On November 1, 1997, PolyGram enforced the sale and 14 weeks later closed Go! Discs offices down, making many of the staff redundant. This must have been a blow to Andy, as he had built the label up from ground zero, turning it into a prosperous and very successful indie label, with a very talented artist roster. No matter how much Andy was paid for his label, and I've no doubt he did ok, it must have been difficult from him to walk away from Go! Discs. There was such a personal commitment by Andy to his artist that it would have been difficult, but not impossible, for PolyGram to fill his shoes. However, the corporate company took the easy option by closing Go! Discs down, and absorbing the artists on to the various labels they owned. It was a case of asset stripping and short-term thinking by PolyGram's corporate management. Whilst consuming the artists on the label, they cut off a vital artery of new blood, which would have supplied the company with new bands for at least another decade, if not longer. Andy took this on the chin and went on to create Independiente, which has much the same musical policy and he is as successful as ever. This decision must have come as a surprise to Paul and John. Indeed, it was their worst nightmare come true, and they were going to have to deal with PolyGram again. They decided to make Paul's new home Island Records, and during one meeting, a top executive at PolyGram said they hoped Paul would be happy on the pink label that housed one of his favourite artists, Steve

Winwood. This might have been the case before PolyGram had bought Island, when it too was an independent record label and ran by the great modern A&R man Chris Blackwell, but now, it was just another record label owned by a major record company.

The end of the Council had left a bitter taste in Paul and John's mouths, but there was something they could have done when they first signed to Go! Discs. It is unusual, but not unknown, for an artist to have a *Main Man* clause inserted in to their contract. Whitney Houston had this with Clive Davis at Arista Records. This means that if the main man (Andy in Paul's case) leaves the label, the artist has the option to move on, or stay. As Paul did not have this clause in his contract, he had to stay with PolyGram, which meant working with his old foes. Paul and John's view on PolyGram was a little jaundiced, as the majority of execs who were around at the end of the Council had long gone, or moved up the chain of command, and the company was full of new faces who'd played no part in the Council's downfall. This didn't matter to Paul and John; they had long memories and what had happened in the past had cut deep. They were never going to forgive and forget, no matter how much the personnel had changed. There was much talk that Paul might deliberately deliver a duff album, but this would have been a mistake. In doing so, they would have given PolyGram the opportunity to turn it down, as they did with the last Council album. Much better to knuckle down, see out the contract, and move on to pastures new, hoping that PolyGram wouldn't gobble up his next label as well.

Because of the protracted negotiations that took place with Island and PolyGram, it meant *Heavy Soul* wasn't fully marketed. Following the release of the album there were three more singles, but none faired that well in the charts. A month after the album came out, on July 28, they released 'Brushed', which went to 14, and on September 29, 'Friday Street' came out and went to 21. 'Mermaids', the most commercial track on the album, was released on November 24, and it just squeezed in the top thirty. It was a case of a little too late, and had this single been released earlier, I'm sure it would have been a much bigger hit. By the time the last single came out, the album had slipped out of the chart and it would have been lost amongst the Christmas pap. It is corporate policy at big companies to flog an album to death, but there was no real return on the last two singles, and it may have been better to wait for something new in the New Year.

On November 29, he appeared on Jools Holland's *Later* show and I went along to Shepherd Bush to see it recorded. Jane Hitchen, who ran Polydor's tape library, and was a great help while I was putting together The Jam box set, accompanied me. Jane was a big fan of Paul's and while the other bands were performing, I took her backstage to introduce her. As we waited, I noticed she was shaking, more than a little nervous, and asked if everything was ok. She replied, "I'm meeting PAUL WELLER, I'm shitting myself." I can honestly say I'd never really saw Paul this way, and he was just Paul Weller to me, and it came, as a bit of shock. The incredible success of *Stanley Road* had raised Paul's stature, and although it didn't really change him, even I now realised he was PAUL WELLER!

In 1998, there was another break, with only one single and album released, and only about thirty gigs played. On November 2, Island released a new track 'Brand New Start', which went to 16 in the charts. The B-side featured two tracks, a new song entitled, 'Underneath It' and 'The Riverbank', which is a re-working of the Jam classic 'Tales From The Riverbank'. It's slower, less psychedelic, but it's not a patch on the original. 'Brand New Start' was included on *Modern Classics: The Greatest Hits*, which came out on November 9, and went to number seven and stayed in the charts for 19 weeks. Strangely enough, given how big Paul had become, it didn't fare as well in the charts as The Jam's, or The Style Council's *Greatest Hits.*

The hits CD was a contract filler, which left Paul owing Island one more studio album and once delivered, he could leave. When this compilation came out, I wondered whether Paul was having a little pop at PolyGram as the title bore more than a similarity to the rejected Council album, *Modernism: A New Decade.*

Looking at his solo career what's interesting is that singles haven't played as big a part in his success as they did with both The Jam and the Council. There's no doubt with the rise of the CD, the singles market was taking a hammering and sales were dropping each year, with the emphasis now shifting to artists like Paul who could write an album full of tunes. With this change, it meant Paul could shift albums without the pressure of having to write hit records.

In 1999, Paul played fewer dates than at any other time during his solo career, and was very frugal, releasing just a solitary single that year. On December 28, Island re-issued 'Wild Wood', and its appeal to his fans would have been the B-sides, which contained different tracks to the original. It went to 22 in the charts, eight places lower than the first time, which ain't bad considering there was a gap of six years.

Having gaps between albums isn't a bad thing either, as it gives the artist plenty of time to write the next album's worth of songs, and without pressure. However, unless you are a megastar, with albums regularly selling millions worldwide, you can't afford too long a gap. You need to keep the momentum of your success going between albums with singles, touring, and the gap between his last album *Heavy Soul* and the next studio album would be nearly three years, which is perhaps a year too long.

Between the release of *Heavy Soul* in June 1997 and his fifth studio album released in April 2000, he played less than a hundred gigs, and only released five singles, including the re-issue of 'Wild Wood'. There were three in 1997, two in 1998 and one in 1999, with only two managing to get into the top twenty. The *Greatest Hits* was released as a stopgap, and 17 months before his fifth studio album. This interval would have been ok had this followed *Stanley Road,* as the album was in the charts for more than a year and a half. *Heavy Soul* only hung around for 13 weeks, and never realised anything like the million plus sales that *Stanley Road* achieved. Releasing an album as successful as *Stanley Road* would create problems, as the record company would expect the follow up albums to be just as successful, which is only natural for today's money hungry industry.

There's no doubt that Paul was unhappy being tied to Island and PolyGram and this might have affected his thinking, but I'm not sure he was at a level where he could afford to take a long break without it affecting his career. Had his recordings sold in the USA or significantly in the other big markets, it would have been different. The problem that artists face with long careers is that, regardless of their talent, the later into their career they get their album sales yo-yo from year to year. There's no doubt that he was doing it live, as he was headlining mega festival after mega festival, but his CD sales were on a downward trend.

On April 3, 2000, Island released the first single from Paul's new studio album, and managed to cock it up completely. As it had the wrong bar code strip, the single was ineligible for the charts, making this the only single that Paul's released to date that hasn't charted. This is one piece of news I wouldn't have wanted to pass on to him, and I can't imagine what he told his record company! 'He's The Keeper' sets the tone of the album, and not the best track to open with, or release as a single, although there isn't a track on the album that really snaps your head off. The B-side, Sonny and Cher's 'Bang-Bang', would have raised a few eyebrows, but this cover came via Stevie Wonder, who'd recorded this tune on his 1967 Motown album, *Down To Earth.*

Heliocentric, came out on April 10, 2000, and the back line featured Ocean Colour Scene's guitarist Steve Craddock, and their bassist, Damon Minchella, with Steve White on drums. Paul played all the other instruments and there are only a few guest musicians. The album is consistent, but has no stand out tracks and no 'real' singles, which is unusual for Paul. The songs are generally lighter, more reflective than those on *Heavy Soul*, perhaps too reflective, giving the album a listless feel.

Following the first single, 'Frightened' doesn't get out of the blocks, and is on the lumpy side. The lilting 'With Time And Temperance' features Brendan Lynch on mini-moog and glockenspiel, and is reminiscent of his Council days, circa *Our Favourite Shop*. All that's missing is Mick's tinkling piano, which may have given this song a lift. 'There's No Drinking After You're Dead' deals with a subject that Paul knows a bit about and might be borne from experience. 'Back In The Fire' sees Paul at his melancholic best, and 'Love-Less' covers a subject he's written about many times during his career, but there's nothing smaltzy about this tune.

As we all know, love is a double sided coin, when it works it's great, when it doesn't life can be shit. 'Dust And Rocks' aptly deals with this, whilst 'Picking Up Sticks' sees Paul playing everything but the kitchen sink. Cliff Stapleton plays the hurdy-gurdy and Steve White takes a rare drum solo, something he usually saves for live appearances. 'A Whale's Tale' clumps along with lyrics that seem to reflect Paul's unhappiness with being back with PolyGram. A recent convert to Nick Drake, whom most of Paul's generation wouldn't even have heard of, he hired Drake's arranger Robert Kirby to score the strings. This was a logical move, and whilst Kirby's scores are nicely understated, they tend to fit the melancholic mood of the album.

The album went to number two, but only hung around in the charts for eight weeks before quickly dropping out of the top 75. As I have said before, it's how many weeks in the charts that matter, not the chart position. The record companies in my day were amateur compared to the Big Four now; these well oiled-machines have slick marketing department that rarely lose a record, and are very adept at hitting the top end of charts. As with The Jam and The Council, his loyal fan base is extremely dedicated and rush out to buy Paul's CDs as soon as they hit the streets, and what is clear from the stats is that *Heliocentric* never went beyond his large fan club. It's an ok album rather than great, in a similar vein to his first two solo records, but without their sparkle. The production values aren't up to the past albums either, and several of the songs sound jaded. Possibly the combination of Paul producing with Brendan was reaching an end, they'd been together for nearly eight years, and it was Paul's sixteenth studio album, if you include the unreleased Council album.

On August 21, Island released a second single from the album, 'Sweet Pea, My Sweet Pea'. It was dedicated to his daughter Leah, ensuring that his

Sweet Pea will be forever immortalised. This was PolyGram/Island's last throw of the dice, but it wasn't really a single, just a belated effort to shift some CDs, and it only just scraped into the top fifty. Paul could now move on and he re-signed with Andy McDonald's new label Independiente, finally saying goodbye to PolyGram, all assuming they don't wolf down his next record company.

Steve Craddock, Damon Minchella, and Whitey are still with Paul to this day, it's very hard not to draw a comparison between this, and Neil Young's backing band Crazy Horse, given that Young's music was influencing him. However, with the type of music he was writing and playing, he needed a backing band that could fall in behind him. As ever, he prefers to surround himself with like-minded people whom he can trust to perform the songs the way he wants to hear them. Paul rarely steps out of his circle when looking for musicians and has always chosen solid and dependable players. He isn't the easiest person to work with, ask anyone who's played with him, and there would be no point in him hiring musicians if he couldn't get along with them. Paul picks his band members precisely because they give him what he wants, and a list of musicians who can do this is pretty short.

The comparisons with Neil Young, Steve Winwood, Nick Drake, Van Morrison are obvious, but I'd rather Paul travelled down this road than playing the standard rock 'n' roll boogie music that many older musicians bang out in the later years. There's nothing unusual about Paul dipping into someone else's pot before adding his own ingredients, and he's gone about his business this way for pretty much the whole of his career. Personally, I've never quite understood the fuss made about Paul and other artists who borrow from the past and other artists' work. Maybe it's because I grew up listening to modern jazz, and worked in this idiom for four years prior to working with The Jam. Charlie 'Yardbird' Parker, considered to be the greatest jazz improviser of all time, often borrowed bits from the George Gershwin song 'I Got Rhythm' to came up with great and original jazz tunes. Since 'Birds' death, there hasn't been an alto player in the universe who wasn't influenced by him. Most tenor players are from the Coleman Hawkins, Ben Webster or Lester Young school – even the great John Coltrane took his influences from Hawkins and Webster but he still went on to stamp his own personality on the tenor saxophone. I worked with Oscar Peterson who was greatly influenced by Art Tatum, Nat 'King' Cole, and Teddy Wilson but only the most churlish of reviewers wrote negatively about these influences. When starting out their careers, all the great jazz artists were influenced by the previous generation of players before going on to make their own mark. This was the norm in jazz, and provided they added to the pot it was perceived as a plus not a minus. It's precisely what you add to the pot that makes the difference between being a journeyman player, or a great musician.

During the nineties, there was a trend for artists to record a *wooden* (acoustic) album of their present and past repertoire for broadcast on MTV's *Unplugged* series. As was his wont, Paul ignored this trend, putting any ideas of acoustic sets or recordings on the back burner. Perhaps he was reluctant because there would have been a demand for him to play songs from Jam and The Style Council. It was certainly too early in his solo career, which was just taking off, but in 2001 he put this right. In February, he undertook a world tour performing acoustic numbers from all three songbooks, showing a very intimate side of the man and a good way of joining up the songs he'd written since first recording with The Jam.

On October 8, 2001, Independiente released *Days Of Speed*, a live album of recordings taken from this very popular acoustic tour. Both the Council's *Home And Abroad* and his *Live Wood* albums were a tad premature, and fleeting moments of Paul's career. *Days Of Speed* is not just an overview, it shows how he's developed his career from a promising teenage songwriter to a mature tunesmith who with every decade has taken his craft to another level. You won't learn anything new about him from this album, although there is a charm and intimacy that his studio albums don't always capture. It's unusually relaxed, and there's a looseness about the tracks and the man that doesn't always come across when he plays the full band versions.

The songs from his two previous bands are a bit predictable but fit in nicely among the songs from his solo career. His homage to his country, 'English Rose', lacks the *yearning* that the original had, but is still a nice tune, and 'That's Entertainment' still sounds great. Paul wrote this tune quickly, conjuring up strong urban images while gazing out of the window of his London home, and when I complimented him on a memorable portrait of the city, he dismissed the compliment, pointing out how quickly he'd knocked it out. Listening to this song I'm reminded of that other great British song writer Ewan McColl whose song 'Dirty Old Town' painted an even starker picture of grimy urban life. The Pogues covered this song to great acclaim.

'Town Called Malice' lacks the edge of the original, although listening to this version it's hard to believe that both this, 'That's Entertainment' and 'English Rose' were recorded more than 20 years ago. Divorced from the riff that sounds like 'You Can't Hurry Love', the original melody comes through and shows just how little the song owes to the Supremes' song. From his Council days, he plays just two tunes, 'Headstart For Happiness', one of the first he recorded in 1983 after splitting up The Jam, and 'Down In The Seine' from his French period. The vocals are a little gruffer than the originals, which is probably down to all those cigarettes he smokes. I could come up with another half a dozen tunes from these periods that he could include in his set but this album is more about the decades that followed than his seventies and eighties songbooks.

Throughout the performances, he's laid back and knocks his songs out with effortless ease, as if he has been doing this for a long time, which he has. The sign of a good songwriter is when his songs still stand up when stripped to the bone. On this album, the songs not only stand up but singing them solo give Paul and his lyrics an added dimension. My only complaint is I would have liked to have heard him accompany himself on the piano on a couple of numbers, as he's an underrated pianist, but given that critics were calling him a third rate Eric Clapton, whatever that is, had he done this he would have probably been labelled a fourth rate Reg Dwight! Of the solo songs 'Brand New Start', 'Science', 'Above The Clouds' and 'Wild Wood' are outstanding, but then so are the rest of the tracks on this album.

In every aspect, this is a raw album that didn't need too much tinkering with in the studio, and like fine leather, there's the occasional scars, but it's one of the finest albums in his catalogue. I was recently asked by a fanzine to name my favourite Weller solo album and I chose this one. It went to number three and stayed in the charts for 16 weeks, twice as long as his previous studio album and sales went on to exceed over half million copies.

When Paul started out again for the third time, he was almost back to where he started, playing pubs, clubs, Universities and remote venues. The success of the first three solo albums changed all this, and he went on to play bigger venues than he'd ever played with either The Jam, or the Council, and not just in the UK. From April 1996 to December 2001, Paul played nearly 250 concerts worldwide. On June 9, 1996, he headlined his own festival, *A Lazy Afternoon With Paul Weller*, in Finsbury Park, a stone's throw away from one of his old haunts, The Rainbow. The title was a nod to his fixation with Steve Marriot and The Small Faces and the line-up featured bands like Reef, The Bluetones, and his mate Dr Robert. An amazing 35,000 fans turned out, which this must have given Paul one of his biggest ever blasts, and as for John, this gig must have fulfilled his dreams, even more than wanting to see The Jam play Madison Square Garden. As big as The Jam became, they were never capable of pulling an audience this size; mind you, if they reformed, Finsbury Park might not be big enough. Shortly after this event, he found the time to jam in a boozer with his guitar roadie's band, Dave Liddle's Blues Express, singing on Tommy Tucker's 'High Heel Sneakers'.

John was rubbing his hands with glee, as by now Paul could really put bums on seats, and the odd acre of grass. During 1997, it was more of the same, and he played over 60 concerts. In July, to support the release of *Heavy Soul*, he played 15 dates, making appearances at T-In-The-Park festival in Scotland, A Day-At-The Races in Sheffield, two festivals in Belgium, plus on August 2, another Day At The Races at that well-known racetrack, Crystal Palace Sports Centre. In the autumn, he blitzed the USA, Canada, and Japan, as well as squeezing in a few gigs in Holland and Germany, ending the year with his annual UK tour. This consisted of 20 dates with the last four in London, two at Battersea Power Station, one at the Kilburn National, with the last gig at the incongruous, but famous London Palladium.

In 1998 and 1999, it was a different story, and he played less than forty gigs. In August '98 he played a festival at the Victoria Park, Hackney, with Ian Dury on the under card. Dury had previously supported Paul when the Council played the Glastonbury Festival in June 1985. Sadly, it would be one of Ian's last appearances as later he lost his battle with cancer and died, leaving the record business bereft of one if its real characters.

As we entered a new decade in 2000, he notched up just over 50 concerts, commencing in April with a large UK tour to support the release of *Heliocentric.* When it came to the summer, there wasn't a festival in Europe where Paul Weller didn't make an appearance. At the end of year, he played *The Ideal Pop Exhibition* at Earls Court, which almost sold out the 30,000 tickets before they announced the rest of the bill!

In 2001, he undertook an acoustic tour and with his other shows played nearly 80 gigs. Playing these enormous venues and festivals must have seemed a far cry from the early days of The Jam, where once they played to three men and a dog, and venues like Tumbledown Dick in Farnborough, The Nags Head in High Wycombe, West Runton (cricket) Pavilion, and The Village Bowl Discotheque in Bournemouth.

There was no doubt he was doing the business live, and *Days Of Speed* did well, however, his last studio album, *Heliocentric,* hadn't sold as well as either *Stanley Road* or *Heavy Soul.* What would 2002 bring, and would his first studio album for Independiente, turn this around?

CHAPTER 20

Going Places

Paul is renowned for speaking his mind and in interviews has rapaciously criticised many of his contemporaries as well as newer acts that have come along during his long career. For the most part, he gets it right, and often says what people are thinking but are too scared to say. When first meeting him, or reading his interviews, his no nonsense, shoot from the hip, abrasive character is always to the fore, especially if anyone dares to challenge him. Attack has always been his first (and only) line of defence, as many journalists have found out. However, there is another side of his character that is often overshadowed by the aggressive persona that he portrays. Throughout The Jam and the Council's career, Paul's support of left wing politics, CND and Animal Rights was well known, and he was one of few pop stars who took the political fight into the enemy's camp, which could have had a damaging affect on his career. You won't find Paul's name associated with the trendy causes, nor does he advertise or try to make gain from his charity appearances, even though he knows he's only on the bill to put bums on seats.

During his solo career, he's gone about his charity work quietly, and supported many good causes, including Phil Morris's testicular cancer awareness site (www.checkemlads.com), where he and Steve White both lent their support. I recall going to Great Ormond Street with Paul, Bruce and

Rick to visit a Jam fan who was dying of cancer, and their surprise visit brought much joy into this young man's tragically short life. On February 9, 2002, he was at the Royal Albert Hall lending his support for a Teenage Cancer Trust gig (www.teenagecancertrust.org/main). The Who's Roger Daltrey makes a significant contribution organising the events for this very worthwhile charity.

When it came time to record the new songs for his album Paul decided to dispense with Brendan Lynch's services and once again produce himself. This was a shame, as Brendan had served him well and worked with Paul for longer than either Vic Smith or Peter Wilson. It's quite possible, that the relationship had run its course and it was time for a change. I'm not casting aspersions on Brendan's abilities, as up to this album he'd done a fine job, but the production on *Heliocentric* suffered. Although I must say in his defence, just listening to the CD and not being in the studio, it's hard to point the finger. The songs on the album were Paul's weakest to date, there weren't any up-front singles, and a few songs were on the ordinary side. I know how difficult Paul can be when he's in the studio, although he's no different from many artists. They hear their songs the way they wrote and demoed them, and don't see any other way of playing them – or don't want to. It's not always easy to deliver the goods, and many factors contribute towards making a great album, but a good producer can make the difference between an album sounding ordinary, or great.

Independiente released *Illumination* on September 16, 2002, and it went to number one, although it stayed on the charts for only seven weeks, one week less than *Heliocentric.* The engine room on this album is once again Steve White, Steve Craddock and Damon Minchella, and there is a guest appearance by Simon Dine, who co-produced a couple of the tracks. Carleen Anderson seems to have filled the vocal slot that Dee C. Lee had with the Council and Jocelyn Brown lends her voice.

Unlike *Heliocentric,* there were genuine singles on *Illumination* and on September 2, 'It's Written In The Stars' preceded the album and was released as two CDs. The first single was b/w 'Horseshoe Drama' and 'Push Button Automatic', while the second CD featured two Jam classics taken from the 2001 acoustic tour, 'The Butterfly Collector' and 'Carnation'. The A-side, co-produced by Simon Dine, is a little slicker than the other tracks on the album, the looped brass synth on the intro is peppered throughout, and the song is nice drop of Weller soul.

The album opens up with 'Going Places', a road song in the classic tradition. As a fan of The Flying Burrito Brothers since hearing their first album in 1969, I didn't have to read the reviews to know that Paul had dipped his bread in their gravy. There is a familiarity about this tune as soon as you hear the opening chords. It's like pulling on those old loafers you've had for years, the ones that fit you like a glove, and it's a song that no matter how many times you hear it, you never tire of hearing it. 'A Bullet For Everyone' sees Paul back on the rampage with a great mixture of guitar, Hammond organ and echoes of Norman Greenbaum's 'Spirit In The Sky'. The lyrics talk of the haves and have nots, always a subject close to Paul's heart. 'Leafy Mysteries' was taken off as the second single and released on November 18, but didn't have the same impact as the first, and only reached 23. It's a solid album track, but it might have been better to go with 'A Bullet', which is more direct and a real foot-tapper. 'Who Brings You Joy', is a love song that reminds me of Traffic's Dave Mason's early solo material, although Paul's vocal is a little affected. Since 1977 with 'I Need You', Paul has been able to write songs of this genre that are emotive and hit the heart spot. This is not a song that drools over a loved one; it's a tender soliloquy to someone special. Both 'Now The Night Is Here' and 'One X One' are a bit downy and could have been on the previous album. Even though Noel Gallagher and Gem Archer of Oasis make a guest appearance on the latter track, neither really go anywhere.

'Spring (At Last)'is a downbeat instrumental, which would have benefited from some of Brendan's touches and, it might have been better to leave it off the album all together. 'Standing Out In The Universe' has a similar breeze to Thunderclap Newman's 'Something In The Air' with some great backing vocals from Carleen Anderson and Jocelyn Brown. The title track, 'Illumination', is another Weller acoustic classic, whose lineage dates back to his Jam and Council days and has a great vocal. 'Bag Man' is of the same ilk, but not as good and has a mannered vocal that neither feels, or sounds comfortable. 'All Good Books', which deals with religion and the problems that plague the world, contain some of the best lyrics on the album, and features Aziz Ibrahim, who replaced John Squire in The Stone Roses, on acoustic guitar. 'Call Me No. 5' sees Paul swapping Joe Cocker like vocals with Kelly Jones of The Stereophonics.

There were no further singles released, reducing the album's shelf life to a couple of months. It's certainly more satisfying than the previous outing, but I feel a co-producer may have got more out of Paul, and his songs. Even the graphics suffered and weren't up to his previous albums, with an unclear image of his face. Inside, the psychedelic tie-died images are ok, but you can't read the lyrics, making it a pointless exercise printing them.

With both this and *Heliocentric*, it sounds like Paul's treading water, and it's possible that he was finding it hard to come up with the songs, which isn't strange considering he'd was in the 25th year of his career. No matter how talented you are, it's not possible to write great song after great song. Perhaps with these two albums Paul was going through a mid-life crisis, or there was nothing out there to get his creative juices flowing. Although the chart position for both albums looks great, it hides the fact that neither of these albums crossed over, and went beyond the fans. It was going to be interesting to see how his record company would view this, and his sales, which were on a downward trend. There's no doubt that when Andy McDonald re-signed Paul, it would have been for a hefty advance, and the next album wouldn't come cheap. Although I doubt that anyone thought it would be another three years, before his next studio album would surface.

In 2002, Virgin Radio conducted a poll to find the top 100 British artists and placed Paul at number 21. He was in front of The Clash, as well as The Who, although The Jam was ahead of him at five, with the Council sneaking in the top 100 at 97.

During his career, Paul has castigated the music business on many occasions. When Polydor dropped him the invective flowed and still does to this day, and he is one of the few (big) artists that constantly rails against record companies. He can take this stance as he's been at the top for nearly thirty years and more importantly, he did it his way. However, he can only take this stance as long as he is selling records. The Roman Senate is a nursery school compared to the Machiavellian goings on in the record business, and like him, it has a long memory.

We are now midway through the first decade of the 21st century and there seems to be no change in the industry. Even though sales are dropping, if you do not conform to the uniformity that the characterless record business has become, you've no chance. This is a shame, and it's possible that we will not see the likes of Paul and his breed again, and if the business is not careful, it will bore itself to death.

In 2003, the record business went through another crisis; single sales had been steadily declining for the past decade, but that year, in the first quarter alone they dropped 43%. For many years, the record companies were reliant on the quick fix artist, the pretty boy, and mini skirted good-looking girl bands. These boy and girl vocal groups had very little talent other than looking good and being able to dance and sing at the same time, usually on a cover version of an old hit. This was nothing new as this kind of facile music has been around for years, and even Messrs Weller and Gallagher have pointed out that each new generation of teenagers re-cycles the past and puts their own slant on pop music.

CDs were introduced in the early eighties and when this became the main format, with nearly 80 minutes of music, it was blindingly obvious that the single format would become redundant. While Bill Gates and his mates changed the world with innovation, the music industry was slow to change. Typically, it buried its head in the sand and since the mid '80's marketing and sales became the keywords. Why do they have to look for talent, when they could manufacture it! Had these execs looked at the history of pop music they would have seen that every decade threw up (sic) bands of this ilk – The Archies, 1910 Fruit Gum Company, Brotherhood Of Man, Edison Lighthouse, New Seekers, The Rubettes, Bananarama – which gave the companies instant success and turnover, but none of these artists had a long-term future.

This is A&R by numbers and requires no flair whatsoever, the talent shows on national TV and the viewing public does the job for them. They don't have to slog round the pubs, clubs, and all the toilet gigs that every previous generation of A&R men did. These superficial programmes mimic the likes of Hughie Green's *Opportunity Knocks*, which at least gave us the likes of Les Dawson and many other great comedians. Lena Zavaroni, Peters & Lee and Mary Hopkins all got their start on this show, but *Op Knocks* never unearthed great pop talent. The business has always needed the here-today gone-tomorrow artists to bring in instant cash, but in the '60's, '70's and the early '80's the emphasis was always on breaking more serious artists, which could take up two or three albums. These three decades had their fair share of disposable pop bands whose lifespan was short, so you milked it dry, knowing that your back catalogue would still be selling and you could deep mine your talented artists. These were the days though when A&R departments ruled, when music makers decided the music policy, not the artful marketing mangers and Armani-clad lawyers who hold sway these days.

As far as the record companies go, A&R is a lost science. I recall a conversation at the start of Paul's solo career, and he reckoned that if he was starting out again no record company would sign him. Even sadder, it's unlikely that any of the modern A&R men would recognise the latent talent of the likes of Bob Dylan, Bruce Springsteen, and Lennon & McCartney – and if they appeared on any of these reality TV talent contests, they'd be lucky to come third.

The steady decline in the demand for CDs throughout the world appears to have bottomed out, and for the rock stars of tomorrow, there is a light at the end of the tunnel and that is the net. At last, the record companies are finally – six or seven years too late – starting to get to grips with the electronic delivery of music. The A&R function will in time pass totally to the net and new talents will be able to promote their music to a cult level on the net, with the majors then picking it up to take it to a national and global level. Today's Wellers and Dylans will have no trouble finding an outlet for their music via the net. A couple of months ago the first single went to number one on downloads alone so it seems that the single may not die after all. I-Pods are doing the same for music now that Walkmans did in the late seventies.

In another interview, Paul was vehement about the record business, saying: "I think they're all scum really and always have been. They've treated me awfully (but) I don't expect anything else really. They're only there to make a quick buck, the quickest, fastest way they can do that the better for them. It would be nice if they could also make their quick buck but you'd be allowed to do your own thing and be creative as well." This is not strictly true, and until his excesses got the better of him, when he was signed to Polydor, he did exactly what he wanted, and the problem lay in taking such huge advances and producing albums that didn't sell. If you don't want to lose the right to be creative, then you have to look at your deal and the money you want up front, especially if you're only selling in your home market. I've always agreed with his sentiments towards the record business, but when you accept large advances, you're bartering with the freedom to do what you like, and there is no room for experiment, as the record company will demand a return for their investment. As long as your records are selling and you are at the top end of the charts, the record companies will leave you alone. At this point, they need you more than you need them, but when your sales and chart profile slip, as it did towards the end of the Council's career, record companies will shed you, regardless of how much money you have made for them in the past. I'm afraid history is full of artists who have sold records, but past sales are a collateral that has no value. In the music business, it's the present that counts.

Illumination turned out to be his last album for Independiente, which came as a surprise as after the problems with Island and PolyGram it seemed to be the ideal home for Paul. The problem was money, and the advances demanded didn't match the sales of his albums, which had slipped since *Heavy Soul*. Paul wasn't doing the business overseas to supplement his UK sales, and as much as Andy McDonald was into Paul, the asking price was too high and he was unwilling to pick up the option, although their parting of the ways was amicable. As far as John goes, he will always ask for big numbers, having said that, there are some idiots working in the music business today who will pay out telephone numbers, as in the huge advances that Mariah Carey and Robbie Williams have received. Following *Stanley Road,* none of Paul's album came close to selling a million copies. When it came to doing a deal, John should have taken a leaf out of Abba manager Stig Anderson's book. He went for the record label he believed would do the best for the band, which wasn't always the one that offered the most money. Abba were signed to different record companies around the world and weren't exclusive to one label, and whilst he would take less money upfront, he made sure they received maximum points. This enabled them to recoup the advance faster, and they would earn serious money when the royalties came rolling in.

Sanctuary thought they had him, but in the end, he signed for Richard Branson's new label V2. Branson was a very successful entrepreneur who has a penchant for self-publicity and when he started Virgin records and the Virgin Megastore chain, it was a breath of fresh air. However, it developed into just another over sized label, and nineteen years after its inception he sold it off to EMI and picked up a cool £500 million. Paul might even have considered his nemesis Polydor, as it has gone through a real purple patch the last ten years, and although attached to an octopus like conglomerate, it has once again become a decent record label.

While Paul is delivering the goods, everything in the garden will be rosy, but should he go through a barren period, which is not impossible, he may wish he were talking to Andy than the executives at Branson's new company, or the man himself. In the past, Paul has always confounded his critics and only time will tell if this partnership is successful. If V2 have paid a king's ransom for his signature, I am sure there are clauses in the contract to cover their arses; Branson's no fool, he's an astute businessman with the smile of a crocodile. One thing for sure, there will be no room for records that are anything less than successful.

The only album released during 2003 was the 39-track three-CD mini box set entitled *Fly On The Wall: B-sides & Rarities 1991–2000* which contained songs that Paul had demoed during his solo career. The Jam and The Style Council had released this type of compilation, but they were only single CDs, and not so in-depth. Along with Andy Street at Universal, he compiled the CDs, as well as adding his comments on the tracks in the booklet, making it a very personal collection. These compilations are for the genuine fans, acknowledging their loyal support, and Paul is lucky as his fans, whether they are Jam, Council, or Weller fans, have stuck by him through thick and thin. He himself is an avid collector of these kinds of recordings by his own favourite acts, which probably motivates him to release such compilations himself.

The three CDs are chock full of B-sides, re-mixes, rarities, and unreleased tracks both vocal and instrumental. The first two cover his solo work, and include 'Here's A New Thing', the very first song he recorded after the demise of the Council. The third CD contains the cover versions taken from his heroes and influences. The Beatles are never far away with 'Sexy Sadie', 'Instant Karma' and 'Don't Let Me Down' joining 'And Your Bird Can Sing' and 'Rain' from his early days. There's Traffic's 'Feelin' Alright', and 'Ohio' by Neil Young and not CSN&Y as is often quoted. Sonny and Cher's 'Bang Bang' was a surprise but Weller wouldn't be Weller if he didn't throw the odd bouncer down the wicket.

Paolo Hewitt summed up this type of compilation perfectly when he wrote on the Council rarities CD insert: "Albums such as these, which don't dwell on the obvious always, tell us so much more about the artist motivation. The wide style of music that is evident here, the growing maturity of so many of his songs, compared to Weller's previous work, which seek to reflect a myriad of moods and feelings. The sheer energy and joy that seeps through so many of the tunes captures an artist who's given us many musical highlights over the past three decades." This was written some 10 years before *Fly On The Wall*, but is equally applicable to this box set. It went to 22 in the charts, which isn't bad for a three-CD package.

After giving us an insight into the way he works, and the artists he personally likes, it was time for his debut on V2, and his first offering was an album of covers. Many in the business were chuckling over this, as it isn't the norm for a known artist who's just signed to a new record company to kick off with this kind of album. Most record companies would have frowned at this idea, not least because Paul is a talented songwriter.

Covering other artist's songs is always a difficult task, as it's nigh on impossible to top the original versions, as Paul often points out, and at best, if you do justice to the original, it's a great accomplishment. What's interesting about this album is Paul's choice of songs. When he's dabbled with cover versions in the past, they've been the usual suspects, but as Paul is fond of telling us, nobody really knows him and many of his choices came as a genuine surprise.

Along with Messers Craddock, Minchella, and White, Carleen Anderson makes her usual appearance, as does Sam Brown and Claudia Fontaine, who, with Caron Wheeler, sang on a number of Jam tracks. They recorded the album over five weeks in Amsterdam at Studio 150, where the title comes from. Looking at the track listing only Paul could come up with such a mix. What do The Carpenters, Gil Scott-Heron, Neil Young, Rose Royce, Nolan Porter, Sister Sledge, The Neville Brothers share? Nothing, except that each tune is a great song in its own right, which is why this album works. Paul also included an unrecorded song written by his mate, and fellow Beatles fanatic, Noel Gallagher.

A single of Gil Scott-Heron's (tragic) autobiographical 'The Bottle' preceded the album, which also included two covers that didn't appear on the album, the traditional 'Corrina Corrina', as recorded by Taj Mahal, and The Lovin' Spoonful's 'Coconut Grove'. Gil Scott-Heron's classic is a tough one to cover, and is played Ritchie Haven's like, and at much faster speed, than the original. The sax and flute really add to the arrangement, and it went to 13 in the charts. Rose Royce's 'Wishing On A Star' was the next single, which also contained two more unreleased covers. The great French songwriter Gilbert Becaud's 'Let It Be Me', which The Everly Brothers scored a hit with in 1960, plus Sly Stone's 'Family Affair'. This went to number 11 and was Paul's favourite track. It's a pulsating string laden ballad, although his voice by now had changed from his Council days. All those cigarettes and booze have taken their toll, and his voice is not as smooth as it once was.

Paul's version of 'All Along The Watchtower' differs from both the well-known Dylan and Hendrix versions, leaning towards gospel. 'Close To You' is probably the strangest choice, with the arrangement a nod to Curtis Mayfield, although the brass is more Tijuana than Chicago! He'd been playing Allen Toussaint's 'Hercules' in his live act for sometime and it was no surprise to see it surface on this album. Northern Soul has always been a favourite with Paul, and he includes Nolan Porter's 'If I Could Only Be Sure' and turns in a cracking rendition of this little known classic. Noel Gallagher's 'One Way Road' starts like a Woody Allen movie, clarinet and all, before breaking into a more traditional soul/rock number.

The traditional Scottish folk song 'Black Is The Colour' hearkens back to the sixties and great British folk singers like Martin Carthy, Davey Graham, John Renbourne, and Bert Jansch. Gordon Lightfoot's 'Early Morning Rain' is a classic singer songwriter's tune, and Paul is ably backed by Martin Carthy's daughter Eliza Carthy's violin on both these tunes. Tim Hardin's 'Don't Make Promises' has a very sixties flavour with Steve White playing brushes, and the re-working of Sister Sledge's 'Thinking Of You' is stripped to the bone, giving this tune another dimension. On both these songs, Danny Thompson, a legend of the folk/jazz world, plays the double bass. Thompson is at home whether he's playing Miles Davis or a traditional folk song, and he'd played with the likes of Alexis Koerner, John Martin, Nick Drake as well as being in the legendary folk group Pentangle. 'Birds' is one of Neil Young's earlier songs, and I've always considered his stuff difficult to cover, even for an artist of Paul's stature. However, he does justice to this plaintive tune and the girls on backing vocals giving it an added dimension. One song left off the album was the Stones 'Gimme Shelter'. I know it was Merry Clayton's version they were trying to copy but this is exactly the type of song that wouldn't sit well with the other tracks. I suspect the lads had been out on the town that night, had a few Heinekens, gotten into some of that Dutch ganja, and decided to tear some arse out of this song. No doubt, it will surface on the next rarities collection.

The album came out on September 13, went to number two in the charts, and was his most successful album for a long time, outselling both his previous albums. 'Thinking Of You', was released as the third single on the 15 November and went to number 18. Paul contributed 50p from the sale of each copy to the Children In Need campaign, and performed the track in the Children In Need Studios.

Paul and Jan 'Stan' Kybert produced the album, with Steve White receiving co-production credits on a number of the songs. Many artist and producers make the mistake of over producing a cover so they sound different to the original. The understated production of these songs, gives them an uncomplicated feel, and a different touch to the originals. Having a template to work from and a band who can give him what he wants must have helped. Paul's records generally have a 'blokish' feel to them, but his version of 'Thinking Of You' would have made him well popular with gals. Unusual as it was for a new label debut, the whole project was a genuine success.

Although Paul has successfully covered many other songwriters' tunes, it's a different story when it comes to his own songs. Yes, there was the tribute album *Fire & Skill* put together by Simon Halfon, and there have been bands that have tucked away a Weller song on the B-side of a single. However, no known artist has attempted to cover a song in the same way that Joe Cocker covered The Beatles' 'With A Little Help From My Friends'. The problem is that Paul writes very singular and personal songs that rarely lend themselves to reinterpretation. Not only does he write with conviction, he also sings them with the same conviction. From the days of The Jam, he stamped an indelible mark on his songs that make it almost impossible for other artists to cover them. They know that if they screw it up, not only will the music press give them a hard time, but they will have to contend with Paul, who has never been short in coming forward with his criticisms. He recently stated: "I don't get Coldplay and James Blunt. They bore the shit out of me. I've met Chris Martin before and I don't want to slag him off because he's a lovely lad, but his music is too fucking bland," which show that old age and four kids hasn't mellowed the man.

During 2002, he played just over forty concerts, which included a summer tour, where he played a large outdoor festival at the Old Trafford Cricket Ground in Manchester. Joe Strummer, his old sparring mate from his punk days was on the under card, and who would have predicted in 1977 that Paul would eclipse both The Clash and their front man. The tour ended on July 28, in Hyde Park, London, and in August, he took a nice little break with only one date in Spain at the Benicassim Festival. Following this, he didn't go on the road until October, to support the release of *Illumination*, which started at The Brighton Conference Centre, the scene of the last Jam gig, and ended at Wembley Arena. November saw a date at the Marquee cancelled which was a shame, and he spent the rest of the month touring Europe, and in December, played a solitary date at the Shepherds Bush Empire.

In 2003, Paul played around fifty gigs, which commenced in February with a tour of America. In March, there were a couple of gigs in London at the Shepherds Bush Empire and The Royal Albert Hall, and in June, there were two gigs at Sheffield and Newcastle City Halls. These were as a warm up for the main event when Paul headlined the famous Isle Of Wight Festival, which The Who and Jimi Hendrix had performed at several decades earlier, and 14,000 fans made the trip across, making it yet another special event. July saw a short burst of gigs all in the northern half of England and Scotland. In August, Paul played an acoustic gig at HMV, where my career started, which attracted 400 fans, who repaid the free gig by buying autographed copies of the mini box of rarities. During October and November he was back in America, and played one gig in Canada, before going on to tour Europe. December saw him play another short tour of the UK as well as two shows in Belfast and Dublin, ending with three concerts in London.

In 2004, he played just over twenty shows and his first appearance was at The Festival Hall in a concert that paid respect to one of the hottest rhythm sections in pop music, Tamla Motown's Funk Brothers. This engine room played on many of the classic Motown recordings, and are as much a part of the Motown sound as Smokey Robinson, and Holland, Dozier & Holland.

On March 30, Paul made an appearance at another Teenage Cancer Trust Event at the Royal Albert Hall, and turned up at the same venue on April 8, to pay homage to Ronnie Lane of The Small Faces. He indulged himself singing many of their songs, which he knows as well, if not better than the remaining members of the band do. For his summer tour, having put behind him the jibes about being a second rate Eric Clapton, in June he opened his tour with three nights at The Royal Albert Hall. He then lent his support to the Forestry Commission's *Music In The Forest* project, and during July, he played a couple of gigs in Japan, and two festivals in Europe during August. There was a massive UK tour booked, for the end of the year, but all the dates cancelled, as he was suffering from quinsy, an inflammation of the tonsils that leads to abscesses, and he ended the year on a quiet note.

There's no doubt that the low sales of both *Heliocentric* and *Illumination* had an effect on his profile, and not just in the UK. The failure of both albums to crossover in the UK would have had a knock-on effect throughout the world and sales outside of his home market would have dipped. Between 2002 and 2004, he only played five dates in Italy, France and Spain and, surprisingly, only two in Japan. I say surprisingly because the Japanese label Pony Canyon kick-started his solo career, and he was always popular there with The Jam and the Council. During this period, he concentrated on his strongholds in the UK and Northern Europe, as well as playing in the USA and Canada. However, the trips across the Atlantic would have been at his own expense as he wasn't shifting CDs on this vast continent, and it ain't cheap touring there, not even for a couple of weeks.

As far as song writing goes, it was a fallow period, but to be expected and a natural phenomena with any artist that has a career spanning three decades. *Days Of Speed* and *Studio 150* were stopgaps, although the live acoustic CD was a logical release, and not just another live album banged out to fill a gap. As far as the covers album goes, fair play to the man, as it could have backfired, given his choice of songs and the arrangements. Many of my colleagues in the biz had a good laugh when the idea was first proposed, and his fans weren't exactly happy with his choice of songs. Had he gone down this road just to pacify his tifosi, I doubt that it would have sold beyond his fan club, which *Studio 150* clearly did.

Songwriters work to a rhythm, and like any other profession they have to work at it week in week out. It's a job, just like a master carpenter, or any other person working in a skilled occupation. We all know what it's like going back to the grind after a couple of weeks in the sun, bloody difficult, but thank God, unlike Paul we're not in the spotlight. Throughout the gaps in his solo career, Paul would have had to keep the rhythm going, and no doubt he has quite a few demos of his own unreleased songs in that box under the stairs, just like he did with The Jam and the Council. Whatever is said about Paul, you can't write as many quality songs as he's written over the last 30 years without grafting. No matter where he is, a line will appear in his head, he'll hear a tune on the radio, or notice something (pebbles on a beach) and it will be filed away, and these ideas eventually get turned into songs. Great songwriters are not referred to as tunesmiths for nothing. The piano and guitar are their equivalent of the smithy's anvil and hammer, and like the blacksmith their work is born of talent, a long apprenticeship and perspiration.

The New Year saw Paul entering his 28th year in the music business, and although *Studio 150* was a resounding success, his critics will always judge him by his own songs. It was time to deliver his seventh solo studio album but we would have to wait until the end of 2005 to hear his new set of tunes.

CHAPTER 21

This Is The Modern World

During the first half of his solo career, Paul's success outstripped both The Jam and the Council put together. However, the studio albums that followed *Heavy Soul*, haven't sold as well, or anywhere near the 1.5 million selling *Stanley Road*. *Days Of Speed* stayed on the charts twice as long as *Illumination*, but sales dipped enough for Andy McDonald at Independiente to pass on re-signing Paul. Throughout his long career, several times it's been necessary to go back to the drawing board and rethink where he's coming from and where he goes next. All artists who've been at the top for so long need to take the odd time out, as the longer the career, the harder it is to keep the creative juices flowing. The release of *Studio 150,* certainly gave him a breathing space, and time to write the next album.

As well as shedding his record company, he stopped working with Brendan Lynch, and after 28 years parted company with his agent Martin Hopewell, which surprised me as Martin was the only person other than John and Kenny Wheeler that had worked with Paul since the seventies. A good agent makes life much easier for a manager and is an important cog in the machinery of an artist of Paul's stature, as he takes care of everything relating to booking dates and touring. Although the split with Martin was amicable, it left Paul a little isolated, and short on long standing mates in the business.

While Paul has never had a problem selling records or touring in the UK, elsewhere there have been problems. When you're selling overseas and you release a not so commercial album or you go through a fallow patch, these sales help to take up the slack. This is a luxury that Paul's never had, with the possible exception of Japan. On an international level, he has never reached anywhere near the lofty heights he's reached in the UK. There's no doubt the records he's made since going solo, are the most commercial as far as the rest of the world go, but to date he has failed to break into the big time outside of the UK.

In February 2005, he kicked off a two-month tour of the UK, and on March 14, some six months after the release of the *Studio 150* album, V2 released 'Early Morning Rain' as a limited edition single, on vinyl only. As the Beeb had thrown all their turntables away years ago, there was a promo CD. The B-side contained another Beatles cover, 'Come Together', and the single went to number 40. I'm not sure why this single was released as the album had peaked by this time, and Paul certainly wasn't having problems selling out his tour, or at least he shouldn't have. The track itself was no way a single, and given that it only just made the top 40, the airplay would have been minimal. Living in Italy this single passed me by, and I phoned a big Weller fan and asked if there was anything special about this release. He replied: "No mate, it's just another record company scam to make more money out of us loyal fans." I always admired The Jam for the stand they took on singles and fought their corner when Polydor tried it on, but I can't help but feel a little cynical about this single, and the many other singles that have been released with many different versions.

The unreleased Beatles cover was clearly there to entice the fans who collect everything, which would insure a chart position. This kind of thing is nothing new, and has been going on since the record companies introduced the 12 inch vinyl in the eighties. I've never been a fan of these marketing ploys; if the record's good enough, it will sell, and if doesn't so be it. There's no doubt that V2's marketing wallahs saw this as a good wheeze, and gave it the old bollocks that you have to do this kind of thing, as every other band does, and you need to compete in the market place. I was told this kind of shit over 20 years ago when 'Speak Like A Child', was released, but it still went on to sell over 250,000 copies and was a top five record. These days single sales are meaningless, and just another marketing tool, and unless you hit the top end of the chart, you ain't going to make any money from their sales. Paul's solo career hasn't been as reliant on hit singles as either The Jam or the Council were, and while his albums have regularly made appearances in the top five, with the exception of 'Peacock Suite' every other single has failed to penetrate the top five, with only a few hitting the top ten.

It's not the packaging, or how many versions you release, it's what's in the grooves that counts. All these multi-release packages are negative marketing, and just negate what other record companies are doing to their artist's records. In the case of Paul, his record company know he has a big hard-core following that snap up every release, and it makes for a nice earner. The whole ploy has always had a Del Boy feel about it, and instead of wasting vast amounts of money on multi-release singles and albums, it would be better if the big four invested this money into the business end, the music, but what a stupid idea that is!

Since his days in The Jam, Paul has demoed his songs on his own, and it was no different during his solo career and for the next album, he spent time in his own studio laying down songs. During the spring tour he acquainted the band with many of the new songs during sound checks and, hoping to recreate the intensity and energy of the band's live performances, they went into Noel Gallagher's' Wheelers End studio and in just two weeks recorded the album, with the tracks eventually being re-mixed at Studio 150 in Amsterdam. As with the covers album the new tracks were co-produced by the same team of Paul and Jan 'Stan' Kybert, and recorded by Joeri Saal.

Following this, Paul was back on the road, and on July 16, along with legendary rockers Status Quo, played the annual Guilfest at Stoke Park in Guildford. A pass for the weekend set you back £75, and BBC's Radio 2 broadcast the event. Paul, Rick Parfitt, and Francis Rossi were all Woking lads, and the gig brought them back to their roots. To coincide with this event, on thc 18 July, V2 released the first single from the new album, 'From The Floorboards Up' b/w 'Oranges And Rosewater'. As well as a CD single there were two 7 inch disc sets released, with alternative mixes on the B-sides. At two minutes and 27 seconds, the track is one of the shortest tunes he's recorded, ten seconds longer than The Jam's 'Start!'. Like 'Start!', it's stripped down to the minimum, and its choppy guitar gives it a real sense of urgency, and went to number 18 in the charts.

A second single preceded the album and 'Come On Let's Go' came out on September 26, going three places higher to number 15. Opening with an acoustic guitar with chords not unlike 'That's Entertainment', before Steve Craddock chimes in with some nice power chords, and hats off to Damon Minchella, whose bass playing on this track is superb. Like the first single, it certainly hearkens back to his Jam days, but lacks the explosive punch of 'Eton Rifles'.

V2 released *As Is Now* on October 10 and 'Blink And You Miss It' opens up the proceedings, with a spiteful guitar intro. There's an urgency about this track and Paul's vocals that wasn't on the songs he'd recorded on his last two studio albums. Why this wasn't the first single is beyond me, although like 'Come On Let's Go' there is a distinct lack of production, which is a shame as this has big hit written all over it. If this song had the same production values as 'Going Underground', it would have been the dog's bollocks and perhaps emulated the chart success. 'Paper Smiles' follows this and stomps along whilst 'Here's The Good News' is very sixties with a very wild and woolly trombone solo.

'The Start Of Forever' is another one of those very good lilting 'Weller' acoustic ballads, that drifts along nicely with a brass arrangement that's out of the Bacharach & David songbook. 'Pan' is a little on the pretentious side, whilst 'All On A Misty Morning', is back in *Wild Wood* territory and hearkens back to Traffic, particularly Dave Mason, who wrote a tune with a similar title. 'I Wanna Make It Right', bounces along nicely but has a mannered vocal on the verses, which suits neither Paul, nor the song. It would have been better if he'd recorded it, à la Kinks, and bit more snappy. 'Savages' is another good song undone by the arrangement, which would have been meat and drink to the Council. 'Fly Little Bird' has echoes of Neil Young's 'Birds', with some nice backward tape affects, and a surprise in the middle when the band comes crashing in.

'Roll Along Summer' is a look through Paul's back pages and is a tune that would have fitted on any of his first three albums. With its 'Long Train Running' guitar, 'Bring Back The Funk Part 1 & 2' is a Weller soul number and a great tune, but like the first two singles it needed a more dynamic production to bring out the best in it. 'The Pebble And The Boy', is full of melancholy and reminiscent of songs that he's recorded before, with the string arrangement underscoring the despondent feeling that permeates this track.

As Is Now received the acclaim of the press, with many viewing it as return to form. *NME* boldly declared: "Weller's back and this time he rules." *Uncut* said: "A work of rejuvenation power – an icon reawakens," while Mojo described it as his most consistent album since *Wild Wood*. Another reviewer even proclaimed the album to be a milestone record in his solo career. It went to number four in the charts with sales emulating his previous two studio albums, and dropped out quickly.

The main reason for the failure of this album to ignite the public is the flat production, or as one of my mates said when he heard the record, "what production?" There's no problem with the band, the energy is close to what they achieve in concert, and the playing is excellent throughout. The songs are great, but lack the dynamics to make them jump out at you, and what should have been a great record is just a very good record,

As a fan, I really like this album, and songwise the man is back to his best but if I put on my A&R ears, it's a different story. There's no doubt Paul wanted his songs recorded this way, it has his mark running throughout and he was well pleased with the final mixes. Two weeks recording wasn't enough time to do justice to the tunes, and to get the best out of the songs, it would have been a better idea to record the songs over a longer period and more conventionally.

Like many artists, Paul strives to get the feel of playing live on his recordings, but it's something that rarely happens. Also, what's the point of recording in a multi-track studio when you can go and record on to two-track stereo as they did in the fifties and sixties. The sixties records had a live feel to them for several reasons, the songs were recorded with all the band members playing at the same time, with maybe just the vocals overdubbed at the end of the session. Multitrack recording was in its infancy, the equipment was minimal and most studios were equipped with Fairchild valve compressors and plate reverb that required a room the size of a small warehouse, and the mikes were almost as big as your head. The first time I stepped into a recording studio in the mid-sixties the soundproofing was state of the art – the walls and ceiling were lined with cardboard egg trays. Acoustic tiles were expensive and would have cost about £2 each, while the cost of soundproofing the whole room with egg trays was about the same price as one tile. The recordings sounded ok, well ok for the sixties, and I recall The Equals recorded 'Baby Come Back' in this studio.

Modern studios are designed with digital technology in mind and have a sterile atmosphere, and there is a need for the songs to be *produced* to supplement the missing 'live' dynamics. We also live in the age of digital music, which is antiseptic clean and shows up deficiencies, often hidden, and a part of the sound when music was recorded on to analogue tape and released on vinyl. In the sixties you only got a couple of shots at recording your tunes, and many bands would record a whole album in a day, now you're lucky if you get a couple of backing tracks down.

For those retro folk who yearn for the good old days, I am afraid you'll have to wait until a time machine has been invented. Technology marches on and, as someone once said, this is the modern world! It's no different when it comes to radio, which is now broadcast digitally, and when the tracks on this album are played next to modern recordings, the flatness of production stands out.

Whenever I was faced with a band who wanted to produce themselves, I had one answer, if The Beatles needed George Martin, then you will need two producers. Abba were one of the few successful mega bands who were capable of producing themselves, as Benny Andersson and Bjorn Ulvaeus were consummate musicians who understood counterpoint and arranging, and with their engineer Michael Tretow, they produced quality pop records. They're not one of my favourite bands, but as an old pro, I admire their professionalism, and they sold a lot records.

Throughout Paul's career, I knew it would never work pairing him with a big name producer, and he's not the only artist like this. You won't find the likes of Neil Young or Bob Dylan going down this road. What these artists need is someone by their side that is sympathetic, to their music and their personality. Listening to *As Is Now* it strikes me that he didn't learn from the mistakes made at the end of the Council's career. I just wish Paul would listen to his own back catalogue, and look at the records he made with Vic Smith ('Start' and 'Going Underground'), Peter Wilson ('Town Like Malice' and 'Long Hot Summer') or Brendan Lynch ('The Changing Man' and 'Peacock Suite') – they're all Weller classics, well produced, and big hits.

After *Heliocentric* and *Illumination*, it must have been a difficult time for Paul, and I have no idea why he parted company with Brendan. Jan 'Stan' Kybert is probably a good man, but knowing Paul as I do, it's unlikely that he has the personality to deal with his bloody mindedness. Paul's always had a one-eyed approach towards recording, but needs to look no further than the very members of his band, and listen to their input when it comes to production. They've never let him down on stage and are hardly likely to in the studio.

There is no doubting his talents as songwriter, and the list of names below Paul Weller is miles longer than the names above. However, it was patently obvious at the end of the Council's career that the production value of his albums suffered as well as his ability to write meaningful songs. With Paul's solo career, Brendan's role in the production of his records was more than just a walk-on part. There's no doubt that the songs on this album show Paul back to his best, and they are quality tunes, but I can't help but wonder what the album would have sounded liked with a better co-producer.

On December 5, a second single was released, 'Here's The Good News' b/w 'Alone' and 'Super Lekker Stoned', with two 7 inch vinyl singles released with alternative mixes and extra tracks. The single went to number 21 in the charts, but nowhere near high enough to revive the album's fortunes. V2 then tried to revive the album, by re-releasing it as a double CD, in December, hoping to catch the Christmas market, which was the last throw of the dice. It was to no avail and the double CD didn't trouble the chart compilers.

As far as touring goes, in 2005 Paul played nearly 70 concerts and regardless of his record sales, he was still doing it on the road. During February and March, he undertook a UK tour, playing double nighters at many venues, ending up with three nights at the Hammersmith Odeon. He was quiet until July, and then it was only four gigs, however he was saving himself for the end of the year, and he played 43 shows in the UK and Northern Germany during the last third of the year to support the release of *As Is Now.* September saw the band touring America with dates in his strongholds, Chicago, Boston and New York, as well as one in Toronto. There were two dates on the West Coast in Los Angeles and San Francisco, and they played the *Late, Late Show* for CBS TV, a very popular coast-to-coast chat show. This would have given Paul exposure throughout the States, but to capitalise on this appearance you needed to follow up with a twenty to thirty date tour of key cities. There was one festival played in Spain during November, but southern Europe was given the elbow, and there were no gigs in Japan. The tour climaxed in Ireland, where he played both sides of the border, and his last appearance was supporting Dogs, a new band influenced by The Jam at their London gig.

Over the last couple of years, as far a playing live goes, Paul has lost a few territories. He is no longer as big in Japan as he was, America is a lost cause, and it will be necessary to re-conquer Southern Europe.

As Paul moved into the New Year, he could look forward to receiving a special prize, and there was no doubt, it was an honour he richly deserved.

With the exception of the *Novellos* and the *Mercurys,* I'm no fan of these over-the-top, back-slapping award ceremonies. They get it right occasionally, but most awards relate to the turnover of the artists rather than real talent. Can someone explain to me why Georgie Fame goes unrecognised? He's been on the scene for over 45 years, introduced the sound of the Hammond to us Mods in the sixties, and was one of the first musicians to play West Indian Blue Beat music, nearly two decades before the 2-Tone crowd were strutting their stuff. The music he recorded with the Blue Flames is now recognised as seminal recordings of the sixties, which included *Sound Venture*, a big band album that featured the cream of British jazz musicians. His biggest hit was 'Yeh Yeh', which went to number one in the UK in 1964 (it reached 21 in USA) and sold over a million copies, knocking The Beatles' 'I Feel Fine' off the top slot – no mean feat. He's played with Count Basie, Van Morrison and is a much respected artist amongst his peers. What chance does Georgie have of The Brits recognising him? None, he doesn't have enough tattoos for a start, and he's got too much talent, and as far as these awards go, that's a big drawback.

On February 15, Paul appeared at the Brits to pick up the award for his outstanding contribution to British music, and there's no doubt he thoroughly deserved this, as his contribution over thirty years has been phenomenal. Paul's racked up eight number one singles and albums, which is none too shabby by anyone's standards, spread over two very different bands and a solo career. It's quality that counts, and he has songbook that most songwriters would die for. When Britpop exploded, the likes of Blur and Oasis were quoting The Jam as an influence, and now it's Hard-Fi and The Arctic Monkeys. This award, and the respect paid to Paul, is not meant to massage his ego, or curry favour, it's respect for him being a unique and gifted songwriter.

That night the band played a great set, featuring 'Come On Let's Go', 'The Changing Man', 'From The Floorboards Up', 'Broken Stones', and a thundering encore of 'Town Called Malice'. To coincide with this on February 13, V2 released a Brits special edition of *As Is Now* as a 2-CD with 14 tracks, and included live versions of 'From The Floorboards Up', 'Come On Let's go', 'The Changing Man' and 'Town Called Malice' recorded at Alexandra Palace, on December 5, 2005. When I read about this release, like other fans I was under the assumption that tunes played at the Brits were going to be released as the bonus CD, and not songs from a previous live performance.

At the same time, V2 released a limited edition of 6,000 copies of a 7 inch vinyl containing 'Blink And You'll Miss It' and the three previous singles off the album, which was ineligible for the singles chart. On top of this, Paul released a 7 inch vinyl single on his website of the four live titles, initially it was only going to be a limited edition, but because of the demand the number was increased.

During an interview with *Uncut* magazine in March 2006, Paul scathingly castigated many former winners of the Brit lifetime award winners, among them Bob Geldof, Bowie, Bono, and Freddie Mercury. On hearing that Geldof had won a Brit, Paul voiced an opinion, which is probably shared by many when he stated: "It can't have been for his music, it must have been for Africa." More than likely, the Brits committee awarded this honour for Geldof's staging of two of the biggest events in the last 100 years, bringing together the worlds top artists (and largest egos) playing for free and for a worthwhile cause. Sir Bob was a tad more magnanimous about Paul when it came to his participation in the original Live Aid single, explaining: "I never got on with him. I respected him musically though, and felt the record needed him. But, I thought he'd think, a) this is naff and b), Geldof is a cunt. But he put it all aside. That always impressed me that he could do that. I was wrong about him."

While many of the past winners are not my cup of tea, some of his comments were a little over the top. The *Uncut* interview was open and frank, and no doubt sold many extra copies of the magazine, but I'm not sure what it says about Paul, considering he retaliates at the slightest criticism. In an interview with David Lodge for the *Boys About Town* fanzine, he vented his spleen about ceremonies like the Brits, describing them as "a silly fucking circus", a comment I don't agree with, as circuses have acts that are talented and clowns that are funny, unlike the Brits! However, at the time of the 2006 awards, *As Is Now* needed a leg up, so an appearance in the big top was deemed necessary.

The award nominations don't stop with Brits as along with Johnny Cash, The Fall, Buzzcocks, and Sparks, Paul was nominated for *Mojo*'s Inspiration Award. The event was created to recognise those artists that have enriched our rich musical culture and is not about the biggest names, or the hottest acts. Have to say though mate, I think this one belongs to Johnny, or if there's any justice it will be. Cash's track record is awesome.

On June 12, 2006, V2 released a double live CD entitled *Catch-Flame*, which is a recording of The Alexandra Palace gig played on December 5, 2005. Once again, there will be multiple versions released, to tempt the fans into buying every variation. Yep Roc, his American record company have even gone to the trouble of manufacturing a limited edition 1,000 copies that will be individually hand-numbered and include five collector buttons!

It's certainly a blast through his back pages, with tracks from every solo album, with the exception of his debut, which is a shame as there are quality tracks on this album. His Jam days are represented by 'In The Crowd', 'That's Entertainment' and 'Town Called Malice', whilst 'Long Hot Summer' and 'Shout To The Top' are from the Council's songbook. 'In The Crowd' is a nice touch, but he's been playing the other two titles for a long time, and he should have picked different Jam songs that he hasn't recorded before. The same goes for the Council songs. On the night, one of Paul's biggest influences was in the audience, Wilko Johnson.

There's a familiarity about the set, and it's one he's been playing for a long time, with just the additions of tracks from *As Is Now*. Paul seems to be a little bit too comfortable and set in his ways when playing live these days. The band are on form, but it's very good gig, rather that a great one.

It entered the charts at 17, and gave him his lowest chart entry of his solo career, save for the 3-CD box set of rarities. It seems that many of his die-hard fans have passed this one by, with many feeling let down about the packaging, something unusual for Paul. It came as a gatefold double with no booklet, giving the impression that it was promo copy. In the past with The Jam, the Council, and most of his solo albums, he always gave good value for money when it came to his sleeves. I recall all the fights I had with Polydor over his packaging and if I didn't know better, I would say he doesn't care any more.

With all the activity around the Brits and his last studio album and singles, I'm not sure why it was necessary to release this live CD so soon after. Judging by its sales, there doesn't appear to have been a demand for it, and it's a little too soon after *As Is Now*, hence the lowly chart position.

As far as gigs, it was a quiet start to the year; there's were a couple of dates in Tokyo at the Zepp club, and a small tour of Germany. In the summer, he's booked to play festivals in Scotland, Ireland, Italy, and both V Festivals at Weston Park, Staffordshire, and Hylands Park Chelmsford. The rest of 2006 is blank at the time writing this book. At the end of the year, he will again undertake his annual tour of the UK and after this, he's announced that he will take a year out to spend with his family – a wise move at this point of his career.

There is a similarity between the end of the Council's career and the years prior to *As Is Now*. After *The Cost Of Loving*, Paul had clearly lost the plot, although from *Heliocentric* onwards, he'd only lost his way. On his return from the wilderness the first time around, his debut album was better than most expected and set up his solo career and his next two albums. *As is Now* wasn't a return to form, as many reviews stated, form is fleeting while class is forever, and the songs on this album are a cut above everything he'd recorded on the previous two studio albums. Notwithstanding my comments about the production of *As Is Now,* Paul is on the way up again, and his future looks set to run into a fourth decade.

There are still a few problems to deal with as Paul carries on; his fan club is naturally diminishing as it does when artists have been around for so long. While they can sell out concerts, their record sales dwindle, and like The Rolling Stones and many other vintage acts, Paul has now reached a stage where he plays to more fans live than actually buy his new recordings.

Another problem that Paul faces is airplay, or the lack of it. As far as Radio 1 goes, it's unlikely that they will play list his singles any more, unless they break into the top five. Radio 1 and most of the independent radio stations formats are identical, churning out the same pop pap week in week out. Radio 2 will support him, which only leaves the rock stations, who play his records heavily as well as recording sessions. Most artists with long careers suffer this problem, as the producers of most radio programs are obsessed with a fast disappearing teenage market, and missing out the now vast middle age market. In February 2006, Virgin held a Paul Weller weekend, but this was more likely to generate interest in his whole catalogue rather than *As Is Now.* He regularly appears on TV and there is plenty of interest from the media, even if he is selective about which papers and music mags he speaks too. Paul's appeal now is to the thirty-plus market, which is catered for by the likes of XFM, Virgin and Radio 2, but the saturation airplay he once received is history. All of his singles save one have charted, but this is down to a phenomenal fan club that buys and collects every single and album, no matter how many formats they're released on. This lack of airplay is a problem not easily solved, and the older you get the more difficult it becomes.

2006 will be tricky for Paul, as John is now in his seventies, has had serious heart surgery, and is now suffering from emphysema. The music industry is a young man's game and going on the road and the day-to-day running of a major artist like Paul takes up a considerable amount of time and energy. Things have changed in the record business with the rapid advance of technology, where even the recently developed CD is now out of date. It's all about downloads, iPods, MP3s and the phone is no longer the primary mode of communication. These technological changes, and the need to be cognisant with e-mail and the internet are alien to the way John works and, come to that, Paul, given that he still releases songs on vinyl, a sound carrier that has been out of date for quarter of a century.

Parting company with Martin Hopewell who was Paul's agent for nearly thirty years will have put an even greater strain on John. They have retained Helter Skelter as their agent, but it will take them time to get used to the way Paul works. From the old days, there's only Kenny left. Like most artists, Paul surrounds himself with friends who are in his fan club and maybe too frightened to speak out candidly for fear of losing his patronage. True friendship isn't about whether you're the kind of person who sends Christmas cards or not, it's about how you value friendship and no matter how much money you have, you still need real mates.

The time when John won't be around can't be that far away, which will cause problems as Paul is reluctant to trust anyone as he does his father.

Managing himself while leading the band is going to be difficult, as that side of the business takes up as much time as recording and playing live gigs. Paul is no stranger to change and although *As Is Now* hasn't quite done the business expected, it doesn't mean the wheels are coming off. Perhaps following the release of *Catch-Flame*, it might be advisable to step back and take a time out, and think about what comes next.

While researching this book I've read many comments on John's management style, mostly negative. Certainly when I started working with him, he didn't know his way around a major record company, and his knowledge of marketing and recording was zilch. Coming from a similar background, I understood the way he went about his wheeling and dealing, and his attitude towards cash. John would have first hand knowledge of what it was like to grow up in the post war years in England and having had to deal with the austerity of the fifties, he made sure that Paul and his sister Nicky wouldn't have to suffer. By doing this, he was no different from any other (working class) father – you look after your own. What can be said categorically is that he has been the driving force behind Paul's career, perhaps not so much now, but certainly during the first two and half decades. John has made the occasional dodgy decision, but what manager hasn't?

Over the years, I have heard many faces in the biz go on about how they would change things if they'd managed Paul, and even though many are more knowledgeable about the business than John is, I doubt that anyone of them could have persuaded Paul to change direction. Once he's made his mind up, he's immoveable – if his *old man* couldn't shift him, who could? For over thirty years, through the good and the bad times, John has championed Paul and been by his side, never once doubting his son's ability and talent. A bond developed between them that went beyond father and son, and it's impossible to think, or talk about Paul, without John coming into the equation. There's never been a doubt in my mind that no one else could have managed Paul other than John, who knows his moods better than most. Their loyalty to each other is paramount and comes before anyone else, whoever they are. When Paul picked up his Brit award, he knew a part of that award, and the accolades that came with it, went to his dad. John was a real character, and one of the few left in the record business. In the modern music business, well-heeled lawyers and professional managers have taken over, and there's no place for the likes of the colourful characters like John. When John goes, which is inevitable, whoever follows him will need a gum shield and the hide of an elephant.

My one criticism of the Wellers is that their loyalty tends to be a one-way street, which is not unusual in the music business. They dropped Bruce and Rick and well before the infamous court case, there was no love lost between them, which I saw at first hand. With every change, Paul shed the old skin and moved on quickly, never looking back, and the same goes for the Council, where Mick has all but disappeared off the radar screen. I have seen many people who worked conscientiously for them disappear when they had outlived their usefulness, or perhaps demanded fair remuneration for their labour. Dave Liddle, Paul's guitar roadie and a loyal foot soldier for nearly 20 years, was very embittered about the way he was treated, and when he died, I commented adversely on this on Drew Hipson's *allmodicon* website. It was a knee-jerk reaction to learning of Dave's death, and although Drew offered the chance to rescind the comments, I chose not to. In 2006, Paul phoned me in Italy to give me a right bollocking for my forthright statement, made more than three years ago, which shows just what a long memory he has. Once Paul found out Dave was dying he made amends, did the right thing, and visited him in hospital, which made Dave very happy. There's no doubt that Paul deserves the accolades he's received and not just at the Brit awards, but many people have contributed to his success, and when you tally up the small contributions, they count as much as the big ones.

I first met Paul as a callow 18-year-old teenager, and although it was difficult in the beginning, I went on to have a good working relationship with him for nearly 30 years – although I think this book will test this relationship to the full! Perhaps being a first generation Mod helped, and I came from a similar working class background as his dad. In his teens, Paul was frighteningly serious and unlike most other teenagers of the day, or any other era, there was a touch of the Victor Meldrews about him, even at this age. When I was his age, it was all about having a good time, girls, music, going to see bands. On Saturday nights, the cry was, "Where's the Mori" (Moriarty/party), and we would breeze up west, returning home the next morning bombed out and the worse for wear.

When success came Paul's way, he had a few problems when the money really started rolling in and he became wealthy. They say that ordinary people from a working-class background have a problem with this and feel a sense of guilt. John certainly didn't suffer from this (nor would I) but he would have known what it felt like to be skint, and what a struggle it was to bring up his family. Paul has never had to deal with this kind of problem and when he left school it was no ordinary job for him, he'd already made his mind up that he was going to become a pop star. When he first became successful, I always felt this fact affected him, and by never having done the nine-to-five daily grind, it would have been difficult for him to understand what it was like to live for the weekend, or enjoy your favourite band on a purely hedonistic level, as his own fans do. I recall talking to John when he was worth quite a few quid and he told me how handy it would be to win a million quid on the lottery. I agreed with his sentiments – you can never have enough money, but you can certainly have too little.

When I worked with Paul, there were very few problems, but I was lucky because whether it was The Jam or the Council, every single and album was a hit. Although this success had little to do with me, it was my job to get the records out on time and keep an eye on Polydor. I never had to market a record like *The Cost Of Loving*, or deal with the excesses that proliferated during the second half of the Council's career. I certainly wouldn't have supported the deal that Polydor gave him after I left, as when you receive large advances, you have to play the game. Because of his seemingly infinite songwriting talent, he has managed to manipulate the system and move the goalposts when and where it suited him. However, with the changes the music business has gone through, and Paul is now approaching fifty, it's going to get difficult. Ultimately, no one beats the system and I hope he hasn't forgotten that after a string of failed singles, and two unsuccessful albums, Polydor dropped him. Success is everything, even when you're an icon of the music business.

How Paul stays so driven is beyond me, although beyond his family there's little else in his life that isn't music related. Genius is a word I wouldn't attribute to any musician; Albert Einstein yes, he changed the world, but music doesn't, although it does help it spin round. The word I would use to describe Paul's talents is unique, and whether you like him or not, there's no denying his songwriting skills.

With The Jam, he reached out to a teenage audience, with songs they could directly relate too, which mirrored their lives and the world they inhabited. The Style Council allowed him a freedom that The Jam couldn't, and his song writing expanded and took in every style of music. The Council's part in his solo success is often understated, and in many ways, it's as important as The Jam contribution, as throughout his solo career, he's dipped his bread in the Council's gravy.

Critics are fond of digging out Paul for his retro style, and playing 'dad rock', but where else can he go for inspiration other than back in time, where there's a rich seam of talent to mine? Coldplay are on everyone's lips and their latest album has sold seven million copies, but they are in their first decade, and while they have already won a Brit and a Grammy, it will be interesting to see whether they will step up to the podium in twenty years time to pick up a lifetime award. Paul will be the Mod Grandfather, and 70 by then, but no doubt still giving it large.

Paul's kept his nose to the grindstone and seems determined to stick at it, and this determination is not just about the financial rewards, he wants to be recognised as an artist. Paul is no different from the great painters, actors, or sportsmen who rise above the mediocre, and are held in the highest esteem not just by their fans, but by their peers as well. In 1998, the *Guinness Book of Hit Records* had Paul as the fourth most successful singer-songwriter of all time and had more self-penned hit records (51 including 'Brand New Start') than any other artists except Paul McCartney (69), Elton John (62) and David Bowie (54, which includes Tin Machine). Given the quality of songs on his last studio album *As Is Now,* there's no doubt that he will be around for another decade, and maybe break Macca's record.

As for being the changing man, I don't see that big a change. Yes, Paul has mellowed a little, but as Chris Martin of Coldplay, David Bowie, Bono, and Bob Geldof found out, this change doesn't measure on the Richter scale. There have been a few cosmetic changes, and there might be a different haircut, but underneath the man's remained the same. The acerbic criticisms, his quick temper, and those ever-changing moods are a part of his character. I know that whenever I talk to him I'm never sure whether to wear a T-shirt or a flak jacket.

Whatever Paul's shortcomings are, in the music business you don't last thirty years, win a Novello, and a Brit award for outstanding achievement unless you have talent, and the respect of your peers. If Paul didn't have real talent he'd have been found out a long time ago.

APPENDICES

1 Discography

There are numerous websites and books which contain complete discographies of The Jam, The Style Council and Paul Weller's solo career. I have therefore decided to include only a UK discography. In addition, I haven't listed flexi discs of others given away with magazines. The Jam recorded six studio albums and eighteen singles, including two imports. The Style Council recorded six studio albums, including the mini album *Introducing The Style Council*, which was originally imported into the UK. Polydor refused to release their fifth album, *Modernism: A New Decade* and it only became available as the fifth CD of the box set in 1988. The Council released 19 singles, including 'Soul Deep', which was released under the name of The Council Collective, as well as a single under the name of King Truman. Paul Weller has released twenty-eight singles, plus 'Wild Wood' and 'Out of The Sinking' were re-released and to date twelve albums, including three live albums, a three-CD box set of rarities and a Greatest Hits compilation, as well as a single released under the name of the Smokin' Mojo Filters. In 2006, Island Records released 'Hit Parade', which chronicles Paul's career, and I've added this compilation at the end of Paul's solo discography.

Most discographies, including books like *The Guinness Book Of British Hit Singles & Albums* generally use the date the single or album/CD entered the charts. Originally, records were shipped on a Monday but given a Friday release date. At some stage, and I am not sure when, record companies changed the release date to Mondays. To obtain the correct release date I had to browse through old copies of *Music Week* at the British Library, and search the internet for accurate information, and I have made every attempt to arrive at the correct dates. *Music Week* relies on the record companies supplying them with the information and there were many re-issues that were not listed.

My thanks go to Shaun Kelly and James Mayes for their sterling help in preparing this discography.

THE JAM

A. In The City
B. Takin' My Love
7 inch Polydor 2058 866
29 April 1977
Highest chart position: 40
Later released on 7 inch Polydor 587611–7 in original picture bag (25th anniversary issue)
Release date: 6 May 2002
Highest chart position: 36

IN THE CITY
LP Polydor 2383 447
MC Polydor 3170 447
20 May 1977
Highest chart position: 20
Later released on LP SPELP 27 MC SPEMC 27 August 1983
Later released on CD 817124-2 LP 817124-1 July 1990
Later released on CD 537 417-2 (Remastered) 4 August 1997

A. All Around The World
B. Carnaby Street
7 inch Polydor 2058 903
8 July 1977
Highest chart position: 13

A. The Modern World
B. Sweet Soul Music (Live) / Back In My Arms Again (Live) /
Bricks And Mortar (Live) Recorded at the 100 Club 11 September 1977
7 inch Polydor 2058 945
21 October 1977
Highest chart position: 36

THIS IS THE MODERN WORLD
LP Polydor 2383 475
MC Polydor 3170 475
18 November May 1977
Highest chart position: 22
Later released on LP SPELP 66 MC SPEMC 66 August 1983
Later released on CD 823281-2 LP 823281-1 June 1990
CD 537 418-2 (remastered) 4 August 1997

A. News Of The World
B. Aunties And Aunties (Impulsive Youths) / Innocent Man
7 inch Polydor 2058 995
24 February 1978
Highest chart position: 27

A. David Watts
AA. 'A' Bomb In Wardour Street
7 inch Polydor 2059 054
11 August 1978
Highest chart position: 25

A. Down In The Tube Station At Midnight
B. So Sad About Us / The Night
7 inch Polydor Posp 8
6 October 1978
Highest chart position: 15

ALL MOD CONS
LP Polydor POLD 5008
MC Polydor POLDC 5008
3 November 1978
Highest chart position: 6
Later released on CD 823282-2 LP June 1989
Later released on CD 537 419-2 (Remastered) 4 August 1997
Later released on deluxe edition with extra tracks added and a DVD of the making of All Mod Cons directed by Don Letts
CD Polydor 9839238
5 June 2006
Highest chart position: 62

A. Strange Town
B. The Butterfly Collector
7 inch Polydor POSP 34
9 March 1979
Highest chart position: 15

A. When You're Young
B. Smithers-Jones
7 inch Polydor POSP 69
17 August 1979
Highest chart position: 17

A. The Eton Rifles
B. See-Saw
7 inch Polydor POSP 83
26 October 1979
Highest chart position: 3

SETTING SONS
LP Polydor POLD 5028
MC Polydor POLDC 50028
16 November 1979
Highest chart position: 4
Later released on CD 831314-2 10 May 1988
Later released on CD 537 420-2 (remastered) 4 August 1997

A. Going Underground
Aa. The Dreams Of Children
7 inch Polydor Posp 113

1A. Going Underground / 1B. The Dreams Of Children
2A. Away From The Numbers (Live) / 2B. The Modern World (Live) / Down In The Tube Station At Midnight (Live) recorded at The Rainbow 3 December 1979
7 inch Double Pack POSPJ 113 (100,000 Limited Edition)
14 March 1980
Highest chart position: 1

All singles prior to 'Going Underground' were re-issued on 18 April 1980. With the exception of 'Down In The Tube Station At Midnight', 'When You're Young' and 'The Eton Rifles', they all re-entered the top 75.

A. Start
B. Liza Radley
7 inch Polydor 2059 266
15 August 1980
Highest chart position: 1

IN THE CITY/THIS IS THE MODERN WORLD
Double LP Polydor 2683 074
Double MC Polydor 3574 088
September 1980
Later released on CD 847730-2 & MC 847730-4 1 February 1991

SOUND AFFECTS
LP Polydor POLD 5035

MC Polydor POLDC 5035
28 November 1980
Highest chart position: 2
Later released on CD 823284-2, LP 823284-1 & MC 823284-4 April 1990
Later released on CD 537 421-2 (Remastered) 4 August 1997

A. That's Entertainment
B. Down In The Tube Station At Midnight (Live) recorded at The Rainbow 3 December 1979
7 inch Metronome 0030 364
30 January 1981
Highest chart position: 21
(German import – later re-issued in 1983 as Polydor POSP 482)
Later released as A. That's Entertainment B. Down In The Tube Station At Midnight (Live) recorded at The Rainbow 3 December 1979
7 inch Polydor PO 155
MC Polydor POCS 155

A. That's Entertainment
B. Down In The Tube Station At Midnight (Live) recorded at The Rainbow 3 December 1979 / Town Called Malice (Live) recorded at Hammersmith Palais 14 December 1981
12 inch Polydor PZ 155
CD Polydor PZCD 155
17 June 1991
Highest chart position: 57

ALL MOD CONS / SETTING SONS
MC Polydor 3574 098
(2 on 1 re-issue)
February 1981 [Pos 83]

A. Funeral Pyre
B. Disguises
7 inch Polydor POSP 257
29 May 1981
Highest chart position: 4

A. Absolute Beginners
B. Tales From The Riverbank
7 inch Polydor POSP 350
16 October 1981
Highest chart position: 4
(Initial copies released with lyric insert)

A. Town Called Malice
AA. Precious
7 inch Polydor POSP 400

A. Town Called Malice (Live) recorded at the Hammersmith Palais 14 December 1981
AA. Precious (Extended Version)
12 inch Polydor POSPX 400
29 January 1982
Highest chart position: 1

THE GIFT
LP Polydor POLD 5055
MC Polydor POLDC 5055
(Limited edition released in striped paper bag)
12 March 1982
Highest chart position: 1
Later released on CD 823284-2 LP 823284-1 & MC 823284-4 29 June 1990
Later released on CD 537 422-2 (Remastered) 4 August 1997

A. Just Who Is The 5 O' Clock Hero?
B. War / The Great Depression
7 inch Polydor 2059 504

A. Just Who Is The 5 O' Clock Hero?
B. War / The Great Depression
12 inch Polydor 2141 558
11 June 1982
Highest chart position: 8
(Dutch import)

A. The Bitterest Pill (I Ever Had To Swallow)
B. Pity Poor Alfie / Fever
7 inch Polydor POSP 505
10 September 1982
Highest chart position: 2
Later Released As The Bitterest Pill (I Ever Had To Swallow) / The Butterfly Collector / That's Entertainment / The Bitterest Pill (I Ever Had To Swallow) – First Version 3:16
7 inch Polydor 571598–7
MC Polydor 571598-4
September 1997

A. Beat Surrender
B. Shopping
7 inch Polydor POSP 540
1A. Beat Surrender / 1B. Shopping
2A. Move On Up / 2B. Stoned Out Of My Mind / War
7 inch Double Pack Polydor POSPJ 540
12 inch Polydor POSPX 540
26 November 1982
Highest chart position: 1

DIG THE NEW BREED (LIVE ALBUM)
LP Polydor POLD 5075
MC Polydor POLDC 5075
10 December 1982
Highest chart position: 2
Later released on LP SPELP 107 & MC SPEMC 107 17 June 1987
Later released on CD 810041-2, LP 810041-1 & MC 810041-4 29 June 1990

All 17 singles (prior to 'Beat Surrender') re-released in picture bags, 14 January 1983. All re-entered the top 75 with the exception of 'Funeral Pyre', 'Absolute Beginners', 'Just Who Is The 5 O' Clock Hero?' and 'The Bitterest Pill'.

SOUND AFFECTS & THE GIFT
MC Polydor TWOMC 1
(2 On 1 Re-issue)
June 1983

SNAP!
Double LP Polydor SNAP 1
Double MC Polydor SNAPC 1
7 inch Vinyl SNAPL 45 (Bonus live single free with the double LP; these tracks also available on the double MC)
A Move On Up / Get Yourself Together
B The Great Depression / Bit I'm Different Now
Recorded live at Wembley Arena, December 2 & 3, 1982
14 October 1983
Highest chart position: 2
Later released on CD 821712-2 September 1984
Later released on CD 815537-2 LP 815537-1 & MC 815537-4 29 June 1990
Later released on CD Polydor 821712-1
20 June 2005
Highest chart position: 39

Later released as a 2-CD set with the same running order as the original 2-LP set plus extra tracks
CD Polydor 821712-1
Bonus live CD Polydor 9818340
A Move On Up / Get Yourself Together
B The Great Depression / But I'm Different Now
Recorded live at Wembley Arena, December 2 & 3, 1982
13 February 2006
Highest UK chart position: 8

SNAP! 3CD Special Edition
CD Polydor 9877182
Released: 13 February 2006
Highest chart position: 8

A. Town Called Malice
B. Absolute Beginners
7 inch Old Gold OG 9894
June 1989

A. Beat Surrender
B. The Bitterest Pill (I Ever Had To Swallow)
7 inch Old Gold OG 9895
June 1989

A. The Eton Rifles
B. Down In The Tube Station At Midnight
7 inch Old Gold OG 9896
June 1989

A. Going Underground
B. Start!
7 inch Old Gold OG 9897
June 1989

THE PEEL SESSIONS EP
In The City / Art School/ I've Changed My Address / The Modern World
MC Strange Fruit SFPS 080
12 inch Strange Fruit SFPSC 080
CD Strange Fruit SFPSCD 080
July 1990
Later released in new sleeve, September 1996

GREATEST HITS
LP Polydor 849 554-1
MC Polydor 849 554-4
CD Polydor 849 554-2
1 July 1991
Highest chart position: 2
Later released on DCC 849554-5

A. The Dreams Of Children
B. Away From The Numbers (Recorded live at the Rainbow Theatre, 3 December, 1979)
7 inch Polydor PO 199

A. The Dreams Of Children
B. Away From The Numbers (Live) / The Modern World (Recorded live at the Rainbow Theatre, 3 December, 1979)
12 inch Polydor PZ 199
CD Polydor PZCD 199
23 March 1992

EXTRAS
LP Polydor 513 177-1
MC Polydor 513 177-4
CD Polydor 513 177-2
6 April 1992
Highest chart position: 15

WASTELAND
CD Pickwick PWKS 4129P
MC Pickwick PWKMC 4129P
October 1992

BEAT SURRENDER
CD Spectrum 550 006-2
MC Spectrum 550 006-4
May 1993

LIVE JAM
LP Polydor 519 667-1
MC Polydor 519 667-4
CD Polydor 519 667-2
25 October 1993
Highest chart position: 28

THE JAM COLLECTION
LP Polydor 531 493-1
MC Polydor 531 493-4
CD Polydor 531 493-2
15 July 1996
Highest chart position: 58

DIRECTION, REACTION, CREATION
5-CD box set Polydor 537 143-2
26 May 1997
Highest chart position: 8
Later released as 4 CD Box Set Polydor 9841221 (comes with hardback version of the book)
23 October 2006

THE VERY BEST OF THE JAM
CD Polydor / Polygram TV 537423-2
MC Polydor / Polygram TV 537423-4
13 October 1997
Highest chart position: 9

THE JAM 45 RPM THE SINGLES 1977–79 BOX 1
CD Box Set Polydor 587 610-2

CD Single 1
In The City / Takin' My Love
(Enhanced Track – In The City Video)

CD Single 2
All Around The World / Carnaby Street

CD Single 3
Modern World / Sweet Soul Music (Live)
Back In My Arms Again (Live) /Bricks & Mortar (Live) Recorded live at The 100 Club, 11 September, 1977

CD Single 4
News Of The World
Aunties And Uncles (Impulsive Youths)/ Innocent Man
(Enhanced Track – News Of The World Video)

CD Single 5
David Watts/ 'A' Bomb In Wardour Street

CD Single 6
Down In The Tube Station At Midnight/ So Sad About Us / The Night

CD Single 7
Strange Town / The Butterfly Collector
(Enhanced Track – Strange Town Video)

CD Single 8
When You're Young / Smithers – Jones
(Enhanced Track – When You're Young Video)

CD Single 9
Eton Rifles / See Saw
2nd April 2001

THE JAM 45 RPM THE SINGLES 1980-82 BOX 2
CD Box Set – Polydor 587 620-2

CD Single 1
Going Underground / The Dreams Of Children
Away From The Numbers (Live at the Rainbow)/ The Modern World (Live at the Rainbow)/ Down In The Tube Station At Midnight (Live at the Rainbow)
(Enhanced Track – Going Underground Video)

CD Single 2
Start! / Liza Radley
(Enhanced Track – Start! Video)

CD Single 3
That's Entertainment/ Down In The Tube Station At Midnight (Live, recorded at the Rainbow, 3 December 1979)
(Enhanced Track – That's Entertainment Video)

CD Single 4
Funeral Pyre / Disguises
(Enhanced Track – Funeral Pyre Video)

CD Single 5
Absolute Beginners / Tales From The Riverbank / (Enhanced Track – Absolute Beginners Video)

CD Single 6
Town Called Malice / Precious
(Enhanced Track – Town Called Malice Video)

CD Single 7
Just Who Is The 5 O'clock Hero/ The Great Depression

CD Single 8
The Bitterest Pill (I Ever Had To Swallow)/ Pity Poor Alfie / Fever
(Enhanced Track – The Bitterest Pill Video)

CD Single 9
Beat Surrender / Shopping / Move On Up / Stoned Out Of My Mind / War
30th April 2001

THE SOUND OF THE JAM
CD Polydor 589 761-2
LP Polydor 589 761-1
6 May 2002
Highest UK chart position: 3

THE JAM AT THE BBC
CD Polydor 589 690-2
LP Polydor 589 761-1
Bonus CD of in concert recorded at the Rainbow, December 4, 1979
27 May 2002
Highest UK chart position: 33

MASTERS SERIES
CD Polydor 539 841-1
10 June 2003

THE STYLE COUNCIL

A. Speak Like A Child
B. Party Chambers (Vocal Version)
7 inch Polydor TSC 1
11 March 1983
Highest chart position: 4
(Only released on 7 inch vinyl)

A. Money-Go-Round (Part 1)
B. Money-Go-Round (Part 2)
7 inch Polydor TSC 2

A. Money-Go-Round (Parts 1 & 2)
B. Headstart For Happiness / Mick's Up
12 inch Polydor Tscx 2
20 May 1983
Highest chart position: 11
(Dance mix unreleased in the UK)

À PARIS EP
A. Long Hot Summer/ Party Chambers (Instrumental)
B. The Paris Match / Lé Depart
7 inch Polydor TSC 3

A. Long Hot Summer (Extended Version) / Party Chambers (Instrumental)
B. The Paris Match / Lé Depart
12 inch Polydor TSCX 3
Also released in a limited edition double pack paired with Money/Go/Round 12 inch
5 August 1983
Highest chart position: 3

À PARIS
CD Video Single Polydor 080 206-2
Audio – Long Hot Summer (Extended Version)
The Paris Match / Le Depart
Video – Long Hot Summer
November 1988

INTRODUCING THE STYLE COUNCIL (MINI LP)
LP Polydor 815 277-1
MC Polydor 815 531-4
2 September 1983
Dutch import later released in the UK on CD 815 277-2

A. A Solid Bond In Your Heart
B. It Just Came To Pieces In My Hands / A Solid Bond In Your Heart (Instrumental)
7 inch Polydor TSC 4
7 inch Gatefold Sleeve TSCG 4
11 November 1983
Highest chart position: 11

A. My Ever Changing Moods
B. Mick's Company
7 inch Polydor TSC 5

A. My Ever Changing Moods (Long Version)
B. Mick's Company / Spring, Summer, Autumn
12 inch Polydor TSCX 5
10 February 1984
Highest chart position: 5

CAFE BLEU
LP Polydor TSCLP 1
MC Polydor TSCMC 1
March 16 1984
Later released on CD 817 535-2
Later released on CD 557 915-2 (remastered) 21 August 2000
Highest chart position: 2

GROOVIN' EP
A. You're The Best Thing
AA. The Big Boss Groove
7 inch Polydor TSC 6

A. You're The Best Thing (Long Version)
Aa. You're The Dub Thing / The Big Boss Groove (Long Version)
12 inch Polydor TSCX 6
18 May 1984
Highest chart position: 5

A. Shout To The Top
B. Ghosts Of Dachau
7 inch Polydor TSC 7

A. Shout To The Top (Extended Version) / Shout To The Top (Instrumental)
B. The Piccadilly Trail / Ghosts Of Dachau
12 inch Polydor TSCX 7
5 October 1984
Highest chart position: 7

A. Soul Deep (Part 1)
B. Soul Deep (Part 2)
7 inch Polydor MINE 1

A. Soul Deep (Parts 1 & 2)
B. A Miners Point
12 inch Polydor MINE X1

A. Soul Deep (Club Mix)
B. Soul Deep
Limited edition 12 inch MINEX 1
14 December 1984
Highest chart position: 24
Released under the name 'The Council Collective'

A. Walls Come Tumbling Down
B. The Whole Point II / Blood Sports
7 inch Polydor TSC 8

A. Walls Come Tumbling Down / Spin' Drifting
B. The Whole Point II / Blood Sports
12 inch Polydor TSCX 8
3 May 1985
Highest chart position: 6

OUR FAVOURITE SHOP
LP Polydor TSCLP 2
MC Polydor TSCMC 2
31 May 1985
Later released on CD 825 700-2
Highest chart position: 1
Later released on CD 559 050-2 (Remastered) 21 August 2000
To be released as a Deluxe Edition with extra tracks added in the autumn of 2006
CD Polydor 9838703

A. Come To Milton Keynes
B. (When You) Call Me
7 inch Polydor TSC 9
7 inch Gatefold Sleeve TSCG 9

A. Come To Milton Keynes / Our Favourite Shop (Club Mix)
B. (When You) Call Me / The Lodgers (Club Mix)
12 inch Polydor TSCX 9
28 June 1985
Highest chart position: 23

A. The Lodgers
B. Big Boss Groove (Live) / You're The Best Thing (Live)
7 inch Polydor TSC 10

A. The Lodgers (Extended Mix)
B. Big Boss Groove / Move On Up / You're The Best Thing / Money-Go-Round / Soul Deep / Strength Of Your Nature – Medley (Live)
12 inch Polydor TSCX 10
7 inch Double Pack Single Polydor TSCDP 1
20 September 1985
Highest chart position: 13

A. Have You Ever Had It Blue
B. Mr. Cool's Dream
7 inch Polydor CINE 1

A. Have You Ever Had It Blue (Uncut Version)
B. Have You Ever Had It Blue (Cut Version) / Mr. Cool's Dream
12 inch Polydor CINEX 1
Limited 7 inch & MC pack in plastic blue embossed sleeve CINEC1
28 March 1986
Highest chart position: 14

Have You Ever Had It Blue
CC Video Single Polydor 080 336-2
Audio – Have You Ever Had It Blue (Uncut Version)
Mr Cools Dream / With Everything To Lose
Video – Have You Ever Had It Blue
November 1988

HOME & ABROAD (LIVE)
LP TSCLP 3
MC TSCMC 3
CD 829 143-2 (With two extra tracks)
9 May 1986
Highest chart position: 8

A. It Didn't Matter
B. All Year Round
7 inch Polydor TSC 12

A. It Didn't Matter
B. It Didn't Matter (Instrumental) / All Year Round
12 inch Polydor TSCX 12
9 January 1987
Highest chart position: 9

COST OF LOVING
LP Polydor TSCLP 4
MC Polydor TSCMC 4
CD 831 443-2
Later released on CD 557 917-2 (Remastered) 21 August 2000
6 February 1987
Highest chart position: 2

A. Waiting
B. Françoise
7 inch Polydor TSC 13

A. Waiting (Vocal) / Françoise (Vocal)
B. Françoise (Theme From 'Jerusalem') / Waiting (Instrumental)
12 inch Polydor TSCX 13
6 March 1987
Highest chart position: 52

A. Wanted *Or Waiter There's Some Soup In My Flies
B. The Cost Of Loving (Vocal) / The Cost (Instrumental)
7 inch Polydor TSC 14

A. Wanted *Or Waiter There's Some Soup In My Flies
B. The Cost / The Cost Of Loving
12 inch Polydor TSCX 14
CD Polydor TSCCD 14
Cassette Polydor TSCCS 14
23 October 1987
Highest chart position: 20

CAFÉ BLEU EP
A. Headstart For Happiness / Here's One That Got Away
B. Blue Café / Strength Of Your Nature
7 inch Polydor TSCEP 1
CD Polydor TSCCD 1
4 December 1987

THE BIRDS & THE B'S EP
A. The Piccadilly Trail / It Just Came To Pieces In My Hands
B. Spin' Drifting / Spring, Summer, Autumn
7 inch Polydor TSCEP 2
CD Polydor TSCCD 2
4 December 1987

MICK TALBOT IS AGENT 88 EP
A. Mick's Up / Party Chambers
B. Mick's Blessing / Mick's Company
7 inch Polydor TSCEP 3
CD Polydor TSCCD 3
4 December 1987
Highest chart position: 100

A. Life At A Top Peoples Health Farm
B. Sweet Loving Ways
7 inch Polydor TSC 15

A. Spank (Live At A Top Peoples Health Club) /
Life At A Top Peoples Health Farm (7 inch Version)
B. Life At A Top Peoples Health Farm (Um & Argh Mix) /
Sweet Loving Ways
12 inch Polydor TSCX 15
CD Polydor TSCCD 15
20 May 1988
Highest chart position: 28

Life At A Top Peoples Health Farm
CD Video Single Polydor 080 560-2
Audio – Life At A Top Peoples Health Farm (Extended Remix)
Spank! (Life At A Top Peoples Health Club) / Sweet Loving Ways
Video – Life At A Top Peoples Health Farm (7 inch Version)
April 1989

CONFESSIONS OF A POP GROUP
LP Polydor TSCIN 1
Interview with Mick and Paul by Sasha Stojanovic
Interview Disc – Style 7
7 inch Picture Disc 2000 Copies
7 inch Blue Vinyl 1000 Copies
7 inch Clear Vinyl 100 Copies
7 inch Black Vinyl 250 Copies
April 1988

CONFESSIONS OF A POP GROUP
LP Polydor TSCLP 5
MC Polydor TSCMC 5
CD Polydor 835 785-2
Later released on CD 557 916-2 (Remastered) 21 August 2000
24 June 1988
Highest chart position: 15

A. How She Threw It All Away / In Love For The First Time
B. Long Hot Summer / I Do Like To Be B-Side The A-Side*
7 inch Polydor TSC 16

A. How She Threw It All Away / In Love For The First Time
B. Long Hot Summer (Tom Mix) / I Do Like To Be B-Side The A-Side*
12 inch Polydor TSCX 16
CD Polydor TSCCD 16
15 July 1988
Highest chart position: 41
How She Threw It All Away
CD Video Single Polydor 080 400-2
Audio – How She Threw It All Away
Love For The First Time / Long Hot Summer (Tom Mix)
Video – How She Threw It All Away
November 1988

A. Promised Land
B. Can You Still Love Me?
7 inch Polydor TSC 17
7 inch Limited edition box set Polydor TSCB 17
12 inch Polydor TSCX 17

A. Promised Land (Longer Version) / Promised Land (Pianopella Version)
B. Can You Still Love Me? (Dub) / Can You Still Love Me? (Vocal)
CD Polydor TSCD 17

A. Promised Land (Radio Edit) / Promised Land (Longer Version)
B. Can You Still Love Me? (Vocal) / Can You Still Love Me? (Dub)
CD Polydor TSCCD 17
A Promised Land (Longer Version) / Promised Land (Pianopella Version)
B Can You Still Love Me? (Dub) / Can You Still Love Me? (Vocal)

A. Promised Land (Joe Smooth's Alternate Mix)
B. Can You Still Love Me? (Club Vocal) / Can You Still Love Me? (12 O' Clock Dub)
12 inch Limited Edition Polydor TSCXS 17
10 February 1989
Highest Chart Position: 27

Acid Jazz JAZID 9T
A. Like A Gun (12 inch Mix) / Like A Gun (Safe Sax Mix)
B. Like A Gun (Dub Version) / Like A Gun (Radio Edit)
17 February 1989
Released under the name 'King Truman'

THE SINGULAR ADVENTURES OF THE STYLE COUNCIL
LP Polygram TSCTV 1
MC Polygram TSCTVMC 1
CD Polygram 837 896-2
10 March 1989
Highest chart position: 3

A. Long Hot Summer '89
B. Everybody's On The Run
7 inch Polydor LHS 1

A. Long Hot Summer '89 (Extended Version)
B. Everybody's On The Run (Version One) / Everybody's On The Run (Version Two)
12 inch Polydor LHSX 1
CD 889 341-2
19 May 1989
Highest chart position: 48

A. Long Hot Summer
B. Speak Like A Child
7 inch Old Gold OG 9924
1990

You're The Best Thing
My Ever Changing Moods
7 inch Old Gold OG 9929
1990

HEADSTART FOR HAPPINESS
CD Pickwick PWKS 4090 P
MC Pickwick PWKMC 4090 P
29 November 1991

HERE'S SOME THAT GOT AWAY
CD Polydor 519 372-2
MC Polydor 519 372-4
2 July 1993
Highest chart position: 39

THE STYLE COUNCIL COLLECTION
CD Polydor 529 483-2
MC Polydor 529 483-4
23 February 1996
Highest chart position: 60

THE STYLE COUNCIL IN CONCERT
CD Polydor 533 143-2
MC Polydor 533 143-4
14 February 1998

THE COMPLETE ADVENTURES OF THE STYLE COUNCIL
5-CD Box Set Polydor 557 789–2
23 October 1998

MASTERS SERIES
CD Polydor 539 841-1
31 December 1999

GREATEST HITS
CD Polydor 557 900-2
LP Polydor 549 134-1
14 August 2000
Highest chart position: 28

THE SOUND OF THE STYLE COUNCIL
CD Polydor 065 643-2
LP Polydor 065 643-1
17 March 2003

PAUL WELLER

THE PAUL WELLER MOVEMENT
A. Into Tomorrow
B. Here's A New Thing
7 inch Freedom High FHP 1
MC Freedom High FHP MC 1

A. Into Tomorrow / Here's A New Thing
B. That Spiritual Thing / Into Tomorrow (8 Track Demo)
12 inch Freedom High FHTP 1
CD Freedom High FHPCD 1
6 May 1991
Highest chart position: 36

A. Uh Huh Oh Yeh
B. Fly On The Wall
7 inch Go! Discs GOD 86
MC Go! Discs GOD MC 86

A. Uh Huh Oh Yeh / Arrival Time
B. Fly On The Wall / Always There To Fool You
12 inch Go! Discs GOD X 86
CD Go! Discs God CD 86
3 August 1992
Highest chart position:18

PAUL WELLER
LP Go! Discs 828 343-1
MC Go! Discs 828-343-4
CD Go! Discs 828 343-2
31 August 1992
Highest chart position: 8

A. Above The Clouds
B. Everything Has A Price To Pay
7 inch Go! Discs GOD 91
MC Go! Discs GOD MC 91

A. Above The Clouds / Everything Has A Price To Pay
B. All Year Round (Live at The Ritz, New York, 25 July 1992) / Feeling Alright
12 inch Go! Discs GOD X 91
CD Go! Discs GOD CD 91
28 September 1992
Highest chart position: 47

A. Sunflower
B. Bull Rush/Magic Bus
7 inch Go! Discs GOD 102
MC Go! Discs GOD MC 102

A. Sunflower / Kosmos Sxdub 2000
B. Bull-Rush/Magic Bus / That Spiritual Feeling (New Mix)
12 inch Go! Discs GOD X 102
CD Go! Discs GOD CD 102
5 July 1993
Highest chart position: 16

A. Wild Wood
B. Ends Of The Earth
7 inch Go! Discs GOD 104
MC Go! Discs GODMC 104
10 inch GOD T 104 (Limited Edition – Numbered C/W Poster)
CD GOD CD 104
23 August 1993
Highest chart position: 14

A. Wild Wood
B. Wild Wood (Paul Weller Vs Portishead – The Sheared Wood Remix)
7 inch Island IS 734 – 572 526-7

A. Wild Wood / Science (With The Psychonauts – A Lynch Mob Remix)
B. Wild Wood (Paul Weller Vs Portishead – The Sheared Wood Remix)
12 inch Island 12IS 734 – 572 527-1
CD Island CID 734 – 572 526-2
Later released on 28 December 1998
Highest chart position: 22

WILD WOOD
LP Go! Discs 828 435-1
MC Go! Discs 828 435-4
CD Go! Discs 835 435-2
6 September 1993
Highest chart position: 2

All formats later released in April 1994 and included the single "Hung Up"
LP Go! Discs 828 513-1
MC Go! Discs 828 513-4
CD Go! Discs 828 513-2
On both releases the LP came with an "Obi" and Initial Copies With A Poster.

THE WEAVER EP
A. The Weaver / This Is The Time
B. Another New Day / Ohio (Live at The Royal Albert Hall, London 13 October 1992)
7 inch Go! Discs GOD 107
10 inch GOD T 107
CD GOD CD 107
MC Go! Discs GOD MC 107
1 November 1993
Highest chart position: 18

A. Hung Up / Foot Of The Mountain (Live at The Royal Albert Hall, London 23 November 1993)
B. The Loved / Kosmos (Lynch Mob Bonus Beats)
7 inch Go! Discs GOD T 111
12 inch Go! Discs GOD X 111
MC Go! Discs GOD MC 111
CD Go! Discs GOD CD 111
28 March 1994
Highest chart position: 11

LIVE WOOD
LP Go! Discs 828 561-1
CD Go! Discs 828 561-2
MC Go! Discs 828 561-4
12 September 1994
Highest chart position: 13

A. Out Of The Sinking
B. Sexy Sadie / Sunflower (Lynch Mob Dub)
7 inch Go! Discs GOD 121
12 inch GOD X 121
MC Go! Discs GOD MC 121
CD GOD CD 121
24 October 1994
Highest chart position: 20

A. Out Of The Sinking (LP Version) / I Shall Be Released
B. Broken Stone / Porcelain Gods (Recorded 1 October 1995 at K.R.O. Radio 3 Leidsekade Live)
7 inch Go! Discs GOD 143
CD GOD CD 143
Later released on 26 February 1996
Highest chart position: 16
(Available for one week only)

A. The Changing Man / I'd Rather Go Blind
B. It's A New Day, Baby / I Didn't Mean To Hurt You (Live at The Royal Albert Hall, London, December 1993)
7 inch Go! Discs GOD 127
12 inch GOD X 127
MC GOD MC 127
CD Go! Discs GOD CD 127
24 April 1995
Highest chart position: 7

STANLEY ROAD
LP Go! Discs 828 619-1
MC Go! Discs 828 619-4
CD Go! Discs 828 619-2
Limited edition box set 850 070-7 / 828 620-2
15 May 1995
Highest chart position: 1
Deluxe edition double CD + DVD
Island 9828401
30 May 2005

A. You Do Something To Me / My Whole World Is Falling Down (Radio 1 evening session May 1995)
B. A Year Late / Woodcutter's Son (Radio 1 evening session May 1995)
7 inch Go! Discs GOD 130
12 inch Go! Discs GOD X 130
Mc Go! Discs GODMC 130
CD GOD CD 130
10 July 1995
Highest chart position: 9

A. Broken Stones
B. Steam
7 inch Go! Discs GOD 132
MC Go! Discs GODMC 132

CD GOD CD 132
18 September 1995
Highest chart position: 20

The Smokin' Mojo Filters
Come Together B/W The Beautiful South: A Minute's Silence; Black Grape: In The Name Of The Father; Dodgy: Is It Me
7 inch Go! Discs GOD 136
CD Go! Discs GODCD 136
11 December 1995
Highest chart position: 19

A. Peacock Suit
B. Eye Of The Storm
7 inch Go! Discs GOD 149
MC Go! Discs GODMC 149
CD Go! Discs GODCD 149
5 August 1996
Highest chart placing: 5

HEAVY SOUL
LP Go! Discs / Island ILPS 8058 – 524 277-1
MC Go! Discs / Island ICT 8058 – 524 277-4
CD Go! Discs / Island CID 8058 – 524 277-2
23 June 1997
Highest chart position: 2

A. Brushed / Ain't No Love In The Heart Of The City
B. Shoot The Dove / As You Lean Into The Light (Acoustic)
7 inch Island IS 666 – 572 098-7
MC Island CIS 666 – 572 098-4
CD Island CID 666 – 572 098-2
28 July 1997
Highest chart placing: 14

A. Friday Street / Sunflower (Live)
B. Brushed (Live) / Mermaids (Live)
(Live tracks recorded at The Southbank, London 24 June 1997)
7 inch Island IS 676 – 572 130-7
MC Island CIS 676 – 572 131-4
CD Island CID 676 – 572 131-2
29 September 1997
Highest chart placing: 21

A. Mermaid's / Everything Has A Price To Pay (1997 Version)
B. So You Want To Be A Dancer
7 inch Island IS 683/572 184-7
MC Island CIS 683 – 572 184-4
CD Island CID 683 – 572 184-2
24 November 1997
Highest Chart Placing: 30

A. Brand New Start
B. Right Underneath It / The Riverbank
7 inch Island IS 711- 572 370-7
MC Island CIS 711- 572 370-4
CD Island CID 711 – 572 370-2
2 November 1998
Highest chart placing: 16

MODERN CLASSICS – THE GREATEST HITS
LP Island ILPS 8080 – 524558-1
CD Island CID 8080 – 524558-2 (Single Cd)
CD Island CIDD 8080 – 524609-2 (Double Cd With "Live Classics")
MC Island ICT 8080 – 524558-4
Limited edition box set IBX 8080 572/472-7
Later released in February 2006
9 November 1998
Highest chart position: 7

A. He's The Keeper
B. Heliocentric / Bang-Bang
12 inch Island 12IS 760 – 562 655-1
CD Island CID 760 – 562 655-2
3 April 2000
Owing to a wrong bar code, this single wasn't eligible for the charts

HELIOCENTRIC
LP Island ILPS 8093 – 542-394-1
CD Island CID 8093 – 542-394-2
MC Island ICT 8093 – 542-394-4
10 April 2000
Highest chart position: 2

A. Sweet Pea, My Sweet Pea / Back In The Fire (BBC Radio 2 Session)
B. There's No Drinking After You're Dead (Noonday Underground Remix)
12 inch Island 12IS 764 – 562-869-1
CD Island CID 764 – 562 869-2
21 August 2000
Highest chart position: 44

DAYS OF SPEED (LIVE)
LP Independiente ISOM 26LP
CD Independiente ISOM 26CD
8 October 2001
Highest chart position: 3

A. It's Written In The Stars
B. Horseshoe Drama / Push Button, Automatic
10 inch Independiente ISOM 63TE
CD 1 Independiente ISOM 63MS
It's Written In The Stars / The Butterfly Collector (Live At The Shepherds Bush Empire, London 02.06.01) / Carnation (Live At The Paradiso, Amsterdam 0702.01)
CD 2 Independiente ISOM 63SMS
2 September 2002
Highest chart position: 7

ILLUMINATION
LP Independiente ISOM 33LP
CD Independiente ISOM 33CD
CD/DVD Independiente ISOM 33CDL
16 September 2002
Highest chart position: 1

A. Leafy Mysteries
B. Talisman
7 inch Independiente ISOM 65S
Leafy Mysteries / Talisman / Wild Wood (Live At The Route Of Kings, Hyde Park, London 28 July 2002)
CD 1 Independiente ISOM 65MS
Leafy Mysteries (Live)/ Broken Stones (Live) / Peacock Suite (Live)
(All Songs Live At The Route Of Kings, Hyde Park, London 28 July 2002)
CD 2 Independiente ISOM 65SMS
18 November 2002
Highest chart position: 23

FLY ON THE WALL – B SIDES AND RARITIES 1991–2000
LP Island 0635271 – Triple LP (Omits certain tracks that are on the CD)
CD Island 0635272 – 3CD
25 August 2003
Highest chart position: 22

A. The Bottle
B. Corrina Corrina / Coconut Grove
7 inch V2 VVR 5026917
CD V2 VVR 5026913

A. The Bottle (Big Boss Man Vocal Mix)
B. The Bottle (Big Boss Man Instrumental Mix)
7 inch V2 VVR 5026910
14 June 2004
Highest chart position: 13

A. Wishing On A Star
B. Family Affair / Let It Be Me
7 inch V2 VVR 5026927
CD 1 V2 VVR 5026923
Wishing On A Star / Let It Be Me
CD 2 V2 VVR 5026928
30 August 2004
Highest chart position: 11

STUDIO 150
LP V2 VVR 1026901
CD V2 VVR 1026902
CD/DVD V2 VVR 1026908
13 September 2004
Highest chart position: 2
Later Released On CD + Bonus Live Disc
V2 VVR1032132
13 September 2005

A. Thinking Of You
B. Don't Go To Strangers / Needles & Pins
7 inch V2 VVR 5028467
CD V2 VVR 5028463
Thinking Of You (Audio – Live At The Riverside Studios 14 September 2005) / Wishing On A Star (Audio – Beta Band Remix) / Early Morning Rain (Video – Live At The Riverside Studios 14 September 2005)
DVD Single V2 VVR 8028469
15 November 2004
Highest chart position: 18

A. Early Morning Rain
Aa. Come Together
7 inch V2 VVR 5030397
14 March 2005
Highest chart position: 40

A. From The Floorboards Up
B. Oranges And Rosewater
7 inch Multi Coloured V2 VVR 5033417

A. From The Floorboards Up
B. From The Floorboards Up (Lynchmob Remix – Instrumental)
7 inch Gatefold V2 VVR 5033410
From The Floorboards Up / Oranges And Rosewater / From The Floorboards Up (Video)
V2 CD VVR 5033413
18 July 2005
Highest chart position: 18

A. Come On/Let's Go (Acoustic Demo)
B. Into Tomorrow (Live From Guilfest)
7 inch Multi Coloured V2 VVR 5033227

A. Come On/Let's Go
B. Shine On
7 inch Gatefold V2 VVR 5033220
Come On/Let's Go / Shine On / Come On/Let's Go (Video)
CD V2 VVR 5033223
26 September 2005
Highest chart position: 15

AS IS NOW
LP V2 VVR 1033201
CD V2 VVR 1033202
CD/DVD V2 VVR 1033208
10 October 2005
Highest chart position: 4

A. Here's The Good News
B. Paper Smile (Audio Twitch Remix)
7 inch Multi Coloured V2 VVR 5034607

A. Here's The Good News
B. Super Lekker Stoned (Richard Fearless Remix)
7 inch Gatefold V2 VVR 5034600
Here's The Good News / Alone / Super Lekker Stoned
CD V2 5034603
5 December 2005
Highest chart position: 21

AS IS NOW

2-CD 14-track set released in celebration of his 'Lifetime Achievement Award' at the Brits 2006

CD V2 VVR 1038232

13 February 2006

Highest chart position: 64

Bonus CD Featuring four live tracks: From The Floorboards Up / Come On / Let's Go / The Changing Man / Town Called Malice recorded at Alexandra Palace, London 5 December 2005

AS IS NOW EP

A. Blink & You'll Miss It / From The Floorboards Up

B. Here's The Good News / Come On / Let's Go

Strictly limited edition 4-track 7 inch vinyl single released to coincide with his 'Outstanding Contribution To Music' Award at Brits 2006

Limited to 6,000 copies and available for one week only

7 inch V2 VVR 5036267

13 February 2006

(Not eligible for the charts)

CATCH-FLAME!

2CD V2 VVR1039392 (Standard Version)

2CD V2 VVR1039398 (Special Edition)

2LP V2 VVR1039391

12 June 2006

Highest chart position: 17

HIT PARADE

CD Island 9842593

4 CD box set Island 9842615 with 64 Page Book (Limited Edition)

2 DVD Double CD 9843252

6 November 2006

Highest Chart Position: 7

A. Wild Blue Yonder

B. Small Personal Fortune / To The Start Of Forever (acoustic)

CD V2 VVR5043983

6 November 2006

Highest chart position: 22

2 Gig List

THE JAM, THE STYLE COUNCIL AND PAUL WELLER SOLO LIVE CONCERTS

My gig listing is as definitive as I could make it. I checked the dates against four separate sources; Karl Gonzalez website, Neil Allen's from The Jam Box Set, Iain Munn's from *Mr Cool's Dream* and Graham Willmott's from his book, *The Sound Of The Jam*. I spent a day at the British Library going through back issues of all the music papers but it was impossible to check every gig, and would have taken years rather than months.

Special thanks to Karl Gonzalez, for giving up so much time and his invaluable help.

THE JAM

1973

April

22 – Sheerwater Community Centre, Woking

May

12 – Community Centre Old, Woking – (*Win Talent Contest Performing 'Reelin' & Rockin'*)

1974

January

22 – Audition for residency at Michael's Club, Woking

26 – Michael's Club, Woking

February

2 & 16 – Michael's Club, Woking

March

2, 16 & 30 – Michael's Club, Woking

April

7 – Working Men's Club, Woking

13, 26 & 27 – Michael's Club, Woking

May

3 – Michael's Club, Woking

4 – Parkside Club, Frimley

10, 17 & 24 – Michael's Club, Woking

26 – Parkside Club, Frimley

31 – Michael's Club, Woking

June

1 – British Legion Club, Ripley

7, 9 & 14 – Michael's Club, Woking

15 – Sheerwater Youth Club, Woking

21 & 28 – Michael's Club, Woking

29 – West End Club, Woking

July

5 – Michael's Club, Woking

6 – Working Men's Club, Woking

7 – Bunter's Club, Guildford

12 – Michael's Club, Woking

13 – Working Men's Club, Woking

19 – Michael's Club, Woking

21 – Bunter's Club, Guildford

26 – Michael's Club, Woking

27 – Parkside Club, Frimley

28 – Michael's Club, Woking

August

2 – Michael's Club, Woking

3 – Working Men's Club, Woking

17 & 23 – Michael's Club, Woking

26 – Parkside Club, Frimley

30 – Michael's Club, Woking

September

6 – Michael's Club, Woking

13 – Michael's Club, Woking

14 – British Army Cannon Club, Aldershot
20 – Michael's Club, Woking
21 – Parkside Club, Frimley
27 – Michael's Club, Woking
28 – British Legion Club, Leatherhead

October

2 – Gaiety Bar, Aldershot
4 – Michael's Club, Woking
5 – Bunter's Club, Guildford *(Cancelled due to bombing in the town)*
6 & 12 Michael's Club, Woking
13 – British Legion Club, Hindhead
19 – Michael's Club, Woking
20 – Darts Club Party, Basingstoke
25 – Michael's Club, Woking
26 – Gladstone Club, Reading
27 – Greyhound, Croydon

November

1 – Michael's Club, Woking
2 – Working Men's Club, Woking
8, 10 & 15 – Michael's Club, Woking
17 – HM Prison Coldingley, Bisley
20 – Gaiety Bar, Aldershot
22 & 29 Michael's Club, Woking
30 – Sheerwater Community Centre, Woking

December

1 – Michael's Club, Woking
4 – Tumbledown Dick, Farnborough
6 & 13 – Michael's Club, Woking
14 – Lansing Bagnall Dance, Surrey
15 – The Hatch, Surrey
16 – Winning Post, Twickenham
18 – Tumbledown Dick, Farnborough
19 – Highlands School, Woking
20 – Michael's Club, Woking
21 – Working Men's Club, Woking
26 – The Hare & Hill Club, Ottershaw
29 – Michael's Club, Woking
31 – Woking Liberal Club

1975

January

3 – The Country Club, Fleet
4 – Leatherhead Football Club

5 – Working Men's Club, Woking
10 – Michael's Club, Woking
11 – Woking Liberal Club
15 – Tumbledown Dick, Farnborough
17 – Michael's Club, Woking
18 – Working Men's Club, Stouton
24 – Michael's Club, Woking
25 – West End Club, Woking
30 – Michael's Club, Woking

February

1 – The Ivy League Club
2 – Working Men's Club, Woking
5 – Tumbledown Dick, Farnborough
7 – Michael's Club, Woking
8 – The Queens Hotel, Send, Farnborough
9 – Woking Liberal Club
14 – Michael's Club, Woking
15 – Sheerwater Community Centre
21, 22, 23 & 28 – Michael's Club, Woking

March

2 – Byfleet Social Club
7 – Michael's Club, Woking
8 – The Bison Club, Hounslow
9 – Michael's Club, Woking
14 – Aldershot Cricket Club
15 – The Bison Club, Hounslow
19 – Tumbledown Dick, Farnborough
21 – Michael's Club, Woking
23 – Woking Liberal Club
28 – Michael's Club, Woking
29 – Sheerwater Community Centre
31 – The Queens Hotel, Send, Farnborough

April

04 – Michael's Club, Woking
06 – Working Men's Club, Woking
09 – Tumbledown Dick, Farnborough
11 – Michael's Club, Woking
12 – Parkside Social Club, Frimley
13 – New Haw Club, Byfleet
18 & 20 – Michael's Club, Woking
21 – Stamford Bridge (Chelsea FC), London
25 – Michael's Club, Woking
26 – The Peabody Club, Farnborough

May
02 – Tumbledown Dick, Farnborough
03 – Working Men's Club, Woking
04 – Sheerwater Community Centre
16 – Michael's Club, Woking
17 – Sheerwater Community Centre
23 – Woking Football Club
25 – Michael's Club, Woking
31 – The Bison Club, Hounslow
June
01 – Working Men's Club, Woking
06 – Lightwater Social Club
07 – The Bison Club, Hounslow
13 & 15 – Michael's Club, Woking
18 & 20 – Tumbledown Dick, Farnborough
21 & 22 – Michael's Club, Woking
28 – West End Club, Woking
29 – Michael's Club, Woking
July
5 – Greyhound, Fulham
6 – Greyhound, Croydon
9 & 11 – Tumbledown Dick, Farnborough
12 – Sheerwater Youth Club, Woking
13, 20 & 25 – Michael's Club, Woking
August
12 – Town Hall, Surbiton – *(Audition for Opportunity Knocks – Failed)*
September
20 – Greyhound, Fulham
26 – Michael's Club, Woking
December
26 – Tumbledown Dick, Farnborough

1976
March
9 & 20 – Greyhound, Fulham
May
8 – Hope & Anchor, Islington
June
6 – Windsor Castle, London
7 – Kensington, London
16 – Windsor Castle, London (*Unconfirmed)*
17 – Greyhound, Fulham
29 – Hope & Anchor, Islington (*Unconfirmed)*
Teacher Training College, Canley

July
05 – Windsor Castle, London (*Unconfirmed)*
September
8 – Upstairs At Ronnie Scott's, London
17 – Greyhound, Fulham (*Unconfirmed)*
October
16 – Soho Market, London
21 – Queensway Hall, Dunstable
November
9 & 16 – 100 Club, London
23 – Upstairs At Ronnie Scott's, London
December
13 – Greyhound, Fulham
14 & 28 – 100 Club, London

1977
January
11 – 100 Club, London
22 – Marquee, London
25 – 100 Club, London
February
2 – Nashville, West Kensington, London (*Unconfirmed)*
3 – Nags Head, High Wycombe
7 – Nashville, West Kensington
11 – Roxy Club, Covent Garden, London
19 – Hunt Hotel, Leighton Buzzard
21 – Nashville, West Kensington
24 – Roxy Club, Covent Garden
25 – Greyhound, Fulham
26 – Hunt Hotel, Leighton Buzzard
March
1 – Railway Hotel, Putney
2 – Red Cow, Hammersmith
5 – Leicester Polytechnic
9 – Red Cow, Hammersmith
11 – Canterbury University, Kent
15 – Hope & Anchor, Islington
16 – Red Cow, Hammersmith
18 – Hope & Anchor, Islington (*Advertised, but later changed to Southbank Polytechnic, London*)
22 – Roxy Club, Covent Garden
23 – Red Cow, Hammersmith
24 – Rochester Castle, Stoke Newington

25 – Royal College Of Art, London
28 – Palais De Glace Punk Festival, Paris
29 – 100 Club, London
30 – Red Cow, Hammersmith
31 – Rochester Castle, Stoke Newington

April

1 – Leeds Polytechnic
5 – Nashville, West Kensington
6 – Hope & Anchor, Islington
7 – Manor Ballroom, Ipswich
9 – Rochester Castle, Stoke Newington
12 – Nashville, West Kensington
15 – Embassy Cinema, Brighton
16 – Rochester Castle, Stoke Newington
17 – Roundhouse, London
19 – Nashville, West Kensington
20 – Roundabout Club, Newport
22 – North London Polytechnic, Kentish Town
23 – Marquee, London
26 – Dingwalls, Camden *(Cancelled)*
28 – Hope & Anchor, Islington
29 – Royal College Of Art, London

May

3 – Dingwalls, Camden
5 – Oaks Hotel, Chorlton, Manchester
7 – Playhouse Theatre, Edinburgh
8 – Electric Circus, Manchester
9 – Rainbow Theatre, Finsbury Park
12 – Nag's Head, High Wycombe
20 – Newcastle University *(Cancelled)*
21 – City Hall, St Albans *(Cancelled)*
22 – Civic Hall, Wolverhampton *(Cancelled)*
23 – Top Of The World, Stafford *(Cancelled)*
24 – Top Rank, Cardiff *(Cancelled)*
25 – Woking Park Swimming Pool Area *(Cancelled) [The Woking Conference Of Youth Organisations 'Jubilee Youth Week' held a "Fashions Of Yesteryear by Sheerwater Youth Club with rock bands." The local paper reported that The Jam was unable to appear.]*
25 – Brighton Dome *(Cancelled)*
26 – Colston Hall, Bristol *(Cancelled)*
27 – West Runton Pavilion *(Cancelled)*
28 – Odeon, Canterbury *(Cancelled)*
29 – Chancellor Hall, Chelmsford *(Cancelled)*

28 – Portsmouth Polytechnic *(Cancelled)*
30 – California Ballroom, Dunstable *(Cancelled)*

June

4 – Nag's Head, High Wycombe
7 – Barbarella's, Birmingham
8 – Winning Post, Twickenham
9 – Winter Gardens, Eastbourne
10 – Corn Exchange, Cambridge
11 – Bristol Polytechnic
12 – Stamford Bridge (Chelsea FC), London *(Cancelled)*
13 – Top Rank, Reading
14 – Portsmouth Locarno
15 – Village Bowl Discotheque, Bournemouth
16 – Leeds Town Hall
17 – Seaburn Hall, Sunderland
18 – Civic Hall, Poplar, London
18 – U.C.L., London
19 – Electric Circus, Manchester
20 – Outlook Club, Doncaster
21 – Top Rank, Cardiff
22 – Lafayette, Wolverhampton
23 – Huddersfield Polytechnic
24 – Brunel Rooms, Swindon
25 – Winter Gardens, Malvern
26 – Greyhound, Croydon
27 – Battersea Town Hall, London
28 – Drill Hall, Lincoln *(Cancelled)*
29 – Cat's Whiskers, York
30 – Rebecca's, Birmingham *(Cancelled)*

July

1 – Mayfair Ballroom, Newcastle
2 – Middleton Town Hall, Manchester
4 – London Venue, Unknown
5 – Top Rank, Brighton
6 – Top Rank, Portsmouth
7 – Mr Digby's, Birkenhead
8 – Middlesbrough Town Hall
9 – Harrogate Spa Hall *(Originally advertised but later changed to the California Ballroom, Dunstable)*
10 – Top Rank, Sheffield
12 – Tiffany's, Shrewsbury
13 – Shuffle's, Glasgow
14 – Maniqui Hall, Falkirk

15 – Clouds, Edinburgh
16 – Eric's, Liverpool
17 – Maxims, Barrow In Furness
22 – West Runton Pavilion, Cromer
23 – High Wycombe Town Hall
24 – Hammersmith Odeon, London

August

8 – Punk Rock Festival, Mont De Marson, France *(Band arrive but don't play)*
16 – 100 Club, London

September

10 – Nashville, West Kensington
11 – 100 Club, London
17 – Chelmsford City FC, Essex *(Afternoon)*
17 – Roxy Theatre, Harlesden, London
23 – Malmo, Sweden
24 – Ronneby, Sweden *[Gig abandoned after crowd invade stage and smash up equipment]*
25 – Stockholm *[Cancelled]*
30 – Paradiso, Amsterdam

October

8 & 9 – Whiskey-A-Go-Go, Los Angeles
10 & 13 – Rat's Kellar, New York
15 & 16 – CBGBs, New York

November

17 – Huddersfield Polytechnic
18 – Newcastle Mayfair Ballroom
19 – Leeds University
20 – Empire Theatre, Liverpool
22 – Top Rank, Cardiff
24 – Leicester University
25 – Kings Hall, Derby
26 – Friars, Aylesbury *(Afternoon & evening shows)*
27 – Top Rank, Sheffield
28 – Top Rank, Birmingham
29 – Apollo, Manchester
30 – Apollo, Glasgow

December

2 – Bracknell Sports Centre
3 – Civic Hall, Wolverhampton
4 – Bristol Locarno
5 – Bournemouth Village Bowl
7 – Top Rank, Brighton
8 – Coventry Locarno

9 – Odeon, Canterbury
11 – Greyhound, Croydon
14 – Lancaster University
15 – Victoria Hall, Stoke Hanley
16 – Corn Exchange, Cambridge
18 – Hammersmith Odeon, London

1978

February

13 – L'ancienne, Brussels
14 – Le Sporté Hall, Paris
16 – Salle De Concerts, Le Mans
18 – Palais Des Sports, Lille *(Tickets stated 13th but clashes with Brussels gig, and may have been postponed until 18th)*
24 & 25 – Marquee Club, London
27 – 100 Club, London

March

2 – Music Machine, London
16 – University Of Bridgeport, CT, USA *(Supporting Blue Oyster Cult)*
18 – Tower Theatre, Philadelphia, PA
19 – Agricultural Hall, Allentown, PA
20 – Four Acres Club, Utica, NY
21 & 22 – Colonial, Toronto, Canada
24 – Hammond Civic Centre, IN
25 – Richfield Coliseum, Cleveland, OH *(Supporting Blue Oyster Cult)*
26 – Civic Centre, Wheeling, WV *(Supporting Blue Oyster Cult)*
27 – Coliseum, Fort Wayne, IN *(Supporting Blue Oyster Cult)*
29 – Paradise Rock Club, Boston, MASS
30 & 31 – CBGBs, New York, NY

April

2 – Rupp Arena, Lexington, KY *(Supporting Blue Oyster Cult)*
3 – River Daze, St Louis, MO
4 – Bunky's, Madison, WI
5 – BJ's Concert Club, Detroit, MI
6 – Bogart's, Cincinnati, OH
7 – Riviera Theatre, Chicago, ILL
11 & 12 – Celebrity Theatre, Phoenix, AZ *(Supporting Be Bop Deluxe)*
14 – Starwood, Santa Monica, CA
15 – Winterland, San Francisco, CA
16 – Exhibition Hall, San Jose, CA

June

1 – BBC Paris Theatre, London
12 – King George's Hall, Blackburn

13 – Victoria Hall, Keighley *(Cancelled)*
14 – The Pier, Colwyn Bay *(Cancelled)*
15 & 16 – Barbarella's, Birmingham
17 – Friars, Aylesbury
18 – Lyceum, London

July

30 – Guildford Civic Hall
31 – Town Hall, Torquay

August

1 – Fiesta Club, Plymouth
2 – Village Bowl Discotheque, Bournemouth
4 – Brunel Rooms, Swindon
13 – Bilsen Festival, Limburg, Belgium
25 – Reading Festival
27 – Groningen Festival, Holland

October

20 – Top Hat Club, Dublin
21 – Leisureland, Galway

November

1 – Empire Theatre, Liverpool
2 – De Montfort Hall, Leicester
3 – St Georges Hall, Bradford
4 – Newcastle City Hall
5 – Apollo, Glasgow
6 – Capitol Theatre, Aberdeen
7 – University Of St Andrews, Fife
10 – Sheffield Polytechnic
12 – Leeds University
13 – Apollo, Manchester
14 – Odeon, Birmingham
15 – Coventry Theatre, Coventry
17 – Corn Exchange, Cambridge
18 – ABC Cinema, Great Yarmouth
20 – Cardiff University
21 – Dome, Brighton
22 – University Of Kent, Canterbury *(Cancelled)*
24 – Guildhall, Portsmouth
26 – Colston Hall, Bristol
29 – Great British Music Festival, Wembley Empire Pool

December

7 – University Of Kent, Canterbury
21 – Music Machine, London

1979

February

16 – Reading University
20 – Metropole, Berlin
21 & 22 – Star Club, Hamburg
23 – Wartburg Wiesbaden, Germany
26 – Stadium, Paris
27 – L'espace Club, Rennes
28 – Le Royale, Lyon

March

4 – Marseille, France

April

10 – Rex Theatre, Toronto
11 – Unknown Venue, Chicago, ILL
12 – Paradise Rock Club, Boston, MASS
13 – Tower Theatre, Philadelphia, PA
14 – Palladium, New York, NY
16 – Agora Ballroom, Cleveland, OH
17 – Punch & Judy Theatre, Detroit, MI
20 – Auditorium, Oakland, CA
21 – UCLA Royce Hall, Los Angeles, CA
24 – Commodore Ballroom, Vancouver

May

4 – Sheffield University
5 – Sheffield University
6 – Newcastle City Hall
8 – Salford University
10 & 11 – Rainbow Theatre, Finsbury Park
12 – Loughborough University
14 – Exeter University
15 – Liverpool University
16 – Liverpool University
18 – Strathclyde University, Glasgow
19 – Strathclyde University, Glasgow
21 – Colston Hall, Bristol
22 – Odeon, Birmingham
24 – Guildhall, Portsmouth

June

9 – Saddleworth Arts Festival

August

29 – Moonlight Club West, Hampstead *(Cancelled)*
30 – Bridgehouse, Canning Town *(Cancelled)*
31 – Nashville, West Kensington *(Cancelled)*

November

2 – Marquee Club, London *(Secret gig, billed as "John's Boys")*

3 – Nashville, West Kensington (*Secret gig, billed as "The Eton Rifles" and "La Confiture"*)

17 – Friars, Aylesbury

18 – Poole Arts Centre

20 – Apollo, Manchester

21 – Apollo, Manchester

22 – Civic Hall, Wolverhampton

23 – Gaumont, Southampton

24 – Gaumont, Southampton

25 – Bingley Hall, Stafford

26 – Trentham Gardens, Stoke On Trent

27 – Royal Spa, Bridlington

29 – Deeside Leisure Centre

30 – Lancaster University

December

1 – Sophia Gardens, Cardiff *(Cancelled)*

2, 3 & 4 – Rainbow, Finsbury Park

6 & 7 – Newcastle City Hall

08 – Apollo, Glasgow

09 – Caird Hall, Dundee

10 – Odeon, Edinburgh

11 – Queen's Hall, Leeds

12 – King George's Hall, Blackburn

13 – Sophia Gardens, Cardiff

15 – Brighton Centre

16 – Guildhall, Portsmouth

18 & 19 – De Montfort Hall, Leicester

20 & 21 – Pavilion, Bath

1980

February

11 – Corn Exchange, Cambridge

12 – University Of Kent, Canterbury

13 – Winter Gardens, Malvern

15 – Woking YMCA Centre

27 – Emerald City, NJ

28 – Stage West West, Hartford, CT

29 – Palladium, New York, NY

March

1 – Triangle Theatre, Rochester, NY

3 – JB Scott's, Albany, NY

5 – Motor City Roller Rink, Detroit, MI
6 – Park West, Chicago, ILL
7 – Old Chicago Amusement Park, ILL
9 – St Paul's Civic Centre, Minnesota, MN
13 – Shoe Box, Seattle, WA
15 – Fox Warfield Theatre, San Francisco, CA
16 – Santa Monica Civic Centre, CA
21 – Palace, Houston, TX (*Cancelled*)
22 – Armadillo World Headquarters, Austin, TX
27 – Ontario Theatre, Washington DC (*Cancelled*)
28 – Capitol, Passaic, NJ (*Cancelled*)

April

7 & 8 – Rainbow, Finsbury Park
18 – Civic Hall, Guildford

May

17 – Pavilion Baltard, Paris
26 – Pink Pop Festival, Holland

June

2 – Civic Hall, Wolverhampton
3 – King George's Hall, Blackburn
4 – Victoria Hall, Hanley, Stoke On Trent
21 – Loch Lomond Festival, Scotland

July

3 – Mainichi Hall, Osaka
4 – Kaiken Hall, Kyoto
6 – Nakano Sun Plaza, Tokyo
7 & 8 – Nihon Seinenkan, Tokyo
10 – Unknown Venue, Tokyo (*Cancelled*)
22 – Guildford Civic Hall

August

2 – Friars, Aylesbury
3 – Poole Arts Centre
9 – Ruisrock Festival, Turku, Finland

October

18 – Technical College, Bromley (*Charity event organised by Wing Music In Bromley For Save The Children Fund*)
26 – Top Rank, Sheffield
27 & 28 – Newcastle City Hall
29 – Playhouse, Edinburgh
30 – Apollo, Glasgow
31 – Apollo, Manchester

November

1 – Apollo, Manchester

2 – Leisure Centre, Deeside
3 – Queen's Exhibition Hall, Leeds
5 & 6 – Brighton Conference Centre
7 & 8 – Bracknell Sports Centre
9 – Poole Arts Centre
10 – Sophia Gardens, Cardiff
11 – Bingley Hall, Stafford
12 & 13 – De Montfort Hall, Leicester
15 & 16 – Rainbow, Finsbury Park
18 & 19 – Hammersmith Odeon, London
22 – Unknown Venue, Gothenburg
23 – Christiana Centre, Stockholm
24 – Unknown Venue, Oslo *(Cancelled)*
25 & 26 – Gota Lejon, Stockholm
27 – Unknown Venue, Lund, Sweden
29 – Carregat, Eindhoven, Holland
30 – Westfalenhalle, Dortmund

December

1 – Vredenburg Concert Hall, Utrecht
2 – Oosterpoort Groningen, Holland
3 – Hofterlo, Antwerp
6 – Fort Regent, Jersey
8 – St Austell Coliseum *(Cancelled)*
9 – Colston Hall, Bristol
10 – Winter Gardens, Malvern
11 – Guildford Civic Hall
12 – Music Machine, London
14 – Coliseum, St Austell

1981

February

14 – Cricketers Pub, Westfield, Woking *(Secret gig billed as The Jam Road Crew)*
16 – Woking YMCA
17 – Sheerwater Youth Club, Woking
21 – Norwich University
22 – Nottingham University
23 – Crawley Leisure Centre
26 – Pavilion Baltard, Paris

March

1 – Olympen, Lund
2 & 3 – Oddfellows, Copenhagen
5 – Market Hall, Hanover
6 – Markthalle, Hamburg

8 – Metropole, Berlin
10 – L'ancienne, Brussels
12 – Tivoli Hall, Strasbourg *(Cancelled)*
13 & 14 – Paradiso Club, Amsterdam
15 – Palais St Sauvre, Lille
16 – Studio 44, Rouen

April
27 – Royal Court, Liverpool

May
13 – Aichi Kinro Kaikan, Nagoya
14 – Mido Kaikan Hall, Osaka
15 & 16 – Nakano Sun Plaza, Tokyo
21 – Le Club, Montreal
22 & 23 – Masonic Hall, Toronto
24 – Technical High School, Ottawa
26 – Ritz, New York, NY
29 – Channel Club, Boston, MASS

June
10 – Grona, Lund
12 – Unknown Venue, Borlanger, Sweden
17 – Rainbow, Finsbury Park
20 – Festival Pavilion, Skegness
22 – Granby Hall, Leicester
23 – Guildhall, Portsmouth
25 – St Austell Coliseum
27 – Bingley Hall, Stafford
30 – Magnum Centre, Irvine

July
2 – Royal Hall, Bridlington
4 – Market Hall, Carlisle
5 – Guildhall, Preston
7 & 8 – Guildford Civic Hall

October
23 – Rainbow, Finsbury Park *(CND Benefit)*
24 – Embankment, London *(CND Benefit)*

December
12 & 13 – Michael Sobell Sports Centre, Finsbury Park
14 & 15 – Hammersmith Palais, London
19 – Hippodrome (BBC TV Theatre), Golders Green, London

1982

February
24 – Central London Polytechnic

March
6 – Guildford Civic Centre
11 – Canterbury *(Cancelled)*
12 – Guildhall, Portsmouth
13 & 14 – Brighton Conference Centre
15 – Fair Deal, Brixton
16 – Alexandra Pavilion, London
17 – Royal Bath & West Showground, Shepton Mallet
18 – Afan Lido, Port Talbot
20 & 21 – Bingley Hall, Stafford
22 & 23 – De Montfort Hall, Leicester
25 & 26 – Apollo, Manchester
27 – Leisure Centre, Deeside
28 – Opera House, Blackpool
29, 30 & 31 – Top Rank, Sheffield
April
1 – The Queens Hall, Leeds
3 & 4 – Newcastle City Hall
5 & 6 – Playhouse Theatre, Edinburgh
7 & 8 – Apollo, Glasgow
16 – Johaneshov's Isstadion, Stockholm
18 – Olympen, Lund
20 – Falkoner Theatre, Copenhagen
21 – Vejlby Risskov Hall, Arhous, Denmark *(Cancelled)*
24 & 25 – Paradiso Club, Amsterdam
26 – De Vereniging Nijmegen, Amsterdam
27 – L'ancienne, Brussels
29 – Pantin Hippodrome, Paris
30 – Palais D'hiver, Lyon
May
14 – University Of Maryland, Washington DC
15 – Palladium, New York, NY
16 – North Stage, Long Island, NY
18 – Palladium, New York, NY
19 – Trenton Hall, NJ
20 – Orpheum Theatre, Boston, MASS
22 – Verdun Auditorium, Montreal
24 – Coliseum, Toronto
25 – Michigan Theatre, Ann Arbor, MI
26 – Aragon Ballroom, Chicago, ILL
29, 30 & 31 – Perkins Palace, Pasadena, CA
June
2 – Fox Warfield Theatre, San Francisco, CA

5 – Kerrisdale Arena, Vancouver
11 – Kosei Nenkin Kaikan Hall, Tokyo
14 – Nakano Sun Plaza Hall, Tokyo
15 – Mainichi Hall, Osaka
16 – Seinenkan Hall, Tokyo
17 – Kinro Kaikan, Nagoya
26 – QPR Football Ground, Shepherds Bush, London *(Cancelled)*

July

10 – QPR Football Ground, Shepherds Bush *(Cancelled)*

September

20 – Leas Cliff Pavilion, Southend
21 – Showground, Shepton Mallet
22 – Brighton Conference Centre
23 – Granby Halls, Leicester
24 & 25 – Royal Court, Liverpool
27 – Edinburgh Ingliston Highland Centre
28 & 29 – Whitley Bay Ice Rink
30 – Queen's Hall, Leeds

October

1 – New Bingley Hall, Stafford
9 – Gloucester Hall, Jersey
11 – Beau Sejour Leisure Centre, Guernsey
13 – Paris *(Cancelled)*
14 – Strasbourg *(Cancelled)*
15 – Genk, Belgium *(Cancelled)*
16 – Popperinge, Belgium *(Cancelled)*
17 & 18 – Amsterdam *(Cancelled)*

November

25 – Apollo, Glasgow
27 – Poole Arts Centre
28 – St Austell Coliseum
29 – Afan Lido, Port Talbot

December

1, 2, 3, 4 & 5 – Wembley Arena
6 – Royal Spa Bridlington
7 – Apollo, Manchester
8 – Bingley Hall, Stafford
9 – Guildford Civic Hall
11 – Brighton Conference Centre

THE STYLE COUNCIL

1983
January
5 – ICA, London
May
1 – Empire Theatre, Liverpool
7 – Brockwell Park, London
25 – BBC Paris Theatre, London
October
24 – Volkhaus, Zurich
26 – Le Palace, Paris
28 – VUB University, Brussels
31 – De Meervaart, Amsterdam
November
1 – Trinity, Hamburg
December
7 – Hammersmith Odeon, London *(Cancelled)*
8 – Gaumont, Liverpool *(Cancelled)*
10 – Apollo, Coventry *(Cancelled)*
11 – Gaumont, Ipswich *(Cancelled)*
12 – City Hall, Sheffield *(Cancelled)*
13 – Halifax Civic Hall *(Cancelled)*
18 – Apollo Theatre, London

1984
March
10 – Goldiggers, Chippenham
13 – Gaumont, Liverpool
14 & 15 – Dominion Theatre, London
16 – Odeon, Birmingham
17 – Gaumont, Ipswich
18 – Nottingham Sports Centre
19 – Newcastle City Hall
20 – Apollo, Glasgow
25 – L'ancienne, Brussels
27 – Palais D'hiver, Lyon
29 – L'Eldorado, Paris
30 – Zeche Bochum, Germany
April
1 – Metropol, Berlin
3 – Vredenberg Concert Hall, Utrecht
8 – 100 Club, London
30 – Koseinenkin Hall, Tokyo

May
2 – Joh Hall, Osaka
4 – Nakano Sun Plaza, Tokyo
7 & 8 – Wilshire Theatre, Los Angeles, CA
10 & 11 – Savoy Theatre, New York, NY
26 – Apollo, Coventry
July
7 – Liverpool University *(Miners Benefit)*
September
7 – Royal Festival Hall, London *(Miners Benefit)*
October
4 – Civic Hall, Wolverhampton *(Miners Benefit)*
6 – Apollo, Oxford
7 – Hippodrome, Bristol
8 – St David Hall, Cardiff
9 – St Austell Coliseum
11 – Sheffield City Hall
12 – Apollo, Manchester
14 – Playhouse Theatre, Edinburgh
15 – Royal Court, Liverpool
16 – De Montfort Hall, Leicester
22 – Rome
23 – Bologna
24 – Teatro Tenda, Milan
29 – Alabamahalle, Munich
November
1- Robert Schumann, Düsseldorf
4 – Carré, Amsterdam
5 – Linz, Austria
6 – Innsbruck, Austria
December
1 – Winter Gardens, Margate
3 & 4 – Royal Albert Hall, London

1985
June
5 – Brixton Academy
6 – Windsor Hall, Bournemouth
7 – The Guildhall, Portsmouth
8 – Brighton Conference Centre
9 – Odeon, Birmingham
10 – Odeon, Birmingham
11 – City Hall, Sheffield

13 – Royal Centre, Nottingham
14 – Apollo, Manchester
15 – Empire, Liverpool
16 – Apollo, Glasgow
22 – Glastonbury Festival
29 – Roskilde Festival, Denmark

July

6 – Torhout Festival, Belgium
8 – Werchter Festival, Belgium
13 – Live Aid, Wembley Stadium

August

6 – Castle Hall, Osaka
11 – Arena, Yokohama *(Might be on another date as some lists show the band flying to Australia on this date. There might have been other dates in Japan as well)*
18 – Sports & Entertainment Centre, Melbourne
19 – Venue, Melbourne (Benefit/charity gig)
21 & 22 – The Horden Pavilion, Sydney

September

8 – Festa De L'unita, Ferrara, Italy
10 – Teatro Tendra, Rome
11 – Palasport, Florence
12 – Modena, Italy
13 – Teatro Tenda, Milan
14 – Parco Pellerina, Turin

October

10 – Musikhalle, Hamburg
11 – Tempodrom, Berlin
13 – Ludwigshafen Pfalzau, Germany
17 – Phillipshalle, Düsseldorf
19 – Deinze Brielpoort, Brussels

December

3 – De Montfort Hall, Leicester
4 – Leisure Centre, Gloucester
5 – King George's Hall, Leicester
6 – Playhouse Theatre, Edinburgh
8, 9 & 10 – Wembley Arena, London

1986

January

25 – Apollo, Manchester
26 – St David's Hall, Cardiff
27 – Odeon, Birmingham
28 – De Montfort Hall, Leicester

29 – St George's Hall, Bradford
30 – Playhouse, Edinburgh
31 – Newcastle City Hall
March
21 – Hammersmith Odeon
June
28 – Clapham Common, London
July
20 – Shaw Theatre, London *(Billed as The Party Chambers Group)*

1987
February
14 & 15 – Newport Centre
16, 17, 18 & 19 – Royal Albert Hall, London
20 – International Centre, Bournemouth
21 & 22 – NEC, Birmingham
25 – St George's Hall, Bradford
26 & 27 – Newcastle City Hall
28 – SEC Glasgow
March
7 – Ahoy, Rotterdam
8 – Cirque Royale, Koninklijk Circus, Brussels
10 – Düsseldorf
11 – Halle Munsterland, Munster
12 – Capital, Hanover
13 – CCH Hamburg
15 – Frankfurt
16 – Stadthalle, Heidelberg
18 – Paris
April
2 – World Kinen Hall, Kobe
3 & 4 – Ryogoku Kokugikan, Tokyo
6 – Bunka Taiikukan, Yokohama
7 – Lobe, Nr Osaka
25 – Hyde Park, London
May
6 – Palasport, Florence
7 – Palasport Venue, Turin
8 – Palasport, Varese, Italy
23 – Eindexamen Festival, Den Bosch, Belgium
July
19 – Brixton Academy, London

September
4 – Festa De L'unita Reggio, Emilia, Italy
7 – Palatrussardi, Milan
October
15 – Barrowlands, Glasgow *(Cancelled)*
16 – Caird Hall, Dundee *(Cancelled)*
17 – Apollo, Manchester
18 – Conference Centre, Harrogate
22 – Sheffield City Hall
23 – De Montfort Hall, Leicester
24 – Crawley Leisure Centre
25 – Winter Gardens, Margate
November
24 & 25 – Hammersmith Odeon

1988
March
6 – Hackney Empire, London

1989
June
7 – Arena, Yokohama
8 – Joh Hall, Osaka
9 – Shiodome, Tokyo
July
4 – Royal Albert Hall, London

PAUL WELLER (SOLO) LIVE

1990
February
11 – Dominion Theatre, London
November
1 – Dingwalls, London
5 – Turin
6 – The Rolling Stone, Milan
8 – Vidia Cesena, Italy
11 – Tor 3, Düsseldorf
12 – Capitol, Hanover
13 – The Docks, Hamburg
14 – Berlin
16 – Paradiso, Amsterdam
18 – Goldiggers, Chippenham

23 – Leeds Polytechnic
24 – Queen Margaret's Union, Glasgow University
25 – Manchester Academy
27 – UEA, Norwich
28 – Nottingham Polytechnic
29 – Coventry Polytechnic
December
1 – Bradford University
2 – Cardiff University
4 – Leicester University
5 & 6 – Town & Country Club, London

1991
April
4 – Subterrania, London
9 – St Albans, Arena
10 – Civic Centre, Aylesbury
12 – City Hall, Hull
14 & 15 – Birmingham Institute
16 – Guildford Civic Hall
17 – The Centre, Newport
18 – Cambridge Corn Exchange
20 – Brixton Academy, London
21 – Apollo, Oxford
22 – Event, Brighton
24 – Rock City, Nottingham
25 – Octagon, Sheffield
26 – Town House, Middlesbrough
27 – Royal Court, Liverpool
29 – Guildhall, Portsmouth *(Cancelled)*
November
17 – Zap Club, Brighton
22 & 23 – Club Quattro, Nagoya
25 – Club Citta, Kawasaki
26 – On Air, Shibuya, Tokyo
27 – Wohol, Osaka
28 – Fish Dance Hall, Kobe
29 – Club Citta, Kawasaki
December
4, 5, 6, 7 & 8 – Variety Arts Centre, Los Angeles, CA
12 – The Ritz, New York, NY
17 – Guildhall, Portsmouth
18 – Kilburn National, London

1992
March
2 – Yello Club, Tokyo
June
21 – Waterfront, Norwich
23 – Town & Country Club, London
24 – Clapham Grand, London
25 – Mean Fiddler, Harlesden, London
26 – Subterrania, London
28 – The Centre East Wing, Brighton
29 – Leadmill, Sheffield *(Cancelled)*
July
8 – Nakano Sun Plaza, Tokyo
9 – Akhi Kinro Kaikan, Nagoya
10 – Maruparuku Hall, Fukuoka
12 – Shibuya Nhk Hall, Tokyo
13 – Nakano Sun Plaza, Tokyo
14 – Koseinenkin Kaikan, Osaka
16 – Shibuya Nhk Hall, Tokyo
23 – Concert Hall, Toronto
25 – Ritz, New York, NY
27 – Vic Theatre, Chicago, ILL
29 – Greek Theatre, Los Angeles, CA
31 – Warfield Theatre, San Francisco, CA
August
6 – Mean Fiddler, Harlesden, London *(Guest of Dr Robert)*
October
5 – Sheffield City Hall *(Cancelled)*
7 – Barrowlands, Glasgow
8 – Apollo, Manchester
9 – Newcastle City Hall
10 – Aston Villa Leisure Centre, Birmingham
11 – Sheffield University *(Cancelled)*
12 – Poole Arts Centre
13 – Royal Albert Hall, London
19 – City Square, Milan
20 – Vox Pop Nonantola, Modena, Italy *(Cancelled)*
22 – La Cigale, Paris
23 – Concert Hall, Gent, Belgium
24 – Music Hall, Cologne
26 – The Docks, Hamburg
28 – Paradiso, Amsterdam

November
3 – Park West, Chicago, ILL
5 – Chestnut Cabaret, Philadelphia, PA
7 – Roxy, Atlanta, GA *(Cancelled)*
9 – Gaston Hall, Washington DC
11 – Berklee Performance Centre, Boston, MASS
13 – Intersection, Grand Rapids, MI *(Cancelled)*
14 – Majestic Theatre, Detroit, MI
17 – Roxy, Los Angeles, CA
19 – Montezuma Hall, San Diego, CA
21 – Ballroom, Austin, TX *(Cancelled)*
23 – Tippitina's, New Orleans, LA
25 – Tower Records, Greenwich Village, New York, NY
25 – Irving Plaza, New York, NY

1993
March
9 – Town & Country Club, Leeds
10 – Rock City, Nottingham *(Cancelled)*
11 – Town & Country Club, London
16 – Theatre Ventura, CA
18 – Warfield Theatre, San Francisco, CA
20 – Under The Rail, Seattle, WA
21 – The Commodore Ballroom, Vancouver
September
9 – HMV Records, Oxford Street, London
October
20 – Kings College, London
27 – Sun Plaza, Tokyo
30 – Izumity – Sendai, Japan
31 – Shibuya Kokaido, Tokyo
November
1 – Gotanda U-Port, Tokyo
3 – Kyushi Koseinenkan, Fukuoka
5 – Festival Hall, Osaka
6 – Kokaido, Nagoya
7 – Nhk Hall, Tokyo
12 – St David's Hall, Cardiff
13 – Aston Villa Leisure Centre, Birmingham
14 – Newcastle City Hall
16 – Corn Exchange, Cambridge
17 – Town & Country Club, Leeds
18 – Barrowlands, Glasgow

20 – Apollo, Manchester
21 – Royal Centre, Nottingham
22 & 23 – Royal Albert Hall, London
24 – Dome, Brighton
27 & 28 – Stockholm *(Cancelled)*
28 – Regent, Ipswich
December
2 – The Docks, Hamburg
4 – The Bockenheimer Depot, Frankfurt
6 – Music Hall, Cologne
10 – Lupo's Heart Break Hotel, Providence, RI
11 – Academy, New York, NY
14 – WEQX Radio Session, Latham, New York, NY

1994
February
26 – National Stadium, Dublin
27 – City Hall, Cork
March
1 – Ulster Hall, Belfast
4 – Playhouse Theatre, Edinburgh
5 – Capitol, Aberdeen
6 – King George's Hall, Blackburn
8 – Colston Hall, Bristol
9 – Civic Hall, Wolverhampton
11 – Guildhall, Portsmouth
12 – Guildford Civic Hall
13 – Apollo Theatre, Oxford
April
11 – Alabama Hall, Munich
12 – Zeche Carl, Essen
14 – Capitol, Hanover
15 – PC69, Bielfeld, Germany
16 – Paradiso, Amsterdam
17 – La Luna, Brussels
20 – Aqualung, Madrid
21 – Zeleste 1, Barcelona
May
3 – Avalon, New York
4 – Toad's Place, New Haven, CT *(Cancelled)*
5 – The Clubhouse, Plainfield, NJ
6 – Town Hall, New York, NY
7 – Theatre Of Living Arts, Philadelphia, PA

9 – Graffiti Showcase, Pittsburgh, PA
12 – Phoenix Club, Toronto
13 – St Andrews, Detroit, MI
14 – The Metro, Chicago, ILL
16 – First Avenue, Minneapolis, MN
18 – Moore Theatre, Seattle, WA *(Cancelled)*
21 – Pantages Theater, Los Angeles, CA
24 – Fillmore West, San Francisco, CA

June

10 – Freizeitpark, Alsdorf, Germany
11 – Ruhrstadion, Bochum, Germany
12 – Albert Thaer Platz, Uelzen, Germany
14 – Waldbuehne, Berlin
15 – Waldbuehne, Schwarzenberg, Germany
16 – Inselwiese, Lichtenfels, Germany
18 – Bodenseestadion, Konstanz, Germany
19 – Neustadt Stadion, Vienna
21 – Waldbuehne, Berlin
25 – Glastonbury Festival

July

16 – Phoenix Festival, Stratford-Upon-Avon

October

2 – Koseinenkan Kaikan, Hiroshima
3 – Sun Palace, Fukuoka
4 – Koseinenkan Hall, Osaka
5 & 7 – Yu Port, Tokyo
9 – Izumity 21, Senday
10 – Nhk Hall, Tokyo

November

6 – La Luna Theatre, Brussels
7 – Tor 3, Düsseldorf
8 – Muffathalle, Munich
10 – La Bataclan, Paris
11 – Paradiso, Amsterdam
13 – Metropole, Berlin
14 – The Docks, Hamburg
19 – The Point Depot, Dublin
20 – Ulster Hall, Belfast
22, 23 & 24 – Royal Albert Hall, London
26 & 27 – Aston Villa Leisure Centre, Birmingham
29 – Newcastle City Hall
30 – Barrowlands, Glasgow

December
1 – Barrowlands, Glasgow
2 – G-Mex Centre, Manchester
4 – Shepherds Bush Empire, London *(Joe Awome Benefit Gig)*
15 – Shepherds Bush Empire, London *(Guest Of Primal Scream)*

1995
June
1 – 100 Club, London
4 – Junction, Cambridge
6 – Leadmill, Sheffield
9 – Sonoria Festival, Italy
17 – Halfway Festival, Amsterdam
July
2 – Roskilde Festival, Denmark
7 – Out In The Green Festival, Switzerland
8 – Belfour Festival, France
14 – Roadmenders, Northampton
16 – Phoenix Festival, Stratford-Upon-Avon
21 – Beachrock / Belga Festival, Zeebrugge, Belgium
28 – Lollipop Festival, Stockholm
August
1 – Paulio Festival, Geneva
5 – T In The Park Festival, Strathclyde Park
6 – Feile Festival, Cork
13 – Rock Karacala Festival, Gent, Belgium
14 – Leuven Markt Rock Festival, Belgium
23 – Riviera Centre, Torquay
24 – Poole Arts Centre
26 – Reading Festival
September
9 – El Pop Barcelona
21 – Pampehset, Copenhagen *(Cancelled)*
22 – Mejeriet, Lund *(Cancelled)*
23 – Old University, Gothenberg *(Cancelled)*
25 – The Kircus, Stockholm *(Cancelled)*
27 – Tavastia, Helsinki *(Cancelled)*
29 – Rockefellows, Oslo *(Cancelled)*)
October
17 – Aqualung, Madrid
18 – Arena, Valencia
21 – Vox Club, Modena
22 – Rolling Stone, Milan

23 – Teatro Comunale Belluno, Italy
24 – Tenax, Florence
26 – Palladium, Rome
28 – Volkeshaus, Zurich
30 – Posthous, Linz
31 – Messepalast, Vienna

November

2 – Belmondo, Prague
4 – La Cigalle, Paris *(Cancelled)*
4 – Music Nights Festival, Maastricht, Holland
8 & 9 Barrowlands, Glasgow
11 – Ice Arena, Hull
12 – Whitley Bay Ice Rink
14 – Brighton Conference Centre
15 – Cardiff International Arena *(Cancelled)*
17 & 18 – Aston Villa Leisure Centre, Birmingham
20 & 21 – Apollo, Manchester
23 – The Sanctuary, Milton Keynes
24 – Towerlands Arena, Braintree
25 – Bournemouth International Centre
27, 28, 29 & 30 – Brixton Academy, London

December

2 – Cardiff International Arena
3 – La Bataclan, Paris *(Cancelled)*
5 – Vredenberg Concert Hall, Utrecht
6 – The Docks, Hamburg
7 – Aladin, Bremen
9 – Live Music Hall, Cologne *(Re-scheduled from The Rudolfplatz Theatre, 8 December)*
10 – Kick Herford, Germany
12 – Ludwigsburg, Germany *(Cancelled)*
13 – Muffathalle, Munich
14 – Erlangen, Germany *(Cancelled)*
15 – Huxley's Neue Welt, Berlin

1996

April

9 – Virgin Megastore, Oxford Street, London

June

6 – Royal Spa, Bridlington
7 – De Montfort Hall, Leicester
9 – Lazy Sunday Afternoon, Finsbury Park, London

July

5 – Sovereign's Pub, Woking *(Joins Dave Liddle's band Blues Express for a version of Hi-Heeled Sneakers)*

7 – Ronnie Scott's, London

August

12 – Royal Centre, Nottingham

13 – Victoria Hall, Hanley

15 – Empress Ballroom, Blackpool

16 – Leisure Centre, Gloucester

18 – V96 Festival, Chelmsford

October

12 – Hexagon, Reading *(Guest of Ocean Colour Scene)*

November

8 – Aston Villa Leisure Centre, Birmingham *(Support and guest of Ocean Colour Scene)*

1997

February

17 – Royal Albert Hall, London *(Supporting Ocean Colour Scene)*

May

11 – Big Noise Festival, Cardiff Bay

17 – Brixton Academy, London

June

24 – Southbank Heyward Gallery, London

30 – Guildhall, Portsmouth

July

1 – The Winter Gardens, Margate

2 – Guildford Civic Hall

5 – Rock Torhout Festival, Belgium

6 – Werchter Festival, Belgium

9 – Bridlington Royal Spa

10 – Middlesbrough Town Hall

11 – Sands Centre, Carlisle

13 – T In The Park Festival, Scotland

22 – St Austell Coliseum

23 – Riviera Centre, Torquay

24 – Cheltenham Town Hall

26 – A Day At The Races, Don Valley Stadium, Sheffield

28 – Cliff Pavilions, Southend

30 – Leas Cliff Hall, Folkestone

31 – Poole Arts Centre

August

2 – A Day At The Races, Crystal Palace Sports Centre, London

September
25 – Lincoln Theatre, Washington DC
27 – Roseland, New York, NY
28 – Avalon, New York, NY
30 – Concert Hall, Toronto
October
1 – The Royal Oak, Detroit, MI
3 – Vic Theatre, Chicago, ILL
4 – First Avenue, Minneapolis, MN
5 – Ogden Theatre, Denver, CO
9 – The Warfield Theatre, San Francisco, CA
10 – Hollywood Palladium, Los Angeles, CA
16 – Koseinenkin Hall, Osaka
17 – Liquid Room, Tokyo
19, 20, 21 & 22 – Asaka Blitz, Tokyo
29 – Vredenberg Concert Hall, Utrecht
30 – The Docks, Hamburg
November
1 – E-Werk, Cologne
2 – Muffathalle, Munich
3 – Waltshaus, Zurich *(Cancelled)*
5 – Propaganda, Milan *(Cancelled)*
7 – Vox Club, Modena, Italy *(Cancelled)*
7 – Radio Clyde Session, Scotland
8 – Velvet, Rimini, Italy *(Cancelled)*
10 – Bataclan, Paris
12 – L'ancienne, Brussels
19 – Virgin Megastore, Kings Road, London *(Cancelled)*
23 – Towerlands Arena, Braintree
24 – Rivermead, Reading
26 & 27 – Crawley Leisure Centre
29 – Bournemouth International Centre
30 – Cardiff International Arena
December
1 – Kettering Arena
3 – Aston Villa Leisure Centre, Birmingham
6 – Hull Arena
7 – Whitley Bay Ice Rink
9 & 10 – Barrowlands, Glasgow
12, 13 & 14 – The Apollo, Manchester
15 – Trentham Gardens, Stoke
17 & 18 – Battersea Power Station, London
20 – Kilburn National, London
21 – London Palladium

1998
March
29 – Unknown Venue, London
April
20 – Royal Albert Hall, London *(Supporting Ben Harper)*
June
23 – King George's Hall, Blackburn
24 – St George's Hall, Bradford
25 – Sheffield City Hall
28 – Parkpop Festival, Den Haag, Holland
July
6 – Civic Hall, Wolverhampton
7 – Colston Hall, Bristol
9 – Pavilions, Plymouth
11 – Cactus Festival, Bruges, Belgium
28 – Playhouse, Edinburgh
29 – Newcastle City Hall
30 – Sands Centre, Carlisle
August
1 – The Point, Dublin
4 – Royal Centre, Nottingham
6 – The Centre, Newport
8 – Hackney Victoria Park, London
November
23 – Arena, Vienna
24 – Posthof, Linz, Austria
25 – Muffathalle, Munich
27 – Alacatraz, Milan
30 – E-Werk, Cologne
December
2 – Columbia Hall, Berlin
3 – The Docks, Hamburg
6 – La Cigale, Paris
7 – L'ancienne, Brussels
8 & 9 – The Paradiso, Amsterdam
11 – Brixton Academy, London

1999
March
27 – Vereeniging Nijmegen, Holland
28 – Oosterpoort Groningen, Holland
30 – Theaterhaus, Stuttgart
31 – Forum, Nurnberg

April
1 – Huguenottenhalle, Neu-Isenberg, Germany
5 – Philipshalle, Düsseldorf
May
30 – Forum, London
June
1 – Royal Naval College, Greenwich
October
28 – NIA, Birmingham *(Guest of Ocean Colour Scene)*

2000
April
12 – Rehearsals at Brixton Academy
14 – Waterfront, Norwich
15 – L2, Liverpool
17 – Trentham Gardens, Stoke On Trent
18 & 19 – Newcastle City Hall
21 – Bridlington Spa
22 – Guildhall, Preston
23 – De Montfort Hall, Leicester
25 – Rivermead, Reading
26 – Pavilions, Plymouth
27 – Colston Hall, Bristol
29 & 30 – Guildford Civic Hall
May
2 & 3 – Royal Albert Hall, London
5 – Nottingham Arena
6 & 7 – The Apollo, Manchester
9 & 10 – Leisure Centre, Aston Villa
12 & 13 – The Barrowlands, Glasgow
14 – Playhouse Theatre, Edinburgh
17 – Towerlands Arena, Braintree
18 – Bournemouth International Centre
19 – Cardiff Arena
21 – Brixton Academy, London
July
2 – Werchter Festival, Belgium
7 – Swinging Groningen Festival, Holland
8 – Bospop Festival, Weert, Holland
22 – Doctor Music Festival, Asturias, Spain
August
6 – Witnness Festival, Eire
12 – Halderner Festival, Germany

13 – Stadtpark, Hamburg *(Cancelled)*
19 – V2000 Festival, Staffordshire
20 – V2000 Festival, Chelmsford
25 – Glasgow Green Festival

September

9 – Zepp, Osaka
10 – Zepp, Fukuoka
12 – Akasaka Blitz, Tokyo
13 & 14 – Kokusai Forum Hall A, Tokyo
16 – Zepp, Sendai, Japan
17 – Rock Farm, Iwate Koiwai, Japan

October

6 – Avalon, New York, NY *(Cancelled)*
7 – Roseland, New York, NY *(Cancelled)*
10 – Massey Hall, Toronto *(Cancelled)*
11 – Vic Theatre, Chicago, ILL *(Cancelled)*
12 – Clutch Cargos, Detroit, MI *(Cancelled)*
15 – Wiltern Theatre, Los Angeles, CA *(Cancelled)*
17 – Fillmore, San Francisco, CA *(Cancelled)*
28 – Poole Arts Centre
29 – Hereford Leisure Centre
31 – Empress Ballroom, Blackpool

November

1 – Sands Centre, Carlisle
2 – Hull Arena
4 – Earls Court, London
27 – Royal Albert Hall, London *(Guest supporting The Who)*

2001

February

3 & 4 – Le Botanique, Brussels
6 & 7 – Paradiso, Amsterdam
09 – La Scene, Paris

March

19, 20 & 21 – Olympia, Dublin
22 & 23 – Limelight, Belfast
25 – University Concert Hall, Limerick

April

1 – Bahnhof Langendreer, Bochum, Germany
2 – Gloria Theatre, Cologne
3 – Centralstation, Darmstadt
5 – Muffathalle, Munich
7 – Sendesaal Des Sfb, Berlin

8 – Fabrik, Hamburg
9 – Savoy Theatre, Düsseldorf
10 – Tolhaus Karlsruhe, Germany
15 – Apollo, Oxford *(Support To OCS – Cancelled)*
20 – Astoria, London
23 – BBC Theatre, London
26 – Apollo, Barcelona
27 – Roxy, Valencia
28 – Teatro Isabel La Catolica, Grenada, Spain
30 – Teatro Cervantes, Malaga

May

2 – Auditorium De Murcia, Spain
3 – Sala Arena, Madrid
4 – Palais De Congresse, Salamanca, Spain
15 – Conrad Sohm, Dornbirn, Austria
17 – Fillmore Club, Piacenza, Italy
18 – Velvet, Rimini, Italy
19 – Teatro Goldoni, Venice
21 – Teatro Franco Parenti, Milan
22 – Barrumba, Turin

June

28 – Guildhall, Liverpool
29 – St David's Hall, Cardiff

July

1 – Civic Hall, Wolverhampton
2 – Shepherds Bush Empire, London
4 – Academy, Manchester
5 – Newcastle City Hall
7 – T In The Park, Scotland
12 – Ax, Tokyo
13 – Mother Hall, Osaka
14 – Logos, Fukuoka
16 – Blitz, Tokyo
17 – Club Quattro, Tokyo
20, 21 & 22 – House Of Blues, Los Angeles, CA
25 – Town Hall, New York, NY
26 – Berklee Performance Centre, Boston, MASS

August

3 – Dranouter Folk Festival, Belgium
5 – Witnness Festival, Ireland

September

4 – Brixton Academy, London

October
7 – Shepherd's Bush Empire, London *(Guest of Oasis)*
28 – South Tramore
31 – Music Centre, Utrecht
November
1 – Modernes, Bremen
2 – Burgerhaus, Rees-Haldern, Germany
4 – Forum, Bielefeld, Germany
5 – Tuchfabrik, Trier, Germany
6 – Jazzhaus, Freiburg, Germany
8 – Scala, Ludwigsburg, Germany
9 – Kolossal, Aschaffenburg, Germany
11 & 12 – Schlachthof, Hamburg
13 – Nikolaisaal, Potsdam
28 – Corn Exchange, Edinburgh
29 – St George's Hall, Bradford
30 – King George's Hall, Blackburn
December
2 – Poole Arts Centre
3 – Rivermead, Reading
5 – Corn Exchange, Cambridge
6 – Fairfield Halls, Croydon
7 – Colston Hall, Bristol
10 & 12 – Royal Albert Hall, London

2002
February
7 – Royal Albert Hall, London *(Guest of Oasis)*
9 – Teenage Cancer Trust Event, Royal Albert Hall, London
July
3 – Leas Cliff Hall, Folkestone
4 – Winter Gardens, Margate
6 – Beach Festival, Belgium
9 – Town Hall, Middlesbrough
10 – Sands Centre, Carlisle
12 – Old Trafford Cricket Ground, Manchester
22 – Pavilions, Plymouth
23 – Guildhall, Liverpool
24 – De Montfort Hall, Leicester
26 – Marlay Park, Dublin
28 – Hyde Park, London
August
3 – Benicassim Festival, Spain

October
12 – Brighton Conference Centre
13 – Sanctuary, Milton Keynes
15 & 16 – Braehead Arena, Glasgow
18 – Telewest Arena, Newcastle
19 – NEC, Birmingham
21 – Cardiff International Arena
22 & 23 – Apollo Manchester
26 – Hull Arena
27 – Nottingham Arena
29 – Bournemouth International Centre
30 – Wembley Arena, London
November
1 – The Marquee, London *(Cancelled)*
6 – Vega Musikkenshus, Copenhagen *(Cancelled)*
7 – Gr. Freiheit 36, Hamburg
8 – Columbia Halle, Berlin
10 – E-Werk, Cologne
11 – Heineken Music Hall, Amsterdam
12 – L'ancienne, Brussels
14 – Bataclan, Paris
17 – Razzmatazz, Barcelona
19 – La Riviera, Madrid S
20 – Pabellon De La Casilla, Bilbao *(With Oasis)*
23 – Loewensaal, Nurnberg *(Cancelled)*
24 – Gaallter, Vienna
25 – Muffathalle, Munich
27 – Velvet, Rimini, Italy
28 – Alacatraz, Milan
29 – 041 Marghera (Ve), Italy *(Cancelled)*
December
5 – Shepherds Bush Empire, London

2003
February
6 – Spreckels Theatre, San Diego, CA
7 – Wiltern Theatre, Los Angeles, CA
8 – Warfield Theatre, San Francisco, CA
11 – Paramount Theatre, Denver, CO *(Cancelled)*
11 – House Of Blues, Los Angeles, CA
13 – Fitzgerald Theatre, St. Paul, MN *(Cancelled)*
15 – Vic Theatre, Chicago, ILL
17 – Massey Hall, Toronto

18 – Majestic Theatre, Detroit, MI *(Cancelled)*
19 – 9:30 Club, Washington DC
21 – Hammerstein Ballroom, New York, NY
22 – Orpheum Theatre, New York, NY
23 – Electric Factory, Philadelphia, PA *(Cancelled)*

March

15 – Shepherds Bush Empire, London
26 – Royal Albert Hall, London

June

11 – Sheffield City Hall
12 – Newcastle City Hall
14 – Isle Of Wight Festival

July

13 – Barbican, York
14 – Civic Hall, Wolverhampton
16 – King's Dock Arena, Liverpool
17 – Academy, Glasgow
18 – Crathes Castle, Aberdeen
20 – Hyde Park, London *(Cancelled)*

August

27 – HMV Store, Oxford Street, London

October

8 & 9- House Of Blues, Los Angeles, CA
10 – Fillmore, San Francisco, CA
11 – 4 & B, San Diego, CA
14 – House Of Blues, Anaheim, CA
17 – Palais Royale, Toronto
19 – House Of Blues, Chicago, ILL
20 – House Of Blues, Chicago, ILL *(Cancelled)*
23 – Webster Theatre, Hartford, CT *(Cancelled)*
24 – Avalon, New York, NY
26 – Recher Theatre, Baltimore, MD *(Cancelled)*
27 – Town Hall, New York, NY
28 – Irving Plaza, New York, NY

November

15 – Jovel, Munster
16 – Elizabeth Hall, Antwerp
17 – Pepsi Stage, Amsterdam
19 – Mousonturn, Frankfurt
20 – Star Club, Dresden
21 – Colombia Fritz, Berlin
22 – Musikhalle, Hamburg
24 – Gloria, Cologne

25 – Manufaktur, Schorndorf, Germany
27 – Metropole, Vienna
28 – Muffathalle, Munich
December
5 – Colston Hall, Bristol
6 – Guildhall, Portsmouth
7 – Academy, Birmingham
9 – Waterfront Hall, Belfast
10 & 11 – Olympia Theatre, Dublin
14 & 15 – Brixton Academy, London
16 – Shepherds Bush Empire, London

2004
March
30 – Teenage Cancer Trust Event, Royal Albert Hall, London
April
8 – Ronnie Lane Memorial Concert, Royal Albert Hall, London
June
1, 2 & 3 – The Royal Albert Hall, London
12 – Bedgebury Forest, Kent
13 – Thetford Forest, Norfolk
19 – Dalby Forest, North Yorkshire
20 – Delamere Forest, Cheshire
26 – Sherwood Forest, Nottinghamshire
July
4 – Petworth House, West Sussex
24 – Rock Odyssey Festival Stadium, Yokohama
25 – Dome, Osaka
August
7 – Haldern Festival, Germany
8 – Lokerse Festival, Lockeren, Belgium
September
13 – Virgin Megastore, Oxford Street, London
18 – HMV Store, Dublin
27 – Tower Records, New York
October
24 – Cirque Royalle, Brussels
25 – Vredenberg Concert Hall, Utrecht
26 – E-Werk, Cologne
27 – Stadthalle, Heidelberg
29 – Rbb Sendesaal, Berlin
30 – Kampnagel, Hamburg

2005

February

2 – Cargo, London *(Cancelled)*
11 – Cargo, London
13 – Victoria Hall, Keighley
14 & 15 – Royal Court, Liverpool
17 & 18 – Apollo, Manchester
19 – Hull Arena
21 & 22 – Armadillo, Glasgow
24 & 25 – Newcastle City Hall
27 – Nottingham Arena
28 – Opera House, Blackpool

March

2 & 3 – The Civic Hall Wolverhampton
4 – International Arena, Cardiff
6 – Pavilions, Plymouth
7 – Brighton Conference Centre
9, 10 & 11 – The Hammersmith Apollo London

July

4 – Stadtpark, Hamburg *(Cancelled)*
5 – Amphitheatre Gelsenkirchen, Germany *(Cancelled)*
14 – St George's Hall, Bradford
15 – International Centre, Telford
16 – Guilfest, Guildford
17 – Powderham Castle, Exeter *(Cancelled)*
20 – Summer Pops, Liverpool

September

8 – 100 Club, London
16 – Wiltern Theatre, Los Angeles, CA
17 – Warfield, San Francisco, CA
20 – Vic, Chicago, ILL
22 – Kool Haus, Toronto
24 – Roseland, New York, NY
25 – Avalon, New York, NY
26 – 9.30 Club, Washington DC *(Cancelled)*

October

10 – HMV Store, London
13 – 013, Tilburg, Holland
14 – Oosterpoort, Groningen, Holland
15 – The Paradiso, Amsterdam
18 – Columbiahalle, Berlin
19 – The Docks, Hamburg
20 – Ringlokschuppen, Bielefeld, Germany

21 – E-Werk, Cologne
23 – Capitol, Offenbach
24 – Muffathalle, Munich
26 – Alcatraz, Milan
27 – Vox Club, Nonantola
29 – Teatro Tendastriscie, Rome
November
1 – Razzmatazz, Barcelona
3 – La Riviera, Madrid *(Cancelled)*
10 – Usher Hall, Edinburgh
11 – Caird Hall, Dundee
13 – SECC, Glasgow
15 – Dome, Doncaster
16 – Leeds, University
18 – Brentwood Leisure Centre
19 – Corn Exchange, Cambridge
20 – Metro Radio Arena, Newcastle
22 – Brighton Conference Centre
23 – NIA Arena, Birmingham
24 – MEN Arena, Manchester
26 – International Arena, Cardiff
27 – New Theatre, Oxford
29 – Bournemouth International Centre
30 – Colston Hall, Bristol
December
2 – Empress Ballroom, Blackpool
04 – Nottingham Arena
05 – Alexandra Palace, London
11 – Ulster Hall, Belfast
12 & 13 – Olympia Theatre, Dublin
15 – ULU London *(Supporting The Dogs)*

2006
February
13 – Gibson Studios, London *(Afternoon)*
13 – 100 Club, London
15 – Brit Awards, Earls Court, London
March
29 Nakano Sun Plaza, Tokyo
31 Zepp Club, Tokyo
April
1 & 3 – Zepp Club, Tokyo

19 – Hafen, Innsbruck, Austria
20 – Gasometer, Vienna
21 – Orpheum, Graz, Austria
23 – Huxley's Neue Welt, Berlin
25 – Tor 3, Düsseldorf
26 – Theaterhuus, Stuttgart
June
1 – Stadtpark, Hamburg
2 – Rock Am Ring Festival, Volkespark, Nurenberg
3 – Pinkpop Festival, Landgraaf
13 – Koko, Camden Town, London
24 – Metrorock Festival, Madrid
July
8 – T In The Park Festival, Kinross, Scotland
9 – Oxegan Festival, Punchestown Racecourse, Ireland
13 – Istanbal Jazz Festival
16 – North Sea Jazz Festival, Rotterdam
21 – Flippaut Festival, Milan
22 – Cavea Auditorium, Rome
August
3 – City Festivities, La Coruna, Spain
13 – Lokeren Festival, Belgium
19 – V Festival, Weston Park, Staffordshire
20 – V Festival, Hylands Park, Chelmsford
September
16 – Teenage Cancer Trust Gig, The Sage, Gateshead
October
25 – BBC Electric Proms, The Roundhouse, London
November
14 & 15 – Kentish Town Forum, London
17 & 18 – Olympia, Dublin
20 & 21 – Newcastle City Hall
23 – Octagon, Sheffield
24 & 25 – Barrowlands, Glasgow
27 & 28 – Apollo, Manchester
30 – Civic Hall, Wolverhampton
December
2 – Brighton Centre
3 – Lighthouse, Poole
4 – Gloucester Leisure Centre
6 & 7 – Forum Kentish Town, London

2007

January

21 – Dear Mr. Fantasy Charity Concert, The Roundhouse, London

29, 30 & 31 – Irving Plaza, New York, NY

February

3 & 4 – Avalon Theatre, Los Angeles, CA

3 WEBSITES & BOOKS

There are a number of web sites dedicated to The Jam, The Style Council, and Paul Weller. Listed below are some of the best.

Official Paul Weller site
www.paulweller.com

Rick Buckler's sites
www.thejamfan.net
http://com1.runboard.com/bthegift

Iain Munn's Style Council website
www.wholepoint.co.uk

Steve White's official site.
www.whiteydrums.com

Neil 'Twink' Tinning (Official Jam photographer)
www.thejamarchive.com

Karl Gonzalez website
http://members.lycos.co.uk/pwla/

Julie Kershaw's website
http://www.geocities.com/julieoapw

Drew Hipson's website
www.allmodicon.com

Matteo Sedazzari Positive Energy of Madness website
http://www.peom.co.uk/index.html

www.porcelaingod.co.uk

Books

There are a number of good books on The Jam, The Style Council, and Paul Weller and I would like to acknowledge the following:

Brookes, Steve. *Keeping The Flame* (ISBN 0 9528 0620 7)
Hewitt, Paolo. *Beat Concerto* (ISBN 0 7119 0393 X)
Lines, David. *The Modfather: My Life With Paul Weller* (ISBN: 0 4340 1324 2)
Malins, Steve. *The Unauthorised Biography* (ISBN 0 7535 0087 6)
Munn, Iain. *Mr Cool's Dream* (ISBN 0 9551 4430 2
Reed, John. *My Ever Changing Moods* (ISBN 0 7719 5495 X)
Willmott, Graham. *The Sound Of The Jam* (ISBN 1 9031 1166 8)

Acknowledgements

I would like to thank the following without whose help this book wouldn't have been written: Brett 'Buddy' Ascott and Sean Body for their helpful (ouch) comments on the early manuscripts; Jim Cook for taking care of business, and all his help; Mark Pritchard and Colin Clive for their support that went beyond friendship.

To my boss and editor at Omnibus Chris Charlesworth for the guidance and a job well done, and to Sarah Holcraft for being one of the few business affairs persons that I've come across, that understands that a contract must be fair to both parties. Also at Omnibus: Sarah Bacon, Sharon Kelly, George Goble, Steve Jackson and Susan Currie. My thanks also go to Dan Level who was a great help and gave me some sage advice along the way. A lot of skin goes to Iain 'Painstakingly Accurate' Munn for all the help he has given me, in the past, present and the future on his beloved Style Council. David Lodge and Paula Cuccurullo, who published the best ever fanzine on Paul Weller, *Boys About Town*, which since its demise, is sadly missed. Thanks go to Karl Gonzalez, Sean Kelly, James Mayes and Jon Abnett for giving up so much of their time to help me. I hope it was worth it.

From my Polydor days, thanks to George McManus, Lionel Burdge, Gordon Gray, John Perou, as well as Zoe Roberts and Jane Hitchen who do a thankless task looking after Polydor's tape library wonderfully well. Robin Jackson for his continuous support and Dizzy Holmes at Detour for making me a punk star. Special thanks to Laurie Adams, who gave me my first job at Polydor, which kick-started my career. To Frank O'Donnell, the nicest man in the record business, who passed away far too young as did my best friend Rob Johnston, my Italian *brother* Mario Sandrigo and my Welsh rugby chum, Jack Williams, the world's a sadder place without you guys! To my mother, who has always been there for me, and my family, brother Robert, sister Janet and my niece Carrie Higgins and Jimmy Carter. Although we have never met, I feel like I've known Roger Farrow all my life, and he's been a great e-mail mate.

I would also like to thank Ken Dixon for being the only mate that's never refused to help me when I've asked, you're a diamond. As well as Bernie Hogg and Charly Traude in Essen, and look forward to having a beer with you! In Kent where I lived for many years I would like thank Joe Underwood, Danny 'Wizza' Rice-Wilson and his family for their total support, as well his bruvver, Raymondo Wilson. I have to thank Mike and Sue Buttonshaw, and Dave and Sheila Edwards for helping out at a time I really needed it, and when a lot of my so called friends deserted me. Al Beech for leading me astray and always talking me into having just one more beer for the road. Jan Williams for the best Christmas cake in the world, and Glenn Nash and Angie Green for their support through my Argentinean winter, and the use of the phone. Thanks to all my mates at The Red House Pub, Boughton Monchelsea, The Buffalo's Head, and Andrew at the Lord Raglan in Chart Sutton, as well as Dave Nash and Duncan McKellar, both great guys. G'day to the Hoggs-on-the-hill, Derek, Sarah and Chester down under in Australia.

I have to thank my oldest mate Colin King who musically was a big influence on me during my teenage years, and Famiglia Martin, Jeff, Anna, Kris and Stefan. I must also thank Alan and Audrey Lowrie for their constant support.

In Italy, I would like to say molto grazie to mia famiglia, Sandra and Terrazina Blazzista, Efrem and Giulia Sandrigo, Fabio Lorenzon, and Theresa *the terrible*, Roberta Glavich and Famiglia Carabeni, Angelo, Daniela, Roberta and Davide! Big Mick Antonelli and Piero *the* Donat *man*. Franco Visintin and Gabriella Borgia at the Bar 33 Ronchi Dei legionary for looking after me, and my mates in the freccette squadre, Scerifo and Mickey Visintin, Marco Fumis, Claudio *Poldo* Benvegnu, Mauro Gerin, Franco 'Croatia' Manzin. Alberto Lorenzi, Gabriella Vatta, Mad Max Clarig, Nicola 'Indian' Miani, Christian Bratovich, Giauluca But, Davide 'Macchina' Visitin and my amicos in the Joe Bar sqaudre.

Special molto grazie go to Livio and Dana Bagon, my closest mates in Ronchi and Zamir Laverencic for being a special friend. Grazie to Enrico Lehman, a real pal, who listened to all my problems and didn't moan! Ivan Battistella and Paolo Nicola who like a drink or three! Also my amici at

Bar Viale as well as Nadia and Paolo at the Alburgo Furlan. Thanks to Giovanni *Nino* Zupelli and Lorenzo Novati, at Bar Mocambo, for always making me feel welcome, and a bit of a star. Molto grazie to Ezio Brunetta and Sabina Furlani, Eric Anderson, sound man extraordinaire and, last but not least Rita *Piglet* Daniotti, who introduced me to Winnie The Pooh!

To Paul and John Weller, Bruce Foxton, Rick Buckler, Mick Talbot, Steve White and Big Kenny Wheeler, they were great times.

Lastly, thanks to all the fans of The Jam, the Council and Paul Weller – you put them and me where we are - respect, by the shed load.

Dennis Munday, June 2006.

02/07 (61255).